T5-BPY-914

FIRST
EDITION

HiGH-interest BOOKS for Teens

Edited by
Adele Sarkissian

A Guide to Book Reviews and Biographical Sources

Gale Research Company
Book Tower • Detroit, Michigan 48226

Editor: Adele Sarkissian

Associate Editor: Kathryn T. Floch

Assistant Editors: Susette A. Balogh, Victoria H. Welling

Editorial Assistants: Deborah Ellens, Sandy Holt, Elizabeth
Mulligan, Michaelene F. Pepera

Production Supervisor: Nancy Nagy

Cover Design: Arthur Chartow

Computerized photocomposition by Computer Composition Corporation
Madison Heights, Michigan

Library of Congress Cataloging in Publication Data

Sarkissian, Adele.
   High-interest books for teens.

   Bibliography: p.
   Includes index.
   1. High interest-low vocabulary books--Bibliography.
2. Books--Reviews--Bibliography. I. Title.
Z1039.S5S27   011'.63   81-6889
ISBN 0-8103-0599-2   AACR2

HiGH-interest BOOKS for Teens

Table of Contents

Introduction

High-Interest Books for Teens is a guide to more than 1,500 authors and 2,000 titles of books of fiction and nonfiction that appeal to students in junior and senior high school. This is a tool for librarians, teachers in classrooms and reading laboratories, and any other adults involved in guiding teens known to have learning disabilities or simply undeveloped reading skills. Providing quick access to several levels of information, *HIBT* lists both classic and contemporary books that have been identified as "high-interest/low-readability level" materials for young adults. Further, it gives a convenient key to review sources with which each book can be evaluated. Finally, it pinpoints sources of information on the author's life which can provide background to spark a student's interest or to help design a booktalk or class assignment.

Features

The Guide to Book Reviews and Biographical Sources, the main section of *High-Interest Books for Teens,* is arranged alphabetically by author. Each entry gives the author's full name (or an identified pseudonym), dates of birth and death (if known), and one or more sources that give further biographical information. A total of 126 carefully selected sources has been cited. A key to the abbreviations used to designate biographical sources appears on the back endsheets. The complete listing of biographical sources cited, including the abbreviations, appears immediately after this Introduction.

Each author entry also includes one or more book titles, each of which is followed by detailed citations of periodical reviews of that title. A key to the abbreviated periodical sources appears on the front endsheets and immediately following this Introduction.

A separate Title Index, located at the back of the book, provides access to the main entries in the Guide to Book Reviews and Biographical Sources when the user does not have the author's name.

Criteria

The books included in *HIBT* have been designated in recommended reading lists and in publishers' catalogs as high-interest/low-readability level materials by authorities in the field—librarians, teachers, publishers, book reviewers, and critics. However, any selection of high/low materials for young adults will surely fail to satisfy everyone. Discounting personal preference, such a selection inevitably suffers from the lack of real standards in the field: there are no firm limits to the concept of a "young adult"; and there is no single, universally-accepted measurement of reading difficulty. But even as standards wait to be defined, guidance for the teachers and librarians working in the field is sorely needed. Therefore, *HIBT* presents the composite choice of those people who are involved in publishing and evaluating reading materials for teens. The individual teacher or librarian must be the final arbiter of what is most suitable for the young adults in his or her charge.

Further Information Sources

The following information sources, selected from the many consulted in the preparation of *HIBT*, will be helpful to anyone with a special interest in the high/low field.

> *The Best in Children's Books*, edited by Zena Sutherland, University of Chicago Press (Chicago, Ill.), 1976.

> *Booklist*, "High-Low Reading" column, American Library Association (Chicago, Ill.), 1977—.

> *Easy Reading: Book Series and Periodicals for Less Able Readers*, by Michael F. Graves, Judith A. Boettscher, Randall A. Ryder, International Reading Association (Newark, Del.), 1979.

> *Easy Reads for Teens*, by Jack Forman, Eastern Massachusetts Regional Library System (Boston, Mass.), 1976.

> *Easy-to-Read Books for Teenagers*, Office of Young Adult Services, New York Public Library (New York City), 1979.

> *Gateways to Readable Books*, 5th ed., by Dorothy E. Withrow, Helen B. Carey, and Bertha M. Hirzel, H.W. Wilson (New York City), 1975.

> *Good Reading for Poor Readers*, 10th ed., by George D. Spache, Garrard Publishing (Champaign, Ill.), 1978.

> *High Interest/Easy Reading for Junior and Senior High School Students*, edited by Marian E. White (with a committee of the National Council of Teachers of English), 2nd ed., Citation Press (New York City), 1972, 3rd edition, NCTE (Urbana, Ill.), 1979.

> *High-Interest Low-Reading Level Booklist*, by the High-Interest/Low Literacy Level Materials Evaluation Committee, Young Adult Services Division, American Library Association (Chicago, Ill.), 1980. Also published as "Getting Reluctant Readers to Read: A Hi-Lo Booklist," *Top of the News*, YASD/ALA, Winter, 1980.

High-Interest/Low Vocabulary Reading Materials, 1978 Supplement.
Journal of Education, Boston University, School of Education
(Boston, Mass.), 1978.

The High/Low Report, edited by Thetis Powers Reeves, Riverhouse
Publications (New York City), 1979—

Kliatt Young Adult Paperback Book Guide, edited by Doris Hiatt and
Claire Rosser (Newton, Mass.), 1967—.

Sample Entry

Main entries in *HIBT* cite the author's name (or pseudonym) as it was
listed in the original book review source. Biographical sources given in
HIBT can be assumed to list the author under the same name form. In the
rare contrary instance, parenthetical information in the entry will direct
the user to an alternate name form.

The typical entry in *HIBT* gives the following items of information:

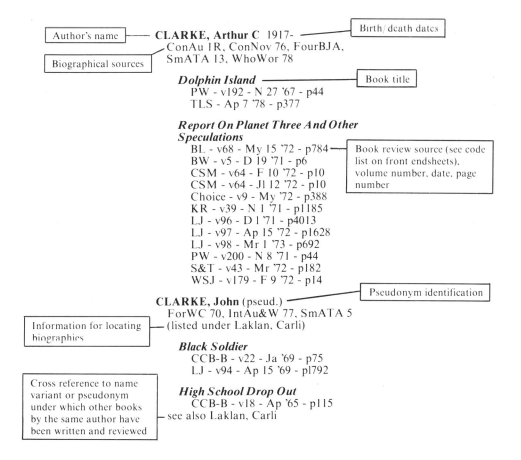

Author's name ⟶ **CLARKE, Arthur C** 1917- ⟵ Birth/death dates
ConAu 1R, ConNov 76, FourBJA,
Biographical sources — SmATA 13, WhoWor 78

Dolphin Island ⟵ Book title
PW - v192 - N 27 '67 - p44
TLS - Ap 7 '78 - p377

Report On Planet Three And Other
Speculations
BL - v68 - My 15 '72 - p784 ⟵ Book review source (see code
BW - v5 - D 19 '71 - p6   list on front endsheets),
CSM - v64 - F 10 '72 - p10   volume number, date, page
CSM - v64 - Jl 12 '72 - p10 number
Choice - v9 - My '72 - p388
KR - v39 - N 1 '71 - p1185
LJ - v96 - D 1 '71 - p4013
LJ - v97 - Ap 15 '72 - p1628
LJ - v98 - Mr 1 '73 - p692
PW - v200 - N 8 '71 - p44
S&T - v43 - Mr '72 - p182
WSJ - v179 - F 9 '72 - p14

CLARKE, John (pseud.) ⟵ Pseudonym identification
ForWC 70, IntAu&W 77, SmATA 5
Information for locating — (listed under Laklan, Carli)
biographies

Black Soldier
CCB-B - v22 - Ja '69 - p75
LJ - v94 - Ap 15 '69 - p1792

Cross reference to name
variant or pseudonym   *High School Drop Out*
under which other books   CCB-B - v18 - Ap '65 - p115
by the same author have — see also Laklan, Carli
been written and reviewed

Entries may lack dates and/or biographical sources when that information was not found in the sources consulted for *HIBT*.

Cross references are used in this guide to indicate the following:

1. Variant name forms for the same author

   COMBER, Lillian
   see Beckwith, Lillian

   The cross reference directs the user to the name under which book reviews have been listed.

2. Co-authorship of all books cited

   CLEAVER, BILL
   see Cleaver, Vera (co-author)

   The cross reference directs the user to the name under which book reviews have been listed and further indicates that all books listed under "Vera Cleaver" in this guide were co-authored by Bill Cleaver.

3. Co-authorship of particular titles among those listed in *HIBT*

   CRAMER, Kathryn
   see Terzian, James (co-author) -
   Mighty Hard Road

   The cross reference directs the user to the name under which book reviews have been listed and further indicates that Cramer co-authored only *Mighty Hard Road* from among the several books listed under "James Terzian" in this guide.

Suggestions for Future Editions

Future editions of *High-Interest Books for Teens* are planned. The editors welcome your comments on this edition as well as your suggestions for additional book titles, information sources, or added features that would be useful in future editions.

Book Review Sources Cited

A Anth	American Anthropologist
A Art	American Artist
AB	AB Bookman's Weekly
ABC	American Book Collector
AC	American City and County
ACSB	Appraisal: Children's Science Books
AF	American Forests
AJA	American Journal of Archaeology
AL	American Literature
A Lead	Adult Leadership
A Lib	American Libraries
ANQ	American Notes and Queries
ARBA	American Reference Books Annual
Am	America
Atl	Atlantic Monthly
BB	Babbling Bookworm
B&B	Books & Bookmen
BIC	Books in Canada
BL	Booklist
BOT	Books of the Times (NYT)
BS	Best Sellers
BW	Book World
BksW	BooksWest
Bl W	Black World
CBRS	Children's Book Review Service
CC	Christian Century
CCB-B	Center for Children's Books. Bulletin
CE	Childhood Education
CF	Canadian Forum
CLW	Catholic Library World
CM	Carleton Miscellany
CR	Contemporary Review
CSM	Christian Science Monitor
CW	Classical World
Cath W	Catholic World
Choice	Choice
Comt	Commentary
Comw	Commonweal
Cr H	Craft Horizons
Cres	Cresset
Crit	Critic
Cu H	Current History
Cur R	Curriculum Review
Dance	Dance Magazine
Dr	Drama: The Quarterly Theatre Review
EJ	English Journal
EL	Educational Leadership
Econ	Economist
Esq	Esquire
FQ	Film Quarterly
Fly	Flying
GJ	Geographical Journal
GP	Growing Point
GW	Guardian Weekly
HB	Horn Book Magazine

HE	Human Events
HM	Harper's Magazine
HR	Hudson Review
HT	History Today
Hi Lo	High/Low Report
Hob	Hobbies
ILN	Illustrated London News
Inst	Instructor
Inter BC	Interracial Books for Children Bulletin
JAF	Journal of American Folklore
JAH	Journal of American History
JB	Junior Bookshelf
JGE	Journal of General Education
J Ho E	Journal of Home Economics
JLD	Journal of Learning Disabilities
JLH	Journal of Library History, Philosophy, and Comparative Librarianship
JNE	Journal of Negro Education
J Pol	Journal of Politics
J Read	Journal of Reading
KR	Kirkus Reviews
Kliatt	Kliatt Paperback Book Guide
LA	Language Arts
LJ	Library Journal
LR	Library Review
LW	Living Wilderness
Life	Life
Lis	Listener
M Ed J	Music Educators Journal
MFS	Modern Fiction Studies
MFSF	Magazine of Fantasy and Science Fiction
Money	Money
Ms	Ms.
NAR	North American Review
NCW	New Catholic World
ND	Negro Digest
NH	Natural History
NHB	Negro History Bulletin
NO	National Observer
NPCM	National Parks
NS	New Statesman
NW	Newsweek
NY	New Yorker
NYRB	New York Review of Books
NYT	New York Times
NYTBR	New York Times Book Review
NYTBR, pt.1	New York Times Book Review, Pt. 1
NYTBR, pt.2	New York Times Book Review. Pt. 2
Nat	Nation
Nat R	National Review
New R	New Republic
Notes	Notes (Music Library Association)
Obs	Observer (London)

(Continued)

P&R	Parks and Recreation		*SN*	Saturday Night
PGJ	Personnel and Guidance Journal		*SR*	Saturday Review
PR	Partisan Review		*SS*	Social Studies
PS	Prairie Schooner		*SWR*	Southwest Review
PT	Psychology Today		*Sci*	Science
PW	Publishers Weekly		*Spec*	Spectator
Pac A	Pacific Affairs		*Spectr*	Spectrum
Par	Parents Magazine		*TCR*	Teachers College Record
Pet PM	Petersen's Photographic Magazine		*TES*	Times Educational Supplement
Poet	Poetry		*TLS*	Times Literary Supplement
Prog	Progressive		*TN*	Top of the News
Punch	Punch		*Teacher*	Teacher
RR	Review for Religious		*Time*	Time
RSR	Reference Services Review		*Trav*	Travel-Holiday
RT	Reading Teacher		*VQR*	Virginia Quarterly Review
SA	Scientific American		*VV*	Village Voice
S&T	Sky and Telescope		*WCRB*	West Coast Review of Books
SB	Science Books and Films		*WLB*	Wilson Library Bulletin
SE	Social Education		*WSJ*	Wall Street Journal
SEP	Saturday Evening Post		*YR*	Yale Review
SLJ	School Library Journal		*Yacht*	Yachting
SMQ	School Media Quarterly			

ABBREVIATIONS OF MONTHS USED IN CITATIONS

Ja	January		Jl	July
F	February		Ag	August
Mr	March		S	September
Ap	April		O	October
My	May		N	November
Je	June		D	December

Biographical Sources Cited

Code	Book Indexed
AfroAA	*Afro-American Artists: A Bio-Bibliographical Directory.* Compiled and edited by Theresa Dickason Cederholm. Boston: Trustees of the Boston Public Library, 1973.

AmM & WS — *American Men and Women of Science.* Edited by Jaques Cattell Press. New York: R.R. Bowker Co., 1971-1973, 1976-1978.

AmM & WS 73P	Physical & Biological Sciences, 12th edition, 1971-1973
AmM & WS 73S	Social & Behavioral Sciences, 12th edition, 1973
AmM & WS 76P	Physical & Biological Sciences, 13th edition, 1976
AmM & WS 78S	Social & Behavioral Sciences, 13th edition, 1978

AmNov — *American Novelists of Today.* By Harry R. Warfel. New York: American Book Co., 1951. Reprint. Westport, Connecticut: Greenwood Press, 1976.

The "Index of Married Names and Pseudonyms," indicated in this index by the code *X*, begins on page 477.

AmSCAP 66 — *The ASCAP Biographical Dictionary of Composers, Authors and Publishers.* Third edition, 1966. Compiled and edited by The Lynn Farnol Group, Inc. New York: American Society of Composers, Authors, and Publishers, 1966.

ArtCS — *The Art of the Comic Strip.* By Judith O'Sullivan. College Park, Maryland: University of Maryland, Department of Art, 1971.

Biographies begin on page 60.

ASpks — *The Author Speaks: Selected "PW" Interviews, 1967-1976.* By *Publishers Weekly* editors and contributors. New York: R.R. Bowker Co., 1977.

Au & ICB — *Authors and Illustrators of Children's Books: Writings on Their Lives and Works.* By Miriam Hoffman and Eva Samuels. New York: R.R. Bowker Co., 1972.

Au & Wr 71 — *The Author's and Writer's Who's Who.* Sixth edition. Darien, Connecticut: Hafner Publishing Co., Inc., 1971.

AuBYP — *Authors of Books for Young People.* By Martha E. Ward and Dorothy A. Marquardt. Metuchen, New Jersey: Scarecrow Press Inc., 1971, 1979.

AuBYP	Second edition, 1971
AuBYP SUP	Supplement to the second edition, 1979
AuBYP SUPA	Addendum to the Supplement begins on page 301

AuNews — *Authors in the News.* A compilation of news stories and feature articles from American newspapers and magazines covering writers and other members of the communications media. Two volumes. Edited by Barbara Nykoruk. Detroit: Gale Research Co., 1976.

AuNews 1	Volume 1
AuNews 2	Volume 2

BiDFilm — *A Biographical Dictionary of Film.* By David Thomson. New York: William Morrow & Co., Inc., 1976.

BiDrAPA 77	*Biographical Directory of the Fellows and Members of the American Psychiatric Association.* Compiled by Jaques Cattell Press. New York: R.R. Bowker Co., 1977.
BiDrLUS 70	*A Biographical Directory of Librarians in the United States and Canada.* Fifth edition. Edited by Lee Ash. Chicago: American Library Association, 1970.
BiE & WWA	*The Biographical Encyclopaedia and Who's Who of the American Theatre.* Edited by Walter Rigdon. New York: James H. Heineman, Inc., 1966. Revised edition published as *Notable Names in the American Theatre.* (See below.)

The "Biographical Who's Who" section begins on page 227.

BioIn	*Biography Index.* A cumulative index to biographical material in books and magazines. New York: H.W. Wilson Co., 1949-1980.

BioIn 1	Volume 1: January, 1946-July, 1949, 1949
BioIn 2	Volume 2: January, 1949-August, 1952, 1953
BioIn 3	Volume 3: September, 1952-August, 1955, 1956
BioIn 4	Volume 4: September, 1955-August, 1958, 1960
BioIn 5	Volume 5: September, 1958-August, 1961, 1962
BioIn 6	Volume 6: September, 1961-August, 1964, 1965
BioIn 7	Volume 7: September, 1964-August, 1967, 1968
BioIn 8	Volume 8: September, 1967-August, 1970, 1971
BioIn 9	Volume 9: September, 1970-August, 1973, 1974
BioIn 10	Volume 10: September, 1973-August, 1976, 1977
BioIn 11	Volume 11: September, 1976-August, 1979, 1980

BioNews	*Biography News.* A compilation of news stories and feature articles from American news media covering personalities of national interest in all fields. Edited by Frank E. Bair. Detroit: Gale Research Co., 1974-1975.

BioNews 74	Volume 1, Numbers 1-12, 1974
BioNews 75	Volume 2, Number 1, January-February 1975

BkP	*Books Are by People: Interviews with 104 Authors and Illustrators of Books for Young Children.* Edited by Lee Bennett Hopkins. New York: Citation Press, 1969.
BlkAW	*Black American Writers Past and Present: A Biographical and Bibliographical Dictionary.* Two volumes. By Theressa Gunnels Rush, Carol Fairbanks Myers, and Esther Spring Arata. Metuchen, New Jersey: Scarecrow Press, Inc., 1975.
BrAu 19	*British Authors of the Nineteenth Century.* Edited by Stanley J. Kunitz. New York: H.W. Wilson Co., 1936.
BrCA	*British Children's Authors: Interviews at Home.* By Cornelia Jones and Olivia R. Way. Chicago: American Library Association, 1976.
CaW	*Canada Writes!* The members' book of the Writers' Union of Canada. Edited by K.A. Hamilton. Toronto: Writer's Union of Canada, 1977.

The "Additional Members" section, indicated in this index by the code *A*, begins on page 387.

CanWW 79	*Canadian Who's Who.* Volume 14, 1979. Edited by Kieran Simpson. Toronto: University of Toronto Press, 1979.
CasWL	*Cassell's Encyclopaedia of World Literature.* Edited by S.H. Steinberg in two volumes. Revised and enlarged in three volumes by J. Buchanan-Brown. New York: William Morrow & Co., Inc., 1973.

Biographies are found in Volumes 2 and 3.

CelR　　　　　　*Celebrity Register.* Third edition. Edited by Earl Blackwell. New York: Simon & Schuster, 1973.

ChLR　　　　　　*Children's Literature Review.* Excerpts from reviews, criticism, and commentary on books for children and young people. Detroit: Gale Research Co., 1976-1978.

ChLR 1	Volume 1, 1976
ChLR 2	Volume 2, 1976
ChLR 3	Volume 3, 1978

ConAu　　　　　*Contemporary Authors.* A bio-bibliographical guide to current writers in fiction, general nonfiction, poetry, journalism, drama, motion pictures, television, and other fields. Detroit: Gale Research Co., 1967-1981.

ConAu 1R	Volumes 1-4, 1st revision, 1967
ConAu 5R	Volumes 5-8, 1st revision, 1969
ConAu 9R	Volumes 9-12, 1st revision, 1974
ConAu 13R	Volumes 13-16, 1st revision, 1975
ConAu 17R	Volumes 17-20, 1st revision, 1976
ConAu 21R	Volumes 21-24, 1st revision, 1977
ConAu 25R	Volumes 25-28, 1st revision, 1977
ConAu 29R	Volumes 29-32, 1st revision, 1978
ConAu 33R	Volumes 33-36, 1st revision, 1978
ConAu 37R	Volumes 37-40, 1st revision, 1979
ConAu 41R	Volumes 41-44, 1st revision, 1979
ConAu 45	Volumes 45-48, 1974
ConAu 49	Volumes 49-52, 1975
ConAu 53	Volumes 53-56, 1975
ConAu 57	Volumes 57-60, 1976
ConAu 61	Volumes 61-64, 1976
ConAu 65	Volumes 65-68, 1977
ConAu 69	Volumes 69-72, 1978
ConAu 73	Volumes 73-76, 1978
ConAu 77	Volumes 77-80, 1979
ConAu 81	Volumes 81-84, 1979
ConAu 85	Volumes 85-88, 1980
ConAu 89	Volumes 89-92, 1980
ConAu 93	Volumes 93-96, 1980
ConAu 97	Volumes 97-100, 1981
ConAu X	This code refers to pseudonym entries which appear only as cross references in the cumulative index to *Contemporary Authors.*

ConAu P-　　　*Contemporary Authors, Permanent Series.* A bio-bibliographical guide to current authors and their works. Detroit: Gale Research Co., 1975-1978.

ConAu P-1	Volume 1, 1975
ConAu P-2	Volume 2, 1978

ConDr　　　　　*Contemporary Dramatists.* Edited by James Vinson. London: St. James Press; New York: St. Martin's Press, 1977.

ConDr 77	Second edition, 1977, "Contemporary Dramatists" begins on page 9
ConDr 77A	Second edition, "Screen Writers" begins on page 893
ConDr 77B	Second edition, "Radio Writers" begins on page 903
ConDr 77C	Second edition, "Television Writers" begins on page 915
ConDr 77D	Second edition, "Musical Librettists" begins on page 925
ConDr 77E	Second edition, "The Theatre of the Mixed Means" begins on page 941
ConDr 77F	Second edition, Appendix begins on page 969

Biographical Sources

ConLC	*Contemporary Literary Criticism.* Excerpts from criticism of the works of today's novelists, poets, playwrights, and other creative writers. Detroit: Gale Research Co., 1973-1980.	

ConLC 1	Volume 1, 1973
ConLC 2	Volume 2, 1974
ConLC 3	Volume 3, 1975
ConLC 4	Volume 4, 1975
ConLC 5	Volume 5, 1976
ConLC 6	Volume 6, 1976
ConLC 7	Volume 7, 1977
ConLC 8	Volume 8, 1978
ConLC 9	Volume 9, 1978
ConLC 10	Volume 10, 1979
ConLC 11	Volume 11, 1979
ConLC 12	Volume 12, 1980
ConLC 13	Volume 13, 1980

ConNov   *Contemporary Novelists.* Edited by James Vinson. London: St. James Press; New York: St. Martin's Press, 1972, 1976.

ConNov 72	First edition, 1972
ConNov 76	Second edition, 1976

Deceased novelists are listed in the Appendix at the end of the second edition.

ConP   *Contemporary Poets.* London: St. James Press; New York: St. Martin's Press, 1970, 1975.

ConP 70	First edition. Edited by Rosalie Murphy, 1970.
ConP 75	Second edition. Edited by James Vinson, 1975.

Deceased poets are listed in the Appendix at the end of each volume.

ConSFA   *Contemporary Science Fiction Authors.* First edition. Compiled and edited by R. Reginald. New York: Arno Press, 1975. Previously published as *Stella Nova: The Contemporary Science Fiction Authors.* Los Angeles: Unicorn & Son, Publishers, 1970.

Conv   *Conversations.* Conversations series. Detroit: Gale Research Co., 1977-1978.

Conv 1	Volume 1: *Conversations with Writers,* 1977
Conv 2	Volume 2: *Conversations with Jazz Musicians,* 1977
Conv 3	Volume 3: *Conversations with Writers II,* 1978

CreCan   *Creative Canada: A Biographical Dictionary of Twentieth-Century Creative and Performing Artists.* Compiled by the Reference Division, McPherson Library, University of Victoria, B.C. Toronto: University of Toronto Press, 1971, 1972.

CreCan 1	Volume 1, 1971
CreCan 2	Volume 2, 1972

CurBio   *Current Biography Yearbook.* New York: H.W. Wilson Co., 1940-1978.

Number after the source code indicates the year covered by the yearbook. Obituaries, located in the back of some volumes, are indicated in this index by the code *N.*

DcAmAu   *A Dictionary of American Authors.* Fifth edition, revised and enlarged. By Oscar Fay Adams. New York: Houghton Mifflin Co., 1904. Reprint. Detroit: Gale Research Co., 1969.

Biographies are found in the "Dictionary of American Authors" section beginning on page 1 and in the "Supplement" beginning on page 441.

DcLB   *Dictionary of Literary Biography.* Detroit: Gale Research Co., 1978-1980.

      DcLB 1   Volume 1: *The American Renaissance in New England.* Edited by Joel Myerson, 1978.

      DcLB 2   Volume 2: *American Novelists since World War II.* Edited by Jeffrey Helterman and Richard Layman, 1978.

      DcLB 3   Volume 3: *Antebellum Writers in New York and the South.* Edited by Joel Myerson, 1979.

      DcLB 4   Volume 4: *American Writers in Paris, 1920-1939.* Edited by Karen Lane Rood, 1980.

DcLEL   *A Dictionary of Literature in the English Language.* Compiled and edited by Robin Myers. Oxford: Pergamon Press, Inc., 1970, 1978.

      DcLEL   *From Chaucer to 1940*, 1970
      DcLEL 1940   *From 1940 to 1970*, 1978

DcNAA   *A Dictionary of North American Authors Deceased before 1950.* Compiled by W. Stewart Wallace. Toronto: Ryerson Press, 1951. Reprint. Detroit: Gale Research Co., 1968.

DrAF 76   *A Directory of American Fiction Writers.* 1976 edition. Names and addresses of more than 800 contemporary fiction writers whose work has been published in the United States. New York: Poets & Writers, Inc., 1976.

      Use the Index, beginning on page 123, to locate listings.

DrAP 75   *A Directory of American Poets.* 1975 edition. Names and addresses of more than 1,500 contemporary poets whose work has been published in the United States. New York: Poets & Writers, Inc., 1974.

      Use the Index, beginning on page vii, to locate listings.

DrAS   *Directory of American Scholars.* Edited by Jaques Cattell Press. New York: R.R. Bowker Co., 1974, 1978.

      DrAS 74H   Sixth edition, volume 1: History
      DrAS 74E   Sixth edition, volume 2: English, Speech, & Drama
      DrAS 74F   Sixth edition, volume 3: Foreign Languages, Linguistics, & Philology
      DrAS 74P   Sixth edition, volume 4: Philosophy, Religion, & Law
      DrAS 78H   Seventh edition, volume 1: History
      DrAS 78E   Seventh edition, volume 2: English, Speech, & Drama
      DrAS 78F   Seventh edition, volume 3: Foreign Languages, Linguistics, & Philology
      DrAS 78P   Seventh edition, volume 4: Philosophy, Religion, & Law

EncMys   *Encyclopedia of Mystery and Detection.* By Chris Steinbrunner and Otto Penzler. New York: McGraw-Hill Book Co., 1976.

EncSF   *The Encyclopedia of Science Fiction: An Illustrated A to Z.* By Peter Nicholls. London: Grenada Publishing Ltd., 1979.

ForWC 70   *Foremost Women in Communications.* A biographical reference work on accomplished women in broadcasting, publishing, advertising, public relations, and allied professions. New York: Foremost Americans Publishing Corp., in association with R.R. Bowker Co., 1970.

FourBJA   *Fourth Book of Junior Authors and Illustrators.* Edited by Doris DeMontreville and Elizabeth D. Crawford. New York: H. W. Wilson Co., 1978.

HerW   *Her Way: Biographies of Women for Young People.* By Mary-Ellen Kulkin. Chicago: American Library Association, 1976.

IIBEAAW   *The Illustrated Biographical Encyclopedia of Artists of the American West.* By Peggy and Harold Samuels. Garden City, New York: Doubleday & Co., Inc., 1976.

IlsBYP   *Illustrators of Books for Young People.* Second edition. By Martha E. Ward and Dorothy A. Marquardt. Metuchen, New Jersey: Scarecrow Press, Inc., 1975.

IlsCB   *Illustrators of Children's Books.* Boston: Horn Book, Inc., 1958, 1968, 1978.

        IlsCB 1946   *1946-1956.* Compiled by Ruth Hill Viguers, Marcia Dalphin, and Bertha Mahony Miller, 1958. Biographies begin on page 62.

        IlsCB 1957   *1957-1966.* Compiled by Lee Kingman, Joanna Foster, and Ruth Giles Lontoft, 1968. Biographies begin on page 70.

        IlsCB 1967   *1967-1976.* Compiled by Lee Kingman, Grace Allen Hogarth, and Harriet Quimby, 1978. Biographies begin on page 93.

IndAu 1917   *Indiana Authors and Their Books, 1917-1966.* A continuation of *Indiana Authors and Their Books, 1816-1916*, and containing additional names from the earlier period. Compiled by Donald E. Thompson. Crawfordsville, Indiana: Wabash College, 1974.

IntAu & W 77   *The International Authors and Writers Who's Who.* Eighth edition. Edited by Adrian Gaster. Cambridge, England: International Biographical Centre, 1977.

        IntAu & W 77   Biographical Section
        IntAu & W 77X   "Pseudonyms of Included Authors" begins on page 1131

IntMPA 78   *International Motion Picture Almanac.* Edited by Richard Gertner. New York: Quigley Publishing Co., Inc., 1978.

    Biographies are found in the "Who's Who in Motion Pictures and Television." The listings are identical to those found in *The International Television Almanac.*

IntWW 78   *The International Who's Who.* Forty-second edition. London: Europa Publications Ltd., 1978. Distributed by Gale Research Co., Detroit, Michigan.

    The "Obituary" section, indicated in this index by the code *N*, is located at the beginning of the volume.

JBA 34   *The Junior Book of Authors.* An introduction to the lives of writers and illustrators for younger readers from Lewis Carroll and Louisa Alcott to the present day. First edition. Edited by Stanley J. Kunitz and Howard Haycraft. New York: H.W. Wilson Co., 1934.

JBA 51   *The Junior Book of Authors.* Second edition, revised. Edited by Stanley J. Kunitz and Howard Haycraft. New York: H.W. Wilson Co., 1951.

LEduc 74   *Leaders in Education.* Fifth edition. Edited by Jaques Cattell Press. New York: R.R. Bowker Co., 1974.

LivBAA   *Living Black American Authors: A Biographical Directory.* By Ann Allen Shockley and Sue P. Chandler. New York: R.R. Bowker Co., 1973.

LongCTC   *Longman Companion to Twentieth Century Literature.* By A.C. Ward. London: Longman Group Ltd., 1970.

McGEWB   *The McGraw-Hill Encyclopedia of World Biography.* An international reference work in 12 volumes including an index. New York: McGraw-Hill Book Co., 1973.

MnnWr	*Minnesota Writers: A Collection of Autobiographical Stories by Minnesota Prose Writers.* Edited and annotated by Carmen Nelson Richards. Minneapolis: T.S. Denison & Co., Inc., 1961.

Use the Table of Contents to locate biographies.

ModBlW	*Modern Black Writers.* Compiled and edited by Michael Popkin. A Library of Literary Criticism. New York: Frederick Ungar Publishing Co., 1978.
MorBMP	*More Books by More People: Interviews with Sixty-Five Authors of Books for Children.* By Lee Bennett Hopkins. New York: Citation Press, 1974.
MorJA	*More Junior Authors.* Edited by Muriel Fuller. New York: H.W. Wilson Co., 1963.
NatCAB	*The National Cyclopaedia of American Biography.* 57 volumes. New York and Clifton, New Jersey: James T. White & Co., 1892-1977. Reprint. Volumes 1-50. Ann Arbor: University Microfilms, 1967-1971.
NatPD	*National Playwrights Directory.* Edited by Phyllis Johnson Kaye. Waterford, Connecticut: The O'Neill Theater Center, 1977. Distributed by Gale Research Co., Detroit, Michigan.
NewYTBE	*The New York Times Biographical Edition: A Compilation of Current Biographical Information of General Interest.* New York: Arno Press, 1970-1973. Continued by *The New York Times Biographical Service.* (See below.)

NewYTBE 70	Volume 1, Numbers 1-12, 1970
NewYTBE 71	Volume 2, Numbers 1-12, 1971
NewYTBE 72	Volume 3, Numbers 1-12, 1972
NewYTBE 73	Volume 4, Numbers 1-12, 1973

NewYTBS	*The New York Times Biographical Service: A Compilation of Current Biographical Information of General Interest.* New York: Arno Press, 1974-1979. A continuation of *The New York Times Biographical Edition.* (See above.)

NewYTBS 74	Volume 5, Numbers 1-12, 1974
NewYTBS 75	Volume 6, Numbers 1-12, 1975
NewYTBS 76	Volume 7, Numbers 1-12, 1976
NewYTBS 77	Volume 8, Numbers 1-12, 1977
NewYTBS 78	Volume 9, Numbers 1-12, 1978
NewYTBS 79	Volume 10, Numbers 1-12, 1979

NewYTET	*The New York Times Encyclopedia of Television.* By Les Brown. New York: New York Times Book Co., Inc., 1977.
NotNAT	*Notable Names in the American Theatre.* Clifton, New Jersey: James T. White & Co., 1976. First edition published as *The Biographical Encyclopaedia and Who's Who of the American Theatre.* (See above.)

NotNAT	"Notable Names in the American Theatre" section begins on page 489
NotNAT A	"Biographical Bibliography" begins on page 309
NotNAT B	"Necrology" begins on page 343

This book often alphabetizes by titles of address, e.g.: Dr., Mrs., and Sir.

ODwPR 79	*O'Dwyer's Directory of Public Relations Executives, 1979.* Edited by Jack O'Dwyer. New York: J.R. O'Dwyer Co., Inc., 1979.
OhA & B	*Ohio Authors and Their Books: Biographical Data and Selective Bibliographies for Ohio Authors, Native and Resident, 1796-1950.* Edited by William Coyle. Cleveland and New York: World Publishing Co., 1962.

Biographical Sources

OxAm   *The Oxford Companion to American Literature.* Fourth edition. By James D. Hart. New York: Oxford University Press, 1965.

OxCan   *The Oxford Companion to Canadian History and Literature.* Toronto: Oxford University Press, 1968, 1973.

      OxCan   Original volume, corrected. By Norah Story, 1968.
      OxCan SUP   Supplement. Edited by William Toye, 1973.

OxEng   *The Oxford Companion to English Literature.* Compiled and edited by Sir Paul Harvey. Fourth edition, revised by Dorothy Eagle. New York: Oxford University Press, 1967.

OxFilm   *The Oxford Companion to Film.* Edited by Liz-Anne Bawden. New York: Oxford University Press, 1976.

OxGer   *The Oxford Companion to German Literature.* By Henry Garland and Mary Garland. Oxford: Clarendon Press, 1976.

OxMus   *The Oxford Companion to Music.* By Percy A. Scholes. 10th edition (corrected). Edited by John Owen Ward. London: Oxford University Press, 1974.

Pen   *The Penguin Companion to World Literature.* New York: McGraw-Hill Book Co., 1969, 1971.

      Pen AM   *The Penguin Companion to American Literature.* Edited by Malcolm Bradbury, Eric Mottram, and Jean Franco, 1971. Biographies are found in the "U.S.A." and "Latin America" sections.
      Pen EUR   *The Penguin Companion to European Literature.* Edited by Anthony Thorlby, 1969.

Prof   *Profiles.* Revised edition. Edited by Irma McDonough. Ottawa: Canadian Library Association, 1975.

      Contains articles from *In Review: Canadian Books for Children,* published quarterly by the Ontario Provincial Library Service.

REn   *The Reader's Encyclopedia.* Second edition. By William Rose Benet. New York: Thomas Y. Crowell Co., 1965.

REnAL   *The Reader's Encyclopedia of American Literature.* By Max J. Herzberg. New York: Thomas Y. Crowell Co., 1962.

RkOn   *Rock On: The Illustrated Encyclopedia of Rock n' Roll.* By Norm N. Nite. New York: Thomas Y. Crowell Co., 1974.

ScF & FL   *Science Fiction and Fantasy Literature.* A checklist, 1700-1974, with *Contemporary Science Fiction Authors II.* By R. Reginald. Detroit: Gale Research Co., 1979.

      ScF & FL 1   Volume 1: "Author Index" begins on page 3
      ScF & FL 1A   Volume 1: Addendum begins on page 581
      ScF & FL 2   Volume 2: *Contemporary Science Fiction Authors II*

SelBAA   *Selected Black American Authors: An Illustrated Bio-Bibliography.* Compiled by James A. Page. Boston: G.K. Hall & Co., 1977.

SmATA   *Something about the Author.* Facts and pictures about authors and illustrators of books for young people. Edited by Anne Commire. Detroit: Gale Research Co., 1971-1981.

      SmATA 1   Volume 1, 1971
      SmATA 2   Volume 2, 1971

SmATA 3	Volume 3, 1972
SmATA 4	Volume 4, 1973
SmATA 5	Volume 5, 1973
SmATA 6	Volume 6, 1974
SmATA 7	Volume 7, 1975
SmATA 8	Volume 8, 1976
SmATA 9	Volume 9, 1976
SmATA 10	Volume 10, 1976
SmATA 11	Volume 11, 1977
SmATA 12	Volume 12, 1977
SmATA 13	Volume 13, 1978
SmATA 14	Volume 14, 1978
SmATA 15	Volume 15, 1979
SmATA 16	Volume 16, 1979
SmATA 17	Volume 17, 1979
SmATA 18	Volume 18, 1980
SmATA 19	Volume 19, 1980
SmATA 20	Volume 20, 1980
SmATA 21	Volume 21, 1980
SmATA 22	Volume 22, 1981
SmATA 23	Volume 23, 1981
SmATA 24	Volume 24, 1981
SmATA X	This code refers to pseudonym entries which appear only as cross references in the cumulative index to *Something about the Author.*

SouST — *A Sounding of Storytellers: New and Revised Essays of Contemporary Writers for Children.* By John Rowe Townsend. New York: J.B. Lippincott, 1979.

St & PR 75 — *Standard and Poor's Register of Corporations, Directors and Executives.* Three volumes. Volume 2: *Directors and Executives.* New York: Standard & Poor's Corp., 1975.

Str & VC — *Story and Verse for Children.* Third edition. By Miriam Blanton Huber. New York: Macmillian Co., 1965.

Biographies begin on page 793.

TexWr — *Texas Writers of Today.* By Florence Elberta Barns. Dallas: Tardy Publishing Co., 1935. Reprint. Ann Arbor: Gryphon Books, 1971.

ThrBJA — *Third Book of Junior Authors.* Edited by Doris DeMontreville and Donna Hill. New York: H.W. Wilson Co., 1972.

TwCA — *Twentieth Century Authors: A Biographical Dictionary of Modern Literature.* New York: H.W. Wilson Co., 1942, 1955.

TwCA	Original volume. Edited by Stanley J. Kunitz and Howard Haycraft, 1942.
TwCA SUP	First supplement. Edited by Stanley J. Kunitz, 1955.

TwCCW — *Twentieth-Century Children's Writers.* Edited by D.L. Kirkpatrick. New York: St. Martin's Press, 1978.

TwCCW 78	"Twentieth-Century Children's Writers" begins on page 9
TwCCW 78A	Appendix begins on page 1391
TwCCW 78B	"Children's Books in Translation" begins on page 1481

TwCW — *Twentieth Century Writing: A Reader's Guide to Contemporary Literature.* Edited by Kenneth Richardson. Levittown, New York: Transatlantic Arts, Inc., 1971.

WebAB	*Webster's American Biographies*. Edited by Charles Van Doren. Springfield, Massachusetts: G. & C. Merriam Co, 1974.
WebE & AL	*Webster's New World Companion to English and American Literature*. Edited by Arthur Pollard. New York: World Publishing Co., 1973.
WhAm 1	*Who Was Who in America*. Volume 1, 1897-1942. A component volume of *Who's Who in American History*. Chicago: A.N. Marquis Co., 1943.

The Corrigenda, indicated in this index by the code *C*, begins on page x.

WhAm 2	*Who Was Who in America*. Volume 2, 1943-1950. A companion biographical reference work to *Who's Who in America*. Chicago: A.N. Marquis Co., 1963.

| **WhoAm 2A** | Addendum begins on page 12 |
| **WhoAm 2C** | Corrigenda begins on page 5 |

WhAm 3	*Who Was Who in America*. Volume 3, 1951-1960. A component of *Who's Who in American History*. Chicago: Marquis Who's Who, Inc., 1966.

The Addendum, indicated in this index by the code *A*, begins on page 952.

WhAm 4	*Who Was Who in America with World Notables*. Volume 4, 1961-1968. A component volume of *Who's Who in American History*. Chicago: Marquis-Who's Who, Inc., 1968.

The Addendum, indicated in this index by the code *A*, begins on page 1049.

WhAm 5	*Who Was Who in America with World Notables*. Volume 5, 1969-1973. Chicago: Marquis Who's Who, Inc., 1973.
WhAm 6	*Who Was Who in America with World Notables*. Volume 6, 1974-1976. Chicago: Marquis Who's Who, Inc., 1976.
WhNAA	*Who Was Who among North American Authors, 1921-1939*. Compiled from *Who's Who among North American Authors*, Volumes 1-7, 1921-1939. Two volumes. Gale Composite Biographical Dictionary Series, Number 1. Detroit: Gale Research Co., 1976.
Who 74	*Who's Who, 1974-1975*. An annual biographical dictionary. 126th year of issue. New York: St. Martin's Press; London: A. & C. Black Ltd., 1974.
WhoAdv 72	*Who's Who in Advertising*. Second edition. Edited by Robert S. Morgan. Rye, New York: Redfield Publishing Co., 1972.
WhoAm	*Who's Who in America*. Chicago: Marquis Who's Who, Inc., 1974, 1976, 1978.

WhoAm 74	38th edition, 1974-1975
WhoAm 76	39th edition, 1976-1977
WhoAm 78	40th edition, 1978-1979

WhoAmA 78	*Who's Who in American Art*. Edited by Jaques Cattell Press. New York: R.R. Bowker Co., 1978.

The Necrology, indicated in this index by the code *N*, is found at the end of the volume.

WhoAmW	*Who's Who of American Women*. Chicago: Marquis Who's Who, Inc., 1958, 1961, 1963, 1965, 1967, 1969, 1971, 1973, 1975, 1978, 1979.

WhoAmW 58	First edition, 1958-1959
WhoAmW 61	Second edition, 1961-1962
WhoAmW 64	Third edition, 1964-1965
WhoAmW 66	Fourth edition, 1966-1967

WhoS & SW   *Who's Who in the South and Southwest.* Chicago: Marquis Who's Who, Inc., 1976, 1978.

      WhoS & SW 76   15th edition, 1976-1977
      WhoS & SW 78   16th edition, 1978-1979

WhoSpyF   *Who's Who in Spy Fiction.* By Donald McCormick. London: Elm Tree Books Ltd., 1977.

WhoTwCL   *Who's Who in Twentieth Century Literature.* By Martin Seymour-Smith. New York: Holt, Rinehart & Winston, 1976.

WhoWest   *Who's Who in the West.* Chicago: Marquis Who's Who, Inc., 1974, 1976, 1978.

      WhoWest 74   14th edition, 1974-1975
      WhoWest 76   15th edition, 1976-1977
      WhoWest 78   16th edition, 1978-1979

WhoWor   *Who's Who in the World.* Chicago: Marquis Who's Who, Inc., 1973, 1976, 1978.

      WhoWor 74   Second edition, 1974-1975
      WhoWor 76   Third edition, 1976-1977
      WhoWor 78   Fourth edition, 1978-1979

WhoWorJ 72   *Who's Who in World Jewry: A Biographical Dictionary of Outstanding Jews.* Edited by I.J. Carmin Karpman. New York: Pitman Publishing Corp., Inc., 1972.

WorAu   *World Authors, 1950-1970.* A companion volume to *Twentieth Century Authors.* Edited by John Wakeman. New York: H.W. Wilson Co., 1975.

WorEFlm   *The World Encyclopedia of the Film.* Edited by John M. Smith and Tim Cawkwell. New York: A. & W. Visual Library, 1972.

WrDr 80   *The Writers Directory, 1980-1982.* London: St. James Press; New York: St. Martin's Press, 1979.

YABC   *Yesterday's Authors of Books for Children.* Facts and pictures about authors and illustrators of books for young people, from early times to 1960. Edited by Anne Commire. Detroit: Gale Research Co., 1977-1978.

      YABC 1   Volume 1, 1977
      YABC 2   Volume 2, 1978
      YABC X   This code refers to pseudonym entries which appear only as cross references in the cumulative index to *Yesterday's Authors of Books for Children.*

HiGH-
inTEREST
BOOKS
FOR
Teens

A

AARON, Chester 1923-
AuBYP SUP, BioIn 11, ConAu 21R,
SmATA 9, WhoWest 74

Catch Calico!
KR - v47 - Jl 15 '79 - p795
SLJ - v25 - My '79 - p69

ABDUL, Raoul 1929-
ConAu 29R, SmATA 12, WhoBlA 75

The Magic Of Black Poetry
BL - v69 - Ja 1 '73 - p447
BL - v69 - My 1 '73 - p837
CCB-B - v26 - Ja '73 - p69
CSM - v64 - N 8 '72 - pB2
LJ - v97 - O 15 '72 - p3450
PW - v202 - O 2 '72 - p54

ABELS, Harriette Sheffer

The Haunted Motorcycle Shop
BL - v75 - N 15 '78 - p551
SLJ - v25 - Ja '79 - p49

ABODAHER, David J 1919-
AuBYP SUP, ConAu 17R, SmATA
17

Compacts, Subs And Minis
SLJ - v23 - D '76 - p58

ADAMS, Charlotte 1899-
AuBYP SUP

The Teen-Ager's Menu Cookbook
BL - v66 - Ap 1 '70 - p966
BS - v29 - D 1 '69 - p350
CCB-B - v24 - Jl '70 - p171
KR - v37 - N 1 '69 - p1155
NYTBR, pt.2 - N 9 '69 - p42
SR - v53 - My 9 '70 - p69

ADAMSON, Joy 1910-1980
ConAu 69, CurBio 72, FourBJA,
SmATA 11, WhoAm 78

Elsa And Her Cubs
B&B - v11 - D '65 - p12
Inst - v75 - Ap '66 - p108
LJ - v91 - F 15 '66 - p1060
NYTBR - v72 - D 3 '67 - p103
Par - v41 - D '66 - p21

Forever Free
BS - v23 - Ap 15 '63 - p36
CSM - Mr 28 '63 - p15
Crit - v21 - Je '63 - p80
HB - v39 - Ag '63 - p405
HM - v226 - Je '63 - p110
LJ - v88 - Mr 1 '63 - p1022
LJ - v88 - My 15 '63 - p2156
PW - v192 - Ag 21 '67 - p77
TLS - N 30 '62 - p940

Pippa, The Cheetah, And Her Cubs
BL - v67 - F 15 '71 - p492
CLW - v42 - My '71 - p578
Comw - v93 - N 20 '70 - p205
LJ - v96 - Je 15 '71 - p2123
PW - v198 - D 28 '70 - p61
SB - v6 - Mr '71 - p324

ADLER, Irving 1913-
ConAu 5R, SmATA 1, ThrBJA

Calendar
BL - v64 - Mr 1 '68 - p777
LJ - v93 - Ja 15 '68 - p287
SB - v3 - Mr '68 - p298

Communication
CCB-B - v21 - Ja '68 - p73
KR - v35 - Je 1 '67 - p646
LJ - v92 - Jl '67 - p2646

ADLER, Irving (continued)

    Language And Man
      BL - v67 - Mr 15 '71 - p618
      CCB-B - v25 - O '71 - p21
      KR - v38 - D 1 '70 - p1292
      SA - v225 - D '71 - p109

    Mathematics: Exploring The
    World Of Numbers And Space
      B&B - v11 - Je '66 - p60

ADLER, Joyce
  see Adler, Irving (co-author) -
    Language And Man

ADLER, Ruth
  see Adler, Irving (co-author) -
    The Calendar
    Adler, Irving (co-author) -
    Communications

ADLER, William
  see David, Jay

ADOFF, Arnold   1935-
  AuNews 1, ConAu 41R, FourBJA,
  MorBMP, SmATA 5

    Brothers And Sisters: Modern
    Stories By Black Americans
      BL - v67 - D 15 '70 - p335
      Comw - v93 - N 20 '70 - p202
      KR - v38 - Ag 1 '70 - p807
      LJ - v95 - D 15 '70 - p4359

    Celebrations: A New Anthology Of
    Black American Poetry
      BL - v74 - F 1 '78 - p901
      CCB-B - v31 - Mr '78 - p105
      Cur R - v17 - Ag '78 - p176
      EJ - v67 - Ap '78 - p97
      HB - v54 - Ap '78 - p180
      SLJ - v24 - Mr '78 - p135

    I Am The Darker Brother
      BL - v65 - Ap 1 '69 - p900
      Bl W - v20 - Ag '71 - p95
      CSM - v61 - My 1 '69 - pB7
      Comw - v89 - F 21 '69 - p645
      Poet - v113 - Ja '69 - p265
      RR - v86 - Mr '69 - p176
      SE - v33 - My '69 - p560

It Is The Poem Singing Into Your
Eyes
  BL - v68 - D 15 '71 - p363
  CCB-B - v25 - Ja '72 - p69
  CE - v48 - My '72 - p424
  CLW - v43 - F '72 - p358
  Comw - v95 - N 19 '71 - p191
  EJ - v61 - Mr '72 - p436
  KR - v39 - O 1 '71 - p1080
  LJ - v96 - S 15 '71 - p2923
  SR - v54 - Ag 21 '71 - p26
  SR - v54 - D 11 '71 - p46

Malcolm X
  BL - v66 - Jl 1 '70 - p1339
  BL - v67 - Ap 1 '71 - p659
  BL - v69 - My 1 '73 - p836
  CCB-B - v24 - S '70 - p1
  Inst - v82 - N '72 - p136
  KR - v38 - Ap 15 '70 - p456
  LJ - v95 - S 15 '70 - p3044
  NYTBR, pt.2 - My 24 '70 - p39
  PW - v197 - Ap 20 '70 - p62
  TN - v27 - Ja '71 - p208
  Teacher - v90 - Mr '73 - p81

My Black Me
  BL - v70 - Jl 1 '74 - p1197
  BL - v71 - Mr 15 '75 - p765
  CCB-B - v28 - O '74 - p21
  Choice - v12 - N '75 - p1130
  KR - v42 - Ap 15 '74 - p427
  LJ - v99 - S 15 '74 - p2258
  NYTBR - My 5 '74 - p38
  PW - v205 - Jl 1 '74 - p82

ADORJAN, Carol   1934-
  ConAu 41R, IntAu&W 77, SmATA
  10

    The Cat Sitter Mystery
      BL - v70 - O 15 '73 - p226
      LJ - v98 - D 15 '73 - p3717
      NYTBR - My 20 '73 - p10

ADRIAN, Mary   1908-
  AuBYP, ConAu X, ForWC 70,
  WhoAmW 75 (also known as
  Jorgensen, Mary Venn; and Venn,
  Mary Eleanor)

    The American Alligator
      BW - v2 - F 25 '68 - p16
      CSM - v59 - N 2 '67 - pB11

ADRIAN, Mary (continued)
  LJ - v93 - F 15 '68 - p857
  NYTBR - v72 - N 5 '67 - p52
  SB - v3 - D '67 - p241

AIKEN, Conrad 1889-1973
  ConAu 5R, ConAu 45, ConLC 10,
  SmATA 3, WhoAm 6, WhoTwCL

  *Cats And Bats And Things With
  Wings: Poems*
    BL - v62 - Mr 1 '66 - p660
    CCB-B - v19 - O '65 - p25
    CSM - v57 - N 4 '65 - pB4
    Comw - v83 - N 5 '65 - p156
    HB - v42 - F '66 - p62
    Inst - v75 - Ja '66 - p140
    KR - v33 - Ag 1 '65 - p746
    LJ - v90 - S 15 '65 - p3776
    NYTBR - v70 - O 24 '65 - p34

AIKEN, Joan 1924-
  ChLR 1, ConAu 9R, SmATA 2,
  ThrBJA, TwCCW 78

  Night Fall
    Am - v125 - D 4 '71 - p490
    B&B - v14 - Ag '69 - p48
    BL - v67 - Jl 15 '71 - p950
    BS - v31 - Jl 15 '71 - p190
    BS - v32 - S 1 '72 - p262
    CE - v48 - D '71 - p149
    Comw - v95 - N 19 '71 - p188
    HB - v47 - O '71 - p487
    KR - v39 - My 1 '71 - p508
    LJ - v96 - My 15 '71 - p1821
    PW - v199 - Je 28 '71 - p63
    SLJ - v24 - F '78 - p35

  The Whispering Mountain
    B&B - v15 - Ag '70 - p54
    BL - v66 - Ja 1 '70 - p563
    CCB-B - v23 - Ap '70 - p123
    CE - v46 - Mr '70 - p319
    Econ - v237 - D 26 '70 - p38
    HB - v46 - F '70 - p39
    KR - v37 - N 1 '69 - p1146
    LJ - v94 - D 15 '69 - p4610
    Obs - D 6 '70 - p23
    PW - v196 - D 29 '69 - p67
    SR - v53 - Ap 18 '70 - p37

  Winterthing
    B&B - v18 - Jl '73 - p140

  BL - v69 - Ja 15 '73 - p490
  CCB-B - v26 - F '73 - p85
  HB - v49 - Ap '73 - p149
  KR - v40 - N 15 '72 - p1314
  LJ - v97 - D 15 '72 - p4075
  NYTBR - pt.1 - F 11 '73 - p8
  TLS - Je 15 '73 - p681
  TN - v29 - Je '73 - p356
  Teacher - v92 - D '74 - p14

AINSWORTH, Norma Ruedi
  ConAu 13R, SmATA 9, WhoAmW
  75, WhoE 77

  Mystery Of The Crying Child
    WCRB - v3 - S '77 - p57

ALBERT, Louise 1928-
  ConAu 69

  But I'm Ready To Go
    BB - v5 - Mr '77 - p4
    CCB-B - v30 - F '77 - p85
    CLW - v48 - My '77 - p442
    Comw - v103 - N 19 '76 - p763
    Cur R - v16 - Ag '77 - p206
    KR - v44 - S 1 '76 - p980
    SLJ - v23 - O '76 - p113

ALDEN, Raymond MacDonald 1873-
1924
  AmAu&B, DcAmAu, DcNAA,
  WhAm 1

  *Why The Chimes Rang, And Other
  Stories*
    NYTBR - D 2 '45 - p42

ALDERMAN, Clifford Lindsey 1902-
  AuBYP, ConAu 1R, SmATA 3

  A Cauldron Of Witches
    BL - v68 - O 15 '71 - p189
    Inst - v82 - My '73 - p78
    KR - v39 - Jl 15 '71 - p747
    LJ - v96 - O 15 '71 - p3472
    NYTBR, pt.2 - N 7 '71 - p42
    Teacher - v90 - Ap '73 - p90

  The Devil's Shadow
    BS - v30 - O 15 '70 - p300
    PW - v198 - S 28 '70 - p82

  Witchcraft In America
    BL - v71 - N 1 '74 - p282

ALDERMAN, Clifford Lindsey
(continued)
> BL - v71 - N 1 '74 - p286
> KR - v42 - O 1 '74 - p1068
> SE - v39 - Mr '75 - p173
> SLJ - v21 - Mr '75 - p103

ALDRIDGE, James 1918-
ConAu 61, ConNov 76, TwCA SUP,
Who 74, WrDr 80

> *A Sporting Proposition*
> BL - v70 - O 15 '73 - p207
> BL - v70 - O 15 '73 - p220
> BS - v33 - O 1 '73 - p289
> BW - v7 - S 23 '73 - p15
> CLW - v45 - Mr '74 - p396
> EJ - v64 - Ja '75 - p112
> KR - v41 - Jl 1 '73 - p697
> KR - v41 - Jl 15 '73 - p764
> LJ - v98 - Ag '73 - p2330
> NYTBR - D 9 '73 - p47
> PW - v204 - Jl 23 '73 - p61

ALEXANDER, Lloyd 1924-
ChLR 1, ConAu 1R, MorBMP,
SmATA 3, ThrBJA, TwCCW 78

> *The Marvelous Misadventures Of
> Sebastian*
> BL - v67 - N 15 '70 - p266
> BL - v67 - Ap 1 '71 - p659
> BW - v4 - N 8 '70 - p10
> BW - v7 - My 13 '73 - p7
> CCB-B - v24 - F '71 - p85
> CE - v47 - My '71 - p437
> CLW - v43 - N '71 - p174
> HB - v46 - D '70 - p628
> LJ - v95 - N 15 '70 - p4040
> LJ - v95 - D 15 '70 - p4324
> NYTBR - N 15 '70 - p42
> PW - v198 - N 2 '70 - p53
> SR - v54 - Ja 23 '71 - p71

> *Time Cat: The Remarkable
> Journeys Of Jason And Gareth*
> LJ - v88 - Je 15 '63 - p2548
> NS - v66 - N 8 '63 - p668
> NYTBR - Ap 14 '63 - p56
> PW - v194 - Jl 22 '68 - p65
> SR - v46 - My 11 '63 - p49
> TLS - N 28 '63 - p980

ALEXANDER, Rae Pace 1898-1974
WhAm 6, WhoBlA 75

> *Young And Black In America*
> BL - v67 - Ja 15 '71 - p418
> BW - v4 - N 8 '70 - p5
> CCB-B - v24 - Ap '71 - p117
> Inst - v130 - Ap '71 - p135
> KR - v38 - S 15 '70 - p1052
> LJ - v96 - F 15 '71 - p729
> NYRB - v15 - D 17 '70 - p10
> NYTBR - D 6 '70 - p58
> NYTBR, pt.2 - N 8 '70 - p2
> NYTBR, pt.2 - N 8 '70 - p36
> PW - v198 - N 9 '70 - p61
> SR - v54 - Mr 20 '71 - p31
> TN - v27 - Ap '71 - p305

ALEXANDER, Sue 1933-
ConAu 53, SmATA 12

> *Finding Your First Job*
> Hi Lo - v2 - S '80 - p3
> KR - v48 - Jl 1 '80 - p842

ALLAN, Mabel Esther 1915-
ConAu 5R, SmATA 5, TwCCW 78

> *The Ballet Family*
> BS - v26 - Ag 1 '66 - p173
> CCB-B - v20 - S '66 - p2
> KR - v34 - F 15 '66 - p185

> *Mystery Began In Madeira*
> B&B - v13 - D '67 - p42
> KR - v35 - My 1 '67 - p564
> LJ - v92 - My 15 '67 - p2039
> PW - v194 - O 7 '68 - p54

ALLEN, Betty 1896-

> *Mind Your Manners*
> BL - v61 - Je 1 '65 - p953
> CC - v82 - Je 30 '65 - p838
> LJ - v90 - Jl '65 - p3129

ALLEN, Elizabeth 1914-

> *You Can't Say What You Think*
> BL - v64 - My 15 '68 - p1085
> BS - v28 - Ap 1 '68 - p17
> BW - v2 - Ag 11 '68 - p12
> CCB-B - v21 - My '68 - p137
> KR - v36 - Mr 1 '68 - p268
> NYTBR - v73 - N 3 '68 - p10

ALLEN, Elizabeth (continued)
PW - v193 - Ap 29 '68 - p78
SR - v51 - Ap 20 '68 - p41

ALLEN, Henry Wilson
see Henry, Will

ALLEN, Maury 1932-
ConAu 17R

> *Reggie Jackson: The Three Million Dollar Man*
> Hi Lo - v2 - O '80 - p6

> *Ron Guidry: Louisiana Lightning*
> CCB-B - v33 - Ja '80 - p86
> Hi Lo - v2 - S '80 - p5
> SLJ - v26 - D '79 - p102

ALLISON, Jon

> *The Pro Basketball Reading Kit*
> Hi Lo - v2 - S '80 - p5

ALMEDINGEN, E M 1898-1971
ConAu 1R, ConLC 12, SmATA 3,
ThrBJA, TwCCW 78 (also known as
Almedingen, Martha Edith Von; and
VonAlmedingen, Martha Edith)

> *Katia*
> BL - v63 - Jl 15 '67 - p1192
> CCB-B - v20 - Jl '67 - p165
> HB - v43 - Ap '67 - p210
> KR - v35 - Ja 15 '67 - p60
> LJ - v92 - Je 15 '67 - p2448
> NYTBR - v72 - Ag 6 '67 - p27
> PW - v191 - Mr 27 '67 - p61
> SR - v50 - My 13 '67 - p56

ALTER, Robert Edmond 1925-1965
AuBYP, ConAu 1R, SmATA 9

> *Two Sieges Of The Alamo*
> BS - v25 - Ag 15 '65 - p214
> HB - v42 - F '66 - p64
> KR - v33 - Jl 1 '65 - p631
> LJ - v90 - S 15 '65 - p3800

> *Who Goes Next?*
> LJ - v91 - N 15 '66 - p5753

AMES, Lee Judah 1921-
ConAu 1R, IlsCB 1967, SmATA 3,
WhoAmA 78

> *Draw 50 Airplanes, Aircraft And Spacecraft*
> BL - v74 - O 1 '77 - p284
> SLJ - v24 - Ja '78 - p84

AMES, Rose Wilder
see Wyler, Rose

AMON, Aline 1928-
AuBYP SUP, ConAu 61, SmATA 9

> *Reading, Writing, Chattering Chimps*
> ACSB - v9 - Winter '76 - p5
> BB - v3 - N '75 - p3
> BL - v72 - N 15 '75 - p448
> CCB-B - v29 - F '76 - p90
> CLW - v47 - Ap '76 - p409
> HB - v51 - D '75 - p604
> KR - v43 - O 1 '75 - p1133
> SA - v235 - D '76 - p134
> SB - v12 - My '76 - p41
> SLJ - v22 - S '75 - p94

ANCKARSVARD, Karin 1915-1969
ConAu 9R, SmATA 6, ThrBJA

> *The Robber Ghost*
> BL - v57 - Je 15 '61 - p642
> CSM - Mr 30 '61 - p7
> HB - v37 - Ap '61 - p157
> KR - v28 - D 15 '61 - p1031
> LJ - v86 - Ap 15 '61 - p1684
> NYTBR, pt.2 - My 14 '61 - p34
> SR - v44 - Je 24 '61 - p20

ANDERSON, Alan H, Jr. 1943-
ConAu 69

> *The Drifting Continents*
> BL - v68 - Ja 15 '72 - p428
> CCB-B - v25 - F '72 - p85
> HB - v48 - Ap '72 - p169
> KR - v39 - O 15 '71 - p1133
> LJ - v97 - Ja 15 '72 - p286
> SB - v8 - My '72 - p38
> SR - v55 - Ja 15 '72 - p47
> TN - v28 - Je '72 - p433

ANDERSON, Joy 1928-
ConAu 25R, SmATA 1

> *The Pai-Pai Pig*
> BL - v64 - N 15 '67 - p384

ANDERSON, Joy (continued)
    BW - v1 - N 5 '67 - p45
    Comw - v87 - N 10 '67 - p180
    KR - v35 - Ag 1 '67 - p875
    LJ - v92 - O 15 '67 - p3845

ANDERSON, Lavere   1907-
WhoAmW 77, WhoS&SW 78

    Allan Pinkerton: First Private Eye
      LJ - v97 - S 15 '72 - p2944

    Balto
      SLJ - v23 - F '77 - p60

    Mary Mcleod Bethune
      Cur R - v16 - D '77 - p363
      SLJ - v23 - S '76 - p93

ANDERSON, Mary   1939-
AuBYP SUP, ConAu 49, IntAu&W
77, SmATA 7

    Step On A Crack
      B&B - v6 - S '78 - p3
      BL - v74 - Ap 1 '78 - p1247
      CCB-B - v32 - S '78 - p2
      CLW - v50 - S '78 - p91
      HB - v54 - Je '78 - p282
      KR - v46 - F 15 '78 - p182
      LA - v56 - Ja '79 - p53
      SLJ - v24 - Ap '78 - p90

ANDES, Eugene

    Practical Macrame
      LJ - v96 - S 15 '71 - p2760

ANDREWS, Julie   1935-
BiDFilm, ConAu 37R, IntWW 78,
OxFilm, SmATA 7, WhoWor 78

    Mandy
      BL - v68 - Mr 15 '72 - p628
      CCB-B - v25 - Je '72 - p154
      CSM - v63 - N 11 '71 - pB5
      Inst - v81 - F '72 - p139
      KR - v39 - O 15 '71 - p1119
      LJ - v96 - D 15 '71 - p4183
      PW - v200 - D 13 '71 - p42
      TLS - N 3 '72 - p1330
      Teacher - v90 - Ap '73 - p85
      Time - v98 - D 27 '71 - p60

ANGELL, Judie   1937-
ConAu 77

    In Summertime It's Tuffy
      BL - v73 - Je 1 '77 - p1492
      BW - Ag 14 '77 - pF4
      BW - Jl 8 '79 - pE2
      CCB-B - v31 - O '77 - p25
      Comw - v104 - N 11 '77 - p730
      KR - v45 - My 1 '77 - p485
      Kliatt - v13 - Fall '79 - p4
      NYTBR - O 9 '77 - p28
      PW - v211 - My 30 '77 - p45
      SLJ - v23 - My '77 - p58

    Ronnie And Rosey
      BB - v6 - My '78 - p3
      CCB-B - v31 - Ap '78 - p121
      HB - v54 - Ap '78 - p161
      KR - v45 - O 15 '77 - p1096
      SLJ - v24 - D '77 - p52

    Tina Gogo
      RT - v32 - Ja '79 - p488

ANGIER, Bradford
  see Dixon, Jeanne (co-author)

ANNIXTER, Jane   (pseud.) 1903-
ConAu X, SmATA 1, WhoAmW 75
(real name: Sturtzel, Jane Levington)

    Ahmeek
      KR - v38 - O 13 '70
      PW - v198 - S 28 '70 - p80
      SR - v53 - S 19 '70 - p35
    see also Annixter, Paul (co-author)

ANNIXTER, Paul   (pseud.) 1894-
ConAu X, SmATA 1 (real name:
Sturtzel, Howard A)

    Swiftwater
      BL - v46 - Ja 1 '50 - p160
      KR - v17 - N 1 '49 - p613
      LJ - v74 - D 1 '49 - p1818
      LJ - v75 - Ap 15 '50 - p706
      NYTBR - Ja 22 '50 - p26
      SR - v33 - F 11 '50 - p36
    see also Annixter, Jane (co-author)

ANONYMOUS

    Go Ask Alice
      B&B - v18 - Ja '73 - p99

ANONYMOUS (continued)
BL - v68 - Mr 15 '72 - p611
BL - v68 - Ap 1 '72 - p663
BS - v32 - S 1 '72 - p263
CLW - v43 - D '71 - p219
CSM - v63 - N 11 '71 - pB6
Comw - v95 - N 19 '71 - p190
EJ - v62 - Ja '73 - p146
KR - v39 - Jl 15 '71 - p776
LJ - v97 - Mr 15 '72 - p1174
LJ - v97 - My 15 '72 - p1884
NYTBR - S 9 '73 - p8
NYTBR, pt.2 - N 5 '72 - p42
PW - v201 - Mr 27 '72 - p80
TLS - S 1 '72 - p1012
TN - v28 - Ap '72 - p311
Teacher - v90 - F '73 - p126
see also Sparks, Beatrice

APSLER, Alfred   1907-
ConAu 5R, IntAu&W 77, SmATA
10, WhoPNW

Fighter For Independence:
Jawaharlal Nehru
HB - v40 - Ap '64 - p186
LJ - v88 - S 15 '63 - p3360
SR - v47 - Ap 25 '64 - p41

ARCHER, Elsie

Let's Face It: The Guide To Good
Grooming For Girls Of Color
KR - v36 - Ag 15 '68 - p909

ARCHER, Jeffrey Howard   1940-
Who 74

Shall We Tell The President?
BL - v74 - N 15 '77 - p525
BS - v37 - D '77 - p259
BW - Ag 28 '77 - pF2
KR - v45 - Ag 1 '77 - p796
LJ - v102 - O 15 '77 - p2178
NS - v94 - N 4 '77 - p625
NYT - v127 - O 10 '77 - p33
NYTBR - O 23 '77 - p36
Obs - N 27 '77 - p28
PW - v212 - Ag 8 '77 - p63
PW - v214 - Ag 7 '78 - p81
SLJ - v24 - D '77 - p65
SR - v5 - O 15 '77 - p36
TLS - O 28 '77 - p1258

VV - v22 - O 24 '77 - p105

ARCHIBALD, Joe   1898-
AuBYP, ConAu 9R, SmATA 3

Commander Of The Flying Tigers:
Claire Lee Chennault
BL - v62 - Jl 1 '66 - p1042
BS - v26 - Jl 1 '66 - p140
KR - v34 - Ja 15 '66 - p62
LJ - v91 - Ap 15 '66 - p2215

Go, Navy, Go
KR - v24 - Ag 1 '56 - p525
NYTBR, pt.2 - N 18 '56 - p30

Phantom Blitz
PW - v203 - Ja 22 '73 - p70

Southpaw Speed
KR - v34 - F 15 '66 - p191
LJ - v91 - Jl '66 - p3550

ARMSTRONG, Fiona

Getting Ready For The World Of
Work
Hi Lo - Je '80 - p4

You And The World Of Work
Hi Lo - Je '80 - p4

ARMSTRONG, Louise
AuBYP SUP

Saving The Big-Deal Baby
CBRS - v8 - Jl '80 - p124
Hi Lo - v2 - S '80 - p3
KR - v48 - Jl 1 '80 - p840

ARMSTRONG, William H   1914-
ChLR 1, ConAu 17R, MorBMP,
SmATA 4, ThrBJA, TwCCW 78

Sounder
A Lib - v1 - Ap '70 - p384
Am - v121 - D 13 '69 - p594
BL - v66 - D 1 '69 - p454
BL - v69 - My 1 '73 - p838
BS - v29 - N 1 '69 - p305
CCB-B - v23 - D '69 - p54
CE - v46 - Mr '70 - p319
CE - v46 - Ap '70 - p368
CLW - v41 - Mr '70 - p477
CSM - v61 - N 6 '69 - pB9

ARMSTRONG, William H (continued)
  Comw - v91 - N 21 '69 - p257
  Comw - v93 - F 26 '71 - p522
  HB - v45 - D '69 - p673
  Inst - v79 - D '69 - p114
  KR - v37 - O 1 '69 - p1063
  LJ - v94 - D 15 '69 - p4580
  LJ - v94 - D 15 '69 - p4610
  Lis - v86 - N 11 '71 - p661
  NO - v8 - D 29 '69 - p17
  NS - v81 - Je 4 '71 - p778
  NYTBR - O 26 '69 - p42
  NYTBR - D 7 '69 - p66
  NYTBR, pt.2 - N 9 '69 - p60
  NYTBR, pt.2 - F 13 '72 - p14
  NYTBR, pt.2 - N 5 '72 - p42
  Obs - Ap 4 '71 - p36
  PW - v196 - N 24 '69 - p42
  SR - v52 - D 20 '69 - p30
  TLS - Jl 2 '71 - p765
  TLS - Ap 6 '73 - p381
  TN - v26 - Ap '70 - p307
  Teacher - v90 - Ja '73 - p90
  WSJ - v175 - F 18 '70 - p18

ARQUETTE, Lois S
see Duncan, Lois

ARRICK, Fran

  Steffie Can't Come Out To Play
  BL - v75 - D 1 '78 - p606
  BS - v38 - Mr '79 - p406
  CCB-B - v32 - Mr '79 - p110
  EJ - v68 - Mr '79 - p82
  Hi Lo - v1 - O '79 - p4
  KR - v46 - D 15 '78 - p1361
  Kliatt - v14 - Winter '80 - p4
  WLB - v53 - D '78 - p341

ARTHUR, Robert   1909-1969
AuBYP SUP, WhoHr&F

  ***Alfred Hitchcock And The Three
  Investigators In The Mystery Of
  The Green Ghost***
  LJ - v90 - N 12 '65 - p5106

  ***Alfred Hitchcock And The Three
  Investigators In The Mystery Of
  The Talking Skull***
  Teacher - v96 - O '78 - p177

  ***Alfred Hitchcock And The Three
  Investigators In The Mystery Of
  The Vanishing Treasure***
  LJ - v91 - N 15 '66 - p5773

  Spies And More Spies
  BS - v27 - N 1 '67 - p312
  LJ - v92 - D 15 '67 - p4619

ARTHUR, Ruth M   1905-1979
ConAu 9R, ConAu 85, ConLC 12,
SmATA 7, SmATA 24N, TwCCW 78

  A Candle In Her Room
  BL - v63 - S 1 '66 - p36
  CCB-B - v19 - My '66 - p142
  HB - v42 - Ap '66 - p195
  KR - v34 - F 1 '66 - p111
  LJ - v91 - Ap 15 '66 - p2215
  NYTBR - v71 - Ag 7 '66 - p24
  Obs - N 27 '66 - p28
  PW - v189 - My 2 '66 - p57
  Spec - N 11 '66 - p628
  TLS - N 24 '66 - p1070

  Portrait Of Margarita
  BL - v64 - Je 1 '68 - p1137
  CLW - v41 - O '69 - p139
  KR - v36 - F 1 '68 - p121
  LJ - v93 - Ap 15 '68 - p1806
  NS - v75 - My 24 '68 - p694
  Punch - v255 - Jl 3 '68 - p33
  TLS - Je 6 '68 - p579

  The Whistling Boy
  BL - v65 - Je 15 '69 - p1173
  BW - v3 - My 4 '69 - p32
  CSM - v61 - Jl 17 '69 - p5
  HB - v45 - Je '69 - p310
  KR - v37 - Mr 1 '69 - p244
  LJ - v94 - Ap 15 '69 - p1789
  PW - v195 - My 12 '69 - p58
  TLS - O 16 '69 - p1199

ARUNDEL, Honor   1919-1973
ConAu P-2, FourBJA, SmATA 4,
SmATA 24N, TwCCW 78

  Emma In Love
  BL - v68 - Jl 15 '72 - p996
  BL - v68 - Jl 15 '72 - p1002
  BS - v32 - S 15 '72 - p284
  EJ - v61 - D '72 - p1384
  KR - v40 - My 15 '72 - p589

ARUNDEL, Honor (continued)
    LJ - v97 - S 15 '72 - p2958
    Obs - D 6 '70 - p27
    TLS - D 11 '70 - p1453

    A Family Failing
        BL - v69 - F 15 '73 - p567
        BS - v32 - Ja 15 '73 - p481
        CCB-B - v26 - My '73 - p133
        LJ - v98 - Ap 15 '73 - p1392
        NS - v84 - N 10 '72 - p692
        PW - v202 - D 4 '72 - p62
        TLS - N 3 '72 - p1324

ASHE, Arthur   1943-
    BioNews 74, ConAu 65, WhoAm 78,
    WhoBlA 75

    Getting Started In Tennis
        BL - v74 - Ap 1 '78 - p1263
        CCB-B - v31 - Mr '78 - p105
        EJ - v67 - Mr '78 - p80
        HB - v54 - Ap '78 - p183
        SLJ - v24 - F '78 - p53

ASHFORD, Jeffrey   (pseud.) 1926-
    AuBYP, ConAu X, EncMys (real
    name: Jeffries, Roderic Graeme)

    Grand Prix Monaco
        KR - v36 - Ag 1 '68 - p822
    see also Jeffries, Roderic Graeme

ASIMOV, Isaac   1920-
    ConAu 1R, ConLC 9, ConSFA,
    SmATA 1, ThrBJA, WorAu

    More Words Of Science
        CCB-B - v26 - Ja '73 - p70
        CLW - v44 - N '72 - p247
        KR - v40 - Ap 1 '72 - p410
        LJ - v97 - O 15 '72 - p3458
        NYTBR - S 10 '72 - p10
        SB - v8 - D '72 - p211
        WLB - v47 - Ja '73 - p447

    The Roman Empire
        CCB-B - v21 - Ja '68 - p73
        CW - v61 - F '68 - p220

    The Roman Republic
        BL - v63 - O 1 '66 - p164
        BS - v26 - Ag 1 '66 - p173
        CCB-B - v20 - My '67 - p134
        CSM - v58 - N 3 '66 - pB9

        Comw - v85 - N 11 '66 - p178
        HB - v42 - O '66 - p579
        KR - v34 - My 15 '66 - p515
        LJ - v91 - Jl '66 - p3541
        NYTBR, pt.2 - v72 - My 7 '67 - p20

    Tomorrow's Children
        BL - v63 - Ap 1 '67 - p843
        CCB-B - v20 - Ja '67 - p69
        HB - v43 - F '67 - p69
        KR - v34 - S 15 '66 - p993
        LJ - v91 - D 15 '66 - p6198
        NYTBR - v71 - N 6 '66 - p20
        SR - v49 - N 12 '66 - p54

ATKINS, Thomas
    see Baxter, John (co-author)

ATKINSON, Linda

    Psychic Stories Strange But True
        BL - v76 - O 15 '79 - p347
        Hi Lo - v1 - Ja '80 - p3
        SLJ - v26 - F '80 - p52

ATWATER, James D   1928-
    WhoAm 78

    Out From Under: Benito Juarez
    And Mexico's Struggle For
    Independence
        KR - v37 - Jl 1 '69 - p679
        LJ - v94 - N 15 '69 - p4280

ATWATER, Montgomery M

    Snow Rangers Of The Andes
        BS - v27 - N 1 '67 - p312
        CLW - v39 - My '68 - p665
        CSM - v70 - Ja 30 '78 - p15
        KR - v35 - Ag 1 '67 - p884
        LJ - v92 - D 15 '67 - p4619

AULT, Phil   1914-
    AuBYP SUP, SmATA 23, WhoAm
    78

    These Are The Great Lakes
        LJ - v98 - My 15 '73 - p1687
        SB - v9 - My '73 - p64

AWREY, Don   1943-
    WhoHcky 73

AWREY, Don (continued)

Power Hockey
BL - v71 - My 15 '75 - p961

AXTHELM, Pete

The Kid
BL - v75 - S 1 '78 - p15
BS - v39 - Ap '79 - p16
KR - v46 - O 1 '78 - p1096
KR - v46 - N 1 '78 - p1198
LJ - v103 - Ag '78 - p1527
NYT - v127 - Je 9 '78 - pC25
SLJ - v25 - O '78 - p164

AYLESWORTH, Thomas G   1927-
AuBYP SUP, ConAu 25R, SmATA
4, WhoE 77

Monsters From The Movies
BL - v69 - F 15 '73 - p571
KR - v40 - O 15 '72 - p1203
PW - v202 - D 18 '72 - p39
SR - v55 - N 11 '72 - p79
Teacher - v90 - Ap '73 - p90

Movie Monsters
BB - v3 - O '75 - p3
CLW - v47 - My '76 - p451
Cur R - v16 - Ag '77 - p205
EJ - v65 - My '76 - p91
KR - v43 - S 15 '75 - p1069
SLJ - v22 - Ja '76 - p43
Teacher - v93 - Ap '76 - p125

AYMAR, Brandt   1911-
ConAu 1R, WhNAA

*Laws And Trials That Created
History*
BL - v71 - S 1 '74 - p37
Inst - v84 - O '74 - p205
KR - v42 - Je 15 '74 - p639
LJ - v99 - N 15 '74 - p3050
PW - v205 - Je 17 '74 - p69
SE - v39 - Mr '75 - p174

B

BACH, Alice   1942-
AuBYP SUP, ForWC 70

A Father Every Few Years
BB - v5 - Ag '77 - p4
BL - v73 - My 15 '77 - p1416
BS - v37 - Je '77 - p95
CCB-B - v30 - My '77 - p137
KR - v45 - Ja 15 '77 - p45
PW - v211 - Mr 28 '77 - p79
SLJ - v23 - Ap '77 - p73

The Meat In The Sandwich
BL - v72 - S 15 '75 - p163
CCB-B - v29 - Ja '76 - p73
Comw - v102 - N 21 '75 - p566
KR - v43 - S 1 '75 - p1002
NYTBR - N 2 '75 - p12
PW - v208 - Ag 11 '75 - p117
SLJ - v22 - D '75 - p68

Mollie Make-Believe
BL - v70 - Jl 1 '74 - p1197
BS - v34 - Je 15 '74 - p148
CCB-B - v28 - O '74 - p21
KR - v42 - Ap 15 '74 - p432
LJ - v99 - S 15 '74 - p2282
NYTBR - My 19 '74 - p8
NYTBR - N 3 '74 - p52

*They'll Never Make A Movie
Starring Me*
BS - v33 - Je 15 '73 - p145
KR - v41 - My 15 '73 - p567
PW - v203 - My 7 '73 - p66

BACON, Margaret Hope   1921
ConAu 25R, SmATA 6

*Lamb's Warrior: The Life Of Isaac
T. Hopper*
BL - v67 - O 1 '70 - p142
BS - v30 - My 1 '70 - p59
KR - v38 - My 1 '70 - p515

LJ - v95 - N 15 '70 - p4040
NYTBR - Ag 9 '70 - p22

BACON, Martha   1917-
ChLR 3, ConAu 85, TwCCW 78,
SmATA 18

Sophia Scrooby Preserved
BL - v65 - O 1 '68 - p183
BS - v28 - O 1 '68 - p275
CCB-B - v22 - S '68 - p2
HB - v44 - O '68 - p561
KR - v36 - Ag 1 '68 - p822
LJ - v93 - O 15 '68 - p3975
NYTBR - v73 - O 20 '68 - p38
PW - v194 - Ag 12 '68 - p55
SR - v51 - S 21 '68 - p37

BAILEY, John
AuBYP

Prehistoric Man
KR - v36 - Ap 1 '68 - p405
LJ - v93 - O 15 '68 - p3975

BAKER, A A

Mountain Rescue
BL - v75 - F 15 '79 - p927

BAKER, Betty   1928-
ConAu X, SmATA 5, ThrBJA,
TwCCW 78 (also known as Venturo,
Betty Lou Baker)

Dunderhead War
BL - v64 - D 1 '67 - p443
BW - v2 - Ja 14 '68 - p14
CCB-B - v21 - My '68 - p138
CLW - v39 - D '67 - p297
CSM - v59 - N 2 '67 - pB9
HB - v43 - O '67 - p599
KR - v35 - Jl 1 '67 - p744

BAKER, Betty (continued)
LJ - v92 - O 15 '67 - p3859

Walk The World's Rim
BL - v61 - Je 15 '65 - p995
BS - v25 - My 15 '65 - p96
CCB-B - v18 - Je '65 - p141
CE - v42 - Ja '66 - p314
HB - v41 - Ap '65 - p174
KR - v33 - Ja 15 '65 - p62
LJ - v90 - Mr 15 '65 - p1546
NYTBR - v70 - Jl 11 '65 - p34

BAKER, Laura Nelson 1911-
ConAu 5R, MnnWr, SmATA 3

Here By The Sea
BS - v28 - O 1 '68 - p275
BW - v2 - N 3 '68 - p26
KR - v36 - Ag 1 '68 - p823
LJ - v93 - N 15 '68 - p4410
NYTBR - Mr 9 '69 - p26

BALDWIN, Stan 1929-
ConAu 49

Bad Henry: An Authorized Hank Aaron Story
BS - v34 - My 15 '74 - p78
LJ - v99 - My 15 '74 - p1405
NO - v13 - Ag 17 '74 - p14
NYTBR - Je 2 '74 - p7
PW - v205 - Mr 25 '74 - p55

BALES, Carol Ann 1940-
ConAu 45

Tales Of The Elders: A Memory Book Of Men And Women Who Came To America As Immigrants, 1900-1930
B&B - v5 - Je '77 - p3
BL - v73 - Jl 15 '77 - p1726
CCB-B - v31 - S '77 - p3
Comw - v104 - N 11 '77 - p733
HB - v53 - O '77 - p543
LA - v54 - O '77 - p811
NYTBR - Jl 3 '77 - p11
PW - v211 - My 2 '77 - p70
SE - v42 - Ap '78 - p319
SLJ - v23 - Ap '77 - p74
Teacher - v96 - D '78 - p22

BALL, Charles Elihue

Saddle Up: The Farm Journal Book Of Western Horsemanship
BL - v67 - N 15 '70 - p243
KR - v38 - Mr 15 '70 - p352
LJ - v95 - S 15 '70 - p2931

BALLARD, Martin 1929-
ConAu 25R, SmATA 1, TwCCW 78

The Emir's Son
KR - v35 - O 15 '67 - p1262
LJ - v92 - D 15 '67 - p4608
Spec - v219 - N 3 '67 - p543
TLS - N 30 '67 - p1143

BAMMAN, Henry A 1918-
ConAu 5R, LEduc 74, SmATA 12

Flight To The South Pole
Inst - v75 - F '66 - p160
LJ - v90 - D 15 '65 - p5508

Viking Treasure
Inst - v75 - F '66 - p160
LJ - v90 - D 15 '65 - p5508

BARKIN, Carol

Slapdash Decorating
BB - v6 - Mr '78 - p4
BL - v74 - F 1 '78 - p906
KR - v45 - N 1 '77 - p1149
PW - v213 - Ap 10 '78 - p72
SLJ - v24 - Ja '78 - p93

BARNESS, Richard 1917-
ConAu 65

Graystone College
LJ - v99 - My 15 '74 - p1471

BARNOUW, Victor 1915-
AmM&WS 76P, ConAu 85, WhoAm 74

Dream Of The Blue Heron
BS - v26 - D 1 '66 - p337
KR - v34 - S 15 '66 - p982
LJ - v91 - D 15 '66 - p6198

BARON, Virginia Olsen 1931-
AuBYP SUP, ConAu 25R

BARON, Virginia Olsen (continued)

Here I Am!
BS - v29 - Ja 1 '70 - p387
CCB-B - v23 - Ap '70 - p124
KR - v37 - N 15 '69 - p1204
LJ - v95 - Je 15 '70 - p2306
NO - v8 - N 24 '69 - p25
NYTBR - D 14 '69 - p34
PW - v196 - D 8 '69 - p47
SR - v53 - Ja 24 '70 - p37

The Seasons Of Time: Tanka Poetry Of Ancient Japan
BL - v64 - Jl 15 '68 - p1285
CLW - v40 - O '68 - p146
KR - v36 - My 1 '68 - p519
LJ - v93 - My 15 '68 - p2118
LJ - v93 - Ag '68 - p2875
NYTBR - v73 - My 5 '68 - p44
PW - v193 - Mr 18 '68 - p54

BARRETT, William F 1900-
ConAu 5R, ConSFA, WhoWor 78

The Lilies Of The Field
BL - v58 - My 1 '62 - p606
KR - v30 - F 1 '62 - p128
LJ - v87 - Ap 1 '62 - p1481
NYTBR - Ap 22 '62 - p23

BARTH, Edna 1914-
AuBYP SUP, ConAu 41R, SmATA 7, WhoAmW 77

Turkeys, Pilgrims, And Indian Corn
BB - v3 - N '75 - p3
BL - v72 - D 15 '75 - p575
KR - v43 - O 15 '75 - p1187
PW - v208 - Ag 25 '75 - p294
SLJ - v22 - N '75 - p68

BARTOS-HOEPPNER, Barbara 1923-
ConAu 25R, FourBJA, SmATA 5

Avalanche Dog
BL - v63 - Jl 1 '67 - p1144
CCB-B - v21 - S '67 - p1
HB - v43 - Ag '67 - p474
KR - v35 - Ap 15 '67 - p505
LJ - v92 - Je 15 '67 - p2448
PW - v191 - Ap 10 '67 - p82

TLS - N 24 '66 - p1091

BATES, Betty 1921-
ConAu X, SmATA 19 (also known as Bates, Elizabeth)

Bugs In Your Ears
CCB-B - v31 - F '78 - p89
KR - v45 - S 15 '77 - p989
PW - v212 - D 26 '77 - p68
SLJ - v24 - F '78 - p54

The Ups And Downs Of Jorie Jenkins
KR - v46 - My 1 '78 - p496
SLJ - v24 - My '78 - p62

BATSON, Larry 1930-
ConAu 57

Rod Carew
BL - v73 - Je 15 '77 - p1572
BL - v73 - Jl 1 '77 - p1650
SLJ - v23 - My '77 - p80
SLJ - v23 - My '77 - p81

Walt "Clyde" Frazier
LJ - v99 - D 15 '74 - p3281

BAUER, Marion Dane 1938-
ConAu 69, SmATA 20

Foster Child
BL - v73 - My 1 '77 - p1343
CCB-B - v30 - Je '77 - p153
Comw - v104 - N 11 '77 - p731
KR - v45 - My 1 '77 - p485
NYTBR - My 1 '77 - p46
PW - v211 - My 2 '77 - p69
RT - v32 - O '78 - p42
SLJ - v23 - Ap '77 - p74
WCRB - v4 - Ja '78 - p66

Shelter From The Wind
BB - v4 - Ja '77 - p4
Comw - v103 - N 19 '76 - p762
HB - v52 - Ag '76 - p394
KR - v44 - Ap 1 '76 - p389
Kliatt - v12 - Fall '78 - p4
NYTBR - Je 6 '76 - p54
PW - v209 - Ap 5 '76 - p101
SLJ - v22 - My '76 - p56

BAUM, Myra
see Armstrong, Fiona (co-author)

BAUMANN, Amy Brown Beeching
see Brown, Alexis

BAUMANN, Hans   1914-
ConAu 5R, SmATA 2, ThrBJA

   Lion Gate And Labyrinth
     BL - v64 - Mr 1 '68 - p778
     BS - v27 - Ja 1 '68 - p391
     BW - v2 - Je 23 '68 - p11
     CCB-B - v21 - Mr '68 - p105
     HB - v43 - D '67 - p761
     KR - v35 - N 1 '67 - p1324
     LJ - v93 - F 15 '68 - p877
     PW - v192 - D 25 '67 - p60
     SB - v3 - Mr '68 - p307
     SR - v51 - Ap 20 '68 - p41
     TLS - N 30 '67 - p1162

BAWDEN, Nina   1925-
ChLR 2, ConAu X, FourBJA,
SmATA 4, SouST, TwCCW 78 (also
known as Kark, Nina Mary)

   Squib
     A Lib - v3 - Ap '72 - p419
     BL - v68 - N 15 '71 - p290
     BL - v68 - Ap 1 '72 - p668
     CCB-B - v25 - Jl '72 - p165
     CE - v49 - Ja '73 - p201
     Comw - v95 - N 19 '71 - p188
     GW - v104 - Je 5 '71 - p19
     HB - v47 - O '71 - p482
     KR - v39 - Jl 15 '71 - p738
     LJ - v96 - D 15 '71 - p4198
     NS - v81 - Je 4 '71 - p778
     NYRB - v17 - D 2 '71 - p25
     TLS - Jl 2 '71 - p775
     TN - v28 - Ap '72 - p309

BAXTER, John   1939-
ConAu 29R, EncSF, ScF&FL 1,
ScF&FL 2, WrDr 80

   The Fire Came By
     BL - v73 - O 15 '76 - p312
     Choice - v13 - D '76 - p1313
     KR - v44 - Mr 15 '76 - p352
     Kliatt - v11 - Fall '77 - p36
     LJ - v101 - My 15 '76 - p1217
     NYTBR - Jl 18 '76 - p4
     Obs - D 12 '76 - p26
     PW - v209 - Ap 12 '76 - p64

     PW - v211 - Mr 7 '77 - p98
     SB - v13 - My '77 - p2
     WSJ - v187 - Je 22 '76 - p22
     WSJ - v188 - D 8 '76 - p24

BAYLOR, Byrd   1924-
ChLR 3, ConAu 81, FourBJA,
SmATA 16 (also known as
Schweitzer, Byrd Baylor)

   They Put On Masks
     A Lib - v6 - Mr '75 - p166
     BL - v70 - Je 1 '74 - p1102
     CCB-B - v28 - O '74 - p22
     CE - v51 - N '74 - p94
     KR - v42 - Ap 15 '74 - p428
     LJ - v99 - S 15 '74 - p2239
     PW - v205 - Ap 22 '74 - p74
     RT - v32 - Ja '79 - p444

BEAME, Rona   1934-
ConAu 45, SmATA 12

   Emergency!
     BL - v73 - Je 15 '77 - p1572
     CCB-B - v31 - O '77 - p27
     KR - v45 - Ap 15 '77 - p429
     SB - v14 - My '78 - p40
     SLJ - v24 - S '77 - p120

BEATTY, Patricia Robbins   1922-
ConAu 1R, SmATA 1, ThrBJA,
TwCCW 78

   By Crumbs, It's Mine
     BB - v4 - Ag '76 - p3
     BL - v72 - Ap 15 '76 - p1182
     BL - v73 - My 15 '77 - p1425
     CCB-B - v29 - Jl '76 - p169
     CLW - v48 - O '76 - p137
     KR - v44 - F 1 '76 - p133
     PW - v209 - Ap 26 '76 - p60
     SLJ - v22 - Ap '76 - p80
     SLJ - v22 - My '76 - p34

   Something To Shout About
     BL - v73 - D 1 '76 - p534
     CCB-B - v30 - F '77 - p86
     Comw - v103 - N 19 '76 - p762
     HB - v53 - Ap '77 - p157
     KR - v44 - S 1 '76 - p973
     LA - v54 - Ap '77 - p442
     PW - v210 - O 4 '76 - p74
     SLJ - v23 - N '76 - p52

BEATTY, Patricia Robbins (continued)

Wait For Me, Watch For Me, Eula Bee
    KR - v46 - N 15 '78 - p1246

BECKMAN, Gunnel   1910-
    ConAu 33R, FourBJA, SmATA 6,
    TwCCW 78B

Admission To The Feast
    BL - v69 - Ja 1 '73 - p442
    CCB-B - v26 - Ap '73 - p118
    EJ - v62 - N '73 - p1187
    HB - v48 - O '72 - p474
    KR - v40 - S 15 '72 - p1106
    LJ - v97 - D 15 '72 - p4075
    TLS - O 22 '71 - p1318

BECKWITH, Lillian   1916-
    ConAu X, IntAu&W 77 (also known
    as Comber, Lillian)

The Spuddy
    BL - v72 - F 15 '76 - p847
    BL - v72 - F 15 '76 - p852
    KR - v43 - N 1 '75 - p1248
    LJ - v100 - D 1 '75 - p2263
    NYTBR - Ja 4 '76 - p22
    PW - v208 - D 1 '75 - p60
    SLJ - v22 - N '75 - p95

BEERY, Mary   1907-
    ConAu 5R, WrDr 80

Manners Made Easy
    BL - v63 - O 1 '66 - p164
    BS - v26 - Ag 1 '66 - p173
    LJ - v91 - S 15 '66 - p4346
    NYTBR - v72 - Mr 5 '67 - p30

Young Teens Away From Home
    BS - v26 - S 1 '66 - p201
    NYTBR - v71 - Je 5 '66 - p42

BELTING, Natalia Maree   1915-
    ConAu 1R, DrAS 78H, SmATA 6,
    ThrBJA

Whirlwind Is A Ghost Dancing
    BL - v71 - N 1 '74 - p286
    CCB-B - v28 - Mr '75 - p106
    Choice - v12 - N '75 - p1130
    HB - v50 - D '74 - p688
    KR - v42 - S 1 '74 - p945

    LJ - v99 - N 15 '74 - p3043
    SE - v39 - Mr '75 - p174

BENARY-ISBERT, Margot   1889-
1979
    ConAu 5R, ConLC 12, MorJA,
    SmATA 2, SmATA 21N

The Ark
    BL - v49 - Mr 15 '53 - p241
    CC - v70 - S 2 '53 - p996
    Comw - v59 - N 20 '53 - p178
    HB - v29 - Ap '53 - p102
    HB - v29 - Ap '53 - p124
    KR - v21 - Ja 15 '53 - p41
    LJ - v78 - My 1 '53 - p819
    NY - v29 - N 28 '53 - p194
    NYT - Mr 1 '53 - p32
    NYTBR - My 6 '56 - p32
    SR - v36 - Ap 4 '53 - p64

Rowan Farm
    BL - v51 - S 1 '54 - p20
    HB - v30 - O '54 - p336
    KR - v22 - Je 1 '54 - p341
    LJ - v79 - S 15 '54 - p1670
    NY - v30 - N 27 '54 - p212
    NYTBR - O 10 '54 - p38
    SR - v37 - Ag 21 '54 - p35

BENCHLEY, Nathaniel   1915-
    ConAu 1R, FourBJA, SmATA 3,
    TwCCW 78, WorAu

Gone And Back
    BS - v31 - My 15 '71 - p98
    BW - v5 - My 9 '71 - p18
    CLW - v43 - Ap '72 - p481
    KR - v39 - F 15 '71 - p179
    LJ - v96 - Ap 15 '71 - p1511
    NYTBR - D 5 '71 - p86
    NYTBR, pt.2 - My 2 '71 - p4
    NYTBR, pt.2 - N 7 '71 - p28
    NYTBR, pt.2 - F 13 '72 - p14
    NYTBR, pt.2 - N 5 '72 - p42
    PW - v199 - Mr 22 '71 - p53
    Time - v98 - D 27 '71 - p61

BENDICK, Jeanne   1919-
    BkP, ConAu 5R, IlsCB 1957, MorJA,
    SmATA 2

Electronics For Young People
    LJ - v97 - F 15 '72 - p782

BENDICK, Jeanne (continued)

The Emergency Book
BL - v64 - Ja 15 '68 - p590
CCB-B - v21 - F '68 - p90
HB - v44 - F '68 - p78
Inst - v77 - F '68 - p190
KR - v35 - O 1 '67 - p1221
LJ - v92 - D 15 '67 - p4619
PW - v192 - D 11 '67 - p45
SR - v50 - N 11 '67 - p47

Filming Works Like This
BL - v67 - Ap 1 '71 - p662
CCB-B - v24 - My '71 - p133
FQ - v24 - Spring '71 - p14
Inst - v81 - Ag '71 - p180
LJ - v96 - O 15 '71 - p3464
NYTBR, pt.2 - N 8 '70 - p18

The First Book Of Automobiles
BL - v62 - Jl 1 '66 - p1049
BL - v68 - F 1 '72 - p468
LJ - v91 - Jl '66 - p3552
SLJ - v25 - N '78 - p55

BENDICK, Robert
see Bendick, Jeanne (co-author) -
Filming Works Like This

BENNETT, Jay   1912-
AuBYP SUP, ConAu 69, WhoAm 78

***The Birthday Murderer: A
Mystery***
BL - v74 - O 15 '77 - p366
BW - v9 - O 7 '79 - p15
CCB-B - v31 - F '78 - p90
EJ - v68 - Ja '79 - p57
KR - v45 - N 15 '77 - p1205
PW - v212 - Ag 22 '77 - p66
SLJ - v24 - D '77 - p62

The Dangling Witness
BS - v34 - N 15 '74 - p377
NYTBR - N 10 '74 - p8
PW - v206 - Ag 12 '74 - p58

Deathman, Do Not Follow Me
BS - v28 - Jl 1 '68 - p154
KR - v36 - Ap 15 '68 - p465
LJ - v93 - Jl '68 - p2736
NYTBR - v73 - Jl 7 '68 - p16

The Long Black Coat
KR - v41 - Ap 1 '73 - p395
LJ - v98 - My 15 '73 - p1702
PW - v203 - My 7 '73 - p65

The Pigeon
SLJ - v26 - My '80 - p86

Say Hello To The Hit Man
BL - v72 - Ap 1 '76 - p1100
BL - v72 - Ap 1 '76 - p1108
BS - v36 - Ag '76 - p148
KR - v44 - Ap 15 '76 - p481
NYTBR - My 2 '76 - p36
PW - v209 - Mr 8 '76 - p67
SLJ - v22 - My '76 - p77

BERGAUST, Erik   1925-1978
ConAu 73, ConAu 77, SmATA 20

Colonizing Space
KR - v46 - Mr 1 '78 - p249
SLJ - v25 - S '78 - p153

BERGER, Melvin   1927-
ConAu 5R, ConLC 12, SmATA 5

The Funny Side Of Science
KR - v41 - Ap 15 '73 - p458
LJ - v98 - N 15 '73 - p3447

Police Lab
BL - v72 - Ap 1 '76 - p1108
KR - v44 - Ap 15 '76 - p474
SB - v13 - My '77 - p39
SLJ - v22 - F '76 - p43

The Story Of Folk Music
BL - v73 - D 15 '76 - p603
CE - v53 - Mr '77 - p260
KR - v44 - O 1 '76 - p1096
PW - v210 - O 18 '76 - p63
SE - v41 - Ap '77 - p348
SLJ - v23 - N '76 - p54

The Supernatural
BB - v6 - Ap '78 - p4
BL - v74 - Ja 15 '78 - p809
CCB-B - v31 - Je '78 - p154
HB - v54 - Je '78 - p308
KR - v45 - N 15 '77 - p1200
SB - v14 - D '78 - p142
SLJ - v24 - Mr '78 - p135

BERGER, Phil   1942-
AuBYP SUP, ConAu 61

> *Championship Teams Of The NFL*
> BL - v65 - Ap 15 '69 - p959
> CSM - v60 - N 7 '68 - pB12
> KR - v36 - S 1 '68 - p980
> PW - v194 - O 7 '68 - p55

BERGER, Terry   1933-
ConAu 37R, SmATA 8, WrDr 80

> *How Does It Feel When Your
> Parents Get Divorced?*
> BL - v73 - My 15 '77 - p1423
> CLW - v49 - D '77 - p229
> KR - v45 - Mr 1 '77 - p225
> SLJ - v24 - N '77 - p53

> *Stepchild*
> Hi Lo - v2 - S '80 - p4

BERKOW, Ira   1939?-
BioIn 10

> *Beyond The Dream: Occasional
> Heroes Of Sports*
> BL - v72 - D 1 '75 - p487
> KR - v43 - Jl 15 '75 - p810
> LJ - v100 - S 15 '75 - p1647
> PW - v208 - Jl 28 '75 - p117
> SLJ - v22 - F '76 - p58
> WLB - v50 - Mr '76 - p545

BERLONI, William
see Thomas, Allison (co-author)

BERMAN, Connie   1949-
ConAu 93

> *Leif Garrett*
> SLJ - v25 - Mr '79 - p135

> *The Shaun Cassidy Scrapbook*
> Hi Lo - v1 - N '79 - p6

> *Top Recording Artist And Tv Star!
> Shaun Cassidy*
> Hi Lo - v1 - N '79 - p6
> SLJ - v26 - S '79 - p129

BERNA, Paul   1910?-
ConAu 73, SmATA 15, ThrBJA

> *The Clue Of The Black Cat*
> BL - v62 - O 15 '65 - p218
> CCB-B - v19 - N '65 - p42
> CSM - v57 - N 4 '65 - pB12
> Comw - v83 - N 5 '65 - p157
> HB - v41 - D '65 - p631
> KR - v33 - S 1 '65 - p910
> LJ - v90 - N 15 '65 - p5103
> NS - v80 - N 6 '70 - p616
> NYTBR - v70 - N 7 '65 - p59
> Obs - Ja 10 '71 - p23
> Par - v41 - Jl '66 - p98
> SLJ - v24 - F '78 - p35

> *The Mule On The Expressway*
> BL - v65 - F 15 '69 - p650
> HB - v45 - Ap '69 - p168
> KR - v36 - S 15 '68 - p1047

> *The Mystery Of Saint-Salgue*
> CSM - N 5 '64 - p5B
> HB - v40 - D '64 - p618
> LJ - v89 - S 5 '64 - p3480
> NS - v66 - N 8 '63 - p670
> NYTBR, pt.2 - N 1 '64 - p55
> TLS - N 28 '63 - p974

BERNHEIM, Evelyne
see Bernheim, Marc (co-author)

BERNHEIM, Marc   1924-
ConAu 21R

> *African Success Story: The Ivory
> Coast*
> BL - v66 - Jl 1 '70 - p1339
> BS - v30 - Mr 15 '71 - p548
> CCB-B - v24 - S '70 - p3
> Comw - v93 - F 26 '71 - p521
> HB - v46 - O '70 - p487
> SR - v53 - Jl 25 '70 - p29

BERRY, Barbara J   1937-
ConAu 33R, SmATA 7, WrDr 80

> *Shannon*
> BW - v2 - N 3 '68 - p22
> KR - v36 - Je 1 '68 - p595
> LJ - v93 - N 15 '68 - p4411

BERRY, Erick   (pseud.) 1892-1974
ConAu X, IlsCB 1946, JBA 51,
SmATA 2 (real name: Best, Allena
Champlin)

BERRY, Erick (continued)

When Wagon Trains Rolled To Santa Fe
LJ - v91 - D 15 '66 - p6209

BERRY, James R   1932-
AuBYP SUP, ConAu 21R

Kids On The Run
B&B - v7 - F '79 - p3
BL - v74 - My 1 '78 - p1420
BS - v38 - D '78 - p270
CCB-B - v32 - S '78 - p3
KR - v46 - Mr 1 '78 - p249
NYTBR - Ap 30 '78 - p53
PW - v213 - My 29 '78 - p52
SE - v43 - Ap '79 - p299
SLJ - v24 - Mr '78 - p136

BESSER, Marianne
ForWC 70

The Cat Book
KR - v35 - S 15 '67 - p1137
LJ - v92 - D 15 '67 - p4608
NYTBR - v72 - N 5 '67 - p6
Obs - N 30 '69 - p35
PW - v192 - S 4 '67 - p57
SB - v3 - D '67 - p246

BEST, Allena Champlin
see Berry, Erick

BETHANCOURT, T Ernesto   (pseud.)
1932-
ChLR 3, ConAu X, SmATA 11 (real name: Paisley, Tom)

Dr. Doom: Superstar
BL - v75 - O 15 '78 - p366
HB - v55 - F '79 - p67
KR - v46 - S 15 '78 - p1020
PW - v214 - Ag 28 '78 - p395
SLJ - v25 - D '78 - p69

Doris Fein: Superspy
BL - v76 - F 1 '80 - p763
CBRS - v8 - My '80 - p97
CCB-B - v33 - My '80 - p167
PW - v217 - Ap 11 '80 - p78
SLJ - v26 - My '80 - p86

New York City Too Far From Tampa Blues
BL - v71 - My 15 '75 - p963
CCB-B - v28 - Jl '75 - p174
KR - v43 - Ap 15 '75 - p464
NYTBR - My 4 '75 - p28
PW - v207 - Ap 28 '75 - p45
SLJ - v22 - S '75 - p117

Tune In Yesterday
BL - v74 - My 1 '78 - p1420
BS - v38 - Ag '78 - p153
EJ - v67 - S '78 - p90
HB - v54 - Ag '78 - p400
KR - v46 - Mr 15 '78 - p311
NYTBR - Ap 30 '78 - p44
PW - v213 - Mr 6 '78 - p101
SE - v43 - Ap '79 - p302
SLJ - v24 - My '78 - p73

BETHEL, Dell   1929-
ConAu 29R

Inside Basketball
LJ - v94 - D 15 '69 - p4620
SR - v52 - Je 28 '69 - p1884

BIBBY, Violet   1908-
AuBYP SUP, SmATA 24, TwCCW 78

Many Waters Cannot Quench Love
BL - v72 - D 15 '75 - p575
CCB-B - v29 - F '76 - p91
KR - v43 - O 1 '75 - p1136
PW - v208 - S 29 '75 - p50
SLJ - v22 - N '75 - p86

BIBER, Yehoash

The Treasure Of The Turkish Pasha
CLW - v41 - O '69 - p139
KR - v36 - Ag 1 '68 - p815
LJ - v94 - F 15 '69 - p880
NYTBR - v73 - N 24 '68 - p42

BIEMILLER, Ruth   1914-
ConAu 37R, WhoAmW 77, WhoE 77

Dance
CCB-B - v22 - My '69 - p138
KR - v37 - Mr 1 '69 - p241
LJ - v94 - O 15 '69 - p3827

BIEMILLER, Ruth (continued)
LJ - v98 - O 15 '73 - p3123

BIRO, Val 1921-
ConAu 25R, IlsCB 1967, SmATA 1,
TwCCW 78 (also known as Biro,
Balint Stephen)

Gumdrop
B&B - v12 - Mr '67 - p60
LJ - v93 - F 15 '68 - p857
Spec - N 11 '66 - p627
TLS - N 24 '66 - p1083

BISHOP, Claire Huchet
BkP, ConAu 73, JBA 51, SmATA 14,
TwCCW 78, WrDr 80

Martin De Porres, Hero
Comw - v99 - N 23 '73 - p212
Teacher - v91 - Ja '74 - p107

BISHOP, Curtis Kent 1912-1967
ConAu P-1, SmATA 6

Fast Break
BL - v64 - F 15 '68 - p697
KR - v35 - S 1 '67 - p1054
LJ - v92 - D 15 '67 - p4633

Sideline Pass
KR - v33 - Jl 1 '65 - p630
LJ - v90 - O 15 '65 - p4638

BLACKBURN, Joyce Knight 1920-
ConAu 17R, IndAu 1917, WhoAmW
74

Martha Berry
CCB-B - v22 - My '69 - p138
KR - v36 - O 1 '68 - p1116
PW - v194 - O 14 '68 - p65

BLANTON, Catherine 1907-
AuBYP, ConAu 1R

Hold Fast To Your Dreams
BL - v51 - My 15 '55 - p391
CE - v46 - Ap '70 - p368
EJ - v57 - My '68 - p757
KR - v23 - Ja 1 '55 - p4
LJ - v80 - Ap 15 '55 - p1008
NYTBR - Ap 24 '55 - p32

BLASSINGAME, Wyatt 1909-
ConAu 1R, SmATA 1, WhoHr&F,
WhoS&SW 76, WrDr 80

*The Story Of The United States
Flag*
Am - v121 - D 13 '69 - p598

BLATT, Joseph
see Sullivan, Mary Beth (co-author)

BLAU, Melinda 1943-
ForWC 70

*Whatever Happened To Amelia
Earhart?*
CCB-B - v31 - Je '78 - p155
Cur R - v17 - Ag '78 - p228

BLINN, William
NewYTET

Brian's Song
BS - v32 - O 1 '72 - p316

BLIVEN, Bruce, Jr. 1916-
ConAu 17R, SmATA 2, WhoAm 78,
WhoWor 78

New York
NYTBR - Ja 4 '70 - p12
PW - v196 - D 8 '69 - p49

The American Revolution
BL - v55 - N 1 '58 - p135
KR - v26 - Jl 15 '58 - p510
NY - v34 - N 22 '58 - p215
NYTBR, pt.2 - N 2 '58 - p3

BLIVEN, Naomi
see Bliven, Bruce, Jr. (co-author) -
New York

BLOUGH, Glenn O 1907-
ConAu P-1, LEduc 74, MorJA,
SmATA 1, WhoAm 78

Discovering Insects
LJ - v92 - D 15 '67 - p4609
SA - v217 - D '67 - p146

BLUE, Betty A 1922-
ConAu 45, DrAS 78F

BLUME, Judy (continued)
> LJ - v97 - Ap 15 '72 - p1612
> NYTBR - Ja 16 '72 - p8
> NYTBR, pt.2 - My 6 '73 - p28
> PW - v200 - D 13 '71 - p42
> SR - v54 - S 18 '71 - p49
> TN - v28 - Ap '72 - p309
> Teacher - v90 - Ap '73 - p90

BOLIAN, Polly   1925-
ConAu 33R, IlsBYP, SmATA 4

> *Growing Up Slim*
> BL - v68 - S 15 '71 - p99

BOND, Gladys Baker   1912-
ConAu 5R, SmATA 14, WhoAmW
77, WhoPNW

> *A Head On Her Shoulders*
> HB - v40 - Ag '64 - p373
> LJ - v89 - Mr 15 '64 - p1446
> NS - v67 - My 15 '64 - p776
> PW - v193 - F 12 '68 - p79
> TLS - Jl 9 '64 - p602

BONHAM, Frank   1914-
ConAu 9R, ConLC 12, MorBMP,
SmATA 1, ThrBJA, TwCCW 78

> *Chief*
> BL - v68 - Ja 1 '72 - p390
> BL - v68 - Ja 1 '72 - p392
> BS - v33 - S 1 '73 - p258
> BW - v7 - Ag 26 '73 - p13
> CCB-B - v25 - D '71 - p55
> CSM - v63 - N 11 '71 - pB1
> EJ - v61 - Mr '72 - p435
> KR - v39 - Ag 1 '71 - p813
> LJ - v96 - N 15 '71 - p3906
> PW - v200 - O 18 '71 - p50
> SR - v54 - N 13 '71 - p62

> *Cool Cat*
> BL - v67 - Je 1 '71 - p832
> CCB-B - v24 - Je '71 - p152
> CSM - v63 - My 6 '71 - pB6
> KR - v39 - F 15 '71 - p179
> LJ - v96 - My 15 '71 - p1810
> NYTBR - Ag 8 '71 - p8
> PW - v199 - Mr 22 '71 - p53

> *Devilhorn*
> BL - v74 - Jl 1 '78 - p1676

> CCB-B - v32 - O '78 - p23
> KR - v46 - Je 15 '78 - p640
> PW - v213 - My 1 '78 - p85
> Par - v53 - S '78 - p32
> SLJ - v25 - S '78 - p130

> *Durango Street*
> BL - v62 - N 15 '65 - p319
> BS - v25 - S 15 '65 - p251
> CCB-B - v19 - O '65 - p27
> CE - v46 - Ap '70 - p368
> CSM - v57 - N 4 '65 - pB11
> HB - v41 - O '65 - p505
> KR - v33 - Jl 15 '65 - p689
> LJ - v90 - N 15 '65 - p5086
> NYTBR - v70 - S 5 '65 - p20

> *The Golden Bees Of Tulami*
> HB - v51 - Ap '75 - p145
> KR - v42 - N 1 '74 - p1159
> Kliatt - v12 - Winter '78 - p5
> LJ - v99 - D 15 '74 - p3270
> NYTBR - N 10 '74 - p10
> PW - v206 - S 2 '74 - p69

> *Hey, Big Spender!*
> BL - v68 - My 15 '72 - p818
> CCB-B - v26 - Ap '73 - p119
> KR - v40 - F 15 '72 - p201
> LJ - v98 - Ja 15 '73 - p266

> *The Missing Persons League*
> BL - v73 - N 1 '76 - p405
> CCB-B - v30 - N '76 - p39
> KR - v44 - Ag 15 '76 - p909
> NYTBR - Ja 9 '77 - p10
> PW - v210 - Ag 2 '76 - p113
> RT - v31 - O '77 - p20
> SLJ - v23 - D '76 - p31
> SLJ - v23 - D '76 - p53

> *Mystery Of The Fat Cat*
> BL - v64 - Je 15 '68 - p1183
> BW - v2 - O 6 '68 - p20
> CCB-B - v22 - O '68 - p23
> HB - v44 - Ag '68 - p426
> KR - v36 - Ap 1 '68 - p402
> LJ - v93 - My 15 '68 - p2110
> NYTBR - v73 - Ag 25 '68 - p24
> SLJ - v24 - F '78 - p35
> SR - v51 - Ag 24 '68 - p43

> *The Mystery Of The Red Tide*
> BL - v62 - Jl 1 '66 - p1042
> CCB-B - v19 - Jl '66 - p174

BONHAM, Frank (continued)
>   LJ - v91 - My 15 '66 - p2716
>   NYTBR - v71 - Je 5 '66 - p42
>   PW - v189 - Je 6 '66 - p232

>   *The Nitty Gritty*
>   BL - v65 - N 1 '68 - p305
>   BW - v2 - N 3 '68 - p20
>   EJ - v58 - F '69 - p294
>   KR - v36 - S 15 '68 - p1056
>   LJ - v94 - Ja 15 '69 - p292
>   NYTBR - Ja 19 '69 - p28

>   *Viva Chicano*
>   BL - v67 - S 15 '70 - p94
>   CCB-B - v24 - D '70 - p55
>   EJ - v63 - Ja '74 - p62
>   KR - v38 - My 15 '70 - p558
>   LJ - v95 - Jl '70 - p2538
>   NYTBR, pt.2 - My 24 '70 - p20
>   SR - v53 - Ag 22 '70 - p57

>   *War Beneath The Sea*
>   NYTBR - O 7 '62 - p36

BONNELL, Dorothy Haworth   1914-
AuBYP SUP, ConAu 1R, ForWC 70

>   *Passport To Freedom*
>   BL - v27 - O 1 '67 - p261
>   KR - v35 - S 15 '67 - p1142
>   LJ - v92 - O 15 '67 - p3859

BONTEMPS, Arna Wendell   1902-
1973
ConAu 1R, ConAu 41R, JBA 51,
ModBlW, SmATA 2, SmATA 24N

>   *Chariot In The Sky*
>   BL - v47 - My 15 '51 - p332
>   BL - v68 - Ja 15 '72 - p435
>   BS - v31 - F 15 '72 - p521
>   HB - v27 - S '51 - p333
>   KR - v19 - Mr 1 '51 - p129
>   KR - v39 - O 15 '71 - p1133
>   LJ - v76 - Je 1 '51 - p970
>   LJ - v97 - Ap 15 '72 - p1612
>   NYTBR - Je 17 '51 - p24
>   Notes - v8 - S '51 - p717
>   SR - v34 - Jl 21 '51 - p47

>   *Famous Negro Athletes*
>   BL - v61 - Mr 15 '65 - p710
>   CCB-B - v19 - S '65 - p3
>   LJ - v89 - O 15 '64 - p4202

NYTBR, pt.2 - N 1 '64 - p54

>   *Free At Last: The Life Of*
>   *Frederick Douglas*
>   Am - v125 - O 16 '71 - p295
>   Choice - v8 - S '71 - p901
>   KR - v39 - F 15 '71 - p204
>   LJ - v96 - Ap 15 '71 - p1358

>   *Golden Slippers: An Anthology Of*
>   *Negro Poetry For Young Readers*
>   BL - v38 - D 15 '41 - p135

BOOKER, Simeon   1918-
ConAu 9R, LivBAA, SelBAA,
WhoBlA 77

>   *Susie King Taylor, Civil War*
>   *Nurse*
>   BL - v66 - D 15 '69 - p513
>   CLW - v42 - O '70 - p135
>   KR - v37 - Jl 15 '69 - p720
>   LJ - v94 - N 15 '69 - p4292
>   NYTBR - Je 22 '69 - p22

BOONE, Pat   1934-
ConAu 1R, IntMPA 78, RkOn,
SmATA 7, WhoAm 78

>   *'Twixt Twelve and Twenty*
>   KR - v26 - O 15 '58 - p814
>   LJ - v84 - Ja 15 '59 - p255

BORISOFF, Norman

>   *The Goof-Up*
>   Hi Lo - v1 - N '79 - p4

BORLAND, Hal   1900-1978
ConAu 1R, ConAu 77, SmATA 5,
SmATA 24N, WhoAm 78, WorAu

>   *Penny: The Story Of A Free-Soul*
>   *Basset Hound*
>   BL - v68 - Jl 15 '72 - p965
>   BL - v68 - Jl 15 '72 - p997
>   BS - v32 - Je 15 '72 - p150
>   HB - v48 - Je '72 - p292
>   KR - v40 - Mr 15 '72 - p359
>   PW - v201 - Mr 20 '72 - p67

>   *When The Legends Die*
>   Am - v108 - My 18 '63 - p717
>   Atl - v212 - Ag '63 - p125
>   BS - v23 - My 1 '63 - p54

BORLAND, Hal (continued)
  CSM - Ap 25 '63 - p11
  EJ - v63 - D '74 - p93
  HM - v227 - S '63 - p115
  LJ - v88 - Ap 15 '63 - p1682
  NYTBR - My 19 '63 - p32
  NYTBR - My 19 '63 - p33
  SR - v46 - My 25 '63 - p34
  TLS - My 19 '66 - p442
  TLS - D 4 '69 - p1384
  TLS - Ap 6 '73 - p381

BOSWORTH, J Allan   1925-
AuBYP, SmATA 19

  Among Lions
    BL - v70 - N 15 '73 - p336
    KR - v41 - Jl 1 '73 - p691
    LJ   v98   S 15 '73 - p2661

  A Darkness Of Giants
    BL - v69 - O 1 '72 - p138
    BL - v69 - O 1 '72 - p147
    KR - v40 - Je 15 '72 - p678
    LJ - v97 - S 15 '72 - p2944

BOTHWELL, Jean
ConAu 1R, JBA 51, SmATA 2

  The First Book Of India
    BL - v62 - Jl 1 '66 - p1046
    BL - v68 - Ap 15 '72 - p727
    LJ - v91 - Je 15 '66 - p3255
    LJ - v97 - My 15 '72 - p1910
    NYTBR - v71 - S 4 '66 - p16
    NYTBR - F 27 '72 - p8
    SLJ - v25 - N '78 - p56

  Mystery Cup
    KR - v36 - Ap 1 '68 - p391
    LJ - v93 - My 15 '68 - p2127
    PW - v193 - My 20 '68 - p62

BOUMA, Hans

  An Eye On Israel
    Kliatt - v13 - Spring '79 - p60

BOVA, Ben   1932-
ChLR 3, ConAu 5R, ConSFA,
SmATA 6, WhoAm 78

  Escape!
    CSM - v62 - My 7 '70 - pB6
    KR - v38 - Ap 1 '70 - p389

NYTBR, pt.2 - My 24 '70 - p20

  Man Changes The Weather
    CCB-B - v27 - Mr '74 - p107
    HB - v50 - Ag '74 - p401
    KR - v41 - S 15 '73 - p1038
    LJ - v99 - Mr 15 '74 - p886
    PW - v204 - S 10 '73 - p52
    SB - v10 - S '74 - p123

  Out Of The Sun
    KR - v36 - Jl 1 '68 - p697
    LJ - v93 - Jl '68 - p2736

  The Weather Changes Man
    BL - v71 - S 15 '74 - p95
    CE - v51 - Mr '75 - p276
    KR - v42 - S 1 '74 - p945
    PW - v206 - Ag 19 '74 - p84
    SB - v10 - Mr '75 - p301
    SLJ - v21 - Ap '75 - p49

BOWEN, J David   1930-
AuBYP, SmATA 22

  The Island Of Puerto Rico
    KR - v36 - My 1 '68 - p520
    LJ - v93 - Je 15 '68 - p2544

BOWEN, Robert Sydney   1900-1977
AuBYP, ConAu 69, ConAu 73,
SmATA 21N

  Wipeout
    BS - v28 - F 1 '69 - p446
    EJ - v58 - My '69 - p778
    KR - v36 - N 1 '68 - p1224
    LJ - v94 - My 15 '69 - p2126

BRADBURY, Bianca   1908-
ConAu 13R, FourBJA, SmATA 3

  Dogs And More Dogs
    CCB-B - v22 - O '68 - p23
    KR - v36 - My 1 '68 - p509
    LJ - v93 - Ap 15 '68 - p1794
    PW - v193 - My 27 '68 - p58

  In Her Father's Footsteps
    CCB-B - v29 - Jl '76 - p171
    CLW - v48 - O '76 - p137
    Cur R - v16 - Ag '77 - p206
    KR - v44 - Mr 15 '76 - p320
    SLJ - v22 - My '76 - p66

BRADBURY, Bianca (continued)

The Loner
CCB-B - v24 - N '70 - p38
CE - v47 - N '70 - p87
Comw - v93 - N 20 '70 - p201
KR - v38 - My 15 '70 - p551
PW - v197 - Je 15 '70 - p64
SR - v53 - O 24 '70 - p67

Red Sky At Night
BS - v28 - My 1 '68 - p63
KR - v36 - F 1 '68 - p121
LJ - v93 - Ap 15 '68 - p1807

Where's Jim Now?
SLJ - v25 - O '78 - p152

BRADBURY, Ray   1920-
ConAu 1R, ConLC 10, ConSFA,
DcLB 2, SmATA 11, TwCW

Dandelion Wine
KR - v43 - Ja 15 '75 - p90
Time - v105 - Mr 24 '75 - p78

BRADFORD, Richard   1932-
ConAu 49

Red Sky At Morning
BS - v34 - D 15 '74 - p428
EJ - v58 - F '69 - p294
NYTBR, pt.2 - F 15 '70 - p22
PW - v195 - My 5 '69 - p55

BRADLEY, James J
see Taylor, Dawson (co-author)

BRADY, Mari

Please Remember Me
BL - v74 - N 1 '77 - p440
KR - v45 - Jl 15 '77 - p755
KR - v45 - Ag 15 '77 - p859
LJ - v102 - S 15 '77 - p1839
PW - v212 - Ag 8 '77 - p55
SLJ - v24 - Ja '78 - p99

BRAGDON, Lillian
AuBYP, ConAu 73, SmATA 24

Luther Burbank, Nature's Helper
BL - v55 - Ap 15 '59 - p456
CSM - My 14 '59 - p11
KR - v27 - F 1 '59 - p92

NYTBR - My 24 '59 - p38

BRAITHWAITE, Edward   1912-
ConNov 72, WrDr 80

To Sir, With Love
BL - v56 - Mr 1 '60 - p408
KR - v28 - Ja 15 '60 - p70
LJ - v85 - F 15 '60 - p754
NS - v57 - Mr 28 '59 - p454
NY - v36 - Mr 26 '60 - p160
NYTBR - My 1 '60 - p6
SR - v43 - Ap 30 '60 - p18
TLS - Ap 3 '59 - p194

BRANCATO, Robin Fidler   1936-
ConAu 69, SmATA 23

Blinded By The Light
BL - v75 - S 15 '78 - p175
BS - v38 - Mr '79 - p406
CCB-B - v32 - F '79 - p94
Inter BC - v10 - '79 - p17
KR - v46 - N 1 '78 - p1191
NW - v92 - D 18 '78 - p102
PW - v214 - N 13 '78 - p63
PW - v215 - My 21 '79 - p69
SLJ - v25 - O '78 - p152

Come Alive At 505
BL - v76 - Mr 15 '80 - p1042
CBRS - v8 - Mr '80 - p75
KR - v48 - Mr 15 '80 - p369
NYTBR - v85 - Ap 27 '80 - p65
PW - v217 - Mr 28 '80 - p49

Something Left To Lose
Kliatt - v13 - Spring '79 - p5

Winning
BB - v6 - My '78 - p3
BL - v74 - S 1 '77 - p30
BL - v74 - S 1 '77 - p36
BS - v37 - D '77 - p261
CCB-B - v31 - My '78 - p138
EJ - v68 - Ja '79 - p58
HB - v54 - Ap '78 - p167
KR - v45 - S 15 '77 - p995
PW - v213 - Ja 2 '78 - p65
SLJ - v24 - O '77 - p120
SMQ - v8 - Fall '79 - p27
WLB - v52 - S '77 - p76

BRANDON, William 1914-
ConAu 77, IndAu 1917

The Magic World
ABC - v22 - N '71 - p33
BL - v68 - S 1 '71 - p24
CSM - v63 - Jl 8 '71 - p9
Choice - v8 - O '71 - p1010
EJ - v60 - D '71 - p1263
EJ - v63 - Ja '74 - p70
LJ - v96 - Je 15 '71 - p2088
NYTBR - Ag 29 '71 - p2

BRANDT, Keith

Pete Rose: "Mr. 300"
KR - v45 - Je 1 '77 - p583
SLJ - v24 - S '77 - p122

BRANDT, Sue Reading 1916-
ConAu 25R

First Book Of How To Write A Report
KR - v36 - Ag 1 '68 - p821

BRANLEY, Franklyn M 1915-
BkP, ConAu 33R, MorJA, SmATA 4

A Book Of Stars For You
BL - v64 - Mr 1 '68 - p778
HB - v44 - Ap '68 - p203
KR - v35 - O 1 '67 - p1211
LJ - v93 - F 15 '68 - p866
PW - v192 - N 13 '67 - p80
S&T - v35 - F '68 - p114
SB - v3 - D '67 - p204
TN - v24 - Je '68 - p447

BRAU, Maria M 1932-

Island In The Crossroads: The History Of Puerto Rico
BL - v65 - My 1 '69 - p1014
Cath W - v209 - Ap '69 - p48
LJ - v94 - Ap 15 '69 - p1790

BRAUN, Thomas 1944-

On Stage: Flip Wilson
SLJ - v23 - S '76 - p110

BRECKLER, Rosemary

Where Are The Twins?
CBRS - v8 - N '79 - p26
Hi Lo - v1 - Ja '80 - p4
SLJ - v26 - O '79 - p158

BREWTON, John
see Brewton, Sara Westbrook (co-author)

BREWTON, Sara Westbrook

America Forever New
BL - v64 - Je 1 '68 - p1138
CLW - v40 - O '68 - p143
HB - v44 - Ag '68 - p433
KR - v36 - Ap 15 '68 - p469
LJ - v93 - Je 15 '68 - p2544
NYTBR - v73 - My 5 '68 - p44
PW - v193 - Mr 18 '68 - p54
SE - v33 - My '69 - p560
TN - v25 - Ap '69 - p309

Shrieks At Midnight
A Lib - v1 - Ap '70 - p384
BL - v65 - Je 1 '69 - p1122
BW - v3 - My 4 '69 - p24
CE - v46 - Ap '70 - p378
HB - v45 - Ag '69 - p419
Inst - v79 - O '69 - p161
KR - v37 - Ap 1 '69 - p379
LJ - v94 - My 15 '69 - p2097
NYTBR - D 7 '69 - p68
NYTBR, pt.2 - N 6 '69 - p61
NYTBR, pt.2 - My 4 '69 - p47
PW - v195 - Ap 7 '69 - p56

BRIGGS, Mitchell Pirie
see Allen, Betty (co-author)

BRIGGS, Peter 1921-1975
ConAu 57, ConAu P-2

Men In The Sea
BL - v65 - S 15 '68 - p112
KR - v36 - My 1 '68 - p520
LJ - v93 - O 15 '68 - p3976
NYTBR - v73 - Jl 7 '68 - p16
SR - v51 - Ag 24 '68 - p43

Science Ship
CCB-B - v23 - O '69 - p23
CSM - v61 - My 15 '69 - p11

BRIGGS, Peter (continued)
    KR - v37 - Ap 1 '69 - p387
    LJ - v94 - N 15 '69 - p4293
    SB - v5 - My '69 - p36

BRIGHTMAN, Alan J
    see Sullivan, Mary Beth (co-author)

BRISCO, Patty   (joint pseud.)
ConAu X (real names: Matthews,
Clayton; and Matthews, Patricia)

    Campus Mystery
        BL - v74 - Mr 15 '78 - p1179

    Raging Rapids
        Hi Lo - v1 - Mr '80 - p4
        Teacher - v96 - My '79 - p127

BROCK, Virginia
AuBYP SUP

    Pinatas
        BL - v62 - My 15 '66 - p916
        CE - v43 - F '67 - p354
        LJ - v91 - Je 15 '66 - p3256

BROCKWAY, Edith   1914-
ConAu 17R

    Land Beyond The Rivers
        BS - v26 - My 1 '66 - p56
        KR - v34 - F 1 '66 - p116
        LJ - v91 - My 15 '66 - p2701

BRODERICK, Dorothy M   1929-
BiDrLUS 70, ConAu 13R, SmATA 5

    Hank
        BL - v63 - Ja 1 '67 - p483
        CCB-B - v20 - Ja '67 - p71
        Comw - v85 - N 11 '66 - p176
        KR - v34 - Jl 1 '66 - p635
        LJ - v91 - O 15 '66 - p5244
        NYTBR - v71 - O 23 '66 - p34

BRODSKY, Mimi

    The House At 12 Rose Street
        PW - v195 - F 17 '69 - p160

BROEGER, Achim   1944-
IntAu&W 77

Running In Circles
    BB - v6 - Je '78 - p4
    BL - v74 - O 15 '77 - p371
    CCB-B - v31 - Ja '78 - p75
    HB - v54 - F '78 - p51
    KR - v45 - Ag 1 '77 - p788
    PW - v212 - O 31 '77 - p59
    SLJ - v24 - N '77 - p66

BROMLEY, Dudley   1948-
ConAu 77

    Bad Moon
        Hi Lo - v1 - D '79 - p4
        SLJ - v26 - D '79 - p98

    North To Oak Island
        Hi Lo - v1 - N '79 - p1

BROOKE, Joshua

    Just A Little Inconvenience
        Kliatt - v12 - Spring '78 - p5

BROOKINS, Dana   1931-
ConAu 69

    Alone In Wolf Hollow
        BL - v74 - Je 1 '78 - p1549
        KR - v46 - Je 15 '78 - p636
        SLJ - v24 - My '78 - p84

    Rico's Cat
        BL - v73 - F 15 '77 - p894
        CLW - v48 - Ap '77 - p406
        KR - v44 - O 1 '76 - p1092
        SLJ - v23 - D '76 - p53

BROOKS, Jerome   1931-
ConAu 49, SmATA 23

    The Big Dipper Marathon
        BL - v75 - Ap 15 '79 - p1286
        BS - v39 - Ag '79 - p166
        CBRS - v7 - Spring '79 - p116
        CCB-B - v33 - S '79 - p2
        HB - v55 - Ag '79 - p420
        KR - v47 - Jl 1 '79 - p744
        SLJ - v25 - Ap '79 - p66

BROOKS, Polly Schoyer   1912-
ConAu 1R, SmATA 12

    When The World Was Rome
        BL - v68 - Je 1 '72 - p855

BROOKS, Polly Schoyer (continued)
BS - v32 - My 15 '72 - p97
CCB-B - v25 - Je '72 - p151
CE - v49 - Ja '73 - p204
KR - v40 - Ja 15 '72 - p74
LJ - v98 - My 15 '73 - p1687

BROWN, Alexis (pseud.) 1922-
ConAu X, SmATA X (real name:
Baumann, Amy Brown Beeching)

Treasure In Devil's Bay
KR - v33 - Ja 15 '65 - p62
LJ - v90 - Je 15 '65 - p2882

BROWN, Fern G 1918-
ConAu 97

Hard Luck Horse
SLJ - v22 - Mr '76 - p99

BROWN, Jackum

Fair Game
Hi Lo - v1 - My '80 - p3
SLJ - v25 - My '79 - p70

BROWN, Larry 1947-
WhoFtbl 74

I'll Always Get Up
BL - v70 - Ja 15 '74 - p508
BS - v33 - N 15 '73 - p359
KR - v41 - Ag 1 '73 - p844
LJ - v98 - S 15 '73 - p2566
PW - v204 - Ag 6 '73 - p56

BROWN, Marion Marsh 1908-
ConAu 1R, DrAS 78E, SmATA 6

The Silent Storm
BS - v23 - O 15 '63 - p263
CC - v80 - D 18 '63 - p1586
Comw - v79 - N 15 '63 - p238
LJ - v88 - S 15 '63 - p3346
NYTBR - Ja 26 '64 - p26

BROWN, Roy Frederick 1921
ConAu 65, FourBJA, TwCCW 78

The Cage
BL - v74 - N 1 '77 - p467
CCB-B - v31 - My '78 - p139
Comw - v104 - N 11 '77 - p731
EJ - v67 - S '78 - p90

HB - v54 - F '78 - p51
KR - v45 - O 15 '77 - p1103
PW - v212 - Ag 29 '77 - p367
SE - v42 - Ap '78 - p321
SLJ - v24 - N '77 - p66
TLS - Mr 25 '77 - p359

The White Sparrow
BL - v71 - Ap 15 '75 - p865
CCB-B - v29 - S '75 - p4
CLW - v47 - D '75 - p234
HB - v51 - Je '75 - p273
KR - v43 - Ap 1 '75 - p371
LR - v24 - Autumn '74 - p320
Obs - Ag 4 '74 - p28
SLJ - v21 - My '75 - p53
TLS - S 20 '74 - p1006

BROWNMILLER, Susan 1935-
CurBio 78, WhoAm 78

Shirley Chisholm
BL - v67 - D 15 '70 - p338
CCB-B - v24 - Je '71 - p152
LJ - v95 - N 15 '70 - p4041
PW - v198 - S 28 '70 - p79

BRUNING, Nancy P

The Kids' Book Of Disco
Kliatt - v14 - Winter '80 - p60

BUCHANAN, William (pseud.) 1930-
AuBYP, ConAu X, WrDr 80 (real
name: Buck, William Ray)

A Shining Season
KR - v46 - O 15 '78 - p1160
PW - v214 - O 23 '78 - p53

BUCHENHOLZ, Bruce 1916-
BiDrAPA 77

A Way With Animals
BL - v74 - Jl 1 '78 - p1671
Comw - v105 - N 10 '78 - p734
LJ - v103 - Jl '78 - p1422
SLJ - v25 - O '78 - p142

BUCK, Margaret Waring 1910-
ConAu 5R, IntAu&W 77, SmATA 3,
WrDr 80

Where They Go In Winter
BL - v65 - O 15 '68 - p240

BUCK, Margaret Waring (continued)
CE - v46 - N '69 - p98
HB - v45 - F '69 - p69
KR - v36 - Jl 1 '68 - p693
LJ - v93 - O 15 '68 - p3965
PW - v194 - S 2 '68 - p60
SB - v5 - My '69 - p52

BUCK, William Ray
see Buchanan, William

BUEHR, Walter   1897-1971
ConAu 5R, ConAu 33R, IlsCB 1957,
SmATA 3, ThrBJA

  ***Storm Warning: The Story Of
  Hurricanes And Tornadoes***
BL - v68 - Jl 15 '72 - p1002
CCB-B - v26 - N '72 - p39
KR - v40 - Ap 1 '72 - p403
LJ - v97 - S 15 '72 - p2944
SB - v8 - D '72 - p231

  Volcano
LJ - v87 - Ap 15 '62 - p1692
NYTBR - Ag 19 '62 - p20

BUNTING, Eve   1928-
AuBYP SUP, ConAu 53, SmATA 18
(listed under Bunting, Anne Evelyn)

  The Big Find
Hi Lo - Je '80 - p3

  Blacksmith At Blueridge
BL - v74 - O 1 '77 - p283
BL - v74 - O 1 '77 - p285
Cur R - v16 - D '77 - p361

  Day Of The Earthlings
BL - v75 - O 15 '78 - p389
SLJ - v25 - Ja '79 - p51

  Fifteen
BL - v74 - Je 15 '78 - p1620
SLJ - v25 - S '78 - p130

  The Followers
BL - v75 - O 15 '78 - p389
SLJ - v25 - Ja '79 - p51

  For Always
BL - v74 - Je 15 '78 - p1620
SLJ - v25 - S '78 - p130

The Girl In The Painting
BL - v74 - Je 15 '78 - p1620
SLJ - v25 - S '78 - p130

The Haunting Of Kildoran Abbey
BL - v74 - Jl 1 '78 - p1677
CCB-B - v32 - O '78 - p24
PW - v213 - My 22 '78 - p233
SLJ - v25 - S '78 - p154
WCRB - v4 - N '78 - p59

The Island Of One
BL - v75 - O 15 '78 - p389
SLJ - v25 - Ja '79 - p51

Just Like Everyone Else
BL - v74 - Je 15 '78 - p1620
SLJ - v25 - S '78 - p130

Maggie The Freak
BL - v74 - Je 15 '78 - p1621
SLJ - v25 - S '78 - p130

The Mask
BL - v75 - O 15 '78 - p389
CCB-B - v32 - Ja '79 - p74
SLJ - v25 - Ja '79 - p51

The Mirror Planet
BL - v75 - O 15 '78 - p389
SLJ - v25 - Ja '79 - p51

Nobody Knows But Me
BL - v74 - Je 15 '78 - p1621
SLJ - v25 - S '78 - p130

Oh, Rick!
BL - v74 - Je 15 '78 - p1621
SLJ - v25 - S '78 - p130

One More Flight
Am - v135 - D 11 '76 - p428
B&B - v22 - N '76 - p78
HB - v53 - Ap '77 - p158
JB - v41 - Ap '77 - p85
KR - v44 - Mr 15 '76 - p321
PW - v209 - Ap 26 '76 - p60
Par - v51 - N '76 - p28
SE - v41 - Ap '77 - p348
SLJ - v22 - My '76 - p57

A Part Of The Dream
BL - v74 - Je 15 '78 - p1621
SLJ - v25 - S '78 - p130

The Robot People
BL - v75 - O 15 '78 - p389

BUNTING, Eve (continued)
SLJ - v25 - Ja '79 - p51

The Space People
BL - v75 - O 15 '78 - p389
SLJ - v25 - Ja '79 - p51

Survival Camp!
BL - v74 - Je 15 '78 - p1621
SLJ - v25 - S '78 - p130

Two Different Girls
BL - v74 - Je 15 '78 - p1621
SLJ - v25 - S '78 - p130

The Undersea People
BL - v75 - O 15 '78 - p389
SLJ - v25 - Ja '79 - p51

BURCH, Robert   1925-
ConAu 5R, MorBMP, SmATA 1,
ThrBJA, TwCCW 78

*Hut School And The Wartime
Home-Front Heroes*
BL - v70 - My 1 '74 - p998
CCB-B - v28 - S '74 - p2
Comw - v101 - N 22 '74 - p193
HB - v50 - Ag '74 - p374
Inst - v84 - N '74 - p134
J Ho E - v67 - Ja '75 - p58
KR - v42 - Ap 15 '74 - p423
LJ - v99 - N 15 '74 - p3044
NYTBR - My 5 '74 - p40
Teacher - v92 - S '74 - p129

Queenie Peavy
BL - v62 - Je 15 '66 - p998
CCB-B - v19 - Je '66 - p159
HB - v42 - Ag '66 - p433
KR - v34 - Ap 15 '66 - p428
LJ - v91 - Je 15 '66 - p3256
NYTBR - v71 - My 8 '66 - p33
PW - v189 - Je 13 '66 - p128
TCR - v68 - F '67 - p451

The Whitman Kick
BL - v74 - N 1 '77 - p467
BS - v37 - Mr '78 - p398
CCB-B - v31 - Mr '78 - p107
EJ - v67 - Mr '78 - p80
HB - v54 - Ap '78 - p168
KR - v46 - Ja 1 '78 - p7
Par - v53 - Je '78 - p40
SLJ - v24 - N '77 - p66

BURCHARD, Marshall
AuBYP SUP

Sports Hero: Brooks Robinson
CCB-B - v25 - Mr '72 - p103
KR - v39 - D 1 '71 - p1258
LJ - v97 - My 15 '72 - p1930

Sports Hero: Joe Morgan
BL - v74 - Je 15 '78 - p1621
KR - v46 - Jl 1 '78 - p690
SLJ - v25 - S '78 - p131

Sports Hero: Johnny Bench
BL - v70 - S 1 '73 - p48
CCB-B - v26 - Je '73 - p151
KR - v41 - F 1 '73 - p118
LJ - v98 - My 15 '73 - p1703

*Sports Hero: Kareem Abdul
Jabbar*
KR - v40 - Jl 15 '72 - p804
LJ - v97 - D 15 '72 - p4089

BURCHARD, Peter Duncan   1921-
ConAu 5R, IlsCB 1967, SmATA 5,
ThrBJA, WhoAmA 78

A Quiet Place
BL - v69 - Ja 15 '73 - p488
KR - v40 - N 15 '72 - p1311
LJ - v98 - Ja 15 '73 - p266
NYTBR - N 12 '72 - p14
PW - v202 - D 4 '72 - p62

BURCHARD, Sue H   1937-
AuBYP SUP, ConAu 53, SmATA 22

Sports Star: Dorothy Hammill
Hi Lo - v1 - S '79 - p4

Sports Star: Nadia Comaneci
AB - v60 - N 14 '77 - p2819
BL - v74 - Ja 1 '78 - p750
KR - v45 - O 15 '77 - p1098
SLJ - v24 - D '77 - p64

Sports Star: Reggie Jackson
Hi Lo - v2 - O '80 - p6
KR - v47 - Jl 15 '79 - p794
SLJ - v25 - My '79 - p83

Sports Star: Tony Dorsett
Hi Lo - v1 - S '79 - p4
RT - v33 - O '79 - p36
SLJ - v25 - D '78 - p70

BURCHARD, Sue H (continued)
see also Burchard, Marshall (co-author) -
Sports Hero: Brooks Robinson
Sports Hero: Johnny Bench
Sports Hero: Kareem Abdul Jabbar

BURDICK, Eugene
see Lederer, William (co-author)

BURGER, Carl

All About Cats
BL - v63 - N 15 '66 - p372
CLW - v38 - Ja '67 - p336
CSM - v58 - N 3 '66 - pB11
LJ - v92 - Mr 15 '67 - p1314

BURGER, Jack
see Burger, John Robert

BURGER, John Robert 1942-
ConAu 81

Children Of The Wild
BL - v75 - S 1 '78 - p43
CCB-B - v32 - O '78 - p25
SLJ - v24 - My '78 - p73

BURKE, James Lee 1936-
ConAu 13R

To The Bright And Shining Sun
BS - v30 - S 1 '70 - p210
KR - v38 - Je 1 '70 - p617
LJ - v95 - My 15 '70 - p1969
LJ - v95 - Jl '70 - p2514
LJ - v95 - D 15 '70 - p4327
NYTBR - Ag 9 '70 - p33
PW - v197 - Je 1 '70 - p63

BURLESON, Elizabeth

Middl'un
CCB-B - v22 - Mr '69 - p108
KR - v36 - Je 1 '68 - p595

BURNESS, Gordon

How To Watch Wildlife
CLW - v44 - Mr '73 - p509
LJ - v98 - My 15 '73 - p1679

BURNETT, Frances Hodgson 1849-1924
HerW, OxAm, TwCCW 78, WhAm 1, WhoChL, YABC 2

A Little Princess
LR - v25 - Spring '75 - p34
Spec - v234 - Ap 12 '75 - p442
Teacher - v93 - N '75 - p118

The Secret Garden
B&B - v22 - D '76 - p75
B&B - v22 - Ja '77 - p64
LR - v25 - Autumn '76 - p278
NY - v46 - D 5 '70 - p216
NYTBR - My 14 '61 - p793
Obs - D 8 '74 - p25
Spec - v235 - Jl 26 '75 - p116

BURNFORD, Sheila 1918-
ChLR 2, ConAu 1R, FourBJA, OxCan, SmATA 3, TwCCW 78

The Incredible Journey
Atl - v207 - Mr '61 - p117
B&B - v14 - Ag '69 - p38
BL - v57 - My 1 '61 - p545
CC - v78 - S 13 '61 - p1082
CSM - Mr 16 '61 - p11
Comw - v74 - My 26 '61 - p234
HB - v37 - Je '61 - p253
KR - v28 - D 1 '60 - p1007
LJ - v86 - Ja 1 '61 - p110
NYTBR - Ap 23 '61 - p34
SR - v44 - My 13 '61 - p51
TN - v34 - Winter '78 - p189

BURTON, Hester 1913-
ChLR 1, ConAu 9R, SmATA 7, ThrBJA, TwCCW 78, WhoChL

Castors Away
BL - v23 - Je 15 '63 - p116
HB - v39 - Ag '63 - p388
LJ - v88 - Jl '63 - p2780
NS - v63 - My 18 '62 - p725
NYTBR, pt.2 - My 12 '63 - p2
TLS - Je 1 '62 - p398

BURTON, Hester (continued)

Flood At Reedsmere
BL - v64 - Je 1 '68 - p1138
CCB-B - v21 - Jl '68 - p170
HB - v44 - Je '68 - p322
KR - v36 - F 1 '68 - p122
LJ - v93 - S 15 '68 - p3298
NYTBR - v73 - My 5 '68 - p14
PW - v193 - Je 24 '68 - p68

In Spite Of All Terror
CCB-B - v24 - O '70 - p23
HB - v45 - Ag '69 - p414
LJ - v94 - Jl '69 - p2679
LJ - v94 - D 15 '69 - p4380
TLS - O 30 '70 - p1258
TN - v26 - N '69 - p83

Time Of Trial
CSM - My 7 '64 - p8B
Comw - v80 - My 22 '64 - p270
HB - v40 - Je '64 - p302
LJ - v89 - Je 15 '64 - p2666
NYTBR, pt.2 - My 10 '64 - p8
SR - v47 - Ag 15 '64 - p45
TLS - N 28 '63 - p974

BUSCH, Phyllis S   1909-
WhoAmW 70

What About VD?
ACSB - v10 - Winter '77 - p8
BL - v72 - Jl 15 '76 - p1584
BL - v72 - Jl 15 '76 - p1593
BS - v36 - N '76 - p270
CLW - v48 - My '77 - p442
KR - v44 - My 15 '76 - p602
PW - v210 - Jl 12 '76 - p72
SB - v12 - Mr '77 - p214
SLJ - v23 - S '76 - p128

BUTLER, Beverly   1932-
AuBYP, ConAu 1R, SmATA 7

Captive Thunder
BW - v3 - My 4 '69 - p32
CCB-B - v23 - S '69 - p3
KR - v37 - Mr 1 '69 - p245
LJ - v94 - S 15 '69 - p3212

Light A Single Candle
NYTBR - O 14 '62 - p34

BUTLER, Hal   1913-
AuBYP, ConAu 57

Sports Heroes Who Wouldn't Quit
BL - v70 - S 1 '73 - p44
KR - v41 - F 15 '73 - p190
LJ - v98 - My 15 '73 - p1706

BUTLER, Marjorie

Man Who Killed A Bear With A Stick
LJ - v93 - F 15 '68 - p866

BUTTERS, Dorothy Gilman
see Gilman, Dorothy

BUTTERWORTH, Ben

Danger In The Mountains
Hi Lo - v2 - N '80 - p4

The Desert Chase
Hi Lo - v2 - N '80 - p4

The Diamond Smugglers
Hi Lo - v2 - N '80 - p4

The Island Of Helos
Hi Lo - v2 - N '80 - p4

Jim And The Dolphin
Hi Lo - v2 - N '80 - p4

Jim And The Sun Goddess
Hi Lo - v2 - N '80 - p4

Jim In Training
Hi Lo - v2 - N '80 - p4

The Missing Aircraft
Hi Lo - v2 - N '80 - p4

Prisoner Of Pedro Cay
Hi Lo - v2 - N '80 - p4

The Shipwreckers
Hi Lo - v2 - N '80 - p4

The Sniper At Zimba
Hi Lo - v2 - N '80 - p4

The Temple Of Mantos
Hi Lo - v2 - N '80 - p4

BUTTERWORTH, W E   1929-
AuBYP SUP, ConAu 1R, SmATA 5,
WhoS&SW 76

BUTTERWORTH, W E (continued)

Air Evac
BS - v27 - F 1 '68 - p429
KR - v35 - Jl 15 '67 - p814
LJ - v93 - Ja 15 '68 - p301

The Air Freight Mystery
BL - v75 - My 15 '79 - p1435

Black Gold
BL - v71 - Jl 1 '75 - p1123
BS - v35 - Jl '75 - p94
KR - v43 - Je 1 '75 - p614
SB - v11 - Mr '76 - p182
SLJ - v22 - S '75 - p117

Crazy To Race
KR - v39 - Ap 1 '71 - p380
LJ - v96 - My 15 '71 - p1822

*Dave White And The Electric
Wonder Car*
BL - v70 - Je 15 '74 - p1149
BS - v34 - Je 15 '74 - p148
KR - v42 - Ap 1 '74 - p370
LJ - v99 - My 15 '74 - p1471

Grand Prix Driver
BL - v66 - Mr 15 '70 - p910
KR - v37 - S 1 '69 - p936
LJ - v94 - D 15 '69 - p4620
LJ - v95 - D 15 '70 - p4377
LJ - v96 - Ja 15 '71 - p282
PW - v196 - N 3 '69 - p49

Helicopter Pilot
BS - v27 - Ag 1 '67 - p182
KR - v34 - D 15 '66 - p1290
LJ - v92 - Jl '67 - p2658

The Hotel Mystery
Hi Lo - v2 - N '80 - p5

Leroy And The Old Man
BL - v76 - Jl 1 '80 - p1593
BS - v40 - Ag '80 - p191
CBRS - v8 - Ag '80 - p137
CCB-B - v33 - Jl '80 - p209

The Narc
BL - v69 - Mr 15 '73 - p712
CCB-B - v26 - Ap '73 - p121
EJ - v62 - Ap '73 - p647
KR - v40 - O 15 '72 - p1200
LJ - v98 - Ja 15 '73 - p266

NYTBR - N 26 '72 - p8

Orders To Vietnam
BL - v64 - Jl 15 '68 - p1285
BS - v28 - Ag 1 '68 - p194
KR - v36 - Je 1 '68 - p604
LJ - v93 - Jl '68 - p2736

*The Roper Brothers And Their
Magnificent Steam Automobile*
KR - v44 - My 1 '76 - p540
SLJ - v23 - S '76 - p111

Steve Bellamy
BL - v67 - S 1 '70 - p55
BS - v30 - My 1 '70 - p60
KR - v38 - Ap 15 '70 - p464
LJ - v95 - My 15 '70 - p1939
PW - v197 - Je 15 '70 - p64

Stop And Search
BL - v65 - My 15 '69 - p1074
BS - v29 - My 1 '69 - p55
KR - v37 - Ap 15 '69 - p450
PW - v195 - Je 2 '69 - p135

The Tank Driver
BL - v75 - Mr 15 '79 - p1144

Team Racer
KR - v40 - Mr 1 '72 - p266

Under The Influence
BL - v75 - Je 1 '79 - p1485
KR - v47 - My 15 '79 - p579
SLJ - v25 - Ap '79 - p66
see also Douglas, James M

BYARS, Betsy   1928-
ChLR 1, ConAu 33R, MorBMP,
SmATA 4, ThrBJA, TwCCW 78

The Pinballs
Kliatt - v14 - Winter '80 - p5
TES - My 2 '80 - p24

The Summer Of The Swans
BL - v66 - Je 15 '70 - p1276
BL - v67 - Ap 1 '71 - p659
CCB-B - v24 - F '71 - p87
CE - v47 - Mr '71 - p315
CSM - v62 - My 7 '70 - pB6
Comw - v92 - My 22 '70 - p248
HB - v47 - F '71 - p53
KR - v38 - Mr 15 '70 - p320
LJ - v95 - Jl '70 - p2538

BYARS, Betsy (continued)
>   NYTBR, pt.2 - N 5 '72 - p42
>   PW - v197 - My 18 '70 - p38
>   TN - v27 - Ap '71 - p241
>   VV - v19 - D 16 '74 - p51

C

CALDER, Ritchie 1906-
ConAu 1R, CurBio 63, LongCTC,
OxCan, WorAu (also known as
Ritchie-Calder, Peter)

The Evolution Of The Machine
LJ - v94 - F 15 '69 - p882
NYTBR - Je 23 '68 - p3

CALHOUN, Mary Huiskamp 1926-
ConAu 5R, SmATA 2, ThrBJA

The Horse Comes First
BL - v70 - My 15 '74 - p1054
CE - v51 - O '74 - p32
HB - v50 - O '74 - p136
KR - v42 - Mr 15 '74 - p297
LJ - v99 - S 15 '74 - p2262

White Witch Of Kynance
BS - v30 - S 1 '70 - p218
BW - v4 - My 17 '70 - p28
KR - v38 - Jl 1 '70 - p687
LJ - v95 - My 15 '70 - p1951
NYTBR - O 4 '70 - p30
TN - v27 - Je '71 - p431

CALLEN, Larry 1927-
ConAu 73, SmATA 19

Sorrow's Song
BL - v75 - Je 1 '79 - p1488
CCB-B - v33 - N '79 - p43
HB - v55 - Ag '79 - p411
KR - v47 - Jl 15 '79 - p792
SLJ - v25 - My '79 - p58

CAMERON, Eleanor 1912-
ChLR 1, ConAu 1R, SmATA 1,
ThrBJA, TwCCW 78

A Room Made Of Windows
A Lib - v3 - Ap '72 - p419
Am - v125 - D 4 '71 - p488

B&B - v18 - N '72 - p98
BL - v67 - My 15 '71 - p796
BL - v68 - Ap 1 '72 - p668
BS - v31 - My 15 '71 - p98
BW - v5 - My 9 '71 - p5
CCB-B - v24 - Je '71 - p153
CE - v48 - O '71 - p32
CSM - v63 - My 6 '71 - pB6
HB - v47 - Je '71 - p290
LJ - v96 - My 15 '71 - p1780
LJ - v96 - My 15 '71 - p1800
NYT - v121 - D 16 '71 - p67
NYTBR - Ap 25 '71 - p40
NYTBR - D 5 '71 - p86
NYTBR, pt.2 - N 7 '71 - p28
PW - v199 - Ap 12 '71 - p83
SR - v54 - Ap 17 '71 - p45
TLS - N 3 '72 - p1319
TN - v28 - N '71 - p73
TN - v28 - Je '72 - p433

CAMERON, Ian (pseud.) 1924-
ConAu X, ConSFA, WrDr 80 (real
name: Payne, Donald Gordon)

The Lost Ones
BS - v28 - Ap 15 '68 - p25
CLW - v40 - O '68 - p143
HB - v44 - Je '68 - p341
KR - v36 - Ja 15 '68 - p66
LJ - v93 - Mr 15 '68 - p1160
LJ - v93 - Jl '68 - p2739
PW - v193 - Ja 22 '68 - p269
SR - v51 - N 9 '68 - p73
see also Payne, Donald Gordon

CAMPANELLA, Roy 1921-
CurBio 53, WhoAm 78, WhoBlA 77,
WhoProB 73

It's Good To Be Alive
BL - v56 - N 1 '59 - p152

CAMPANELLA, Roy (continued)
    KR - v27 - S 1 '59 - p678
    LJ - v84 - O 1 '59 - p3026
    NYTBR - O 25 '59 - p50
    NYTBR - F 10 '74 - p25
    SR - v42 - N 21 '59 - p46

CAMPBELL, Gail

*Marathon: The World Of The
Long-Distance Athlete*
    Choice - v14 - F '78 - p1679
    LJ - v102 - O 1 '77 - p2077
    PW - v211 - Mr 21 '77 - p82
    SLJ - v24 - My '78 - p90

CAMPBELL, Hope
ConAu 61, SmATA 20

Why Not Join The Giraffes?
    BL - v64 - Ap 1 '68 - p920
    BW - v2 - My 5 '68 - p26
    CCB-B - v22 - S '68 - p3
    CSM - v60 - Je 13 '68 - p5
    KR - v36 - Ja 15 '68 - p56
    LJ - v93 - F 15 '68 - p878
    SR - v51 - My 11 '68 - p42

CAPIZZI, Michael   1941-
ConAu 41R

Getting It All Together
    CCB-B - v26 - Ap '73 - p121
    KR - v40 - O 1 '72 - p1152
    LJ - v98 - Ja 15 '73 - p266
    PW - v202 - S 25 '72 - p60

CAPUTO, Robert

*More Than Just Pets: Why People
Study Animals*
    BL - v76 - My 1 '80 - p1288
    Hi Lo - v1 - My '80 - p4
    Inst - v89 - My '80 - p92
    PW - v217 - Mr 14 '80 - p75

CARABATSOS, James

Heroes
    Kliatt - v12 - Winter '78 - p5

CARAS, Roger A   1928-
ConAu 1R, SmATA 12, WhoAm 78,
WhoWor 74, WhoWorJ 72

*The Custer Wolf: Biography Of An
American Renegade*
    B&B - v12 - D '66 - p48
    BL - v62 - Mr 15 '66 - p686
    BS - v27 - S 15 '67 - p238
    CLW - v37 - Ap '66 - p554
    KR - v33 - D 15 '65 - p1259
    KR - v34 - Ja 1 '66 - p16
    LJ - v91 - F 1 '66 - p705
    LJ - v91 - Ap 15 '66 - p2228
    LW - v30 - Autumn '66 - p33
    NPCM - v40 - Ap '66 - p23
    NW - v67 - Mr 14 '66 - p106
    NY - v42 - Ap 2 '66 - p174
    NYT - v115 - Jl 13 '66 - p45M
    NYTBR - v71 - F 27 '66 - p6
    Obs - N 30 '69 - p35
    PW - v191 - Je 19 '67 - p86
    SB - v2 - S '66 - p132
    TLS - N 24 '66 - p1091

*Sarang: The Story Of The Bengal
Tiger And Of Two Children In
Search Of A Miracle*
    BS - v28 - N 1 '68 - p313
    KR - v36 - Ag 1 '68 - p838
    NYTBR, pt.1 - v73 - N 3 '68 - p54
    PW - v194 - Jl 22 '68 - p56

CARDOZA, Lois Steinmetz
see Duncan, Lois

CAREY, Ernestine Gilbreth   1908-
ConAu 5R, CurBio 49, SmATA 2,
WhoAm 78, WhoWor 74

Cheaper By The Dozen
    NYTBR - Ja 9 '49 - p18

CARLISLE, Norman V   1910-

The New American Continent
    BL - v69 - Jl 1 '73 - p1020
    KR - v41 - Ag 1 '73 - p388
    LJ - v99 - Ja 15 '74 - p206

Satellites: Servants Of Man
    BL - v67 - Je 1 '71 - p833
    KR - v39 - Mr 1 '71 - p238
    LJ - v96 - My 15 '71 - p1810
    SB - v7 - My '71 - p79

CARLSON, Bernice Wells   1910-
ConAu 5R, SmATA 8, WrDr 80

CARLSON, Bernice Wells (continued)

Masks And Mask Makers
BL - v57 - Je 1 '61 - p613
HB - v37 - Ag '61 - p356
KR - v29 - F 1 '61 - p106
LJ - v86 - Ap 15 '61 - p1688
NYTBR - Je 11 '61 - p34

CARLSON, Dale Bick   1935-
ConAu 9R, SmATA 1, WhoAmW 77

Baby Needs Shoes
BL - v71 - S 1 '74 - p38
CCB-B - v28 - My '75 - p143
KR - v42 - Jl 15 '74 - p742
LJ - v99 - S 15 '74 - p2285
PW - v206 - Jl 15 '74 - p115

The Plant People
CCB-B - v31 - S '77 - p9
Hi Lo - v1 - S '79 - p4
JB - v42 - Je '78 - p149
JB - v42 - O '78 - p264
NYTBR - O 9 '77 - p28
SLJ - v23 - My '77 - p66

A Wild Heart
BL - v74 - N 15 '77 - p545
Hi Lo - v1 - S '79 - p6
JB - v42 - Ag '78 - p213
Kliatt - v13 - Spring '79 - p5
SLJ - v24 - D '77 - p53

CARLSON, Diane

You Can't Tell Me What To Do!
Hi Lo - v1 - Ja '80 - p3

CARLSON, Gordon

Get Me Out Of Here!: Real Life Stories Of Teenage Heroism
Hi Lo - v1 - Ja '80 - p3

CARLSON, Natalie Savage   1906-
Au&ICB, ConAu 1R, MorBMP, MorJA, SmATA 2, TwCCW 78

The Half Sisters
Am - v123 - D 5 '70 - p496
B&B - v17 - Ag '72 - p93
BL - v67 - S 1 '70 - p55
BW - v4 - My 17 '70 - p16
CCB-B - v24 - N '70 - p39

CE - v47 - F '71 - p266
CLW - v42 - O '70 - p137
Comw - v93 - N 20 '70 - p200
HB - v46 - Ag '70 - p385
KR - v38 - My 1 '70 - p504
LJ - v95 - Jl '70 - p2531
NYTBR - S 27 '70 - p30
SR - v53 - Jl 25 '70 - p29
TLS - Jl 14 '72 - p805

CARMER, Carl   1893-1976
ConAu 5R, ConAu 69, OxAm, TwCA, TwCA SUP, WhoAm 76

The Boy Drummer Of Vincennes
BW - v6 - N 5 '72 - p4
CCB-B - v26 - My '73 - p135
Inst - v82 - N '72 - p131
LJ - v98 - Mr 15 '73 - p992
NYTBR - Ja 28 '73 - p8
PW - v202 - O 30 '72 - p56

Flag For The Fort
PW - v193 - Ja 15 '68 - p88

CARPELAN, Bo   1926-
ConAu 49, Pen EUR, SmATA 8

Bow Island
HB - v48 - Ap '72 - p143
KR - v39 - N 15 '71 - p1216
LJ - v97 - My 15 '72 - p1911
PW - v200 - S 20 '71 - p48

CARR, Harriet H   1899-
ConAu P-1, MorJA, SmATA 3

The Mystery Of The Aztec Idol
BL - v55 - Jl 15 '59 - p633
HB - v35 - Ag '59 - p287
KR - v27 - F 1 '59 - p89
LJ - v84 - Jl '59 - p2220
NYTBR, pt.2 - My 10 '59 - p26

CARROLL, Jeffrey   1950-
ConAu 85

Climbing To The Sun
BB - v6 - Ap '78 - p3
BL - v74 - Mr 1 '78 - p1099
Cur R - v17 - Ag '78 - p182
KR - v45 - O 15 '77 - p1103
SLJ - v24 - Ap '78 - p92

CARRUTH, Ella Kaiser
AuBYP SUP

> *She Wanted To Read: Story Of*
> *Mary McLeod Bethune*
> BL - v62 - My 1 '66 - p874
> CCB-B - v19 - Je '66 - p160
> LJ - v91 - S 15 '66 - p4328

CARSON, John F   1920-
ConAu 13R, IndAu 1917, SmATA 1

> *The Coach Nobody Liked*
> BL - v56 - Je 15 '60 - p630
> CSM - My 12 '60 - p3B
> KR - v28 - Ja 15 '60 - p51
> LJ - v85 - My 15 '60 - p2047
> NYTBR, pt.2 - My 8 '60 - p32
> PW - v190 - Jl 18 '66 - p79

> *The Twenty-Third Street*
> *Crusaders*
> CSM - My 8 '58 - p14
> Comw - v68 - My 23 '58 - p212
> HB - v34 - Ag '58 - p268
> KR - v25 - D 1 '57 - p863
> LJ - v83 - Ap 15 '58 - p1290

CARSON, Rachel   1907-1964
ConAu 77, CurBio 51, CurBio 64,
OxAm, SmATA 23, TwCW

> *The Sea Around Us*
> BL - v55 - Ja 15 '59 - p265
> CSM - D 18 '58 - p7
> KR - v26 - O 15 '58 - p805
> LJ - v84 - Ja 15 '59 - p255

CATHERALL, Arthur   1906-
ConAu 5R, SmATA 3, TwCCW 78

> *Prisoners In The Snow*
> BL - v64 - F 15 '68 - p697
> CLW - v39 - My '68 - p665
> HB - v44 - F '68 - p64
> KR - v35 - O 1 '67 - p1204
> LJ - v92 - D 15 '67 - p4610
> Par - v43 - Jl '68 - p81

> *Sicilian Mystery*
> BL - v63 - Jl 15 '67 - p1192
> KR - v35 - Mr 1 '67 - p278
> LJ - v92 - My 15 '67 - p2039
> PW - v191 - Je 12 '67 - p59

> *Ten Fathoms Deep*
> KR - v35 - N 1 '67 - p1323
> LJ - v93 - F 15 '68 - p878

CAUFIELD, Don

> *The Incredible Detectives*
> CCB-B - v20 - Ja '67 - p71
> HB - v42 - D '66 - p708
> LJ - v91 - N 15 '66 - p5771
> NYTBR - v71 - D 18 '66 - p16
> PW - v190 - D 26 '66 - p100
> SR - v50 - Ja 28 '67 - p46

CAUFIELD, Joan
see Caufield, Don (co-author)

CAVANNA, Betty   1909-
ConAu 9R, ConLC 12, MorJA,
SmATA 1, TwCCW 78 (also known
as Headley, Elizabeth)

> *Accent On April*
> BL - v57 - O 15 '60 - p128
> CSM - N 23 '60 - p11
> HB - v37 - F '61 - p56
> KR - v28 - Jl 15 '60 - p564
> LJ - v85 - S 15 '60 - p3229

> *Almost Like Sisters*
> BL - v23 - O 15 '63 - p264
> CCB-B - v18 - Je '65 - p143
> HB - v40 - F '64 - p65
> LJ - v88 - N 15 '63 - p4482

> *Angel On Skis*
> BL - v54 - D 15 '57 - p233
> CSM - N 7 '57 - p17
> KR - v25 - Jl 15 '57 - p487
> LJ - v82 - N 15 '57 - p2977
> NYTBR - D 15 '57 - p18

> *The Ghost Of Ballyhooly*
> KR - v39 - Ag 15 '71 - p881
> LJ - v96 - D 15 '71 - p4199

> *Jenny Kimura*
> BL - v24 - O 15 '64 - p288
> BL - v69 - F 15 '73 - p553
> CSM - v57 - Ja 21 '65 - p11
> HB - v40 - D '64 - p619
> LJ - v89 - S 15 '64 - p3487
> SR - v47 - N 7 '64 - p54
> TLS - My 19 '66 - p442

CAVANNA, Betty (continued)

Mystery At Love's Creek
CCB-B - v19 - F '66 - p95
CSM - v57 - N 4 '65 - pB11
HB - v41 - D '65 - p635
KR - v33 - Ag 15 '65 - p834
LJ - v90 - N 15 '65 - p5104
NYTBR - v70 - N 7 '65 - p59

Mystery In Marrakech
BS - v28 - N 1 '68 - p323
KR - v36 - Ag 1 '68 - p823
PW - v194 - O 7 '68 - p54

The Mystery Of The Emerald Buddha
BL - v73 - D 15 '76 - p603
CCB-B - v30 - Ap '77 - p119
KR - v44 - O 1 '76 - p1100
PW - v210 - N 1 '76 - p74
SLJ - v23 - D '76 - p69

Passport To Romance
BL - v52 - S 15 '55 - p38
CSM - N 10 '55 - p5B
HB - v31 - D '55 - p458
KR - v23 - Jl 15 '55 - p497
LJ - v80 - O 15 '55 - p2389
NYT - N 13 '55 - p16
SR - v38 - N 12 '55 - p70

Ruffles And Drums
BB - v4 - F '76 - p4
CCB-B - v29 - Ja '76 - p74
Inst - v85 - N '75 - p154
J Read - v20 - O '76 - p80
KR - v43 - Jl 1 '75 - p716
PW - v208 - Jl 28 '75 - p122
SLJ - v22 - O '75 - p96

Runaway Voyage
BL - v75 - N 1 '78 - p476
KR - v46 - N 15 '78 - p1252
PW - v214 - O 23 '78 - p61
SLJ - v25 - O '78 - p153

A Time For Tenderness
NYTBR - O 14 '62 - p34

Touch Of Magic
BL - v58 - S 1 '61 - p34
CSM - My 11 '61 - p4B
HB - v37 - Je '61 - p273
KR - v29 - Mr 1 '61 - p222

LJ - v86 - My 15 '61 - p1991
see also Headley, Elizabeth Cavanna

CEBULASH, Mel 1937-
ConAu 29R, SmATA 10, WrDr 80

Big League Baseball Reading Kit
Hi Lo - v1 - My '80 - p5

The Champion's Jacket
Hi Lo - v1 - F '80 - p4

CEDER, Georgiana Dorcas
ConAu 1R, SmATA 10

Little Thunder
LJ - v91 - Jl '66 - p3533

CHABER, M E (pseud.) 1910-
ConAu X (real name: Crossen, Kendall Foster)

The Acid Nightmare
CCB-B - v21 - Jl '68 - p170
KR - v35 - O 15 '67 - p1282
LJ - v92 - N 15 '67 - p4257
NYTBR - v73 - Mr 3 '68 - p30

CHADWICK, Roxane

Don't Shoot
BL - v75 - O 15 '78 - p389
PW - v214 - Jl 24 '78 - p100
SLJ - v25 - F '79 - p39

CHANDLER, Caroline A 1906-1979
AmM&WS 78S, ConAu 17R,
SmATA 22N, SmATA 24, WhoAm 78

Nursing As A Career
LJ - v96 - My 15 '71 - p1810
SB - v7 - My '71 - p69

CHAPIN, Victor

The Violin And Its Masters
KR - v37 - Ag 1 '69 - p785
LJ - v94 - N 15 '69 - p4293

CHETIN, Helen 1922-
ConAu 29R, SmATA 6

CHETIN, Helen (continued)

Perihan's Promise, Turkish Relatives, And The Dirty Old Imam
BL - v70 - O 1 '73 - p168
CCB-B - v27 - O '73 - p23
CE - v50 - N '73 - p97
HB - v49 - O '73 - p470
KR - v41 - Je 15 '73 - p641
LJ - v98 - S 15 '73 - p2649

CHICHESTER, Francis   1901-1972
ConAu 37R, ConAu P-1, CurBio 67, NewYTBE 72, WhAm 5

Gypsy Moth Circles The World
Atl - v221 - Mr '68 - p126
B&B - v13 - D '67 - p53
BL - v64 - Ap 15 '68 - p970
BS - v27 - Mr 1 '68 - p458
BW - v2 - F 25 '68 - p1
CLW - v39 - My '68 - p662
Econ - v225 - D 2 '67 - pR9
GJ - v134 - Mr '68 - p135
HM - v236 - Ap '68 - p107
KR - v35 - D 15 '67 - p1499
LJ - v93 - Mr 1 '68 - p1014
LJ - v93 - Mr 15 '68 - p1335
NS - v74 - D 1 '67 - p767
NYTBR - v73 - Mr 10 '68 - p8
PW - v192 - D 25 '67 - p54
SR - v51 - Mr 2 '68 - p27
TLS - D 7 '67 - p1187
WSJ - v171 - Mr 7 '68 - p10
Yacht - v123 - My '68 - p88

CHILDRESS, Alice   1920-
BlkAW, ConAu 45, ConLC 12, SelBAA, SmATA 7, WhoBlA 77

A Hero Ain't Nothin' But A Sandwich
BL - v70 - N 15 '73 - p333
BL - v70 - N 15 '73 - p336
BW - F 10 '74 - p4
BW - v7 - N 11 '73 - p3C
BW - v7 - N 11 '73 - p7C
CCB-B - v27 - F '74 - p91
CLW - v45 - F '74 - p344
CLW - v47 - N '75 - p164
Choice - v12 - N '75 - p1132
EJ - v64 - Ja '75 - p112

EJ - v64 - D '75 - p79
JNE - v43 - Summer '74 - p398
KR - v41 - Ag 1 '73 - p818
KR - v41 - D 15 '73 - p1355
LJ - v98 - O 15 '73 - p3153
LJ - v98 - D 15 '73 - p3689
NYTBR - N 4 '73 - p36
NYTBR - N 4 '73 - p52
NYTBR - D 2 '73 - p79
NYTBR - O 13 '74 - p46
PW - v204 - Ag 6 '73 - p65
Teacher - v92 - Ja '75 - p110

CHITTUM, Ida   1918-
ConAu 37R, SmATA 7, WrDr 80

Tales Of Terror
BL - v72 - F 1 '76 - p765
PW - v208 - N 24 '75 - p52
SLJ - v22 - Mr '76 - p99

CHODES, John   1939-
ConAu 61

Bruce Jenner
BL - v74 - O 15 '77 - p381
SLJ - v24 - D '77 - p65

CHRISTESEN, Barbara

The Magic And Meaning Of Voodoo
SLJ - v25 - N '78 - p55

CHRISTGAU, Alice E   1902-
ConAu P-2, SmATA 13

The Laugh Peddler
BW - v2 - My 5 '68 - p20
HB - v44 - Je '68 - p323
KR - v36 - F 15 '68 - p181
LJ - v93 - Ap 15 '68 - p1797
NYTBR - v73 - My 5 '68 - p34

CHRISTIAN, Mary Blount   1933-
ConAu 45, SmATA 9, WrDr 80

Felina
BL - v75 - My 15 '79 - p1435
Hi Lo - v1 - N '79 - p4

CHRISTIAN, Samuel T
see Gorodetzky, Charles W (co-author)

CHRISTOPHER, John   (pseud.) 1922-
ChLR 2, ConAu X, ConSFA,
FourBJA, TwCCW 78, WorAu (real
name: Youd, Samuel)

An Empty World
B&B - v23 - Ja '78 - p63
BL - v74 - Je 15 '78 - p1614
BW - Je 11 '78 - pE4
CCB-B - v32 - S '78 - p5
GP - v16 - D '77 - p3225
HB - v54 - Je '78 - p274
JB - v42 - Ap '78 - p99
KR - v46 - Ap 1 '78 - p379
NYTBR - My 14 '78 - p45
Obs - N 27 '77 - p29
SLJ - v24 - My '78 - p64
TES - F 3 '78 - p46
TLS - D 2 '77 - p1415

The Lotus Caves
BL - v66 - O 15 '69 - p295
CSM - v61 - N 6 '69 - pB7
Comw - v91 - N 21 '69 - p257
Econ - v241 - D 18 '71 - p70
HB - v45 - D '69 - p673
KR - v37 - Jl 1 '69 - p672
LJ - v94 - O 15 '69 - p3827
LR - v22 - Fall '69 - p153
NO - v8 - N 3 '69 - p20
NS - v78 - O 31 '69 - p623
Obs - D 7 '69 - p31
PW - v196 - S 8 '69 - p57

White Mountains
B&B - v12 - Je '67 - p36
BL - v63 - Jl 1 '67 - p1144
CCB-B - v21 - D '67 - p57
CSM - v59 - Ag 3 '67 - p11
HB - v43 - Je '67 - p351
KR - v35 - F 1 '67 - p136
LJ - v92 - Je 15 '67 - p2448
Lis - v77 - My 18 '67 - p661
NS - v73 - My 26 '67 - p733
NYTBR - v72 - Ag 13 '67 - p26
SR - v50 - Je 17 '67 - p36
Spec - v218 - Je 2 '67 - p656
TLS - My 25 '67 - p459

Wild Jack
BL - v71 - O 1 '74 - p168
CCB-B - v28 - F '75 - p90
CLW - v46 - My '75 - p452
Comw - v101 - N 22 '74 - p194

GP - v13 - Mr '75 - p2569
HB - v50 - Ag '74 - p374
JB - v39 - F '75 - p58
KR - v42 - Ag 1 '74 - p803
KR - v43 - Ja 1 '75 - p5
LJ - v99 - O 15 '74 - p2738
PT - v8 - D '74 - p130
TLS - Ap 4 '75 - p360

CHRISTOPHER, Matt   1917-
ConAu 1R, MorBMP, SmATA 2,
WrDr 80

Shortstop From Tokyo
CCB-B - v24 - Jl '70 - p173
CSM - v62 - My 7 '70 - pB7
KR - v38 - Ap 15 '70 - p451
LJ - v95 - My 15 '70 - p1963
SR - v53 - Je 27 '70 - p38

The Team That Couldn't Lose
KR - v35 - Je 15 '67 - p694
LJ - v92 - D 15 '67 - p4632

The Year Mom Won The Pennant
BL - v64 - My 1 '68 - p1040
CCB-B - v21 - My '68 - p139
Inst - v77 - My '68 - p128
KR - v36 - Mr 1 '68 - p260
LJ - v93 - My 15 '68 - p2128
Teacher - v91 - Ap '74 - p89

CHUTE, Marchette   1909-
ConAu 1R, MorJA, SmATA 1,
TwCA SUP, TwCCW 78, WhoAm 78

Stories From Shakespeare
Atl - v198 - D '56 - p103
BL - v53 - S 1 '56 - p28
HB - v32 - O '56 - p373
KR - v24 - Je 15 '56 - p407
LJ - v81 - S 15 '56 - p2048
NY - v32 - N 24 '45 - p235
NYTBR - Ag 26 '56 - p28
SR - v39 - N 17 '56 - p67

CLAPP, Patricia   1912-
ConAu 25R, SmATA 4, TwCCW 78

*Constance: A Story Of Early
Plymouth*
BL - v64 - My 1 '68 - p1041
BS - v28 - My 1 '68 - p63
BW - v2 - My 5 '68 - p26

41

CLAPP, Patricia (continued)
    CCB-B - v21 - Je '68 - p156
    CLW - v40 - O '68 - p148
    HB - v44 - Je '68 - p328
    KR - v35 - D 15 '67 - p1477
    NYTBR - v73 - Ag 18 '68 - p34
    SR - v51 - My 11 '68 - p42

  Dr. Elizabeth
    BL - v70 - Jl 1 '74 - p1198
    CCB-B - v28 - O '74 - p25
    KR - v42 - Mr 15 '74 - p304

  I'm Deborah Sampson: A Soldier
  In The War Of The Revolution
    BL - v73 - Jl 1 '77 - p1651
    CCB-B - v31 - S '77 - p10
    CLW - v49 - D '77 - p234
    EJ - v67 - Mr '78 - p81
    HB - v53 - Ag '77 - p437
    KR - v45 - Mr 15 '77 - p284
    LA - v54 - S '77 - p690
    SLJ - v24 - N '77 - p68
    Teacher - v95 - My '78 - p102

  Jane-Emily
    BL - v65 - Jl 1 '69 - p1224
    CCB-B - v22 - Jl '69 - p172
    CLW - v41 - F '70 - p381
    Comw - v90 - My 23 '69 - p301
    HB - v45 - O '69 - p538
    LJ - v94 - Je 15 '69 - p2508
    NYTBR - Jl 20 '69 - p22
    PW - v195 - My 12 '69 - p58

CLARK, David A (pseud.) 1940-
  ConAu X (real name: Ernst, John)

  Jokes, Puns, And Riddles
    KR - v36 - Ap 1 '68 - p398
    LJ - v93 - Je 15 '68 - p2536
    NYTBR - v73 - Je 16 '68 - p24
    PW - v193 - Je 17 '68 - p61

CLARK, James L 1883-1969
  IIBEAAW, NatCAB 55

  In The Steps Of The Great
  American Museum Collector, Carl
  Ethan Akeley
    LJ - v93 - Jl '68 - p2732
    SB - v4 - S '68 - p130

CLARK, Mary Higgins 1931-
  ConAu 81, WhoAmW 74

  A Stranger Is Watching
    BL - v74 - Mr 15 '78 - p1164
    BS - v37 - Mr '78 - p377
    KR - v45 - D 15 '77 - p1331
    LJ - v103 - Mr 1 '78 - p589
    Obs - My 7 '78 - p34
    PW - v212 - D 26 '77 - p59
    PW - v215 - Ja 15 '79 - p130
    Prog - v42 - My '78 - p45
    Spec - v241 - Ag 19 '78 - p22
    WLB - v52 - Je '78 - p801

CLARK, Mavis Thorpe 1912?-
  ConAu 57, ConLC 12, FourBJA,
  SmATA 8, TwCCW 78

  If The Earth Falls In
    BL - v72 - Ja 15 '76 - p682
    CCB-B - v29 - Ap '76 - p123
    HB - v52 - Ap '76 - p161
    KR - v43 - N 1 '75 - p1227
    SLJ - v22 - F '76 - p50

CLARKE, Arthur C 1917-
  ConAu 1R, ConLC 13, ConSFA,
  FourBJA, SmATA 13, WhoWor 78

  Dolphin Island
    NYTBR - Je 9 '63 - p28
    PW - v192 - N 27 '67 - p44
    TLS - Ap 7 '78 - p377

  Report On Planet Three And Other
  Speculations
    BL - v68 - My 15 '72 - p784
    BW - v5 - D 19 '71 - p6
    CSM - v64 - F 10 '72 - p10
    CSM - v64 - Jl 12 '72 - p10
    Choice - v9 - My '72 - p388
    KR - v39 - N 1 '71 - p1185
    LJ - v96 - D 1 '71 - p4013
    LJ - v97 - Ap 15 '72 - p1628
    LJ - v98 - Mr 1 '73 - p692
    PW - v200 - N 8 '71 - p44
    S&T - v43 - Mr '72 - p182
    WSJ - v179 - F 9 '72 - p14

CLARKE, John (pseud.) 1907-
  ConAu X, SmATA 5 (real name:
  Laughlin, Virginia Carli)

CLARKE, John (continued)

Black Soldier
CCB-B - v22 - Ja '69 - p75
LJ - v94 - Ap 15 '69 - p1792

High School Drop Out
CCB-B - v18 - Ap '65 - p115
see also Laklan, Carli

CLARKE, Mary Stetson 1911-
ConAu 21R, SmATA 5, WhoAmW
77, WrDr 80

The Iron Peacock
BL - v62 - Je 1 '66 - p958
BS - v26 - Je 1 '66 - p99
BS - v26 - Ag 1 '66 - p173
CCB-B - v20 - My '67 - p136
CSM - v58 - Jl 14 '66 - p4
HB - v42 - Je '66 - p315
KR - v34 - Mr 1 '66 - p252
LJ - v91 - N 15 '66 - p5754
NYTBR - v71 - My 8 '66 - p14

CLARY, Jack 1932-
ConAu 57

The Captains
BL - v74 - Jl 1 '78 - p1656
Comw - v105 - N 10 '78 - p735
KR - v46 - My 1 '78 - p524
LJ - v103 - Jl '78 - p1430
PW - v213 - Je 12 '78 - p76

CLAUS, Marshall 1936-1970
ConAu P-2

Better Gymnastics For Boys
LJ - v95 - D 15 '70 - p4382

CLAY, Catherine Lee

Season Of Love
BL - v65 - F 1 '69 - p579
CLW - v41 - O '69 - p139
HB - v45 - F '69 - p58
KR - v36 - Ag 1 '68 - p824
LJ - v93 - O 15 '68 - p3976

CLAYTON, Ed 1921-1966

*Martin Luther King: The Peaceful
Warrior*
NYTBR - My 4 '69 - p44

Teacher - v95 - Ja '78 - p45

CLAYTON, Robert

China
CCB-B - v26 - N '72 - p40
KR - v40 - Ap 1 '72 - p403
NYTBR - My 14 '72 - p8
Spec - v227 - N 13 '71 - p703
TLS - O 22 '71 - p1344

CLEARY, Beverly 1916-
ChLR 2, ConAu 1R, MorBMP,
MorJA, SmATA 2, TwCCW 78

Fifteen
Atl - v198 - D '56 - p104
BL - v53 - S 1 '56 - p28
KR - v24 - Jl 1 '56 - p442
LJ - v81 - O 15 '56 - p2469
NY - v32 - N 24 '56 - p234
NYT - S 16 '56 - p38
SR - v39 - N 17 '56 - p60

The Luckiest Girl
BL - v55 - S 1 '58 - p28
HB - v35 - F '59 - p54
KR - v26 - Jl 1 '58 - p463
LJ - v83 - O 15 '58 - p3014
NYT - S 14 '58 - p32

Ramona The Pest
BL - v64 - My 1 '68 - p1041
BW - v2 - S 8 '68 - p24
CCB-B - v21 - Je '68 - p157
CSM - v60 - My 2 '68 - pB7
HB - v44 - Ag '68 - p419
KR - v36 - Mr 15 '68 - p335
LJ - v93 - Je 15 '68 - p2536
NYTBR - v73 - My 5 '68 - p32
PW - v193 - Ap 15 '68 - p97
SE - v33 - My '69 - p555
SR - v51 - My 11 '68 - p38
TLS - Mr 29 '74 - p329
TN - v25 - N '68 - p77

CLEAVER, Bill
see Cleaver, Vera (co-author)

CLEAVER, Vera 1919-
ConAu 73, FourBJA, SmATA 22,
SouST, TwCCW 78

CLEAVER, Vera (continued)

Delpha Green And Company
BS - v32 - Ap 15 '72 - p46
CCB-B - v26 - D '72 - p54
EJ - v63 - Mr '74 - p105
GP - v14 - N '75 - p2737
JB - v40 - F '76 - p39
KR - v40 - Mr 15 '72 - p324
LJ - v97 - My 15 '72 - p1911
NYTBR - My 28 '72 - p8
PW - v201 - My 15 '72 - p53
Spec - v235 - D 6 '75 - p733
TLS - D 5 '75 - p1455

Grover
BL - v66 - My 15 '70 - p1158
CCB-B - v24 - Jl '70 - p174
CE - v47 - D '70 - p159
Comw - v92 - My 22 '70 - p248
HB - v46 - Ap '70 - p158
KR - v38 - F 15 '70 - p172
LJ - v95 - My 15 '70 - p1911
LJ - v95 - My 15 '70 - p1939
LJ - v95 - D 15 '70 - p4325
LJ - v96 - Ja 15 '71 - p286
NS - v81 - Je 4 '71 - p779
NYTBR - Mr 15 '70 - p49
NYTBR, pt.2 - N 8 '70 - p38
PW - v197 - F 9 '70 - p83
SR - v53 - Mr 21 '70 - p39
TLS - Jl 2 '71 - p767

I Would Rather Be A Turnip
CCB-B - v24 - Je '71 - p154
CSM - v63 - My 6 '71 - pB6
Choice - v14 - N '77 - p1178
GW - v106 - Ap 15 '72 - p24
HB - v47 - Ap '71 - p171
KR - v39 - F 1 '71 - p105
LJ - v96 - Ap 15 '71 - p1500
NYTBR, pt.2 - My 2 '71 - p4
Obs - Ap 2 '72 - p28
PW - v199 - Mr 22 '71 - p53
SR - v54 - Ap 17 '71 - p45
TLS - Ap 28 '72 - p481
Teacher - v95 - O '77 - p168

The Mimosa Tree
BL - v67 - D 15 '70 - p340
BW - v4 - N 8 '70 - p22
CCB-B - v24 - Mr '71 - p104
Comw - v93 - N 20 '70 - p202
HB - v46 - O '70 - p477

JB - v42 - F '78 - p35
KR - v38 - Ag 1 '70 - p799
LJ - v96 - Ja 15 '71 - p274
NYTBR, pt.2 - N 8 '70 - p10
Obs - S 25 '77 - p25
PW - v198 - S 14 '70 - p70
TES - Ja 6 '78 - p17

The Mock Revolt
BL - v68 - D 15 '71 - p365
BW - v5 - N 7 '71 - p13
HB - v47 - O '71 - p488
KR - v39 - Jl 1 '71 - p681
LJ - v96 - O 15 '71 - p3474
NCW - v216 - Mr '73 - p92
NYTBR - Ja 16 '72 - p8
NYTBR, pt.2 - N 7 '71 - p47
Spec - v229 - N 11 '72 - p747
TLS - N 3 '72 - p1317
Teacher - v90 - My '73 - p73

Where The Lilies Bloom
Am - v121 - D 13 '69 - p595
BL - v66 - D 15 '69 - p513
CCB-B - v23 - D '69 - p56
CSM - v67 - Ja 22 '75 - p8
Comw - v91 - N 21 '69 - p257
Econ - v237 - D 26 '70 - p41
GW - v103 - D 19 '70 - p21
KR - v37 - Ag 15 '69 - p859
LJ - v94 - D 15 '69 - p4581
LJ - v94 - D 15 '69 - p4602
Lis - v84 - N 12 '70 - p671
NO - v8 - D 29 '69 - p17
NS - v81 - Mr 5 '71 - p312
NYTBR - S 28 '69 - p34
NYTBR - D 7 '69 - p68
NYTBR - Ap 14 '74 - p26
NYTBR, pt.2 - N 9 '69 - p62
PW - v196 - S 22 '69 - p85
SR - v52 - S 13 '69 - p37
Spec - v225 - D 5 '70 - pR20
TLS - D 11 '70 - p1457
TN - v26 - Ap '70 - p307

The Whys And Wherefores Of Littabelle Lee
BL - v69 - My 15 '73 - p904
CCB-B - v26 - Jl '73 - p168
CSM - v65 - My 5 '73 - p10
EJ - v63 - Mr '74 - p105
HB - v49 - Ag '73 - p386
KR - v41 - F 1 '73 - p122

CLEAVER, Vera (continued)
NYTBR - Mr 4 '73 - p6
NYTBR - Je 10 '73 - p41
NYTBR - N 4 '73 - p56
NYTBR - D 2 '73 - p79
NYTBR, pt.2 - My 6 '73 - p6
Obs - Ap 14 '74 - p31
PT - v7 - Je '73 - p19
PW - v203 - Ap 16 '73 - p54
SE - v41 - O '77 - p531
TLS - Mr 29 '74 - p326

CLEMENTS, Bruce 1931-
AuBYP SUP, ConAu 53

From Ice Set Free
BL - v68 - Je 15 '72 - p902
BW - v6 - Ag 13 '72 - p6
CCB-B - v25 - Je '72 - p153
EJ - v61 - My '72 - p768
HB - v48 - Ag '72 - p379
KR - v40 - Ap 1 '72 - p412
LJ - v97 - My 15 '72 - p1919
NYTBR, pt.2 - N 5 '72 - p3

CLIFFORD, Eth
see Rosenberg, Ethel Clifford

CLINE, Linda 1941-
ConAu 65, WrDr 80

Weakfoot
KR - v43 - Ap 15 '75 - p452
NYTBR - Mr 30 '75 - p8
SLJ - v22 - O '75 - p96

CLYMER, Eleanor 1906-
ConAu 61, FourBJA, SmATA 9,
TwCCW 78, WhoAm 78

The Case Of The Missing Link
A Anth - v65 - Je '63 - p695
HB - v39 - F '63 - p82
LJ - v87 - N 15 '62 - p4266
NH - v72 - D '63 - p13
NYTBR - N 11 '62 - p30

Modern American Career Women
BL - v55 - My 15 '59 - p510
KR - v27 - Ja 15 '59 - p44
LJ - v84 - F 15 '59 - p590

The Spider, The Cave And The Pottery Bowl
Am - v125 - D 4 '71 - p488
BL - v67 - Je 15 '71 - p870
BL - v69 - O 15 '72 - p177
CCB-B - v24 - Je '71 - p154
CLW - v43 - My '72 - p537
CSM - v63 - Jl 10 '71 - p15
HB - v47 - Ag '71 - p382
KR - v39 - Ap 15 '71 - p431
LJ - v96 - My 15 '71 - p1801
PW - v199 - Mr 8 '71 - p71

The Trolley Car Family
Atl - v180 - D '47 - p144
BL - v44 - O 1 '47 - p53
KR - v15 - Ag 15 '47 - p427
LJ - v72 - S 15 '47 - p1277
NYTBR - N 16 '47 - p40

CLYNE, Patricia Edwards
AuBYP SUP

The Corduroy Road
KR - v41 - Ag 1 '73 - p812
LJ - v99 - Ja 15 '74 - p206
PW - v205 - Ja 21 '74 - p85

COATSWORTH, Elizabeth 1893-
ChLR 2, ConAu 5R, JBA 51, OxAm,
SmATA 2, TwCCW 78

The Hand Of Apollo
CCB-B - v19 - F '66 - p96
CE - v43 - O '66 - p103
CW - v59 - Ap '66 - p253
KR - v33 - O 1 '65 - p1046
LJ - v91 - Ja 15 '66 - p424
NYTBR - v71 - Ja 2 '66 - p18

COBB, Vicki 1938-
ChLR 2, ConAu 33R, SmATA 8,
WrDr 80

Science Experiments You Can Eat
IIB - v49 - O '73 - p490
KR - v40 - Mr 15 '72 - p327
KR - v40 - D 15 '72 - p1415
LJ - v97 - My 15 '72 - p1920
NY - v48 - D 2 '72 - p191
SA - v227 - D '72 - p119
SB - v8 - S '72 - p126

COGGINS, Jack   1911-
ConAu 5R, MorJA, SmATA 2,
WhoAm 78

   Prepare To Dive: The Story Of
   Man Undersea
     KR - v39 - N 15 '71 - p1219
     LJ - v97 - Jl '72 - p2488
     SB - v8 - My '72 - p77

COHEN, Barbara   1932-
AuBYP SUP, ConAu 53, SmATA 10

   Benny
     BL - v74 - S 1 '77 - p37
     CCB-B - v31 - S '77 - p10
     CE - v54 - N '77 - p84
     KR - v45 - Ap 1 '77 - p350
     LA - v54 - O '77 - p808
     SE - v42 - Ap '78 - p320
     SLJ - v24 - S '77 - p124

COHEN, Carl

   Earth's Hidden Mysteries
     Hi Lo - v1 - Ap '80 - p3

COHEN, Daniel   1936-
AuBYP SUP, ChLR 3, ConAu 45,
SmATA 8

   Creatures From UFO's
     SLJ - v25 - Mr '79 - p136

   Famous Curses
     BL - v76 - D 15 '79 - p607
     Hi Lo - v1 - Ja '80 - p4
     SLJ - v26 - F '80 - p52

   Frauds, Hoaxes, And Swindles
     BL - v75 - My 15 '79 - p1445
     Hi Lo - v1 - O '79 - p4
     SLJ - v25 - My '79 - p60

   Great Mistakes
     BL - v76 - N 15 '79 - p496
     Hi Lo - v1 - F '80 - p3

   The Greatest Monsters In The
   World
     BL - v72 - F 15 '76 - p858
     KR - v43 - Jl 15 '75 - p779
     SLJ - v22 - Ja '76 - p44

   The Magic Art Of Foreseeing The
   Future
     BL - v69 - Jl 15 '73 - p1068

   Magicians, Wizards, And
   Sorcerers
     KR - v41 - Ap 15 '73 - p464
     LJ - v98 - Jl '73 - p2199

   Missing! Stories Of Strange
   Disappearances
     BL - v75 - Je 15 '79 - p1541
     Hi Lo - v1 - S '79 - p3
     KR - v47 - Mr 15 '79 - p330
     SLJ - v26 - F '80 - p53

   The Monsters Of Star Trek
     Hi Lo - v2 - S '80 - p5
     Kliatt - v14 - Spring '80 - p14
     SLJ - v26 - My '80 - p65

   Monsters You Never Heard Of
     Hi Lo - v1 - My '80 - p6

   Real Ghosts
     BL - v74 - N 15 '77 - p548
     KR - v45 - Jl 15 '77 - p729
     SLJ - v24 - O '77 - p110

   Supermonsters
     KR - v44 - D 15 '76 - p1308
     PW - v211 - Mr 14 '77 - p95
     SLJ - v23 - My '77 - p67

   Talking With The Animals
     BL - v68 - S 15 '71 - p108
     BW - v5 - My 9 '71 - p14
     Comw - v94 - My 21 '71 - p270
     KR - v39 - F 1 '71 - p114
     LJ - v97 - Jl '72 - p2482
     NYTBR - My 16 '71 - p8

   The World Of UFOs
     BL - v74 - Je 1 '78 - p1543
     Comw - v105 - N 10 '78 - p735
     Cur R - v17 - D '78 - p385
     HB - v54 - D '78 - p667
     KR - v46 - Je 1 '78 - p600
     SLJ - v25 - S '78 - p155

   The World's Most Famous Ghosts
     BL - v74 - Jl 15 '78 - p1738
     Hi Lo - v2 - S '80 - p5
     NYTBR - Ap 30 '78 - p45
     SLJ - v25 - S '78 - p132
     TN - v36 - Winter '80 - p199

COHEN, Daniel (continued)

Young Ghosts
BL - v75 - Ja 15 '79 - p808
CCB-B - v32 - Ap '79 - p132
SLJ - v25 - O '78 - p143

COHEN, Joel H
AuBYP SUP

Jim Palmer: Great Comeback Competitor
KR - v46 - F 1 '78 - p112
SLJ - v24 - My '78 - p86

Steve Garvey: Storybook Star
SLJ - v24 - D '77 - p63

COHEN, Peter Zachary   1931-
ConAu 33R, SmATA 4, WrDr 80

Bee
BL - v71 - Ap 1 '75 - p815
CE - v52 - Ja '76 - p153
HB - v51 - Je '75 - p267
KR - v43 - Mr 15 '75 - p306
LA - v52 - N '75 - p1165
SLJ - v21 - Ap '75 - p50

Foal Creek
CLW - v44 - Mr '73 - p510
EJ - v62 - Ja '73 - p145
HB - v49 - Ap '73 - p141
KR - v40 - Ag 1 '72 - p864
LJ - v98 - Ja 15 '73 - p259

COHEN, Randy

Easy Answers To Hard Questions
Kliatt - v14 - Winter '80 - p70

COHEN, Robert C   1930-
AuBYP SUP, ConAu 57, SmATA 8

The Color Of Man
BL - v65 - S 1 '68 - p61
BL - v65 - Ap 1 '69 - p900
BS - v28 - My 1 '68 - p63
BW - v2 - My 5 '68 - p30
CCB-B - v21 - Jl '68 - p171
CSM - v61 - My 1 '69 - pB7
Comw - v88 - My 24 '68 - p308
Comw - v89 - F 21 '69 - p645
Cres - v33 - D '69 - p23
EJ - v58 - F '69 - p291

HB - v45 - Ag '69 - p420
Inst - v78 - O '68 - p158
KR - v36 - Ap 1 '68 - p406
LJ - v93 - Je 15 '68 - p2545
NYTBR - v73 - My 5 '68 - p5
SB - v11 - My '75 - p5
SE - v33 - My '69 - p562
SR - v51 - My 11 '68 - p41

COLBY, Carroll Burleigh   1904-
ConAu 1R, MorJA, SmATA 3, WhoAm 78

The Weirdest People In The World
Inst - v82 - My '73 - p75
PW - v203 - F 12 '73 - p68

COLES, Robert   1929-
ConAu 45, CurBio 69, SmATA 23, WrDr 80, WhoAm 76

Dead End School
BL - v64 - My 15 '68 - p1092
BL - v69 - My 1 '73 - p837
BW - v2 - S 8 '68 - p24
CLW - v41 - Ja '70 - p321
CSM - v60 - My 2 '68 - pB1
Comw - v88 - My 24 '68 - p304
Comw - v89 - F 21 '69 - p645
HB - v44 - Je '68 - p323
KR - v36 - Ap 15 '68 - p458
LJ - v93 - My 15 '68 - p2112
NYTBR - v73 - My 5 '68 - p32
SR - v51 - My 11 '68 - p39

The Grass Pipe
BS - v29 - My 1 '69 - p56
BW - v3 - My 4 '69 - p28
CCB-B - v23 - My '70 - p141
CLW - v41 - My '70 - p575
CSM - v61 - My 1 '69 - pB7
Comw - v90 - My 23 '69 - p300
KR - v37 - Ap 15 '69 - p451
LJ - v94 - Jl '69 - p2680
NYTBR, pt.2 - My 4 '69 - p10
PW - v195 - My 12 '69 - p58
SR - v52 - My 10 '69 - p59

COLLIER, Christopher
see Collier, James Lincoln (co-author) - The Bloody Country

COLLIER, James Lincoln   1928-
AuBYP SUP, ChLR 3, ConAu 9R,
SmATA 8

The Bloody Country
Am - v135 - D 11 '76 - p430
BB - v4 - D '76 - p4
BL - v72 - Je 1 '76 - p1403
BW - My 2 '76 - pL3
CCB-B - v30 - D '76 - p55
CE - v53 - O '76 - p33
Comw - v103 - N 19 '76 - p759
HB - v52 - Je '76 - p293
KR - v44 - F 15 '76 - p204
LA - v54 - Ja '77 - p83
NO - v15 - Ag 21 '76 - p16
NYTBR - My 2 '76 - p26
PW - v209 - My 10 '76 - p84
SLJ - v22 - My '76 - p67
Teacher - v94 - N '76 - p134

*Rich And Famous: The Further
Adventures Of George Stable*
BL - v72 - N 15 '75 - p451
BS - v35 - D '75 - p299
CCB-B - v29 - F '76 - p93
HB - v52 - F '76 - p48
KR - v43 - S 1 '75 - p997
SLJ - v22 - N '75 - p72

*The Teddy Bear Habit, Or How I
Became A Winner*
KR - v34 - N 15 '66 - p1183
LJ - v92 - Ap 15 '67 - p1746
NYTBR - v72 - Mr 12 '67 - p28
PW - v191 - My 22 '67 - p64
SR - v50 - My 13 '67 - p57

COLLINS, Ruth Philpott   1890-1975
ConAu 1R, ConAu 53

The Flying Cow
CC - v80 - D 18 '63 - p1585
CSM - N 14 '63 - p4B
HB - v40 - F '64 - p58
LJ - v88 - D 15 '63 - p4851
NYTBR, pt.2 - N 10 '63 - p46

COLMAN, Hila
ConAu 13R, MorBMP, SmATA 1,
ThrBJA

After The Wedding
CCB-B - v29 - F '76 - p93

EJ - v66 - Ja '77 - p64
KR - v43 - S 1 '75 - p1004
PW - v208 - S 29 '75 - p50
SLJ - v22 - S '75 - p118

The Amazing Miss Laura
BB - v4 - Ja '77 - p3
CCB-B - v30 - Ja '77 - p73
KR - v44 - Jl 15 '76 - p799
NO - v15 - D 25 '76 - p15
SLJ - v23 - N '76 - p67

Claudia, Where Are You?
Atl - v224 - D '69 - p150
BS - v29 - O 1 '69 - p254
CCB-B - v23 - N '69 - p41
CSM - v61 - N 6 '69 - pB9
EJ - v58 - N '69 - p1257
Inst - v79 - D '69 - p114
KR - v37 - Ag 15 '69 - p859
LJ - v95 - Mr 15 '70 - p1200
NYTBR, pt.2 - N 9 '69 - p48
PW - v196 - S 22 '69 - p85
SR - v52 - N 8 '77 - p71

Daughter Of Discontent
CCB-B - v25 - N '71 - p39
CSM - v63 - N 11 '71 - pB1
KR - v39 - Ag 1 '71 - p814
LJ - v96 - D 15 '71 - p4188
PW - v200 - Ag 16 '71 - p57

The Girl From Puerto Rico
NYTBR - F 25 '62 - p36

*The Happenings At North End
School*
BS - v30 - O 15 '70 - p297
EJ - v60 - Mr '71 - p405
KR - v38 - Ag 1 '70 - p804
LJ - v95 - D 15 '70 - p4360
NYTBR - Ap 25 '71 - p40

Mixed-Marriage Daughter
BS - v28 - O 1 '68 - p276
HB - v49 - Ap '73 - p173
Inst - v78 - N '68 - p154
KR - v36 - S 1 '68 - p986
LJ - v94 - Ja 15 '69 - p308
LJ - v95 - F 15 '70 - p741
NYTBR - Mr 9 '69 - p26

Nobody Has To Be A Kid Forever
BL - v72 - F 15 '76 - p853
CCB-B - v29 - My '76 - p140

COLMAN, Hila (continued)
EJ - v66 - N '77 - p81
KR - v44 - F 1 '76 - p138
LA - v54 - F '77 - p210
PW - v209 - Ja 19 '76 - p102
SLJ - v22 - Ap '76 - p72
Teacher - v95 - O '77 - p168

Sometimes I Don't Love My Mother
BL - v74 - O 1 '77 - p279
BL - v74 - O 1 '77 - p286
CCB-B - v31 - D '77 - p58
Inst - v87 - N '77 - p160
KR - v45 - Ag 1 '77 - p788
PW - v212 - Ag 8 '77 - p69
SLJ - v24 - O '77 - p122

Tell Me No Lies
Cur R - v18 - F '79 - p29
LA - v56 - Ja '79 - p53
RT - v32 - Ja '79 - p487

COLVER, Alice Ross 1892-
AmNov, AuBYP, ConAu 69

Vicky Barnes, Junior Hospital Volunteer
BS - v26 - D 1 '66 - p338

COLWELL, Robert 1931-
ConAu 33R

Introduction To Backpacking
BL - v67 - F 15 '71 - p466
CC - v87 - D 16 '70 - p1517
LJ - v95 - D 1 '70 - p4191
LJ - v95 - D 15 '70 - p4382

COMBER, Lillian
see Beckwith, Lillian

COMPTON, Grant

What Does A Coast Guardsman Do?
BL - v65 - My 1 '69 - p1014
SB - v4 - Mr '69 - p264

COMPTON, Margaret (pseud.) 1852-1903
DcNAA (real name: Harrison, Amelia Williams)

American Indian Fairy Tales
BL - v67 - My 1 '71 - p752
KR - v39 - Ja 15 '71 - p53
LJ - v96 - My 15 '71 - p1801
PW - v199 - My 3 '71 - p57

CONAN DOYLE, Arthur
see Doyle, Arthur Conan

CONE, Molly Lamken 1918-
ConAu 1R, SmATA 1, ThrBJA

Call Me Moose
BB - v6 - S '78 - p4
BL - v74 - Je 15 '78 - p1614
CCB-B - v32 - S '78 - p6
HB - v54 - Je '78 - p275
KR - v46 - My 15 '78 - p547
LA - v55 - O '78 p862
SLJ - v24 - My '78 - p65

CONFORD, Ellen 1942-
AuBYP SUP, ConAu 33R, SmATA 6, WrDr 80

We Interrupt This Semester For An Important Bulletin
BL - v76 - S 15 '79 - p117
CBRS - v8 - D '79 - p36
CCB-B - v33 - Ap '80 - p148
HB - v56 - F '80 - p59
KR - v48 - F 15 '80 - p221
SLJ - v26 - S '79 - p154
WLB - v54 - Mr '80 - p456

CONLON, Jean
see Lawson, Donna (co-author)

CONLY, Robert Leslie
see O'Brien, Robert

CONNOR, James, III
AuBYP SUP

I, Dwayne Kleber
KR - v38 - Ag 15 '70 - p884
LJ - v96 - Je 15 '71 - p2136
NYTBR - N 22 '70 - p38

CONRAD, Dick

Tony Dorsett: From Heisman To Superbowl In One Year
SLJ - v25 - My '79 - p86

CONRAD, Dick (continued)

> *Walter Payton: The Running Machine*
> SLJ - v25 - My '79 - p86

CONSIDINE, Tim

> *The Photographic Dictionary Of Soccer*
> ARBA - v11 - '80 - p321
> BW - Jl 15 '79 - pH2

COOK, David

> *A Closer Look At Apes*
> GP - v15 - Ja '77 - p3053
> JB - v40 - Ag '76 - p197
> SA - v235 - D '76 - p134
> SB - v13 - My '77 - p43
> SLJ - v23 - Ap '77 - p63
> TLS - Jl 16 '76 - p887

COOK, Fred J   1911-
ConAu 9R, DcAmAu, SmATA 2, WhoAm 78

> *City Cop*
> BL - v75 - Je 15 '79 - p1533
> CBRS - v7 - Ag '79 - p136
> CCB-B - v32 - Jl '79 - p187
> Hi Lo - v1 - S '79 - p5
> NYTBR - Mr 25 '79 - p33
> SLJ - v25 - Ap '79 - p67

> *Dawn Over Saratoga: The Turning Point Of The Revolutionary War*
> BL - v70 - S 15 '73 - p110
> BS - v33 - Je 15 '73 - p145
> KR - v41 - My 1 '73 - p523
> LJ - v98 - N 15 '73 - p3462
> NYTBR - Ag 5 '73 - p8

COOK, Joseph Jay   1924-
AuBYP, ConAu 1R, SmATA 8

> *Better Surfing For Boys*
> CCB-B - v21 - Je '68 - p157
> LJ - v92 - D 15 '67 - p4634

> *Famous Firsts In Tennis*
> CCB-B - v31 - Je '78 - p156
> KR - v46 - Ja 15 '78 - p50
> SLJ - v24 - My '78 - p86

COOK, Olive Rambo   1892-
AuBYP, ConAu 13R

> *Serilda's Star*
> BL - v56 - Mr 15 '60 - p456
> HB - v36 - F '60 - p34
> KR - v27 - Jl 1 '59 - p443
> LJ - v85 - Mr 15 '60 - p1301

COOKE, David C   1917-
AuBYP, ConAu 1R, SmATA 2

> *Famous U.S. Navy Fighter Planes*
> KR - v40 - Je 1 '72 - p628
> LJ - v98 - F 15 '73 - p642

> *How Automobiles Are Made*
> LJ - v98 - Mr 15 '73 - p1001

COOKE, Sarah Fabyan
see Palfrey, Sarah

COOKSON, Catherine McMullen   1906-
ConAu 13R, SmATA 9, WrDr 80

> *Our John Willie*
> BL - v71 - D 15 '74 - p405
> PW - v208 - Ag 18 '75 - p70

COOLEN, Norma
see Tuck, Jay Nelson (co-author)

COOMBS, Charles Ira   1914-
AuBYP, ConAu 5R, SmATA 3

> *Auto Racing*
> BL - v68 - Ja 1 '72 - p393
> KR - v39 - Ag 15 '71 - p884
> LJ - v96 - D 15 '71 - p4203

> *Be A Winner In Soccer*
> BL - v74 - S 1 '77 - p37
> Comw - v104 - N 11 '77 - p734
> KR - v45 - Mr 1 '77 - p228
> SLJ - v23 - My '77 - p80

> *Be A Winner In Track And Field*
> BL - v72 - My 1 '76 - p1262
> KR - v44 - Ap 1 '76 - p396
> SLJ - v22 - My '76 - p80

> *Deep-Sea World: The Story Of Oceanography*
> BL - v62 - My 1 '66 - p874

COOMBS, Charles Ira (continued)
BS - v26 - Ap 1 '66 - p17
Inst - v75 - Je '66 - p139
KR - v34 - F 1 '66 - p114
LJ - v91 - O 15 '66 - p5224
NYTBR - v71 - Je 12 '66 - p22
PW - v189 - My 30 '66 - p88
SB - v2 - My '66 - p27

Drag Racing
BL - v67 - N 1 '70 - p226
LJ - v95 - D 15 '70 - p4378

Rocket Pioneer
SB - v1 - Mr '66 - p237

Skylab
HB - v48 - Ag '72 - p391
KR - v40 - F 15 '72 - p196
SA - v227 - D '72 - p116
SB - v8 - D '72 - p264

COOMBS, Orde M
BlkAW, ConAu 73, LivBAA,
SelBAA, WhoBlA 77

Do You See My Love For You Growing?
Am - v128 - Ja 20 '73 - p42
BW - v6 - O 1 '72 - p15
Bl W - v22 - F '73 - p51
KR - v40 - Jl 1 '72 - p761
LJ - v97 - N 15 '72 - p3821
LJ - v98 - F 15 '73 - p557
PW - v202 - Jl 10 '72 - p45

COOPER, Edmund J 1926-
ConAu 33R, ConSFA, WhoSciF,
WhoSpyF, WrDr 80

Let's Look At Costume
CCB-B - v22 - O '68 - p24
TLS - D 9 '65 - p1157

COOPER, Paulette 1944-
ConAu 37R, WrDr 80

Growing Up Puerto Rican
Choice - v10 - Jl '73 - p858
LJ - v97 - Ag '72 - p2626
NO - v11 - Ag 19 '72 - p19
PW - v201 - Je 12 '72 - p60
PW - v203 - My 28 '73 - p42

COPPARD, Audrey 1931-
ConAu 29R

Who Has Poisoned The Sea?
B&B - v15 - My '70 - p38
KR - v38 - Mr 15 '70 - p321
LJ - v95 - Je 15 '70 - p2307
NYTBR - Ag 23 '70 - p20
PW - v197 - My 18 '70 - p39
SR - v53 - My 9 '70 - p69

CORBETT, Scott 1913-
ChLR 1, ConAu 1R, FourBJA,
SmATA 2, TwCCW 78, WrDr 80

The Baseball Bargain
BL - v66 - My 15 '70 - p1158
CCB-B - v23 - Ap '70 - p126
Comw - v92 - My 22 '70 - p247
KR - v38 - Mr 1 '70 - p242
LJ - v95 - My 15 '70 - p1963
SR - v53 - Je 27 '70 - p38

Diamonds Are Trouble
KR - v35 - O 1 '67 - p1217
LJ - v92 - N 15 '67 - p4257
NYTBR - v72 - N 5 '67 - p44

The Home Run Trick
CCB-B - v27 - S '73 - p5
HB - v49 - Je '73 - p270
Inst - v82 - My '73 - p74
KR - v41 - Mr 1 '73 - p254
LJ - v98 - My 15 '73 - p1703
NYTBR - Jl 15 '73 - p10

What About The Wankel Engine?
BL - v71 - Ja 15 '75 - p506
CCB-B - v28 - My '75 - p144
KR - v42 - N 15 '74 - p1203
SB - v11 - My '75 - p27
SLJ - v21 - Mr '75 - p93

What Makes A Plane Fly?
BL - v64 - Ja 15 '68 - p591
CCB-B - v21 - Mr '68 - p107
HB - v44 - Ap '68 - p203
LJ - v93 - Ap 15 '68 - p1797
NYTBR - v73 - My 5 '68 - p52
SB - v3 - Mr '68 - p339
SR - v51 - Mr 16 '68 - p39

CORCORAN, Barbara 1911-
AuBYP SUP, ConAu 21R, SmATA
3, WrDr 80

CORCORAN, Barbara (continued)

A Dance To Still Music
Am - v131 - D 7 '74 - p374
BB - v3 - Ap '75 - p4
BL - v71 - S 1 '74 - p39
CCB-B - v28 - Ja '75 - p75
CE - v51 - F '75 - p215
CLW - v46 - Ap '75 - p404
CLW - v47 - Ap '76 - p397
Choice - v14 - N '77 - p1178
HB - v50 - O '74 - p136
KR - v42 - Jl 15 '74 - p742
KR - v43 - Ja 1 '75 - p5
LA - v52 - S '75 - p857
LJ - v99 - S 15 '74 - p2287
NYTBR - N 17 '74 - p8
PW - v206 - Ag 26 '74 - p306
Teacher - v92 - D '74 - p78

The Faraway Island
BB - v5 - Ag '77 - p2
BL - v73 - Ap 1 '77 - p1165
CCB-B - v31 - O '77 - p31
CLW - v49 - N '77 - p188
Cur R - v17 - My '78 - p127
HB - v53 - Ag '77 - p438
KR - v45 - F 1 '77 - p97
SLJ - v23 - My '77 - p60

Hey, That's My Soul You're Stomping On
BL - v74 - Ap 1 '78 - p1247
CCB-B - v31 - Je '78 - p156
EJ - v67 - S '78 - p90
HB - v54 - Je '78 - p282
KR - v46 - Mr 1 '78 - p247

Make No Sound
BL - v74 - O 15 '77 - p373
CLW - v49 - Mr '78 - p356
KR - v45 - Jl 15 '77 - p727
SLJ - v24 - S '77 - p125

Me And You And A Dog Named Blue
BL - v75 - Mr 15 '79 - p1153
HB - v55 - Je '79 - p300
KR - v47 - Mr 15 '79 - p331
SLJ - v25 - Mr '79 - p136

Rising Damp
BL - v76 - Ap 1 '80 - p1124
SLJ - v26 - Ap '80 - p121

Sam
BL - v64 - Ja 1 '68 - p542
BW - v1 - O 22 '67 - p14
CCB-B - v21 - N '67 - p39
CLW - v39 - D '67 - p291
CSM - v59 - N 2 '67 - pB11
KR - v35 - Jl 15 '67 - p815
LJ - v92 - N 15 '67 - p4258
NYTBR - v72 - N 5 '67 - p68
SR - v50 - N 11 '67 - p48
see also Dixon, Paige

CORDELL, Alexander (pseud.) 1914-
ConAu X, DcLEL 1940, SmATA 7,
TwCCW 78, WrDr 80 (real name:
Graber, Alexander)

Witches' Sabbath
BL - v67 - Ja 1 '71 - p371
CCB-B - v24 - Jl '71 - p168
Comw - v93 - N 20 '70 - p202
KR - v38 - N 1 '70 - p1200
NS - v80 - N 6 '70 - p610
PW - v198 - N 30 '70 - p41
TLS - Jl 2 '70 - p710
TLS - Ap 6 '73 - p382
TN - v27 - Je '71 - p431

CORNELL, Jean Gay 1920-
ConAu 45, SmATA 23, WhoAmW 77

Louis Armstrong: Ambassador Satchmo
JLD - v11 - Ap '78 - p44

Mahalia Jackson: Queen Of Gospel Song
PW - v205 - My 13 '74 - p58
SLJ - v21 - Ja '75 - p43

Ralph Bunche: Champion Of Peace
SLJ - v22 - My '76 - p58

CORRIGAN, Barbara 1922-
ConAu 57, SmATA 8

Of Course You Can Sew!
BL - v67 - Mr 15 '71 - p618
CE - v48 - O '71 - p29
HB - v47 - Je '71 - p298
Inst - v130 - Je '71 - p74
LJ - v96 - Ap 15 '71 - p1502
PW - v200 - Jl 5 '71 - p50

COVINGTON, John P
AuBYP SUP

Motorcycle Racer
LJ - v98 - D 15 '73 - p3723

COX, William R   1901-
AuBYP, ConAu 9R

Battery Mates
BL - v74 - Je 1 '78 - p1550
CCB-B - v31 - Jl '78 - p173
KR - v46 - F 1 '78 - p107
SLJ - v24 - My '78 - p87

Big League Sandlotters
CLW - v43 - N '71 - p174
KR - v39 - Ja 15 '71 - p56
LJ - v96 - My 15 '71 - p1823
SR - v54 - Jl 17 '71 - p36

Rookie In The Backcourt
BS - v29 - F 1 '70 - p422
CSM - v62 - My 7 '70 - pB7
KR - v37 - D 15 '69 - p1322
LJ - v95 - My 15 '70 - p1964

Third And Goal
BS - v31 - O 15 '71 - p334
LJ - v96 - D 15 '71 - p4201

Trouble At Second Base
LJ - v91 - Jl '66 - p3550
NYTBR - v71 - My 8 '66 - p47

CRAIG, Margaret   1911-1964
ConAu 1R, MorJA, SmATA 9

Trish
BL - v47 - Mr 15 '51 - p258
KR - v19 - Ja 1 '51 - p3
LJ - v76 - Mr 15 '51 - p530
NYTBR - Mr 11 '51 - p26
SR - v34 - My 12 '51 - p57

CRAMER, Kathryn
see Terzian, James (co-author) -
Mighty Hard Road

CRANE, Caroline   1930-
AuBYP SUP, ConAu 9R, SmATA
11, WrDr 80

A Girl Like Tracy
BS - v26 - My 1 '66 - p57

CCB-B - v19 - Je '66 - p161
LJ - v91 - My 15 '66 - p2702

Wedding Song
BS - v27 - O 1 '67 - p262
CLW - v39 - D '67 - p291
CSM - v59 - N 2 '67 - pB11
KR - v35 - Jl 15 '67 - p816
LJ - v92 - O 15 '67 - p3861

CRARY, Margaret   1906-
AuBYP, ConAu 5R, SmATA 9

Mexican Whirlwind
KR - v37 - Ap 15 '69 - p451
LJ - v94 - My 15 '69 - p2098

CRAVEN, Margaret   1901?-
BioIn 10, WrDr 80

I Heard The Owl Call My Name
Am - v130 - My 4 '74 - p349
BL - v70 - F 1 '74 - p569
BL - v71 - Mr 15 '75 - p747
BS - v33 - F 1 '74 - p475
CC - v92 - My 14 '75 - p501
CLW - v47 - N '75 - p167
CSM - v66 - Ja 30 '74 - pF5
LJ - v99 - F 15 '74 - p503
LJ - v99 - Mr 15 '74 - p908
LJ - v99 - My 15 '74 - p1452
NS - v88 - Ag 2 '74 - p163
NS - v88 - N 8 '74 - p666
NYTBR - F 3 '74 - p28
PW - v204 - D 3 '73 - p35
TLS - D 6 '74 - p1375
TN - v31 - Ap '75 - p331
Time - v103 - Ja 28 '74 - p73

CRAWFORD, Charles P   1945-
ConAu 45

Letter Perfect
NYTBR - Jl 22 '79 - p27

Three-Legged Race
BS - v34 - D 15 '74 - p430
Comw - v101 - N 22 '74 - p194
EJ - v64 - Ap '75 - p90
KR - v42 - Ag 1 '74 - p809
LJ - v99 - O 15 '74 - p2745
PW - v206 - N 25 '74 - p46

CRAYDER, Dorothy   1906-
AuBYP SUP, ConAu 33R, SmATA 7

   She, The Adventuress
     BL - v69 - Je 1 '73 - p946
     CCB-B - v26 - Jl '73 - p169
     HB - v49 - O '73 - p465
     KR - v41 - F 15 '73 - p186
     LJ - v98 - My 15 '73 - p1680
     Obs - D 7 '75 - p32
     TN - v30 - Ja '74 - p205
     Teacher - v91 - D '73 - p73

CROFUT, William   1934-
ConAu 25R, SmATA 23, WhoE 74

   Troubadour: A Different
   Battlefield
     BL - v65 - S 1 '68 - p28
     KR - v36 - F 15 '68 - p222
     KR - v36 - Mr 1 '68 - p281
     LJ - v93 - Ap 1 '68 - p1473
     PW - v193 - F 19 '68 - p90
     TN - v25 - N '68 - p80

CROMIE, William J   1930-
AuBYP SUP, ConAu 13R, SmATA 4

   Living World Of The Sea
     BL - v63 - D 1 '66 - p395
     CC - v83 - S 14 '66 - p1116
     CLW - v38 - D '66 - p271
     Choice - v4 - Ap '67 - p181
     HB - v43 - F '67 - p95
     KR - v34 - Jl 1 '66 - p669
     KR - v34 - Jl 15 '66 - p702
     LJ - v91 - D 1 '66 - p5986
     NH - v76 - F '67 - p68
     SB - v2 - Mr '67 - p289

CRONE, Ruth
see Brown, Marion Marsh (co-
author)

CROSBY, Alexander L   1906-1980
ConAu 29R, MorBMP, SmATA 2,
SmATA 23N

   One Day For Peace
     CCB-B - v25 - N '71 - p40
     Comw - v94 - My 21 '71 - p268
     KR - v39 - Ap 15 '71 - p431
     LJ - v96 - Jl '71 - p2369

CROSHER, G R   1911-
ConAu 69, SmATA 14

   Pacemaker Story Books
     Inst - v76 - N '66 - p188

CROSSEN, Kendall Foster
see Chaber, M E

CUNNINGHAM, Chet   1928-
ConAu 49, SmATA 23

   Apprentice To A Rip-Off
     Hi Lo - v1 - S '79 - p4

   Locked Storeroom Mystery
     BL - v75 - Mr 15 '79 - p1145
     Hi Lo - v1 - N '79 - p4

   Narc One Going Down
     BL - v74 - O 15 '77 - p370
     Cur R - v16 - D '77 - p361

CUNNINGHAM, Julia Woolfolk
1916-
ConAu 9R, ConLC 12, MorBMP,
SmATA 1, ThrBJA, TwCCW 78

   Dorp Dead
     CCB-B - v19 - O '65 - p30
     LJ - v90 - Ap 15 '65 - p2018
     NYTBR - v70 - Ap 25 '65 - p26
     SR - v48 - Je 19 '65 - p40

   Macaroon
     CSM - v71 - Ap 9 '79 - pB10
     Teacher - v96 - My '79 - p124

   Onion Journey
     BW - v1 - D 10 '67 - p20
     CCB-B - v21 - D '67 - p57
     Comw - v87 - N 10 '67 - p176
     HB - v43 - D '67 - p738
     KR - v35 - O 1 '67 - p1206
     NYTBR - v72 - D 3 '67 - p68

CURRY, Jane Louise   1932-
ConAu 17R, FourBJA, SmATA 1,
TwCCW 78

   The Ice Ghosts Mystery
     B&B - v18 - Je '73 - p133
     BL - v69 - N 15 '72 - p299
     CSM - v64 - N 8 '72 - pB4
     HB - v48 - O '72 - p467

CURRY, Jane Louise (continued)
    KR - v40 - Ag 1 '72 - p859
    LJ - v97 - D 15 '72 - p4086
    NYTBR - N 26 '72 - p8
    TLS - Ap 6 '73 - p383

CURTIS, Robert H
AuBYP SUP

On ESP
    CCB-B - v29 - O '75 - p25
    KR - v43 - My 1 '75 - p515
    SB - v11 - Mr '76 - p207
    SLJ - v22 - Ja '76 - p52

Questions And Answers About Alcoholism
    J Read - v21 - F '78 - p472
    KR - v44 - O 15 '76 - p1147
    SLJ - v23 - Ja '77 - p100

CUTHBERTSON, Tom 1945-
ConAu 45

Anybody's Bike Book
    A Lib - v4 - F '73 - p99
    BL - v68 - N 1 '71 - p244
    BL - v72 - D 15 '75 - p560
    BW - v6 - Ja 2 '72 - p6
    LJ - v96 - D 15 '71 - p4101
    Money - v3 - N '74 - p114
    NYTBR - Je 4 '72 - p8

Anybody's Skateboard Book
    Kliatt - v11 - Winter '77 - p35
    LJ - v101 - S 15 '76 - p1874
    WLB - v51 - N '76 - p209

Bike Tripping
    A Lib - v4 - F '73 - p98
    BL - v72 - D 15 '75 - p560
    BW - v6 - Je 11 '72 - p1
    KR - v40 - Mr 15 '72 - p391
    LJ - v97 - My 15 '72 - p1823
    LJ - v97 - O 15 '72 - p3474
    NYTBR - Je 4 '72 - p8
    NYTBR - Je 2 '74 - p12

CUTTING, Edith

A Quilt For Bermuda
    BL - v74 - My 15 '78 - p1487
    Cur R - v17 - My '78 - p87

D

DAHL, Roald   1916-
ChLR 1, ConAu 1R, ConLC 6,
SmATA 1, ThrBJA, TwCCW 78,
WorAu

> *Charlie And The Great Glass
> Elevator*
> B&B - v18 - Jl '73 - p140
> CCB-B - v27 - S '73 - p5
> HB - v49 - Ap '73 - p142
> KR - v40 - Jl 15 '72 - p802
> Kliatt - v12 - Winter '78 - p6
> LJ - v97 - D 15 '72 - p4070
> Lis - v90 - N 8 '73 - p642
> NYRB - v19 - D 14 '72 - p41
> NYTBR - S 17 '72 - p8
> NYTBR - N 4 '73 - p54
> NYTBR - D 18 '77 - p35
> PW - v202 - S 4 '72 - p51
> SR - v1 - Mr 10 '73 - p67
> TLS - Je 15 '73 - p683

> *The Wonderful Story Of Henry
> Sugar And Six More*
> B&B - v6 - F '78 - p4
> BS - v37 - Ja '78 - p334
> BW - N 13 '77 - pE1
> BW - D 11 '77 - pE4
> HB - v54 - F '78 - p52
> JB - v42 - Ap '78 - p100
> KR - v45 - N 1 '77 - p1148
> NS - v94 - N 4 '77 - p626
> Obs - D 11 '77 - p31
> PW - v212 - O 31 '77 - p59
> Spec - v239 - D 10 '77 - p24
> TES - N 18 '77 - p35

DAHNSEN, Alan

> *Bicycles*
> BL - v75 - D 15 '78 - p693

DALY, Maureen   1921-
ConAu X, MorJA, SmATA 2,
TwCCW 78, WhoAmW 77, WrDr 80
(also known as McGivern, Maureen
Daly)

> *Seventeenth Summer*
> NYTBR - My 3 '42 - p7
> NYTBR, pt.2 - F 16 '69 - p22
> NYTBR, pt.2 - My 4 '69 - p38
> NYTBR, pt.2 - F 13 '72 - p14

DANA, Barbara   1940-
ConAu 17R, ForWC 70, SmATA 22

> *Crazy Eights*
> BB - v7 - Je '79 - p4
> BL - v75 - S 1 '78 - p36
> BS - v38 - F '79 - p371
> CCB-B - v32 - Ja '79 - p77
> KR - v46 - S 15 '78 - p1020
> PW - v214 - Ag 28 '78 - p394
> SLJ - v25 - O '78 - p153

DANZIGER, Paula   1944-

> *Can You Sue Your Parents For
> Malpractice?*
> BL - v75 - My 1 '79 - p1361
> BL - v75 - Jl 15 '79 - p1634
> CBRS - v7 - Ap '79 - p87
> CCB-B - v32 - Je '79 - p172
> EJ - v69 - My '80 - p91
> J Read - v23 - F '80 - p473
> KR - v47 - Je 1 '79 - p641
> NY - v55 - D 3 '79 - p196
> NYTBR - Je 17 '79 - p25
> RT - v33 - N '79 - p217
> SLJ - v25 - Ap '79 - p67

> *The Cat Ate My Gymsuit*
> CCB-B - v28 - Ja '75 - p76
> J Read - v19 - Ja '76 - p333

DANZIGER, Paula (continued)
    J Read - v22 - N '78 - p126
    KR - v42 - N 15 '74 - p1206
    LJ - v99 - N 15 '74 - p3052
    NYTBR - Ja 5 '75 - p8
    PW - v206 - O 7 '74 - p62

    The Pistachio Prescription
    BL - v74 - Ap 15 '78 - p1347
    BS - v38 - Ag '78 - p154
    CCB-B - v31 - My '78 - p140
    EJ - v67 - S '78 - p90
    KR - v46 - Ap 1 '78 - p379
    PW - v213 - My 8 '78 - p75
    SLJ - v24 - My '78 - p75

DAVID, Jay (pseud.) 1929-
ConAu X (real name: Adler, William)

    Growing Up Black
    BL - v65 - Ja 1 '69 - p479
    BS - v28 - N 1 '68 - p323
    CLW - v40 - Ap '69 - p521
    Choice - v6 - S '69 - p862
    EJ - v60 - My '71 - p662
    KR - v36 - Jl 15 '68 - p791
    LJ - v93 - Ag '68 - p2842
    LJ - v94 - Ja 15 '69 - p319
    PW - v194 - Jl 8 '68 - p163
    PW - v196 - Ag 11 '69 - p44
    SR - v52 - Mr 22 '69 - p63
    WSJ - v172 - O 18 '68 - p16

DAVIDSON, Margaret 1936-
AuBYP SUP, ConAu 25R, SmATA 5

    The Golda Meir Story
    BL - v72 - Je 15 '76 - p1466
    BL - v73 - Ap 1 '77 - p1174
    BS - v36 - O '76 - p239
    HB - v52 - O '76 - p509
    KR - v44 - My 1 '76 - p537
    PW - v209 - Ap 5 '76 - p101
    SE - v41 - Ap '77 - p351
    SLJ - v23 - S '76 - p113

    Seven True Horse Stories
    ACSB - v13 - Spring '80 - p24
    Hi Lo - v1 - F '80 - p3
    PW - v216 - S 10 '79 - p74
    SLJ - v26 - Ja '80 - p68

DAVIES, L P 1914-
ConAu 21R, ConSFA, WrDr 80

    Genesis Two
    KR - v38 - Je 15 '70 - p659
    KR - v38 - Jl 15 '70 - p753
    LJ - v95 - Je 15 '70 - p2279
    LJ - v95 - N 15 '70 - p4065
    MFSF - v40 - Mr '71 - p16
    PW - v197 - Je 15 '70 - p59

DAVIES, Peter 1937-
ConAu 53, Prof

    Fly Away Paul
    BS - v34 - O 15 '74 - p329
    KR - v42 - S 1 '74 - p949
    LJ - v99 - O 15 '74 - p2745
    NYTBR - N 24 '74 - p8
    PT - v8 - Ja '75 - p17
    PW - v206 - Ag 5 '74 - p58

DAVIS, Burke 1913-
ConAu 1R, SmATA 4, WhoAm 78,
WrDr 80

    Black Heroes Of The American
    Revolution
    BL - v72 - Jl 15 '76 - p1594
    CCB-B - v29 - Jl '76 - p172
    CE - v53 - O '76 - p37
    Comw - v103 - N 19 '76 - p758
    Cur R - v17 - Ag '78 - p173
    KR - v44 - Ap 15 '76 - p475
    SE - v41 - Ap '77 - p346
    SLJ - v23 - S '76 - p114

DAVIS, Charles
BioIn 9

    On My Own
    LJ - v96 - Ap 15 '71 - p1514

DAVIS, Clive E 1914-
AuBYP, ConAu 17R

    Book Of Air Force Airplanes And
    Helicopters
    BL - v64 - Mr 15 '68 - p867
    SB - v4 - S '68 - p147

DAVIS, Daniel Sheldon 1936-
ConAu 45, SmATA 12, WhoE 77

    Marcus Garvey
    SE - v37 - D '73 - p785
    SS - v65 - Mr '74 - p139

DAY, Beth   1924-
AuBYP SUP, ConAu 9R, WhoAmW
77

*Life On A Lost Continent: A
Natural History Of New Zealand*
BL - v68 - D 15 '71 - p366
CCB-B - v25 - F '72 - p89
KR - v39 - O 1 '71 - p1074
LJ - v97 - F 15 '72 - p783
SB - v8 - My '72 - p83
SR - v55 - Ja 15 '72 - p47

DAY, Nancy Raines

Help Yourself To Health
BL - v76 - Jl 15 '80 - p1662

DAY, Veronique

Landslide!
CCB-B - v18 - Je '65 - p145
PW - v190 - Ag 29 '66 - p351

DEANE, Shirley   1920-
ConAu 1R, IntAu&W 77, WrDr 80

Vendetta
TLS - Ap 3 '69 - p360

DEARMOND, Dale
WhoAmA 78, WhoAmW 74

*Dale DeArmond: A First Book
Collection Of Her Prints*
Kliatt - v14 - Spring '80 - p48
LJ - v105 - Ja 1 '80 - p94

DECKER, Sunny

An Empty Spoon
BL - v65 - Jl 15 '69 - p1244
BS - v29 - My 1 '69 - p52
BW - v4 - F 22 '70 - p13
CLW - v41 - My '70 - p576
EJ - v60 - Ap '71 - p518
JGE - v22 - Jl '70 - p149
KR - v37 - F 1 '69 - p146
KR - v37 - Mr 1 '69 - p253
LJ - v94 - Ap 15 '69 - p1612
LJ - v94 - Jl '69 - p2687
LJ - v94 - D 15 '69 - p4584
PW - v195 - F 17 '69 - p153
PW - v196 - N 24 '69 - p44
SR - v52 - O 18 '69 - p57

TN - v26 - N '69 - p85
TN - v27 - Je '71 - p424

DEE, M M

Mystery On The Night Shift
BL - v75 - F 15 '79 - p927

DEGENS, T

Transport 7-41-R
BL - v71 - S 1 '74 - p39
BL - v71 - Mr 15 '75 - p765
BL - v73 - Mr 15 '77 - p1100
BS - v34 - Ja 15 '75 - p474
BW - N 10 '74 - p8
CCB-B - v28 - Mr '75 - p109
CE - v51 - F '75 - p215
CLW - v47 - D '75 - p208
Choice - v12 - N '75 - p1132
EJ - v64 - Ap '75 - p90
EJ - v65 - Ja '76 - p97
HB - v50 - O '74 - p140
KR - v42 - Ag 1 '74 - p809
KR - v43 - Ja 1 '75 - p9
LA - v53 - My '76 - p521
LJ - v99 - O 15 '74 - p2745
LJ - v99 - D 15 '74 - p3246
NYTBR - F 9 '75 - p8
PW - v206 - N 11 '74 - p49

DEJONG, Meindert   1906-
ChLR 1, ConAu 13R, MorJA,
SmATA 2, TwCCW 78, WhoAm 78

Hurry Home, Candy
BL - v50 - D 15 '53 - p172
Comw - v59 - N 20 '53 - p180
HB - v29 - D '53 - p456
KR - v21 - Ag 1 '53 - p483
LJ - v79 - Ja 1 '54 - p72
SR - v36 - N 14 '53 - p76

DEKAY, James T   1930-
ConAu 25R

*The Natural Superiority Of The
Left-Hander*
Kliatt - v14 - Winter '80 - p70
NYTBR - O 14 '79 - p56

DELANO, Hugh   1933-
ConAu 65, SmATA 20

DELANO, Hugh (continued)

Eddie
CCB-B - v30 - N '76 - p41
KR - v44 - F 15 '76 - p225
LJ - v101 - Ap 15 '76 - p1040
PW - v209 - Mr 1 '76 - p94

DELEAR, Frank J 1914-
AuBYP SUP, ConAu 21R, WhoE 75,
WrDr 80

The New World Of Helicopters
BL - v63 - My 15 '67 - p991
CCB-B - v20 - Jl '67 - p168
CSM - v59 - S 21 '67 - p11
KR - v35 - Ja 15 '67 - p65
LJ - v92 - S 15 '67 - p3196
SB - v3 - S '67 - p160

DELREY, Lester 1915-
ConAu 65, ConSFA, ThrBJA,
WhoAm 78, WhoSciF

Marooned On Mars
BL - v48 - Jl 15 '52 - p384
KR - v20 - Ap 1 '52 - p228
LJ - v77 - Je 15 '52 - p1081
NYT - Je 22 '52 - p15

Nerves
BW - Je 27 '76 - pG4
MFSF - v41 - S '71 - p45

DEMAS, Vida 1927-
ConAu 49, SmATA 9

First Person, Singular
BL - v71 - Mr 15 '75 - p747
KR - v41 - O 15 '73 - p1179
KR - v41 - N 15 '73 - p1278
LJ - v99 - Ja 1 '74 - p65
LJ - v99 - Ja 15 '74 - p225
LJ - v99 - My 15 '74 - p1452
LJ - v99 - D 15 '74 - p3248
TN - v31 - Ap '75 - p331

DENGLER, Marianna

Catch The Passing Breeze
BL - v74 - N 1 '77 - p474
KR - v45 - Ag 15 '77 - p849
SLJ - v24 - S '77 - p126
WCRB - v4 - Ja '78 - p67

DENNY, Norman George 1901-
Au&Wr 71, AuBYP SUP

*The Bayeux Tapestry: The Story
Of The Norman Conquest, 1066*
Am - v115 - N 5 '66 - p556
Atl - v218 - D '66 - p152
B&B - v12 - D '66 - p75
BL - v63 - O 15 '66 - p264
CCB-B - v20 - Ja '67 - p72
CLW - v38 - Ja '67 - p339
CSM - v58 - N 3 '66 - pB9
HB - v42 - O '66 - p581
KR - v34 - Jl 1 '66 - p627
LJ - v91 - S 15 '66 - p4329
NYRB - v7 - D 15 '66 - p29
NYTBR - v71 - O 23 '66 - p34
Nat R - v18 - D 13 '66 - p1285
PW - v190 - S 26 '66 - p133
SR - v49 - D 10 '66 - p57
TLS - Je 9 '66 - p519

DENZEL, Justin F 1917-
ConAu 53

*Genius With A Scalpel: Harvey
Cushing*
BL - v67 - Ap 15 '71 - p696
BS - v31 - My 15 '71 - p98
KR - v39 - F 1 '71 - p115
LJ - v96 - O 15 '71 - p3474
SB - v7 - My '71 - p69

DEROSIER, John

Chuck Foreman
BL - v73 - Je 15 '77 - p1572
SLJ - v23 - My '77 - p81

DEROSSI, Claude J 1942-
ConAu 53

Computers: Tools For Today
LJ - v98 - Mr 15 '73 - p1001

DEVANEY, John 1926-
AuBYP SUP, ConAu 17R, SmATA
12

Baseball's Youngest Big Leaguers
BS - v28 - Mr 1 '69 - p490
CCB-B - v23 - S '69 - p6
CSM - v61 - My 1 '69 - pB10
LJ - v95 - My 15 '70 - p1964

DEVANEY, John (continued)
  SR - v52 - Je 28 '69 - p38

  The Bobby Orr Story
  BL - v70 - N 1 '73 - p285
  BL - v70 - N 1 '73 - p290
  Inst - v83 - N '73 - p125
  KR - v41 - S 15 '73 - p1042
  LJ - v98 - D 15 '73 - p3722

  Tiny: The Story Of Nate Archibald
  BL - v74 - Ja 1 '78 - p750
  Comw - v104 - N 11 '77 - p734
  KR - v45 - S 1 '77 - p939
  SLJ - v24 - D '77 - p63

DEWEESE, Gene   1934-
EncSF, ConAu 65

  Major Corby And The
  Unidentified Flapping Object
  BL - v75 - Ap 15 '79 - p1300
  CBRS - v7 - My '79 - p97
  Hi Lo - v1 - N '79 - p5
  SLJ - v25 - Mr '79 - p138

DEXLER, Paul R

  Vans: The Personality Vehicles
  BL - v74 - F 15 '78 - p1000
  Inst - v87 - My '78 - p116
  SLJ - v24 - F '78 - p56

DIETZ, Lew   1907-
AuBYP, ConAu 5R, SmATA 11,
WrDr 80

  Jeff White: Young Trapper
  HB - v27 - My '51 - p186
  KR - v18 - D 1 '50 - p693
  LJ - v76 - Mr 15 '51 - p530
  NYT - F 4 '51 - p26
  SR - v34 - My 12 '51 - p53

  Jeff White: Young Woodsman
  LJ - v74 - S 15 '49 - p1334
  NYT - N 13 '49 - p33
  SR - v32 - N 12 '49 - p32

DIGGINS, Julia E
AuBYP

  String, Straightedge, And Shadow:
  The Story Of Geometry
  CCB-B - v18 - Jl '65 - p159

Comw - v82 - My 28 '65 - p332
HB - v41 - Ag '65 - p404
LJ - v90 - My 15 '65 - p2416
SA - v213 - D '65 - p114

DINES, Glen   1925-
ConAu 9R, IlsCB 1967, SmATA 7

  Sun, Sand, And Steel: Costumes
  And Equipment Of The Spanish-
  Mexican Southwest
  BL - v69 - F 1 '73 - p527
  KR - v40 - F 15 '72 - p204
  LJ - v97 - O 15 '72 - p3452

DIXON, Jeanne

  The Ghost Of Spirit River
  CLW - v41 - O '69 - p139
  KR - v36 - Ag 1 '68 - p817
  LJ - v93 - O 15 '68 - p3968

DIXON, Pahl

  Hot Skateboarding
  BW - Ap 10 '77 - pE10
  Kliatt - v11 - Spring '77 - p41
  LJ - v102 - My 15 '77 - p1203

DIXON, Paige   (pseud.) 1911-
AuBYP SUP, ConAu X, WrDr 80
(real name: Corcoran, Barbara)

  The Search For Charlie
  BB - v4 - My '76 - p4
  BL - v72 - Mr 15 '76 - p1040
  CSM - v68 - My 12 '76 - p28
  J Read - v21 - O '77 - p86
  KR - v44 - F 1 '76 - p139
  PW - v209 - My 10 '76 - p84
  SLJ - v22 - My '76 - p77

  Summer Of The White Goat
  BL - v74 - S 15 '77 - p192
  CCB-B - v31 - O '77 - p31
  CLW - v49 - N '77 - p188
  KR - v45 - Mr 1 '77 - p223
  LA - v55 - Ja '78 - p49
  SLJ - v24 - N '77 - p55

  Walk My Way
  BL - v76 - My 1 '80 - p1289
  KR - v48 - Je 1 '80 - p716
  see also Corcoran, Barbara

DIXON, Peter
see Dixon, Pahl (co-author)

DIZENZO, Patricia

Phoebe
BL - v67 - F 15 '71 - p489
CCB-B - v24 - D '70 - p57
EJ - v60 - F '71 - p278
KR - v38 - Ag 15 '70 - p885
LJ - v96 - Ja 15 '71 - p274
NYTBR, pt.2 - N 8 '70 - p8
NYTBR, pt.2 - N 7 '71 - p47
PW - v197 - Je 8 '70 - p180
TN - v30 - Ja '74 - p196

DOBLER, Lavinia G   1910-
ConAu 1R, MorBMP, SmATA 6,
WhoAmW 77

*Pioneers And Patriots: The Lives
Of Six Negroes Of The
Revolutionary Era*
CCB-B - v19 - Ja '66 - p81
JNE - v35 - Summer '66 - p266

DOBRIN, Arnold   1928-
ConAu 25R, IlsCB 1967, SmATA 4,
WhoAmA 78

*The New Life - La Vida Neuva:
The Mexican-Americans Today*
BL - v68 - Je 15 '72 - p894
KR - v39 - Jl 1 '71 - p685

DODSON, Susan   1941-
ConAu 97

The Creep
BL - v75 - Je 1 '79 - p1490
CCB-B - v32 - Jl '79 - p189
KR - v47 - My 1 '79 - p522
PW - v215 - Mr 19 '79 - p94
SLJ - v25 - F '79 - p62
WCRB - v5 - My '79 - p38

DOHERTY, C H   1913-
Au&Wr 71, ConAu 9R, SmATA 6

*Roads: From Footpaths To
Thruways*
LJ - v98 - My 15 '73 - p1680

DOLAN, Edward Francis, Jr.   1924-
AuBYP SUP, ConAu 33R

Archie Griffin
CE - v54 - F '78 - p198
SLJ - v24 - D '77 - p64

*The Bermuda Triangle And Other
Mysteries Of Nature*
BL - v76 - Ap 15 '80 - p1196
Hi Lo - v2 - N '80 - p3

Bobby Clarke
BL - v74 - O 1 '77 - p302
KR - v46 - Ja 1 '78 - p5
SLJ - v24 - D '77 - p64

Fred Lynn: The Hero From Boston
BL - v74 - Jl 15 '78 - p1729

*Janet Guthrie: First Woman Driver
At Indianapolis*
BB - v7 - Ap '79 - p2
B&B - v7 - Ap '79 - p2
BL - v74 - Jl 15 '78 - p1729
CCB-B - v32 - O '78 - p27
Hi Lo - v1 - O '79 - p6
J Read - v22 - Mr '79 - p565
SEP - v24 - My '78 - p86

*Jimmy Young: Heavyweight
Challenger*
BL - v75 - Ap 15 '79 - p1301
Hi Lo - v1 - S '79 - p3
SLJ - v25 - My '79 - p88
TN - v36 - Winter '80 - p200

*Kyle Rote, Jr., American-Born
Soccer Star*
Hi Lo - v1 - N '79 - p5
LA - v56 - N '79 - p933
SLJ - v25 - My '79 - p85

Martina Navratilova
BL - v74 - Ja 15 '78 - p808
CCB-B - v31 - Mr '78 - p109
KR - v45 - D 1 '77 - p1272
SLJ - v24 - D '77 - p64

Scott May: Basketball Champion
BL - v74 - Jl 15 '78 - p1730
SLJ - v24 - My '78 - p86

DONOVAN, John   1928-
ChLR 3, TwCCW 78

DONOVAN, John (continued)

Family
  BL - v72 - Ap 1 '76 - p1112
  BS - v36 - Ag '76 - p149
  CCB-B - v29 - Jl '76 - p173
  Comw - v103 - N 19 '76 - p763
  EJ - v65 - O '76 - p87
  HB - v52 - Ag '76 - p404
  KR - v44 - Ap 1 '76 - p405
  Kliatt - v12 - Fall '78 - p6
  LA - v54 - My '77 - p582
  NYTBR - My 16 '76 - p14
  PW - v209 - Ap 26 '76 - p60
  SE - v41 - Ap '77 - p350
  SLJ - v23 - S '76 - p131

I'll Get There. It Better Be Worth The Trip
  Atl - v224 - D '69 - p150
  BL - v65 - Je 15 '69 - p1174
  BS - v29 - Je 1 '69 - p100
  BW - v3 - My 4 '69 - p5
  CCB-B - v22 - Je '69 - p156
  CLW - v40 - My '69 - p589
  CLW - v41 - Ap '70 - p534
  Comw - v90 - My 23 '69 - p300
  HB - v45 - Ag '69 - p415
  KR - v37 - Ap 1 '69 - p385
  LJ - v94 - My 15 '69 - p2072
  LJ - v94 - My 15 '69 - p2111
  LJ - v94 - D 15 '69 - p4581
  Lis - v83 - Ap 16 '70 - p519
  NYTBR - D 7 '69 - p68
  NYTBR, pt.2 - My 4 '69 - p8
  NYTBR, pt.2 - N 9 '69 - p60
  NYTBR, pt.2 - N 7 '71 - p46
  PW - v195 - Mr 17 '69 - p57
  PW - v199 - F 8 '71 - p82
  SR - v52 - My 10 '69 - p59
  SR - v52 - Jl 19 '69 - p42
  TLS - Jl 2 '70 - p712
  TN - v26 - Ja '70 - p207

Remove Protective Coating A Little At A Time
  BL - v70 - D 15 '73 - p440
  BS - v33 - O 15 '73 - p333
  BW - v7 - N 11 '73 - p6C
  CCB-B - v27 - D '73 - p62
  HB - v50 - F '74 - p54
  KR - v41 - Jl 15 '73 - p759
  LJ - v99 - My 15 '74 - p1481

  NYTBR - N 4 '73 - p34
  NYTBR - N 4 '73 - p52
  PW - v204 - Jl 16 '73 - p111
  TN - v30 - N '73 - p81

Wild In The World
  BL - v68 - N 1 '71 - p240
  BS - v31 - Ag 15 '71 - p234
  BW - v5 - N 7 '71 - p8
  CCB-B - v25 - N '71 - p40
  CSM - v63 - N 11 '71 - pB6
  EJ - v61 - Ja '72 - p138
  HB - v48 - F '72 - p56
  KR - v39 - Jl 1 '71 - p682
  LJ - v96 - O 15 '71 - p3475
  LJ - v96 - D 15 '71 - p4158
  NYTBR - S 12 '71 - p8
  NYTBR - D 5 '71 - p86
  NYTBR - My 12 '74 - p39
  NYTBR, pt.2 - N 7 '71 - p28
  PW - v200 - Ag 2 '71 - p64
  SR - v54 - S 18 '71 - p49

DORIAN, Edith   1900-
  ConAu P-1, SmATA 5, WhoAmW 77

No Moon On Graveyard Head
  BL - v50 - D 1 '53 - p148
  HB - v29 - D '53 - p461
  KR - v21 - S 1 '53 - p588
  LJ - v79 - Ja 1 '54 - p76
  NYTBR, pt.2 - N 15 '53 - p10

DOTY, Jean Slaughter   1929-
  AuBYP SUP, ConAu 45

Winter Pony
  CCB-B - v29 - O '75 - p25
  CLW - v47 - D '75 - p234
  KR - v43 - Mr 1 '75 - p238
  LA - v53 - My '76 - p516
  RT - v29 - F '76 - p511
  SLJ - v21 - My '75 - p54
  SR - v2 - My 31 '75 - p34

DOTY, Roy   1922-
  ConAu 53, IlsBYP

Pinocchio Was Nosey
  SLJ - v24 - F '78 - p46

DOUGLAS, James M   (pseud.) 1929-
  SmATA 5 (real name: Butterworth, W E)

DOUGLAS, James M (continued)

Hunger For Racing
BL - v64 - Mr 1 '68 - p773
LJ - v92 - D 15 '67 - p4633
see also Butterworth, W E

DOUTY, Esther Morris   1911-1978
AuBYP SUP, ConAu 5R, ConAu 85,
SmATA 8, SmATA 23N

**The Brave Balloonists: America's
First Airmen**
Inst - v84 - My '75 - p100

DOWDELL, Dorothy   1910-
ConAu 9R, SmATA 12, WhoAmW
77

**The Japanese Helped Build
America**
BL - v67 - S 15 '70 - p105
BL - v69 - F 15 '73 - p553
KR - v38 - Ap 1 '70 - p385
LJ - v95 - O 15 '70 - p3626

DOWDELL, Joseph
see Dowdell, Dorothy (co-author)

DOWLATSHAHI, Ali

**Persian Designs And Motifs For
Artists And Craftsmen**
Kliatt - v14 - Spring '80 - p48

DOYLE, Arthur Conan   1859-1930
CasWL, JBA 34, OxEng, SmATA 24,
WebE&AL, WhoChL, WhoTwCL

**The Adventures Of Sherlock
Holmes**
B&B - v22 - F '77 - p52
BL - v73 - S 1 '76 - p18
CR - v226 - Ja '75 - p45
GP - v13 - Ja '75 - p2565
MFS - v23 - Summer '77 - p297
WLB - v50 - Ja '76 - p367

The Boys' Sherlock Holmes
BL - v58 - S 15 '61 - p74
KR - v29 - Je 15 '61 - p501
LJ - v86 - Jl '61 - p2540
NYTBR, pt.2 - N 12 '61 - p62

The Hound Of The Baskervilles
B&B - v19 - Jl '74 - p111
BL - v65 - Ja 15 '69 - p538
CR - v224 - Ap '74 - p213
Lis - v91 - Ja 10 '74 - p53
MFS - v23 - Summer '77 - p297
NS - v87 - My 24 '74 - p743
NYT - v125 - D 1 '75 - p29
NYTBR - My 3 '02 - p298
Obs - Ja 20 '74 - p26
SLJ - v23 - My '77 - p85
Spec - v232 - F 9 '74 - p172
TLS - F 1 '74 - p113
WLB - v50 - Ja '76 - p367
WLB - v52 - O '77 - p140

DRISKO, Carol F   1929-
WhoAmW 58

**The Unfinished March: The
History Of The Negro In The
United States, Reconstruction To
World War I**
BL - v63 - Jl 1 '67 - p1146
HB - v43 - Ag '67 - p488
KR - v35 - Ja 1 '67 - p11
LJ - v92 - Ap 15 '67 - p1733
NYTBR - v72 - N 5 '67 - p65
NYTBR, pt.2 - v72 - My 7 '67 - p5

DROTNING, Phillip T   1920-
ConAu 25R, WhoPubR 76

Up From The Ghetto
BL - v66 - Je 15 '70 - p1258
BS - v30 - F 1 '71 - p482
Choice - v7 - O '70 - p1096
LJ - v95 - F 15 '70 - p677
NHB - v34 - D '71 - p191
NYTBR, pt.2 - F 21 '71 - p2
PW - v197 - Ja 19 '70 - p74
SR - v53 - My 9 '70 - p70

DRUCKER, Malka   1945-
ConAu 81

The George Foster Story
KR - v47 - Je 1 '79 - p640
PW - v215 - My 21 '79 - p69
SLJ - v25 - My '79 - p83

Tom Seaver: Portrait Of A Pitcher
BL - v74 - Jl 1 '78 - p1683
BS - v38 - Je '78 - p77

DRUCKER, Malka (continued)
KR - v46 - Je 1 '78 - p601
NYTBR - Ap 30 '78 - p49
PW - v213 - F 6 '78 - p102
SLJ - v25 - S '78 - p135

DUBOIS, Shirley Graham
see Graham, Shirley

DUE, Linnea A

High And Outside
KR - v48 - My 15 '80 - p663
PW - v217 - My 16 '80 - p200

DUGDALE, Vera
AmM&WS 12P

Album Of North American Animals
BL - v63 - Mr 15 '67 - p794
BL - v64 - Ja 15 '68 - p592
CCB-B - v21 - S '67 - p4
CSM - v58 - N 3 '66 - pB11
CSM - v60 - N 30 '67 - pB5
KR - v34 - S 15 '66 - p992
KR - v35 - O 15 '67 - p1277
LJ - v91 - N 15 '66 - p5747
NYTBR - v71 - N 6 '66 - p54
PW - v192 - N 13 '67 - p79
SB - v3 - My '67 - p62
SR - v50 - My 20 '67 - p56

Album Of North American Birds
CCB-B - v22 - S '68 - p5
LJ - v93 - F 15 '68 - p866
SB - v3 - Mr '68 - p322

DUJARDIN, Rosamond 1902-1963
ConAu 1R, CurBio 53, MorJA,
SmATA 2, WhAm 4

Double Feature
KR - v21 - Ag 1 '53 - p489
LJ - v79 - Ja 1 '54 - p76
NYTBR, pt.2 - N 15 '53 - p8

DUNCAN, Fred B

Deepwater Family
BL - v66 - D 15 '69 - p508
CCB-B - v23 - Ja '70 - p78
CLW - v41 - My '70 - p590
KR - v37 - Ap 15 '69 - p460

LJ - v94 - Jl '69 - p2675
SR - v52 - S 13 '69 - p37
Yacht - v126 - N '69 - p88

DUNCAN, Lois 1934-
ConAu X, SmATA 1, WrDr 80 (also
known as Arquette, Lois S)

I Know What You Did Last Summer
BL - v70 - Ja 1 '74 - p483
CCB-B - v27 - F '74 - p93
J Read - v22 - N '78 - p127
KR - v41 - S 1 '73 - p972
LJ - v99 - Ap 15 '74 - p1226
PW - v204 - O 29 '73 - p36

Killing Mr. Griffin
BL - v74 - Mr 1 '78 - p1092
BS - v38 - Ag '78 - p154
CCB-B - v32 - O '78 - p27
HB - v54 - Ag '78 - p400
KR - v46 - My 1 '78 - p500
Kliatt - v14 - Winter '80 - p6
NYTBR - Ap 30 '78 - p54
PW - v213 - F 20 '78 - p127
PW - v216 - Ag 27 '79 - p385
SLJ - v24 - My '78 - p86

Peggy
BL - v67 - F 1 '71 - p446
CLW - v43 - O '71 - p116
HB - v46 - D '70 - p622
KR - v38 - S 15 '70 - p1047

Ransom
CCB-B - v20 - Mr '67 - p107
KR - v34 - F 1 '66 - p111
LJ - v91 - S 15 '66 - p4349
NYTBR - v71 - Je 5 '66 - p42

Summer Of Fear
BL - v73 - S 15 '76 - p136
BL - v73 - S 15 '76 - p173
BS - v36 - D '76 - p286
Comw - v103 - N 19 '76 - p763
HB - v53 - Ap '77 - p167
Inst - v86 - N '76 - p146
KR - v44 - Je 15 '76 - p691
Kliatt - v12 - Winter '78 - p6
NYTBR - Mr 6 '77 - p29
PW - v209 - Je 7 '76 - p75
SLJ - v23 - D '76 - p69
WCRB - v3 - S '77 - p58

DUNLOP, Agnes Mary Robertson
see Kyle, Elisabeth

DUNNAHOO, Terry 1927-
ConAu 41R, IntAu&W 77, SmATA 7, WhoAm 78

 This Is Espie Sanchez
  CCB-B - v30 - F '77 - p89
  CLW - v48 - Mr '77 - p358
  HB - v53 - F '77 - p55
  KR - v44 - Ag 15 '76 - p906
  SLJ - v23 - D '76 - p68

 Who Cares About Espie Sanchez?
  BL - v72 - Ja 1 '76 - p624
  CCB-B - v29 - F '76 - p94
  KR - v43 - O 15 '75 - p1183
  SLJ - v22 - F '76 - p51

 Who Needs Espie Sanchez?
  BL - v74 - S 15 '77 - p192
  CCB-B - v31 - My '78 - p140
  KR - v45 - Ag 15 '77 - p849
  SLJ - v24 - N '77 - p55

DUNNING, Stephen 1924-
AuBYP SUP, ConAu 25R, DrAS 74E

 Reflections On A Gift Of Watermelon Pickle And Other Modern Verse
  A Lib - v5 - Je '74 - p297
  BL - v63 - Ap 1 '67 - p856
  BL - v64 - Ja 15 '68 - p597
  CCB-B - v21 - Mr '68 - p107
  CE - v43 - Mr '67 - p412
  CLW - v39 - F '68 - p441
  EJ - v56 - Ap '67 - p635
  EL - v24 - Ja '67 - p358
  HB - v44 - F '68 - p73
  KR - v35 - N 1 '67 - p1326
  LJ - v92 - N 15 '67 - p4259
  NY - v43 - D 16 '67 - p188
  NYTBR - v72 - D 10 '67 - p38
  NYTBR, pt.2 - v73 - F 25 '68 - p20
  RR - v86 - Mr '69 - p176
  PW - v192 - N 13 '67 - p79
  Par - v43 - Ag '68 - p76
  SR - v51 - Ja 27 '68 - p35

DURANT, John 1902-
AuBYP, ConAu 9R, WhoAm 78

 The Heavyweight Champions
  BL - v70 - Ja 15 '74 - p509
  EJ - v64 - F '75 - p104
  LJ - v97 - My 15 '72 - p1931
  WLB - v46 - Ap '72 - p706

DURHAM, Mae
BiDrLUS 70, ConAu 57 (also known as Roger, Mae Durham)

 Tit For Tat And Other Latvian Folk Tales
  BL - v63 - My 15 '67 - p991
  CCB-B - v20 - Jl '67 - p168
  HB - v43 - Ag '67 - p461
  Inst - v77 - Ag '67 - p207
  KR - v35 - F 15 '67 - p203
  LJ - v92 - My 15 '67 - p2020
  NYTBR, pt.2 - v72 - My 7 '67 - p44
  PW - v191 - Ap 10 '67 - p82
  SR - v50 - My 13 '67 - p54

DURHAM, Philip 1912-
ConAu 9R, DrAS 78E

 The Adventures Of The Negro Cowboys
  CCB-B - v19 - Ja '66 - p81
  JAH - v52 - D '65 - p640
  LJ - v91 - Mr 15 '66 - p1716
  PW - v195 - F 24 '69 - p69
  SR - v49 - Ag 20 '66 - p37

DURSO, Joseph

 Amazing: The Miracle Of The Mets
  BL - v67 - S 1 '70 - p23
  BW - v4 - Jl 12 '70 - p13
  CSM - v62 - Je 25 '70 - p13
  KR - v38 - F 1 '70 - p144
  KR - v38 - Mr 1 '70 - p257
  LJ - v95 - My 15 '70 - p1858
  NYT - v119 - Ap 29 '70 - p39
  NYTBR - Ap 26 '70 - p14
  PW - v197 - F 2 '70 - p85
  SR - v53 - My 9 '70 - p68
  SR - v53 - Je 27 '70 - p38

DWYER-JOYCE, Alice 1913-
ConAu 53, WrDr 80

 The Master Of Jethart
  KR - v44 - O 15 '76 - p1150

DYER, Mike

>   *Getting Into Pro Baseball*
>   SLJ - v25 - My '79 - p86

DYGARD, Thomas J   1931-
  ConAu 85, SmATA 24

>   *Point Spread*
>   BL - v48 - Mr 15 '80 - p370
>   BL - v76 - F 1 '80 - p764
>   CCB-B - v33 - My '80 - p170
>   NYTBR - v85 - Ap 27 '80 - p56

>   *Winning Kicker*
>   BB - v6 - N '78 - p2
>   BL - v74 - F 1 '78 - p901
>   BL - v74 - F 1 '78 - p906
>   KR - v46 - F 1 '78 - p110
>   NYTBR - Ap 23 '78 - p32
>   SLJ - v24 - My '78 - p87

E

EATON, Jeanette 1886-1968
ConAu 73, JBA 51, OhA&B, SmATA 24

Trumpeter's Tale: The Story Of Young Louis Armstrong
BL - v51 - Mr 15 '55 - p302
HB - v31 - Je '55 - p195
KR - v23 - F 1 '55 - p87
LJ - v80 - Ap 15 '55 - p1009
NYTBR - F 27 '55 - p32
SR - v38 - Je 18 '55 - p45

ECKERT, Allan W 1931-
ConAu 13R, FourBJA, WhoAm 78

The Crossbreed
BL - v64 - My 15 '68 - p1081
KR - v35 - D 15 '67 - p1503
LJ - v93 - F 1 '68 - p571
LJ - v93 - F 15 '68 - p893
NYTBR - v73 - Mr 3 '68 - p40
PW - v192 - D 11 '67 - p40
TN - v24 - Je '68 - p449

The King Snake
BL - v65 - O 15 '68 - p246
BS - v28 - Ag 1 '68 - p195
BW - v2 - N 3 '68 - p34
HB - v44 - O '68 - p578
KR - v36 - Jl 1 '68 - p697
LJ - v93 - N 15 '68 - p4402
SB - v4 - S '68 - p134

EDELSON, Edward 1932-
AuBYP SUP, ConAu 17R, WhoAm 78

Great Monsters Of The Movies
HB - v49 - Je '73 - p279
Inst - v82 - My '73 - p69
KR - v41 - Je 1 '73 - p602
LJ - v98 - O 15 '73 - p3144

PT - v8 - F '75 - p21

EDMONDS, Ivy Gordon 1917-
AuBYP SUP, ConAu 33R, SmATA 8

Drag Racing For Beginners
BL - v69 - Mr 1 '73 - p646

Hot Rodding For Beginners
BL - v67 - Ap 1 '71 - p656
LJ - v96 - My 15 '71 - p1822

Jet And Rocket Engines
BL - v70 - O 15 '73 - p229
KR - v41 - Je 15 '73 - p649
LJ - v98 - O 15 '73 - p3153

Motorcycle Racing For Beginners
BL - v74 - O 15 '77 - p367
EJ - v67 - Mr '78 - p80
KR - v45 - D 15 '77 - p1325
SLJ - v24 - N '77 - p69

EDWARDS, Audrey 1947-
ConAu 81

Muhammad Ali, The People's Champ
BL - v74 - Ja 1 '78 - p750
EJ - v67 - Ap '78 - p90
KR - v45 - Ag 15 '77 - p857
NYTBR - Ap 30 '78 - p56
PW - v212 - N 7 '77 - p83
SLJ - v24 - D '77 - p63

The Picture Life Of Muhammad Ali
Cur R - v15 - D '76 - p315
SLJ - v23 - D '76 - p72
Teacher - v96 - O '78 - p174

The Picture Life Of Stevie Wonder
BL - v73 - Ap 15 '77 - p1265
Cur R - v15 - D '76 - p315

EDWARDS, Audrey (continued)
    SLJ - v23 - D '76 - p72
    Teacher - v96 - O '78 - p174

EDWARDS, Cecile Pepin   1916-
AuBYP, ConAu 5R

    Roger Williams, Defender Of
    Freedom
      BL - v54 - O 15 '57 - p110
      CSM - N 7 '57 - p12
      KR - v25 - Je 1 '57 - p384
      LJ - v82 - S 15 '57 - p2910
      NYTBR, pt.2 - N 17 '57 - p40

EDWARDS, Julie
see Andrews, Julie

EDWARDS, Phil

    You Should Have Been Here An
    Hour Ago
      CCB-B - v21 - N '67 - p40
      KR - v35 - Ap 1 '67 - p458
      LJ - v92 - S 15 '67 - p3212
      NYTBR, pt.1 - v72 - F 26 '67 - p41
      PW - v190 - D 26 '66 - p94
      PW - v191 - Ap 10 '67 - p79
      Punch - v252 - My 10 '67 - p697
      SR - v50 - F 25 '67 - p58
      SR - v50 - Ag 19 '67 - p35
      TLS - Je 29 '67 - p583
      TN - v24 - Ja '68 - p225

EIMERL, Sarel Henry   1925-
ConAu 21R, WhoWest 74

    Hitler Over Europe
      BL - v68 - Je 15 '72 - p908
      BS - v32 - Ap 15 '72 - p46
      KR - v40 - Ja 15 '72 - p75
      LJ - v97 - My 15 '72 - p1921

EISEMAN, Alberta   1925-
AuBYP SUP, ConAu 77, SmATA 15

    Manana Is Now: The Spanish-
    Speaking In The United States
      BL - v69 - Jl 15 '73 - p1072
      CCB-B - v27 - S '73 - p6
      KR - v41 - Ap 1 '73 - p399
      LJ - v98 - My 15 '73 - p1654
      LJ - v98 - My 15 '73 - p1687
      RR - v33 - Ja '74 - p224

EISENBERG, Lisa

    Falling Star
      BL - v76 - Mr 15 '80 - p1045
      Hi Lo - v1 - Mr '80 - p3
      Kliatt - v14 - Spring '80 - p6

    Fast Food King
      BL - v76 - Mr 15 '80 - p1045
      Hi Lo - v1 - Mr '80 - p3
      Kliatt - v14 - Spring '80 - p6

    Golden Idol
      Hi Lo - v1 - Mr '80 - p3
      Kliatt - v14 - Spring '80 - p6

    House Of Laughs
      BL - v76 - Ap 15 '80 - p1196
      Hi Lo - v1 - Mr '80 - p3
      Kliatt - v14 - Spring '80 - p6

    Killer Music
      Hi Lo - v1 - Mr '80 - p3
      Kliatt - v14 - Spring '80 - p6

    Tiger Rose
      Hi Lo - v1 - Mr '80 - p3
      Kliatt - v14 - Spring '80 - p6

ELBERT, Virginie Fowler   1912-
AuBYP SUP, ConAu 61

    Grow A Plant Pet
      SLJ - v24 - N '77 - p69

ELDER, Lauren

    And I Alone Survived
      BL - v74 - Jl 15 '78 - p1726
      BS - v38 - Ag '78 - p159
      HB - v55 - O '78 - p546
      KR - v46 - F 15 '78 - p215
      LJ - v103 - Je 1 '78 - p1166
      PW - v213 - F 27 '78 - p149
      SLJ - v25 - S '78 - p171

ELFMAN, Blossom   1925-
ConAu 45, SmATA 8

    The Girls Of Huntington House
      BL - v69 - Ja 1 '73 - p423
      BS - v32 - S 15 '72 - p269
      BS - v33 - F 1 '74 - p496
      EJ - v62 - D '73 - p1299
      J Read - v22 - N '78 - p127
      KR - v40 - Je 1 '72 - p650

ELFMAN, Blossom (continued)
    KR - v40 - Je 15 '72 - p684
    LJ - v97 - S 1 '72 - p2720
    LJ - v97 - N 15 '72 - p3819
    PW - v201 - Je 5 '72 - p138
    TN - v29 - Ap '73 - p255
    TN - v30 - Ja '74 - p199

   A House For Jonnie O
    BL - v73 - N 1 '76 - p401
    CLW - v49 - D '77 - p198
    KR - v44 - N 1 '76 - p1182
    KR - v44 - N 15 '76 - p1231
    NYTBR - Ja 30 '77 - p24
    PW - v210 - N 1 '76 - p65
    SLJ - v23 - F '77 - p75
    SLJ - v23 - My '77 - p37
    WCRB - v3 - My '77 - p31

ELGIN, Kathleen   1923-
ConAu 25R, IlsCB 1957, WhoAmW
77

   The Human Body: The Hand
    BL - v65 - O 15 '68 - p247
    CCB-B - v22 - O '68 - p25
    KR - v36 - Je 15 '68 - p646
    LJ - v93 - O 15 '68 - p3968
    Spec - v226 - My 29 '71 - p756

ELISOFON, Eliot
see Newman, Marvin (co-author)

ELLIS, Jim   1893-1978
BioIn 9, BioIn 11

   Run For Your Life
    LJ - v96 - Ap 15 '71 - p1514

ELLIS, Melvin Richard   1912-
ConAu 13R, SmATA 7

   No Man For Murder
    Am - v129 - D 1 '73 - p430
    BL - v70 - N 15 '73 - p338
    BS - v33 - Ag 15 '73 - p232
    BW - v7 - S 16 '73 - p10
    CCB-B - v27 - Mr '74 - p109
    Comw - v99 - N 23 '73 - p216
    HB - v50 - F '74 - p55
    KR - v41 - Je 1 '73 - p607
    LJ - v98 - D 15 '73 - p3719
    PW - v204 - Ag 6 '73 - p65

   Sad Song Of The Coyote
    LJ - v92 - N 15 '67 - p4257
    NYTBR - v72 - Mr 26 '67 - p22

   The Wild Horse Killers
    BB - v4 - My '76 - p4
    BL - v72 - Mr 1 '76 - p974
    BS - v36 - O '76 - p239
    BW   Ap 11 '76 - p4
    CSM - v68 - My 12 '76 - p28
    KR - v44 - F 1 '76 - p134
    LA - 54 - Ja '77 - p85
    PW   209 - Ja 26 '76 - p287
    SLJ   22 - Ap '76 - p85

ELLISON, Elsie C

   Fun With Lines And Curves
    BL - v69 - Je 15 '73 - p984
    BL - v69 - Je 15 '73 - p988
    KR - v40 - N 1 '72 - p1242
    LJ - v98 - My 15 '73 - p1681
    SB - v8 - Mr '73 - p312

ELMAN, Richard
see Spyker, John Howland

EMERY, Anne   1907-
ConAu 1R, CurBio 52, MorJA,
SmATA 1

   A Dream To Touch
    BL - v55 - S 1 '58 - p26
    KR - v26 - Ap 1 '58 - p286
    LJ - v83 - Jl '58 - p2075

   First Love Farewell
    BL - v55 - Ja 15 '59 - p262
    KR - v26 - Ag 1 '58 - p550
    LJ - v83 - O 15 '58 - p3015

   First Orchid For Pat
    CSM - N 7 '57 - p17
    KR - v25 - Ag 1 '57 - p534
    LJ - v82 - O 15 '57 - p2706

   Sorority Girl
    BL - v48 - Mr 15 '52 - p234
    CSM - My 15 '52 - p9
    HB - v28 - Je '52 - p178
    KR - v20 - Ja 15 '52 - p32
    NYTBR - Mr 30 '52 - p30

EMRICH, Duncan   1908-
ConAu 61, CurBio 55, SmATA 11

EMRICH, Duncan (continued)

The Nonsense Book Of Riddles,
Rhymes, Tongue Twisters, Puzzles
And Jokes From American Folklore
BL - v67 - Ap 1 '71 - p659
CCB-B - v24 - Je '71 - p156
JAF - v84 - Jl '71 - p357
TN - v27 - Ja '71 - p208

ENGDAHL, Sylvia Louise   1933-
ChLR 2, ConAu 29R, FourBJA,
SmATA 4, TwCCW 78

Enchantress From The Stars
TLS - S 20 '74 - p1006
TN - v34 - Spring '78 - p265

ENGEL, Lyle Kenyon   1915-
ConAu 85, EncSF

Road Racing In America
BL - v67 - Je 1 '71 - p813

ENGLE, Eloise   1923-
ConAu 1R, IntAu&W 77, SmATA 9

Medic
BS - v27 - Jl 1 '67 - p144
KR - v35 - Ap 1 '67 - p459
PW - v191 - Ap 3 '67 - p52

ENGLEBARDT, Stanley L

How To Get In Shape For Sports
BL - v73 - N 15 '76 - p472
KR - v44 - O 1 '76 - p1098
SLJ - v23 - D '76 - p72

EPSTEIN, Beryl Williams
see Epstein, Sam (co-author)

EPSTEIN, Sam   1909-
ConAu 9R, MorJA, SmATA 1,
WhoWorJ 72

Baseball: Hall Of Fame, Stories
Of Champions
LJ - v90 - Ap 15 '65 - p2019

George Washington Carver: Negro
Scientist
JNE - v38 - Fall '69 - p420

Harriet Tubman
BL - v65 - F 1 '69 - p586
CLW - v41 - O '69 - p138
LJ - v94 - F 15 '69 - p871
Teacher - v93 - Ap '76 - p120

Jackie Robinson: Baseball's
Gallant Fighter
SLJ - v21 - Ap '75 - p52

Winston Churchill
Inst - v81 - Ap '72 - p144
LJ - v97 - Jl '72 - p2483

Young Paul Revere's Boston
CCB-B - v20 - Ap '67 - p119
CE - v44 - S '67 - p54
LJ - v92 - Ja 15 '67 - p334

ERDOES, Richard   1912-
ConAu 77, IlsCB 1957

The Sun Dance People: The Plains
Indians, Their Past And Present
BL - v69 - O 1 '72 - p147
BW - v6 - Jl 16 '72 - p7
CCB-B - v26 - S '72 - p5
KR - v40 - Ap 15 '72 - p488
LJ - v97 - O 15 '72 - p3459
NYTBR - Ag 13 '72 - p8
PW - v202 - Jl 31 '72 - p71

ERLICH, Lillian   1910-
ConAu 1R, ForWC 70, SmATA 10

Modern American Career Women
BL - v55 - My 15 '59 - p510
KR - v27 - Ja 15 '59 - p44
LJ - v84 - F 15 '59 - p590

ERNST, John
see Clark, David A

ERSKINE, H Keith

Know What's Happening
Hi Lo - v2 - S '80 - p6

ESHERICK, Joseph
see Schell, Orville (co-author)

ETS, Marie Hall   1895-
ConAu 1R, IlsCB 1967, JBA 51,
SmATA 2, TwCCW 78, WhoAm 78,
WhoAmA 78

ETS, Marie Hall (continued)

Bad Boy, Good Boy
BL - v64 - Mr 1 '68 - p783
BW - v1 - N 5 '67 - p47
CCB-B - v21 - F '68 - p93
KR - v35 - S 15 '67 - p1130
LJ - v92 - N 15 '67 - p4242
NYTBR - v72 - N 5 '67 - p63
SR - v50 - N 11 '67 - p42

ETTER, Lester Frederick   1904-
ConAu 25R

Bull Pen Hero
BS - v26 - Ag 1 '66 - p174
KR - v34 - My 15 '66 - p512
LJ - v91 - Jl '66 - p3550

The Game Of Hockey
SLJ - v24 - D '77 - p64

Hockey's Masked Men: Three Great Goalies
SLJ - v23 - Ja '77 - p90

EVANS, Harold   1928-
ConAu 41R, IntWW 78, WhoWor 78

We Learned To Ski
BW - Ag 31 '75 - p2
KR - v43 - Ag 1 '75 - p908
NYTBR - N 9 '75 - p4
PW - v208 - Ag 4 '75 - p53
VV - v20 - S 15 '75 - p50

EVANS, Larry   1939-

How To Draw Monsters
A Art - v42 - Je '78 - p16

EVARTS, Hal G, Jr.   1915-
AuBYP SUP, ConAu 49, SmATA 6,
WhoWest 78

The Pegleg Mystery
BS - v31 - Mr 15 '72 - p566
CLW - v44 - O '72 - p193
EJ - v61 - S '72 - p938
HB - v48 - Je '72 - p274
KR - v40 - F 15 '72 - p201
LJ - v97 - My 15 '72 - p1929

Smuggler's Road
BL - v64 - Je 15 '68 - p1184

BS - v28 - My 1 '68 - p64
BW - v2 - My 5 '68 - p24
HB - v44 - Ag '68 - p427
KR - v36 - F 1 '68 - p122
LJ - v93 - Ap 15 '68 - p1809
NYTBR - v73 - Je 16 '68 - p24

EVSLIN, Bernard   1922-
AuBYP SUP, ConAu 21R

Heroes, Gods And Monsters Of The Greek Myths
CC - v84 - D 13 '67 - p1601
LJ - v93 - Ja 15 '68 - p303
NYTBR - v73 - Ja 21 '68 - p26

EWEN, David   1907-
BiE&WWA, ConAu 1R, SmATA 4,
WhoAm 78, WhoWorJ 72

Famous Conductors
BL - v62 - Je 1 '66 - p952
BS - v26 - S 1 '66 - p201
LJ - v92 - Ja 15 '67 - p342

EYERLY, Jeannette   1908-
ConAu 1R, SmATA 4, WhoAm 78,
WhoAmW 77

Escape From Nowhere
BW - v3 - My 4 '69 - p32
CCB-B - v23 - S '69 - p6
Comw - v90 - My 23 '69 - p300
HB - v45 - Ap '69 - p195
KR - v37 - F 15 '69 - p184
LJ - v94 - Ap 15 '69 - p1794
NYTBR - Jc 8 '69 - p44
NYTBR, pt.2 - My 4 '69 - p10
NYTBR, pt.2 - N 9 '69 - p60
PW - v195 - My 12 '69 - p58

The Girl Inside
CCB-B - v22 - O '68 - p25
EJ - v58 - My '69 - p778
HB - v44 - Ag '68 - p428
KR - v36 - Mr 1 '68 - p271
LJ - v93 - Ap 15 '68 - p1810
NYTBR - v73 - Ap 21 '68 - p34

A Girl Like Me
Am - v115 - N 5 '66 - p554
BL - v63 - D 15 '66 - p446
CCB-B - v20 - Ja '67 - p73
CSM - v58 - N 3 '66 - pB1

EYERLY, Jeannette (continued)
       Comw - v85 - N 11 '66 - p176
       EJ - v56 - F '67 - p316
       KR - v34 - Ag 15 '66 - p841
       LJ - v91 - S 15 '66 - p4349
       NYTBR - v71 - N 6 '66 - p16

The Phaedra Complex
       BL - v68 - N 15 '71 - p286
       CCB-B - v25 - F '72 - p90
       CSM - v63 - N 11 '71 - pB1
       EJ - v61 - Ap '72 - p603
       KR - v39 - Jl 1 '71 - p682
       LJ - v96 - O 15 '71 - p3475
       SR - v54 - N 13 '71 - p62

Radigan Cares
       BS - v30 - N 15 '70 - p361
       CCB-B - v24 - D '70 - p58
       EJ - v60 - My '71 - p667
       KR - v38 - Jl 15 '70 - p748
       LJ - v96 - Ja 15 '71 - p275

F

FABER, Doris 1924-
AuBYP, ConAu 17R, ForWC 70,
SmATA 3

Clarence Darrow: Defender Of The People
CC - v82 - Je 30 '65 - p838
CCB-B - v18 - Je '65 - p146
KR - v33 - Ja 15 '65 - p61
LJ - v90 - My 15 '65 - p2404
NYTBR - v70 - Jl 25 '65 - p20

Enrico Fermi: Atomic Pioneer
KR - v34 - Ja 15 '66 - p62
LJ - v91 - F 15 '66 - p1062
SB - v1 - Mr '66 - p208

Horace Greeley: The People's Editor
CSM - My 7 '64 - p9B
LJ - v89 - Mr 15 '64 - p1449
NYTBR - Mr 22 '64 - p22

Lucretia Mott
BL - v68 - F 15 '72 - p506
CCB-B - v25 - Ja '72 - p73
LJ - v96 - D 15 '71 - p4197
NHB - v34 - D '71 - p191

Robert Frost: America's Poet
AL - v36 - Ja '65 - p551
Am - v111 - N 21 '64 - p672
CSM - N 5 '64 - p8B
LJ - v89 - D 15 '64 - p5006
NYRB - v3 - D 3 '64 - p13

FAIR, Ronald L 1932-
BlkAW, ConAu 69, SelBAA,
WhoBlA 77

Hog Butcher
BL - v63 - N 1 '66 - p300
BS - v26 - S 15 '66 - p207
CC - v83 - Ag 31 '66 - p1057

CLW - v38 - N '66 - p209
KR - v34 - Je 15 '66 - p602
KR - v34 - Jl 1 '66 - p636
LJ - v91 - Ag '66 - p3764
NW - v68 - S 5 '66 - p90
PW - v189 - Je 20 '66 - p77
SR - v49 - S 3 '66 - p36

We Can't Breathe
BL - v68 - N 15 '71 - p272
CSM - v64 - D 30 '71 - p6
Choice - v9 - Il '72 - p644
EJ - v62 - D '73 - p1300
EJ - v63 - Ja '74 - p65
KR - v39 - O 15 '71 - p1139
LJ - v96 - D 1 '71 - p4029
NY - v47 - F 5 '72 - p103
NYTBR - F 6 '72 - p6
Nat - v214 - F 21 '72 - p253
PW - v200 - O 18 '71 - p42
SR - v55 - F 19 '72 - p74
TN - v29 - Ap '73 - p257
YR - v61 - Summer '72 - p599

FALES, E D, Jr. 1906-
WhoE 74

The Book Of Expert Driving
KR - v38 - S 15 '70 - p1068
KR - v38 - O 15 '70 - p1173
LJ - v95 - S 1 '70 - p2819

FALL, Thomas (pseud.) 1917-
ConAu X, FourBJA, SmATA 16 (real
name: Snow, Donald Clifford)

Canalboat To Freedom
BL - v63 - O 1 '66 - p187
CCB-B - v20 - N '66 - p40
CE - v44 - S '67 - p48
HB - v42 - O '66 - p568
KR - v34 - My 15 '66 - p513
LJ - v91 - Jl '66 - p3534

75

FALL, Thomas (continued)
NYTBR - v71 - Ag 14 '66 - p24

Dandy's Mountain
BL - v64 - O 1 '67 - p200
BW - v1 - S 24 '67 - p22
CCB-B - v21 - O '67 - p26
HB - v43 - Ag '67 - p469
KR - v35 - My 1 '67 - p560
LJ - v92 - O 15 '67 - p3862
SR - v50 - Jl 22 '67 - p43

FANBURG, Walter H   1936-
BrDrAPA 77

How To Be A Winner
KR - v430 - F 1 '75 - p153
LJ - v100 - Ja '75 - p1336

FARLEY, Walter   1915?-
ConAu 17R, JBA 51, MorBMP,
SmATA 2, TwCCW 78

The Black Stallion
GP - v17 - N '78 - p3406
Teacher - v95 - My '78 - p109

FAUST, S R

Loaded And Rollin'
BL - v72 - Jl 15 '76 - p1560

FEAGLES, Anita MacRae   1926-
ConAu 1R, FourBJA, SmATA 9

Emergency Room
LJ - v98 - Mr 15 '73 - p1020

Me, Cassie
BL - v65 - S 1 '68 - p53
BS - v28 - Jl 1 '68 - p154
BW - v2 - My 5 '68 - p26
CCB-B - v21 - Jl '68 - p173
KR - v36 - Ap 15 '68 - p465
LJ - v93 - Je 15 '68 - p2546
NYTBR - v73 - My 5 '68 - p8
PW - v193 - My 6 '68 - p45
SR - v51 - Jl 20 '68 - p31

Sophia Scarlotti And Ceecee
BL - v75 - Mr 1 '79 - p1048
CBRS - v7 - Ag '79 - p136
CCB-B - v32 - Jl '79 - p190
KR - v47 - Ap 1 '79 - p391
SLJ - v25 - Mr '79 - p147

The Year The Dreams Came Back
BL - v73 - S 15 '76 - p173
CLW - v48 - My '77 - p443
HB - v52 - O '76 - p503
KR - v44 - Jl 1 '76 - p738
LA - v54 - Ap '77 - p443
PW - v210 - D 27 '76 - p60
SLJ - v23 - S '76 - p132

FECHER, Constance   1911-
AuBYP SUP, ConAu 49, SmATA 7,
WrDr 80

*The Last Elizabethan: A Portrait
Of Sir Walter Raleigh*
BL - v68 - My 1 '72 - p765
BL - v68 - Ag 15 '72 - p769
BS - v32 - Ag 15 '72 - p243
BW - v6 - Ag 13 '72 - p6
HB - v48 - Je '72 - p281
KR - v40 - Ja 15 '72 - p75
LJ - v98 - Mr 15 '73 - p1101
NY - v48 - D 2 '72 - p211
PW - v201 - Ap 10 '72 - p59

FEDDER, Ruth   1907-
AmM&WS 12S, ConAu 5R,
WhoWest 74

A Girl Grows Up
BL - v63 - Je 15 '67 - p1096
BS - v27 - My 1 '67 - p64
KR - v35 - Mr 15 '67 - p353

FEELINGS, Thomas   1933-
ConAu 49, IlsCB 1967, SelBAA,
SmATA 8, ThrBJA, WhoBlA 77

Black Pilgrimage
BL - v68 - Je 15 '72 - p903
BL - v69 - My 1 '73 - p837
BW - v6 - My 7 '72 - p13
Bl W - v22 - N '72 - p91
CCB-B - v26 - S '72 - p6
HB - v48 - Ag '72 - p380
KR - v40 - Ap 15 '72 - p489
LJ - v98 - Ja 15 '73 - p267
NYTBR, pt.2 - My 7 '72 - p30
SR - v55 - My 20 '72 - p82

FELSEN, Henry Gregor   1916-
ConAu 1R, JBA 51, SmATA 1

FELSEN, Henry Gregor (continued)

Hot Rod
BL - v47 - S 15 '50 - p44
KR - v18 - Je 1 '50 - p305
LJ - v75 - N 1 '50 - p1913
NYTBR - Jl 30 '50 - p16

Street Rod
KR - v21 - My 15 '53 - p307
LJ - v78 - Ag '53 - p1339
NYTBR - S 6 '53 - p13

To My Son, The Teen-Age Driver
BL - v24 - Ap 15 '64 - p41
CLW - v41 - My '70 - p576
LJ - v89 - Ap 1 '64 - p1603
Par - v40 - Jl '65 - p14

FELSER, Larry

Baseball's Ten Greatest Pitchers
Inst - v89 - Ja '80 - p112
Kliatt - v13 - Fall '79 - p64
SLJ - v26 - D '79 - p102

FELTON, Harold W   1902-
ConAu 1R, MorJA, SmATA 1

James Weldon Johnson
BL - v67 - Jl 1 '71 - p907
CCB-B - v24 - Jl '71 - p169
Comw - v97 - F 23 '73 - p473
LJ - v96 - N 15 '71 - p3900
NYTBR, pt.2 - My 2 '71 - p43
PW - v199 - My 10 '71 - p43

Mumbet: The Story Of Elizabeth Freeman
BL - v66 - Jl 15 '70 - p1407
CCB-B - v24 - S '70 - p7
CSM - v62 - My 7 '70 - pB1
HB - v46 - Ag '70 - p399
KR - v38 - My 1 '70 - p509
PW - v197 - Mr 30 '70 - p65
SR - v53 - Je 27 '70 - p39

Nat Love, Negro Cowboy
LJ - v95 - D 15 '70 - p4382

FENDERSON, Lewis H   1907-
DrAS 74E

Thurgood Marshall: Fighter For Justice
BL - v66 - Ja 1 '70 - p564
CLW - v41 - My '70 - p590
KR - v37 - My 1 '69 - p509
LJ - v95 - Mr 15 '70 - p1194
NYTBR, pt.2 - My 4 '69 - p16

FENNER, Phyllis Reid   1899-
AuBYP, ConAu 5R, SmATA 1,
WhoAmW 77

Lift Line: Stories Of Downhill And Cross-Country Skiing
CSM - v68 - N 3 '76 - p20
KR - v44 - Jl 15 '76 - p799
SLJ - v23 - D '76 - p71

FENTON, Edward B   1917-
ConAu 9R, SmATA 7, ThrBJA,
TwCCW 78

A Matter Of Miracles
Am - v117 - N 4 '67 - p518
BL - v64 - O 15 '67 - p273
BW - v1 - S 10 '67 - p36
CCB-B - v21 - D '67 - p58
CE - v44 - Ap '68 - p501
HB - v43 - O '67 - p592
KR - v35 - Je 1 '67 - p645
LJ - v92 - S 15 '67 - p3185
NYTBR - v72 - Ag 6 '67 - p26
NYTBR - v72 - N 5 '67 - p66
PW - v192 - N 27 '67 - p43

FIFE, Dale   1910-
ConAu 85, FourBJA, SmATA 18

North Of Danger
BL - v74 - Ap 15 '78 - p1348
HB - v54 - Ag '78 - p394
KR - v46 - Je 15 '78 - p636
NYTBR - Ap 30 '78 - p32
SLJ - v24 - My '78 - p66
Teacher - v96 - O '78 - p167

FILMER-SANKEY, Josephine
see Denny, Norman George (co-author)

FILSON, Brent

The Puma
BL - v75 - My 15 '79 - p1435

FILSON, Brent (continued)
> CE - v56 - Ja '80 - p169
> Hi Lo - v1 - S '79 - p2
> SLJ - v25 - My '79 - p88

> *Smoke Jumpers*
> KR - v46 - F 1 '78 - p110
> NYTBR - Ap 30 '78 - p45
> SLJ - v24 - F '78 - p56

FINKEL, George   1909-1975
ConAu P-2, SmATA 8, TwCCW 78

> *Watch Fires To The North*
> BL - v64 - Je 1 '68 - p1133
> BS - v28 - My 1 '68 - p64
> CCB-B - v22 - O '68 - p26
> CLW - v39 - F '68 - p468
> CSM - v60 - My 2 '68 - pB8
> KR - v35 - S 1 '67 - p1055
> KR - v36 - Mr 15 '68 - p343
> LJ - v93 - Je 15 '68 - p2546
> NYTBR - v73 - Ap 14 '68 - p20
> SR - v51 - Jl 20 '68 - p31

FINLAYSON, Ann   1925-
ConAu 29R, SmATA 8

> *Decathlon Men: Greatest Athletes In The World*
> LJ - v92 - My 15 '67 - p2040

> *Redcoat In Boston*
> BS - v31 - Jl 15 '71 - p191
> LJ - v96 - O 15 '71 - p3475
> PW - v199 - My 10 '71 - p43

FINNEY, Jack   1911-
ConSFA, EncSF, ScF&FL 1, WhoSciF

> *Time And Again*
> BL - v67 - S 1 '70 - p36
> BL - v67 - S 15 '70 - p95
> BL - v67 - Ap 1 '71 - p654
> BS - v30 - Jl 15 '70 - p151
> BW - v4 - Je 28 '70 - p6
> HB - v46 - O '70 - p502
> KR - v38 - Mr 1 '70 - p272
> KR - v38 - Ap 15 '70 - p473
> LJ - v95 - O 1 '70 - p3304
> LJ - v95 - O 15 '70 - p3649
> NO - v9 - S 28 '70 - p21
> NYT - v119 - Jl 25 '70 - p21

> NYTBR - Ag 2 '70 - p24
> PW - v197 - Mr 9 '70 - p81
> PW - v199 - My 31 '71 - p136
> SR - v54 - O 23 '71 - p86
> SR - v54 - N 27 '71 - p48
> TN - v27 - Ap '71 - p308
> Time - v96 - Jl 20 '70 - p76

FIORE, Evelyn   1918-

> *Mystery At Lane's End*
> CCB-B - v22 - Jl '69 - p174
> CSM - v61 - Je 26 '69 - p7
> KR - v375 - Mr 1 '69 - p246
> LJ - v94 - My 15 '69 - p2124
> PW - v195 - Ap 7 '69 - p56

FIRST, Julia

> *Amy*
> KR - v43 - S 1 '75 - p998
> SLJ - v22 - N '75 - p76

FISCHLER, Stanley I

> *Getting Into Pro Soccer*
> BL - v75 - Jl 1 '79 - p1583

FISHER, Aileen   1906-
BkP, ConAu 5R, MorJA, SmATA 1, TwCCW 78

> *Jeanne D'Arc*
> BL - v66 - My 1 '70 - p1098
> CCB-B - v24 - O '70 - p24
> Comw - v92 - My 22 '70 - p245
> HB - v46 - Je '70 - p304
> KR - v38 - F 1 '70 - p106
> LJ - v95 - My 15 '70 - p1941
> NYTBR, pt.2 - My 24 '70 - p30
> PW - v197 - Mr 2 '70 - p82
> SR - v53 - Je 27 '70 - p39

FISHER, Leonard Everett   1924-
ConAu 1R, IlsCB 1967, SmATA 4, ThrBJA, WhoAmA 78, WhoWorJ 72

> *Across The Sea From Galway*
> BL - v72 - F 15 '76 - p854
> KR - v43 - Ag 1 '75 - p848
> PW - v208 - S 22 '75 - p132
> SLJ - v22 - Ja '76 - p52

FISK, Nicholas 1923-
ConAu 65, ConSFA, SmATA 24,
TwCCW 78

   Space Hostages
      KR - v37 - F 15 '69 - p184
      LJ - v94 - Jl '69 - p2675
      Punch - v253 - D 6 '67 - p875
      TES - Mr 10 '78 - p52
      TLS - N 30 '67 - p1160

FITZHARDINGE, Joan Margaret
see Phipson, Joan

FITZHUGH, Louise 1928-1974
ChLR 1, ConAu 53, ConAu P-2,
SmATA 1, ThrBJA, TwCCW 78

   Sport
      BL - v75 - My 15 '79 - p1438
      BS - v39 - N '79 - p289
      BW - My 13 '79 - pK2
      CBRS - v7 - Je '79 - p107
      CCB-B - v32 - Jl '79 - p191
      CE - v56 - Ja '80 - p169
      CLW - v51 - D '79 - p233
      HB - v55 - Ag '79 - p413
      KR - v47 - Jl 15 '79 - p793
      LJ - v57 - Ja '80 - p85
      NY - v55 - D 3 '79 - p212
      NYTBR - Je 3 '79 - p44
      PW - v215 - Je 25 '79 - p123
      SLJ - v25 - My '79 - p61
      WCRB - v5 - S '79 - p83

FLEISCHMAN, Albert Sidney
see Fleischman, Sid

FLEISCHMAN, H Samuel

   Gang Girl
      CCB-B - v21 - S '67 - p5
      EJ - v57 - My '68 - p759

FLEISCHMAN, Sid 1920-
ChLR 1, ConAu 1R, SmATA 8,
ThrBJA, TwCCW 78 (also known as
Fleischman, Albert Sidney)

   Chancy And The Grand Rascal
      Am - v115 - N 5 '66 - p553
      BL - v63 - S 15 '66 - p119
      CCB-B - v20 - N '66 - p41
      CE - v44 - S '67 - p50

CSM - v58 - N 3 '66 - pB6
HB - v42 - O '66 - p569
KR - v34 - Jl 1 '66 - p625
LJ - v91 - O 15 '66 - p5226
NYTBR - v71 - N 6 '66 - p40
NYTBR - v71 - D 4 '66 - p66
PW - v190 - Ag 15 '66 - p64
SR - v49 - D 10 '66 - p57
TLS - N 30 '67 - p1145
TN - v23 - Ap '67 - p291

   The Ghost In The Noonday Sun
      Am - v113 - N 20 '65 - p640
      BL - v62 - S 1 '65 - p54
      CCB-B - v19 - N '65 - p43
      HB - v41 - O '65 - p490
      KR - v33 - Mr 1 '65 - p245
      KR - v33 - My 1 '65 - p472
      LJ - v90 - S 15 '65 - p3790
      NYTBR - v70 - O 24 '65 - p34
      Obs - N 27 '66 - p28
      TLS - N 24 '66 - p1069

FLEISCHMANN, Harriet 1904-
ConAu P-2

   The Great Enchantment
      BS - v27 - Ap 1 '67 - p16
      KR - v35 - Ja 1 '67 - p13
      LJ - v92 - Je 15 '67 - p2458

FLETCHER, Alan Mark 1928-
AuBYP SUP, ConAu 73, WrDr 80

   Unusual Aquarium Fishes
      BL - v64 - Jl 1 '68 - p1234
      CE - v45 - Ap '69 - p468
      LJ - v93 - Je 15 '68 - p2538
      SB - v4 - S '68 - p134

FLORENTZ, Christopher

   So Wild A Dream
      BL - v74 - F 15 '78 - p997

FLYNN, James J 1911-1977
AuBYP SUP, ConAu 21R, DrAS
78H, WhoE 74

   Negroes Of Achievement In
   Modern America
      BS - v30 - Ag 1 '70 - p179
      Bl W - v20 - Ja '71 - p97
      KR - v38 - Je 15 '70 - p646

FOLCH-RIBAS, Jacques 1928-
ConAu 69, OxCan SUP

Northlight, Lovelight
KR - v44 - Ag 15 '76 - p917
NYTBR - D 26 '76 - p15
PW - v210 - Ag 9 '76 - p67
SLJ - v23 - Ap '77 - p81

FOLSOM, Franklin Brewster 1907-
AuBYP, ConAu 1R, SmATA 5,
WrDr 80

The Life And Legend Of George McJunkin
ABC - v25 - Jl '75 - p9
BL - v70 - F 15 '74 - p656
KR - v41 - Jl 1 '73 - p694
LJ - v99 - Ja 15 '74 - p217
PW - v204 - D 3 '73 - p40

FORBES, Esther 1894?-1967
ConAu 25R, ConAu P-1, ConLC 12,
MorJA, SmATA 2, TwCCW 78

Johnny Tremain
BL - v40 - D 15 '43 - p150
CSM - N 18 '43 - p10
HB - v19 - N '43 - p413
Inst - v78 - N '68 - p156
LJ - v68 - N 15 '43 - p965
NY - v19 - D 4 '43 - p124
NYTBR - N 14 '43 - p5
NYTBR, pt.2 - F 13 '72 - p14
Nat - v157 - N 20 '43 - p592
PW - v194 - Jl 22 '68 - p65
SR - v26 - N 13 '43 - p44

FORESTER, C S 1899-1966
ConAu 25R, ConAu 73, LongCTC,
SmATA 13, WebE&AL, WhoChL

Last Nine Days Of The Bismarck
BL - v55 - Ap 15 '59 - p448
CSM - Ap 23 '59 - p5
HB - v35 - Ja '59 - p229
KR - v27 - Ja 15 '59 - p75
LJ - v84 - Mr 1 '59 - p754
NY - v35 - Ap 4 '59 - p169
NYTBR - Ap 5 '59 - p14
SR - v42 - My 2 '59 - p38
TLS - My 1 '59 - p260
Time - v73 - Mr 23 '59 - p96

FORMAN, James 1932-
ConAu 9R, SmATA 8, ThrBJA

Ceremony Of Innocence
BL - v67 - D 15 '70 - p336
BL - v67 - D 15 '70 - p341
CCB-B - v24 - Ja '71 - p73
EJ - v60 - My '71 - p668
KR - v38 - Ag 1 '70 - p805
LJ - v95 - N 15 '70 - p4053
LJ - v95 - D 15 '70 - p4325
NYTBR - Ja 10 '71 - p26
SR - v53 - N 14 '70 - p39

Horses Of Anger
BL - v64 - S 1 '67 - p54
BS - v27 - My 1 '67 - p64
CCB-B - v21 - My '68 - p140
HB - v43 - Je '67 - p352
KR - v35 - Mr 1 '67 - p278
LJ - v92 - My 15 '67 - p2027
NYTBR, pt.2 - v72 - My 7 '67 - p2
TN - v24 - N '67 - p99

My Enemy, My Brother
BL - v66 - S 1 '69 - p44
BS - v29 - Jl 1 '69 - p149
BW - v3 - My 4 '69 - p3
CCB-B - v22 - Jl '69 - p174
HB - v45 - Je '69 - p328
J Pol - v94 - My 15 '69 - p2112
KR - v37 - Ap 15 '69 - p452
LJ - v95 - F 15 '70 - p742
NYTBR - My 25 '69 - p32
PW - v195 - My 19 '69 - p70
SR - v52 - Je 28 '69 - p39

People Of The Dream
BL - v68 - Jl 15 '72 - p997
BL - v68 - Jl 15 '72 - p1004
BW - v6 - Jl 16 '72 - p7
CE - v49 - F '73 - p257
KR - v40 - My 15 '72 - p589
LJ - v97 - N 15 '72 - p3813
NYTBR, pt.2 - N 5 '72 - p14

Ring The Judas Bell
BL - v61 - Je 15 '65 - p993
BS - v25 - Ap 15 '65 - p51
CCB-B - v18 - Jl '65 - p160
CLW - v36 - Ap '65 - p573
CSM - v57 - My 6 '65 - p6B
Comw - v82 - My 28 '65 - p329
HB - v41 - Je '65 - p284

FORMAN, James (continued)
    KR - v33 - Ja 1 '65 - p11
    LJ - v90 - Mr 15 '65 - p1558
    NYTBR - v70 - Ap 4 '65 - p22
    SR - v48 - Je 19 '65 - p41

    The Traitors
        BS - v28 - N 1 '68 - p324
        KR - v36 - S 15 '68 - p1058
        NYTBR - v73 - N 3 '68 - p18

FORSYTH, Elizabeth Held
    see Hyde, Margaret Oldroyd (co-
    author) - *Know Your Feelings*

FORSYTH, Frederick   1938-
    ConAu 85, ConLC 5, WhoAm 74,
    WrDr 80

    The Shepherd
        BL - v73 - D 15 '76 - p586
        BL - v73 - D 15 '76 - p606
        CCB-B - v30 - D '76 - p56
        Fly - v99 - D '76 - p115
        KR - v44 - Ag 1 '76 - p874
        LJ - v101 - N 15 '76 - p2393
        NS - v90 - N 28 '75 - p686
        NYTBR - O 16 '77 - p55
        PW - v210 - Ag 2 '76 - p108
        PW - v212 - Ag 22 '77 - p64
        Punch - v269 - O 29 '75 - p788
        SLJ - v23 - F '77 - p75
        TLS - D 19 '75 - p1508

FORTUNATO, Pat

    When We Were Young: An Album
    Of Stars
        CCB-B - v33 - Mr '80 - p132
        Hi Lo - v1 - F '80 - p3
        SLJ - v26 - F '80 - p54

FOSTER, Alan Dean   1946-
    ConAu 53, EncSF, ScF&FL 1,
    ScF&FL 2

    Splinter Of The Mind's Eye
        BL - v74 - My 1 '78 - p1412
        EJ - v68 - D '79 - p77
        KR - v46 - F 1 '78 - p136
        PW - v213 - F 6 '78 - p92

FOSTER, George
    see Drucker, Malka (co-author) -
        The George Foster Story

FOX, Mary Virginia   1919-
    AuBYP, ConAu 29R

    Lady For The Defense: A
    Biography Of Belva Lockwood
        B&B - v3 - Ag '75 - p4
        Comw - v102 - N 21 '75 - p566
        HB - v51 - Ag '75 - p391
        KR - v43 - Ag 15 '75 - p461
        PW - v207 - F 24 '75 - p116
        SLJ - v22 - S '75 - p102

FOX, Paula   1923-
    ChLR 1, ConAu 73, ConLC 2,
    FourBJA, SmATA 17, TwCCW 78,
    WhoAm 78

    Blowfish Live In The Sea
        BL   v67   F 15 '71   p492
        BS - v30 - F 15 '71 - p506
        CCB-B - v24 - Mr '71 - p106
        CSM - v63 - My 6 '71 - pB6
        HB - v46 - D '70 - p623
        HB - v53 - O '77 - p517
        KR - v38 - N 1 '70 - p1200
        LJ - v96 - Ja 15 '71 - p275
        NYRB - v18 - Ap 20 '72 - p13
        NYTBR, pt.2 - N 8 '70 - p12
        Obs - Ap 2 '72 - p28
        PW - v198 - N 30 '70 - p41
        SR - v54 - Ja 23 '71 - p71
        Spec - v228 - Ap 22 '72 - p625
        TLS - Ap 28 '72 - p477
        Teacher - v92 - My '75 - p93

    How Many Miles To Babylon?
        Atl - v220 - D '67 - p136
        BL - v69 - My 1 '73 - p837
        BW - v1 - O 8 '67 - p24
        CCB-B - v21 - D '67 - p59
        HB - v43 - O '67 - p593
        KR - v35 - Jl 15 '67 - p807
        LJ - v92 - D 15 '67 - p4612
        NYTBR - v72 - S 3 '67 - p24
        NYTBR - v72 - S 24 '67 - p34
        NYTBR - v72 - N 5 '67 - p66
        NYTBR, pt.2 - N 8 '70 - p30
        NYTBR, pt.2 - F 13 '72 - p12
        Obs - Ag 4 '68 - p22

FOX, Paula (continued)
　　　Obs - Ja 14 '73 - p30
　　　PW - v198 - Jl 13 '70 - p166
　　　Punch - v255 - Jl 3 '68 - p33
　　　SR - v50 - N 11 '67 - p46
　　　TLS - Je 6 '68 - p583
　　　TN - v24 - Ap '68 - p323

　　Portrait Of Ivan
　　　A Lib - v1 - Ap '70 - p385
　　　BL - v66 - F 1 '70 - p670
　　　BW - v4 - Mr 29 '70 - p12
　　　CCB-B - v23 - F '70 - p96
　　　GW - v103 - D 19 '70 - p21
　　　HB - v46 - Ap '70 - p159
　　　KR - v37 - O 15 '69 - p1112
　　　LJ - v94 - D 15 '69 - p4581
　　　LJ - v94 - D 15 '69 - p4604
　　　NYTBR - D 7 '69 - p68
　　　NYTBR, pt.2 - N 9 '69 - p34
　　　NYTBR, pt.2 - N 9 '69 - p60
　　　PW - v196 - N 24 '69 - p42
　　　SR - v52 - D 20 '69 - p30
　　　TLS - D 11 '70 - p1451
　　　Teacher - v91 - My '74 - p84

　　The Slave Dancer
　　　B&B - v23 - N '77 - p82
　　　BL - v70 - Ja 1 '74 - p484
　　　BL - v70 - Mr 15 '74 - p827
　　　BW - F 10 '74 - p4
　　　CCB-B - v27 - Ja '74 - p77
　　　CE - v50 - Ap '74 - p335
　　　CLW - v47 - N '75 - p165
　　　EJ - v66 - O '77 - p58
　　　HB - v49 - D '73 - p596
　　　HB - v53 - O '77 - p515
　　　KR - v41 - O 1 '73 - p1095
　　　KR - v41 - D 15 '73 - p1350
　　　LJ - v98 - D 15 '73 - p3689
　　　LJ - v98 - D 15 '73 - p3711
　　　Lis - v92 - N 7 '74 - p613
　　　NS - v88 - N 8 '74 - p666
　　　NYTBR - Ja 20 '74 - p8
　　　Obs - D 8 '74 - p30
　　　Obs - Je 26 '77 - p29
　　　PW - v204 - D 10 '73 - p36
　　　TLS - D 6 '74 - p1375
　　　TN - v30 - Ap '74 - p243
　　　Teacher - v91 - My '74 - p79
　　　VV - v19 - D 16 '74 - p52

FRANCHERE, Ruth　1906-
　ConAu 73, FourBJA, SmATA 18,
　WhoPNW

　　Cesar Chavez
　　　BL - v67 - N 1 '70 - p226
　　　BL - v68 - Je 15 '72 - p894
　　　BL - v70 - O 15 '73 - p225
　　　CC - v87 - D 16 '70 - p1516
　　　CCB-B - v24 - F '71 - p90
　　　Comw - v93 - N 20 '70 - p203
　　　Inst - v80 - O '70 - p142
　　　KR - v38 - Ag 15 '70 - p879
　　　LJ - v96 - Mr 15 '71 - p1132
　　　NYTBR, pt.2 - N 8 '70 - p46
　　　Teacher - v91 - S '73 - p154

　　Hannah Herself
　　　HB - v40 - Ap '64 - p181
　　　LJ - v89 - Mr 15 '64 - p1459
　　　NYTBR - Ag 2 '64 - p20

　　*Jack London: The Pursuit Of A
　　Dream*
　　　CSM - N 15 '62 - p6B
　　　HB - v38 - D '62 - p613
　　　LJ - v87 - D 15 '62 - p4623
　　　NYTBR - D 9 '62 - p36

　　The Travels Of Colin O'Dae
　　　BL - v63 - Ja 1 '67 - p488
　　　CCB-B - v20 - Ap '67 - p120
　　　CE - v44 - N '67 - p188
　　　KR - v34 - O 1 '66 - p1052
　　　LJ - v92 - Ja 15 '67 - p334
　　　NYTBR - v72 - Ja 8 '67 - p30
　　　SR - v50 - F 18 '67 - p42

　　*Willa: The Story Of Willa
　　Cather's Growing Up*
　　　Atl - v202 - D '58 - p100
　　　BL - v55 - S 15 '58 - p52
　　　HB - v34 - D '58 - p480
　　　KR - v26 - Ag 15 '58 - p611
　　　LJ - v83 - O 15 '58 - p3007
　　　NYTBR - O 12 '58 - p29
　　　SR - v41 - N 1 '58 - p59

FRANCIS, Dorothy Brenner　1926-
　ConAu 21R, SmATA 10, WhoAmW
　75, WrDr 80

　　The Flint Hills Foal
　　　BB - v5 - Ap '77 - p2
　　　RT - v31 - Ap '78 - p841

FRANCIS, Dorothy Brenner (continued)
  SLJ - v23 - Ja '77 - p91

  Mystery Of The Forgotten Map
    KR - v36 - Je 1 '68 - p596

FRANK, Anne   1929-1944
  BioIn 4, BioIn 5, HerW, REn, TwCW

  Anne Frank: Diary Of A Young Girl
    Atl - v190 - S '52 - p70
    BL - v48 - Je 1 '52 - p318
    CSM - Jl 3 '52 - p13
    Cath W - v175 - Ag '52 - p395
    Comw - v56 - Je 27 '52 - p297
    HB - v28 - Ag '52 - p248
    HB - v28 - D '52 - p425
    LJ - v77 - My 15 '52 - p889
    NS - v43 - My 17 '52 - p592
    NY - v28 - Je 21 '52 - p106
    SR - v35 - Jl 19 '52 - p20
    Spec - v188 - My 30 '52 - p726
    Time - v59 - Je 16 '52 - p102

FRANKLIN, Joe

  Classics Of The Silent Screen
    LJ - v85 - F 15 '60 - p774
    NYTBR - F 21 '60 - p7

FREDERICK, Lee   (pseud.) 1934-
  ConAu X (real name: Nussbaum, Albert F)

  Crash Dive
    BL - v74 - Ja 15 '78 - p808
    BL - v75 - O 15 '78 - p357

FREEDMAN, Benedict   1919-
  AmNov, BioIn 1, BioIn 3, ConAu 69, WhoAm 76

  Mrs. Mike
    BL - v43 - Mr 1 '47 - p205
    CSM - F 28 '47 - p16
    Cath W - v165 - Jl '47 - p380
    Comw - v45 - Mr 28 '47 - p596
    HB - v24 - Ja '48 - p69
    KR - v15 - Ja 1 '47 - p5
    LJ - v72 - F 15 '47 - p319
    NY - v23 - Mr 1 '47 - p92
    NYT - Mr 2 '47 - p5
    SR - v30 - Mr 8 '47 - p31

  WLB - v43 - Ap '47 - p68

FREEDMAN, Florence B   1908-
  LEduc 74

  Two Tickets To Freedom
    BL - v68 - Ja 15 '72 - p433
    CCB-B - v26 - S '72 - p7
    CSM - v63 - N 11 '71 - pB6
    KR - v39 - O 1 '71 - p1075
    LJ - v97 - Ap 15 '72 - p1604
    PW - v200 - N 15 '71 - p72

FREEDMAN, Nancy
  see Freedman, Benedict (co-author)

FREEMAN, Mae Blacker   1907-
  ConAu 73, MorJA

  Finding Out About The Past
    CE - v44 - My '68 - p562
    CLW - v39 - F '68 - p435
    CSM - v60 - My 2 '68 - pB6
    LJ - v93 - Ja 15 '68 - p290
    SB - v4 - S '68 - p114

  When Air Moves
    CCB-B - v22 - S '68 - p7
    KR - v36 - My 15 '68 - p551
    LJ - v93 - S 15 '68 - p3301
    SB - v4 - S '68 - p148
    SR - v51 - Jl 20 '68 - p31

FREIDEL, Frank
  see Sullivan, Wilson (co-author)

FRENCH, Dorothy Kayser   1926-
  AuBYP, ConAu 9R, SmATA 5, WhoAmW 77

  I Don't Belong Here
    Hi Lo - v2 - S '80 - p4
    SLJ - v26 - Ap '80 - p124

  Pioneer Saddle Mystery
    SLJ - v22 - Mr '76 - p102

FRENCH, Michael   1944-
  ConAu 89

  The Throwing Season
    BL - v76 - Je 1 '80 - p1418
    CBRS - v8 - My '80 - p98
    KR - v48 - My 15 '80 - p650
    NYTBR - v85 - Ap 27 '80 - p56

FRESE, Dolores Warwick
see Warwick, Dolores

FRICK, Constance H   1913-
ConAu X, SmATA 6 (also known as
Irwin, Constance Frick)

The Comeback Guy
BS - v25 - N 1 '65 - p310
CSM - My 11 '61 - p5B
HB - v37 - Ag '61 - p346
KR - v29 - Ja 1 '61 - p16
LJ - v86 - Ap 15 '61 - p1694
NYTBR, pt.2 - My 14 '61 - p34

Five Against The Odds
BL - v52 - D 1 '55 - p149
KR - v23 - Je 1 '55 - p362
LJ - v80 - O 15 '55 - p2390
NYT - N 13 '55 - p20
SR - v38 - N 12 '55 - p68

FRIEDMAN, Ina Rosen   1926-
AuBYP SUP, ConAu 53

*Black Cop: A Biography Of
Tilmon O'Bryant*
BL - v70 - Jl 15 '74 - p1253
CCB-B - v28 - O '74 - p27
KR - v42 - Ap 15 '74 - p435
LJ - v99 - S 15 '74 - p2290
PW - v205 - F 18 '74 - p74

FRIEDMAN, Richard
see Fischler, Stanley I (co-author)

FRIES, Chloe

The Full Of The Moon
Hi Lo - Je '80 - p3

No Place To Hide
Hi Lo - v1 - Mr '80 - p4

FRIIS-BAASTAD, Babbis   1921-1970
ConAu 17R, ConLC 12, SmATA 7,
ThrBJA

Don't Take Teddy
CCB-B - v20 - Jl '67 - p169
KR - v35 - F 1 '67 - p137
LJ - v92 - My 15 '67 - p2020
NYTBR - v72 - My 21 '67 - p30
SR - v50 - Ap 22 '67 - p100

Kristy's Courage
KR - v33 - Jl 15 '65 - p678
LJ - v90 - N 15 '65 - p5076
NYTBR - v70 - D 12 '65 - p26

FRITZ, Jean   1915-
ChLR 2, ConAu 1R, MorBMP,
SmATA 1, ThrBJA, TwCCW 78

Brady
B&B - v16 - Ag '71 - pR12
BL - v57 - Ja 15 '61 - p300
HB - v36 - D '60 - p512
KR - v28 - Ag 15 '60 - p682
LJ - v85 - S 15 '60 - p3215
Obs - Ap 10 '66 - p20
Obs - Jl 25 '71 - p23
Spec - Je 3 '66 - p706
TLS - My 19 '66 - p434

Early Thunder
BL - v64 - D 1 '67 - p446
BS - v27 - O 1 '67 - p263
BW - v1 - O 1 '67 - p24
CCB-B - v21 - F '68 - p93
CLW - v39 - F '68 - p438
Comw - v87 - N 10 '67 - p180
HB - v43 - D '67 - p757
Inst - v77 - F '68 - p190
KR - v35 - O 1 '67 - p1218
LJ - v92 - N 15 '67 - p4260
NS - v77 - My 16 '69 - p700
NYTBR - v72 - O 22 '67 - p62
SR - v50 - N 11 '67 - p48
TLS - Ap 3 '69 - p350
TN - v24 - Ja '68 - p223

*What's The Big Idea, Ben
Franklin?*
BL - v73 - S 15 '76 - p174
BW - D 5 '76 - pH5
CCB-B - v30 - S '76 - p10
CE - v53 - Ja '77 - p152
Comw - v103 - N 19 '76 - p758
Cur R - v16 - D '77 - p363
HB - v52 - O '76 - p507
KR - v44 - Je 1 '76 - p636
LJ - v54 - F '77 - p211
NYTBR - Jl 4 '76 - p16
NYTBR - N 14 '76 - p52
PW - v209 - Je 7 '76 - p74
RT - v31 - O '77 - p18
SB - v13 - My '77 - p39

FRITZ, Jean (continued)
    SE - v41 - Ap '77 - p347
    SLJ - v23 - S '76 - p99
    Teacher - v94 - N '76 - p134

   Why Don't You Get A Horse, Sam
Adams?
    BB - v3 - Ap '75 - p3
    BL - v71 - D 15 '74 - p423
    BL - v71 - Mr 15 '75 - p766
    CCB-B - v28 - Ap '75 - p129
    CE - v52 - O '75 - p36
    Choice - v12 - N '75 - p1132
    Comw - v102 - N 21 '75 - p570
    HB - v51 - F '75 - p57
    KR - v43 - Ja 1 '75 - p20
    LJ - v99 - D 15 '74 - p3262
    NYTBR - N 3 '75 - p26
    NYTBR - N 3 '75 - p55
    Teacher - v92 - Ap '75 - p108

FROLOV, Vadim   1913-
AuBYP SUP, TwCCW 78B

   What It's All About
    BW - v2 - N 3 '68 - p30
    KR - v36 - Ag 1 '68 - p824
    NYTBR - v73 - N 3 '68 - p2
    PW - v194 - S 2 '68 - p58
    SR - v51 - N 9 '68 - p71

FROMAN, Robert Winslow   1917-
ConAu 1R, FourBJA, SmATA 8

   Seeing Things
    B&B - v22 - Je '77 - p72
    CCB-B - v28 - S '74 - p7
    EJ - v64 - F '75 - p102
    KR - v42 - Mr 1 '74 - p248
    LJ - v99 - S 15 '74 - p2245
    NYTBR - My 5 '74 - p38
    SLJ - v25 - N '78 - p30
    WLB - v48 - My '74 - p718

FUJA, Abayomi
AuBYP SUP

   Fourteen Hundred Cowries And
Other African Tales
    BL - v68 - S 1 '71 - p56
    CCB-B - v25 - N '71 - p42
    CE - v48 - Ap '72 - p377
    HB - v47 - Ag '71 - p379
    KR - v39 - Ap 1 '71 - p372

    LJ - v96 - D 15 '71 - p4158
    LJ - v96 - D 15 '71 - p4184

FULLER, Elizabeth

   My Search For The Ghost Of
Flight 401
    BL - v75 - Ap 1 '79 - p1212
    Kliatt - v13 - Spring '79 - p33

G

GAINES, Ernest J 1933-
ConAu 9R, ConLC 11, ConNov 76,
DcLB 2, SelBAA, WhoBlA 77

The Autobiography Of Miss Jane Pitman
A Lib - v2 - S '71 - p897
BL - v67 - Jl 15 '71 - p930
BL - v68 - Ap 1 '72 - p664
BS - v31 - N 1 '71 - p354
BS - v32 - Jl 1 '72 - p180
Bl W - v20 - O '71 - p88
CSM - v63 - Je 3 '71 - p9
CSM - v64 - N 26 '71 - pB3
Comw - v95 - Ja 21 '72 - p380
EJ - v63 - Ja '74 - p65
KR - v39 - F 15 '71 - p190
LJ - v96 - Mr 1 '71 - p860
LJ - v96 - Ap 15 '71 - p1536
LJ - v96 - D 15 '71 - p4161
Life - v70 - Ap 30 '71 - p18
Lis - v89 - F 8 '73 - p189
NS - v85 - F 9 '73 - p205
NW - v77 - My 3 '71 - p103
NYTBR - My 23 '71 - p6
NYTBR - D 5 '71 - p82
Nat - v212 - Ap 5 '71 - p436
Obs - F 4 '73 - p36
PW - v199 - Mr 8 '71 - p64
SR - v54 - My 1 '71 - p40
SR - v54 - N 27 '71 - p46
TLS - Mr 16 '73 - p303
TN - v28 - Ap '72 - p312
Time - v97 - My 10 '71 - pK13

GALBRAITH, Catherine Atwater

India: Now And Through Time
BL - v68 - Ap 1 '72 - p671
BS - v31 - D 15 '71 - p433
HB - v48 - Ap '72 - p158
LJ - v97 - F 15 '72 - p784

NYTBR - F 27 '72 - p8

GALLANT, Roy A 1924-
AuBYP, ConAu 5R, SmATA 4,
WrDr 80

Exploring The Universe
CSM - v60 - N 7 '68 - p89
KR - v36 - Je 15 '68 - p653
LJ - v93 - O 15 '68 - p3970
SB - v4 - S '68 - p98

Man Must Speak: The Story Of Language And How We Use It
BL - v66 - Je 15 '70 - p1272
BS - v29 - N 1 '69 - p306
KR - v37 - N 1 '69 - p1158
LJ - v95 - Jl '70 - p2539

Man's Reach For The Stars
BL - v68 - O 1 '71 - p159
BS - v31 - D 15 '71 - p433
CLW - v43 - My '72 - p536
KR - v39 - Ag 1 '71 - p818
LJ - v96 - S 15 '71 - p2928
SB - v7 - Mr '72 - p328

GARDAM, Jane 1928-
ConAu 49, TwCCW 78

The Summer After The Funeral
B&B - v19 - Ja '74 - p93
BL - v70 - F 1 '74 - p592
CCB-B - v27 - Ap '74 - p128
Comw - v99 - N 23 '73 - p216
HB - v50 - F '74 - p55
ILN - v265 - My '77 - p87
KR - v41 - N 1 '73 - p1211
KR - v41 - D 15 '73 - p1356
LJ - v98 - O 15 '73 - p3154
Lis - v90 - N 8 '73 - p641
NO - v12 - D 29 '73 - p15
NS - v86 - N 9 '73 - p699

GARDAM, Jane (continued)
NYTBR - F 17 '74 - p8
Obs - Mr 6 '77 - p22
Spec - v231 - D 22 '73 - p822
TLS - N 23 '73 - p1429

GARDEN, Nancy   1938-
AuBYP SUP, ConAu 33R, SmATA
12, WrDr 80

The Loners
BL - v69 - F 1 '73 - p524
CCB-B - v26 - Ap '73 - p123
KR - v40 - N 1 '72 - p1245
LJ - v98 - Mr 15 '73 - p1012
NYTBR, pt.2 - N 5 '72 - p2

Vampires
KR - v41 - Mr 1 '73 - p261
LJ - v98 - Jl '73 - p2199
Teacher - v90 - My '73 - p78

Werewolves
KR - v41 - Ap 1 '73 - p400
LJ - v98 - Jl '73 - p2199
Teacher - v90 - My '73 - p78

GARDNER, Lewis
see Burger, John Robert (co-author)

GARDNER, Martin   1914-
AuBYP SUP, ConAu 73, SmATA 16,
WhoE 74

*Codes, Ciphers, And Secret
Writing*
BL - v69 - F 15 '73 - p572
CCB-B - v26 - F '73 - p89
Inst - v83 - My '74 - p97
KR - v40 - N 15 '72 - p1316
LJ - v98 - My 15 '73 - p1681
PW - v203 - Ja 15 '73 - p65
Par - v48 - Ap '73 - p67
SB - v9 - My '73 - p62

GARFIELD, Leon   1921-
ConAu 17R, ConLC 12, FourBJA,
SmATA 1, TwCCW 78, WhoChL

Smith
B&B - v12 - Je '67 - p36
B&B - v13 - Ag '68 - p49
BL - v64 - F 1 '68 - p637
BS - v27 - N 1 '67 - p313

BW - v1 - N 5 '67 - p43
CCB-B - v21 - My '68 - p141
Comw - v87 - N 10 '67 - p181
HB - v43 - D '67 - p758
KR - v35 - Jl 1 '67 - p746
LJ - v92 - N 15 '67 - p4250
LR - v21 - Summer '67 - p93
Lis - v77 - My 18 '67 - p660
NS - v73 - My 26 '67 - p732
NYTBR - v72 - N 26 '67 - p62
PW - v192 - O 23 '67 - p52
SR - v51 - F 24 '68 - p51
Spec - v218 - Je 2 '67 - p654
TLS - My 25 '67 - p446

GARLITS, Don

*King Of The Dragsters: The Story
Of Big Daddy Garlits*
KR - v35 - Ag 1 '67 - p923
LJ - v93 - F 15 '68 - p896

GARRATY, John A   1920-
ConAu 1R, DrAS 78H, SmATA 23,
WhoAm 78

*Theodore Roosevelt: The Strenuous
Life*
BL - v64 - S 15 '67 - p130
BS - v27 - Ag 1 '67 - p183
CCB-B - v21 - D '67 - p54
CLW - v39 - Ja '68 - p373
KR - v35 - Je 1 '67 - p652
LJ - v92 - N 15 '67 - p4260
NYTBR - v72 - Jl 16 '67 - p20
PW - v191 - Je 5 '67 - p176

GARRIGUE, Sheila   1931-
AuBYP SUP, ConAu 69, SmATA 21

Between Friends
BB - v6 - N '78 - p4
BL - v74 - Je 15 '78 - p1616
CCB-B - v32 - O '78 - p28
CLW - v50 - S '78 - p92
Cur R - v17 - O '78 - p272
Inst - v88 - N '78 - p140
KR - v46 - Je 15 '78 - p636
NYTBR - Ap 30 '78 - p28
PW - v213 - My 22 '78 - p233
Par - v53 - O '78 - p40
SLJ - v24 - My '78 - p66
Teacher - v96 - O '78 - p162

GARRISON, Webb B   1919-
ConAu 1R, SmATA 24

> *What's In A Word?*
> BL - v62 - D 1 '65 - p344
> LJ - v90 - N 15 '65 - p4979
> SR - v49 - Mr 19 '66 - p35

> *Why You Say It*
> BL - v52 - O 1 '55 - p49
> KR - v23 - Ag 1 '55 - p568

GATES, Doris   1901-
Au&ICB, ConAu 1R, JBA 51,
SmATA 1, TwCCW 78

> *Blue Willow*
> BL - v37 - N 15 '40 - p122
> CSM - N 11 '40 - p9
> HB - v16 - N '40 - p430
> IIB - v16 - N '40 - p437
> LJ   v65   N 15 '40 - p983
> NY - v16 - D 7 '40 - p128
> NYT - Ja 5 '41 - p10
> Nat - v151 - N 9 '40 - p455
> New R - v103 - D 16 '40 - p844

GATHJE, Curtis

> *The Disco Kid*
> BL - v76 - O 15 '79 - p347
> CBRS - v8 - D '79 - p37
> Hi Lo - v1 - D '79 - p4
> SLJ - v26 - N '79 - p77

GAULT, Clare   1925-
ConAu 97

> *Pele: The King Of Soccer*
> Cur R - v15 - D '76 - p315

GAULT, Frank
see Gault, Clare (co-author)

GAULT, William Campbell   1910-
ConAu 49, EncMys, SmATA 8

> *Backfield Challenge*
> BL - v64 - O 1 '67 - p176
> CCB-B - v21 - S '67 - p5
> KR - v35 - Ap 15 '67 - p505
> LJ - v92 - My 15 '67 - p2042
> SR - v50 - Jl 22 '67 - p43

> *The Big Stick*
> BL - v72 - N 1 '75 - p366
> KR - v43 - Ag 1 '75 - p856
> SLJ - v22 - D '75 - p69

> *The Checkered Flag*
> BS - v24 - My 15 '64 - p87
> HB - v40 - Ag '64 - p380
> LJ - v89 - My 15 '64 - p2228

> *Dirt Track Summer*
> BL - v57 - Ap 15 '61 - p523
> CSM - My 11 '61 - p5B
> KR - v28 - D 15 '60 - p1034
> NYTBR, pt.2 - My 14 '61 - p34

> *Drag Strip*
> BL - v56 - Ja 1 '60 - p271
> CSM - N 5 '60 - p3B
> KR - v27 - Ag 1 '59 - p553
> LJ - v85 - Ja 15 '60 - p358
> NYTBR, pt.2   N 1 '59 - p28

> *The Long Green*
> BL - v62 - O 1 '65 - p144
> BS - v25 - Ap 15 '65 - p51
> KR - v33 - Ja 15 '65 - p65
> LJ - v90 - Mr 15 '65 - p1559

> *Quarterback Gamble*
> BL - v67 - Ja 1 '71 - p372
> CLW - v43 - O '71 - p116
> KR - v38 - Jl 15 '70 - p748
> LJ - v95 - D 15 '70 - p4380
> LJ - v96 - Ja 15 '71 - p284

> *Speedway Challenge*
> BL - v53 - O 15 '56 - p96
> KR - v24 - S 1 '56 - p634
> NYTBR - S 16 '56 - p38
> SR - v39 - N 17 '56 - p70

> *Thin Ice*
> BL - v75 - N 1 '78 - p478
> KR - v46 - S 1 '78 - p953

> *Thunder Road*
> BL - v49 - O 15 '52 - p72
> HB - v28 - D '52 - p426
> KR - v20 - S 15 '52 - p606
> LJ - v77 - O 1 '52 - p1668
> NYTBR - S 28 '52 - p38
> SR - v35 - N 15 '52 - p62

GEE, Maurine H
AuBYP SUP

> *Firestorm*
> KR - v35 - D 15 '67 - p1471
> Obs - My 19 '68 - p1309

GELMAN, Steve 1934-
AuBYP SUP, ConAu 25R, SmATA
3, WhoE 74

> *Young Olympic Champions*
> BL - v70 - O 1 '73 - p170
> KR - v41 - Ap 15 '73 - p459

GEMME, Leila Boyle 1942-
ConAu 81

> *Ten-Speed Taylor*
> BL - v75 - O 15 '78 - p390
> RT - v32 - My '79 - p975
> SLJ - v25 - D '78 - p71

GEORGE, Jean Craighead 1919-
ChLR 1, ConAu 5R, IlsCB 1946,
MorJA, SmATA 2, TwCCW 78

> *Julie Of The Wolves*
> BL - v69 - F 1 '73 - p529
> BS - v7 - My 13 '73 - p6
> BS - v33 - Ap 15 '73 - p45
> CCB-B - v26 - Mr '73 - p105
> CE - v49 - Mr '73 - p317
> HB - v49 - F '73 - p54
> KR - v40 - N 15 '72 - p1312
> KR - v40 - D 15 '72 - p1418
> LJ - v98 - Ja 15 '73 - p267
> NYTBR - Ja 21 '73 - p8
> PW - v203 - F 12 '73 - p66
> Teacher - v90 - My '73 - p43

> *River Rats, Inc.*
> BL - v75 - Mr 15 '79 - p1156
> HB - v55 - Ap '79 - p193
> KR - v47 - Jl 1 '79 - p740
> PW - v215 - F 12 '79 - p127
> SLJ - v25 - Mr '79 - p139

> *Who Really Killed Cock Robin?*
> BL - v68 - D 15 '71 - p366
> BW - v5 - N 7 '71 - p14
> CCB-B - v25 - Ja '72 - p74
> CE - v48 - My '72 - p421
> CSM - v64 - D 30 '71 - p6
> HB - v47 - D '71 - p610

> KR - v39 - S 1 '71 - p945
> LJ - v96 - D 15 '71 - p4184
> SB - v8 - My '72 - p49
> SR - v55 - F 19 '72 - p80
> TN - v28 - Ap '72 - p309

GERBER, Dan 1940-
ConAu 33R, DrAF 76, DrAP 75

> *Indy*
> BL - v73 - Jl 1 '77 - p1626
> KR - v45 - Mr 1 '77 - p258
> LJ - v102 - Mr 15 '77 - p724
> SLJ - v24 - Mr '78 - p106

GERINGER, Laura

> *Seven True Bear Stories*
> Hi Lo - v1 - F '80 - p3
> LA - v56 - N '79 - p930
> PW - v215 - Ap 30 '79 - p114
> SLJ - v25 - Ap '79 - p42
> SR - v6 - My 26 '79 - p63

GERSH, Marvin J

> *The Handbook Of Adolescence*
> BL - v68 - D 15 '71 - p345
> KR - v39 - Je 1 '71 - p595
> LJ - v96 - N 15 '71 - p3917

GERSON, Corinne 1927-
ConAu 93

> *Passing Through*
> BL - v75 - O 1 '78 - p284
> SLJ - v25 - O '78 - p154

GIBSON, Walter B 1897-
BioIn 7, EncMys, WhNAA

> *Master Magicians: Their Lives
> And Most Famous Tricks*
> BL - v63 - N 1 '66 - p308
> KR - v34 - Je 1 '66 - p542
> LJ - v91 - S 15 '66 - p4350

GILBER, E S
see Erskine, H Keith (co-author)

GILBERT, Miriam 1919-
ConAu X, WhoAmW 77, WrDr 80
(also known as Presberg, Miriam
Goldstein)

GILBERT, Miriam (continued)

> *Glory Be! The Career Of A Young Hair Stylist*
> KR - v35 - Ap 1 '67 - p423

GILBERT, Sara Dulaney 1943-
AuBYP SUP, ConAu 57, SmATA 11

> *Fat Free*
> BB - v3 - Ag '75 - p4
> BL - v71 - Mr 1 '75 - p690
> CCB-B - v29 - O '75 - p27
> CLW - v47 - N '75 - p187
> Comw - v102 - N 21 '75 - p571
> KR - v43 - F 1 '75 - p129
> NYTBR - My 4 '75 - p25
> PW - v207 - My 26 '75 - p60

GILBRETH, Frank B, Jr 1911-
ConAu 9R, SmATA 2, WhoAm 78

> *Cheaper By The Dozen*
> NYTBR - Ja 9 '49 - p18

GILDEA, William
see Brown, Larry (co-author)

GILFOND, Henry
ConAu 21R, NatPD, SmATA 2

> *Genealogy: How To Find Your Roots*
> BL - v74 - Ap 15 '78 - p1348
> SLJ - v25 - S '78 - p157

GILL, Derek L T 1919-
ConAu 49, SmATA 9

> *Tom Sullivan's Adventures In Darkness*
> BL - v73 - My 1 '77 - p1351
> CCB-B - v30 - Je '77 - p157
> KR - v44 - N 15 '76 - p1227
> Kliatt - v12 - Winter '78 - p22
> SLJ - v23 - F '77 - p71

GILLIS, Ruby

> *Get Where You're Going*
> Hi Lo - v2 - S '80 - p6

GILMAN, Dorothy 1923-
ConAu X, SmATA 5, WhoAm 78
(also known as Butters, Dorothy Gilman)

> *The Elusive Mrs. Polifax*
> BL - v68 - D 15 '71 - p353
> BS - v31 - O 15 '71 - p314
> KR - v39 - Jl 15 '71 - p771
> LJ - v96 - S 1 '71 - p2674
> NYT - v121 - Ja 1 '72 - p17
> NYTBR - D 12 '71 - p39
> PW - v200 - Jl 5 '71 - p49

GIPSON, Fred 1908-1973
ConAu 1R, ConAu 45, SmATA 2,
SmATA 24N, ThrBJA, TwCCW 78

> *Old Yeller*
> BL - v52 - Je 15 '56 - p421
> BL - v53 - S 1 '56 - p21
> CSM - Jl 12 '56 - p7
> HB - v32 - O '56 - p371
> KR - v24 - My 1 '56 - p320
> LJ - v81 - Jl '56 - p1699
> NY - v32 - Jl 14 '56 - p93
> NYTBR - Jl 15 '56 - p5
> SR - v39 - Jl 21 '56 - p17
> SR - v39 - N 17 '56 - p70
> Time - v68 - Jl 23 '56 - p88

> *Savage Sam*
> NYTBR - F 25 '62 - p37

GIRION, Barbara 1937-
ConAu 85

> *A Tangle Of Roots*
> BL - v75 - My 1 '79 - p1356
> CSM - v71 - Jl 9 '79 - pB6
> KR - v47 - Ap 1 '79 - p392
> SLJ - v25 - My '79 - p71

GLASER, Dianne 1937-
ConAu 77

> *The Diary Of Trilby Frost*
> BB - v4 - N '76 - p2
> BL - v72 - My 1 '76 - p1264
> HB - v52 - Ag '76 - p404
> KR - v44 - My 1 '76 - p541
> PW - v209 - Je 28 '76 - p99
> SE - v41 - Ap '77 - p350
> SLJ - v23 - S '76 - p133

GLASNER, Lynne
  see Thypin, Marilyn (co-author)

GLASS, Frankcina

    Marvin And Tige
      BL - v74 - D 1 '77 - p601
      BS - v37 - Ja '78 - p302
      CSM - v70 - Ja 23 '78 - p11
      KR - v45 - Ag 15 '77 - p869
      LJ - v102 - O 15 '77 - p2181
      PW - v212 - Ag 29 '77 - p354
      SLJ - v24 - F '78 - p69
      WCRB - v4 - Ja '78 - p30
      WLB - v52 - Ja '78 - p430

GLENDINNING, Richard 1917-
  ConAu 21R, WhoS&SW 76

    Circus Days Under The Big Top
      LJ - v95 - D 15 '70 - p4371

GLICKMAN, William G

    Winners On The Tennis Court
      BL - v74 - Ap 15 '78 - p1357

GLUBOK, Shirley 1933-
  ChLR 1, ConAu 5R, MorBMP,
  SmATA 6, ThrBJA, WhoAmW 77

    Art And Archaeology
      BL - v62 - Jl 15 '66 - p1086
      CCB-B - v20 - S '66 - p9
      CSM - v58 - N 3 '66 - pB5
      KR - v34 - My 1 '66 - p476
      LJ - v91 - Je 15 '66 - p3258
      NYTBR - v71 - My 8 '66 - p34
      PW - v189 - My 30 '66 - p89
      SB - v2 - D '66 - p198
      SR - v49 - My 14 '66 - p42

    The Art Of Ancient Peru
      BL - v63 - D 1 '66 - p416
      CCB-B - v20 - Ja '67 - p73
      CLW - v38 - Ja '67 - p336
      HB - v43 - F '67 - p87
      LJ - v91 - D 15 '66 - p6191
      NH - v76 - N '67 - p29
      NYT - v116 - F 2 '67 - p26
      SR - v49 - N 12 '66 - p50

    The Art Of Colonial America
      BL - v67 - N 15 '70 - p268
      CE - v47 - F '71 - p266

      CLW - v42 - D '70 - p257
      Comw - v93 - N 20 '70 - p206
      HB - v47 - Je '71 - p299
      KR - v38 - Jl 15 '70 - p745
      LJ - v95 - O 15 '70 - p3626
      NYTBR, pt.2 - N 8 '70 - p3
      PW - v198 - O 19 '70 - p53

    The Art Of The New American
    Nation
      BL - v68 - Jl 1 '72 - p942
      CCB-B - v26 - N '72 - p42
      HB - v48 - Ag '72 - p386
      KR - v40 - My 1 '72 - p538
      NYTBR - Jl 2 '72 - p8
      PW - v201 - My 15 '72 - p54

    The Art Of The Spanish In The
    United States And Puerto Rico
      BL - v69 - Ja 1 '73 - p448
      BL - v69 - Ja 15 '73 - p479
      CC - v89 - N 29 '72 - p1218
      CCB-B - v26 - Mr '73 - p106
      CE - v49 - Ap '73 - p378
      HB - v49 - F '73 - p64
      Inst - v82 - N '72 - p132
      KR - v40 - O 1 '72 - p1147
      LJ - v98 - Mr 15 '73 - p1002
      PW - v203 - Ja 15 '73 - p65

GOFFSTEIN, M B 1940-
  ChLR 3, ConAu 21R, FourBJA,
  IlsCB 1967, SmATA 8, WhoAmW 77

    Daisy Summerfield's Style
      BS - v35 - D '75 - p300
      BW - F 11 '79 - pF2
      CCB-B - v29 - F '76 - p96
      HB - v52 - F '76 - p56
      J Read - v20 - O '76 - p80
      KR - v438 - O 1 '75 - p1137
      PW - v208 - S 8 '75 - p60
      SLJ - v22 - N '75 - p89

    The Underside Of The Leaf
      BL - v69 - S 15 '72 - p86
      BW - v6 - My 7 '72 - p15
      CCB-B - v26 - O '72 - p25
      EJ - v61 - D '72 - p1385
      KR - v40 - Ap 15 '72 - p485
      KR - v40 - D 15 '72 - p1419
      LJ - v97 - N 15 '72 - p3813
      NYTBR - My 28 '72 - p8
      PW - v201 - My 15 '72 - p53

GOGOLAK, Peter 1942-
WhoFtbl 74

> *Kicking The Football Soccer Style*
> BW - v6 - D 3 '72 - p10
> LJ - v98 - Ja 15 '73 - p179
> LJ - v98 - My 15 '73 - p1704

GOHMAN, Fred 1918-
ConAu 5R

> *Spider Webb Mysteries*
> LJ - v94 - My 15 '69 - p2124

GOLD, Sharlya
ConAu 61, SmATA 9

> *Amelia Quackenbush*
> Am - v129 - D 1 '73 - p429
> BL - v70 - Ja 1 '74 - p488
> CSM - v66 - My 1 '74 - pF4
> KR - v41 - N 1 '73 - p1200
> LJ - v99 - Ja 15 '74 - p209

> *Time To Take Sides*
> BB - v5 - My '77 - p4
> CLW - v48 - Mr '77 - p358
> Inst - v86 - N '76 - p146
> KR - v44 - O 1 '76 - p1093
> SLJ - v23 - Ja '77 - p92

GOLDREICH, Gloria

> *Lori*
> BL - v75 - My 15 '79 - p1432
> KR - v47 - My 1 '79 - p522
> SLJ - v25 - My '79 - p72

GOLDSMITH, Howard 1943-
SmATA 24

> *Invasion: 2200 A.D.*
> CBRS - v8 - D '79 - p37
> Hi Lo - v1 - N '79 - p5
> J Read - v23 - Ap '80 - p662
> SLJ - v26 - N '79 - p77

GOLDSTON, Robert C 1927-
ConAu 17R, FourBJA, SmATA 6,
WhoAm 78

> *Pearl Harbor*
> BS - v32 - D 15 '72 - p445
> LJ - v98 - My 15 '73 - p1688

GOLDWATER, Daniel 1922-
WhoAm 76

> *Bridges And How They Are Built*
> BL - v62 - Ja 15 '66 - p486
> CCB-B - v19 - Ap '66 - p129
> Comw - v83 - N 5 '65 - p161
> HB - v41 - D '65 - p646
> KR - v33 - Ag 15 '65 - p825
> LJ - v90 - N 15 '65 - p5090
> NYTBR - v70 - N 28 '65 - p46
> SB - v2 - My '66 - p56

GONZALEZ, Gloria 1940-
ConAu 65, NatPD, SmATA 23

> *The Glad Man*
> CCB-B - v29 - Je '76 - p156
> KR - v43 - S 15 '75 - p1066
> Kliatt - v13 - Fall '79 - p7
> PW - v208 - Ag 25 '75 - p293
> SLJ - v22 - O '75 - p98

GOODMAN, Burton

> *Spotlight On Literature*
> Hi Lo - v2 - O '80 - p3

GOODWIN, Harold L 1914-
ConAu 1R, SmATA 13, WhoE 77

> *All About Rockets And Space
> Flight*
> LJ - v95 - D 15 '70 - p4383
> SB - v6 - S '70 - p165

GORDON, Ethel Edison 1915-
ConAu 53, WrDr 80

> *Where Does The Summer Go?*
> BW - v1 - O 22 '67 - p14
> CCB-B - v21 - Ja '68 - p78
> CSM - v59 - N 2 '67 - pB11
> KR - v35 - Je 1 '67 - p648
> LJ - v92 - O 15 '67 - p3863
> SR - v50 - Ag 19 '67 - p35

GORDON, Gordon 1912-
ConAu 5R, EncMys, IndAu 1917

> *Undercover Cat Prowls Again*
> BS - v26 - O 15 '66 - p264
> HB - v43 - F '67 - p93
> KR - v34 - Jl 15 '66 - p718
> LJ - v91 - O 15 '66 - p5264

GORDON, Gordon (continued)
LJ - v91 - D 1 '66 - p6005
NYTBR - v71 - O 16 '66 - p54
Punch - v252 - Je 14 '67 - p889
SR - v49 - D 31 '66 - p28

GORDON, Mildred D
see Gordon, Gordon (co-author)

GORDON, Sol   1923-
AmM&WS 78S, AuBYP SUP,
ConAu 53, SmATA 11

*Facts About Sex For Today's
Youth*
BL - v70 - O 15 '73 - p221
BL - v70 - O 15 '73 - p232
KR - v41 - Ap 15 '73 - p467
LJ - v98 - S 15 '73 - p2664

Facts About VD For Today's Youth
BL - v70 - O 15 '73 - p221
Inst - v83 - N '73 - p126
KR - v41 - Ag 15 '73 - p890
LJ - v98 - N 15 '73 - p3464

GORENSTEIN, Shirley   1928-
ConAu 73, WhoAmW 75

Introduction To Archaeology
A Anth - v68 - Ag '66 - p1080
BL - v62 - F 15 '66 - p564
CE - v43 - O '66 - p103
Choice - v3 - My '66 - p246
LJ - v91 - Ja 15 '66 - p252
LJ - v91 - F 15 '66 - p1084
NH - v75 - N '66 - p24
NYRB - v6 - F 17 '66 - p20
SA - v215 - D '66 - p144
SB - v1 - Mr '66 - p216
Sci - v151 - Mr 11 '66 - p1210

GORHAM, Charles   1911-1975
AmNov, ConAu 1R, ConAu 61

*The Lion Of Judah: Haile Selassie
I, Emperor Of Ethiopia*
Am - v115 - Jl 2 '66 - p16
BL - v62 - Je 1 '66 - p959
BS - v26 - Ap 1 '66 - p18
CCB-B - v20 - S '66 - p10
KR - v34 - Ja 15 '66 - p66
LJ - v91 - My 15 '66 - p2706
NYTBR - v71 - Ap 17 '66 - p30

NYTBR - v71 - D 4 '66 - p66
SR - v49 - My 14 '66 - p42

GORODETZKY, Charles W   1937-
AmM&WS 76P, AuBYP SUP,
WhoS&SW 78

*What You Should Know About
Drugs*
BL - v67 - D 15 '70 - p341
BL - v67 - Ap 1 '71 - p660
CCB-B - v24 - F '71 - p91
CE - v48 - O '71 - p29
CLW - v42 - My '71 - p578
Comw - v93 - N 20 '70 - p205
HB - v47 - Ap '71 - p181
KR - v38 - O 15 '70 - p1154
LJ - v95 - D 15 '70 - p4350
NYTBR - F 7 '71 - p33
NYTBR, pt.2 - N 8 '70 - p36
PW - v198 - N 16 '70 - p77
SB - v6 - D '70 - p251
TN - v27 - Ap '71 - p305

GRABER, Alexander
see Cordell, Alexander

GRABLE, Ron
see Olney, Ross R (co-author) -
The Racing Bugs

GRAFF, Stewart   1908-
AuBYP, ConAu 49, SmATA 9

The Story Of World War II
BL - v74 - My 15 '78 - p1492
Comw - v105 - N 10 '78 - p734
KR - v46 - Ja 15 '78 - p49
SLJ - v24 - Mr '78 - p128

GRAHAM, Lorenz Bell   1902-
ConAu 9R, SelBAA, SmATA 2,
ThrBJA, TwCCW 78, WhoBlA 77

North Town
Kliatt - v12 - Winter '78 - p7

Whose Town?
BL - v65 - Jl 1 '69 - p1226
BW - v3 - My 4 '69 - p3
CCB-B - v22 - Je '69 - p158
HB - v45 - Ag '69 - p416
KR - v37 - Ap 15 '69 - p452
LJ - v94 - Je 15 '69 - p2509

GRAHAM, Lorenz Bell (continued)
  SR - v52 - My 10 '69 - p59

GRAHAM, Robin Lee   1949-
ConAu 49, SmATA 7

The Boy Who Sailed Around The World Alone
  CCB-B - v27 - Je '74 - p156
  CSM - v65 - N 7 '73 - pB7
  CSM - v67 - Je 10 '75 - p16
  LJ - v99 - S 15 '74 - p2268
  PW - v205 - Ja 28 '74 - p301

Dove
  B&B - v18 - Mr '73 - p83
  BL - v69 - O 1 '72 - p126
  BL - v69 - O 1 '72 - p138
  BS - v32 - Je 1 '72 - p111
  BS - v33 - Ag 1 '73 - p215
  BW - v6 - Je 18 '72 - p5
  BW - v7 - Je 24 '73 - p13
  EJ - v62 - D '73 - p1298
  KR - v40 - Ap 1 '72 - p445
  LJ - v97 - Ag '72 - p2596
  LJ - v97 - D 15 '72 - p4058
  LJ - v97 - D 15 '72 - p4095
  PW - v201 - My 1 '72 - p44
  TN - v29 - Ap '73 - p257
  Yacht - v133 - F '73 - p92

GRAHAM, Shirley   1907?-1977
ConAu X, CurBio 77N, MorJA,
SelBAA, SmATA X, WhoBlA 77
(also known as Dubois, Shirley
Graham)

*The Story Of Phillis Wheatley,
Poetess Of The American
Revolution*
  BL - v46 - O 15 '49 - p69
  KR - v17 - Ag 15 '49 - p432
  LJ - v74 - O 15 '49 - p1549
  LJ - v74 - D 15 '49 - p1920
  NYTBR - N 13 '49 - p30
  SR - v32 - N 12 '49 - p38

GRANT, C L

The Hour Of The Oxrun Dead
  BL - v74 - O 15 '77 - p355
  KR - v45 - Ag 1 '77 - p801

GRAVES, Charles P   1911-1972
AuBYP, ConAu 5R, ConAu 37R,
SmATA 4

John F. Kennedy
  RR - v86 - Mr '69 - p172

GRAY, Elizabeth Janet   1902-
ConAu X, JBA 51, SmATA 6,
TwCCW 78 (also known as Vining,
Elizabeth Gray)

Adam Of The Road
  BL - v38 - My 1 '42 - p334
  CSM - Je 29 '42 - p10
  HB - v18 - My '42 - p178
  Inst - v82 - My '73 - p78
  LJ - v67 - My 15 '42 - p476
  LJ - v67 - O 15 '42 - p890
  NY - v18 - My 23 '42 - p75
  NYTBR - My 17 '42 - p8
  SR - v25 - D 5 '42 - p60

GREAVES, Griselda

*The Burning Thorn: An Anthology
Of Poetry*
  BL - v68 - Mr 15 '72 - p612
  CCB-B - v25 - F '72 - p91
  KR - v39 - S 15 '71 - p1026
  LJ - v96 - D 15 '71 - p4189
  SR - v55 - Ja 15 '72 - p47
  TLS - Jl 2 '71 - p773

GREEN, Gerald   1922-
ASpks, WhoAm 78, WorAu, WrDr 80

Girl
  BL - v74 - N 15 '77 - p527
  KR - v45 - Ag 15 '77 - p870
  LJ - v102 - N 15 '77 - p2367
  PW - v212 - Ag 22 '77 - p60

GREEN, Iris

Anything For A Friend
  Hi Lo - v2 - N '80 - p5

Second Chance
  BL - v75 - Ap 15 '79 - p1290
  Hi Lo - v1 - D '79 - p5

GREEN, Sheila Ellen
see Greenwald, Sheila

GREENE, Bette 1934-
ChLR 2, ConAu 53, SmATA 8,
TwCCW 78, WhoAm 78

The Summer Of My German Soldier
BL - v70 - N 15 '73 - p334
BL - v70 - N 15 '73 - p339
BL - v70 - Mr 15 '74 - p827
BS - v33 - D 15 '73 - p428
BS - v34 - D 15 '74 - p428
CCB-B - v27 - F '74 - p94
CLW - v47 - N '75 - p166
Choice - v12 - N '75 - p1132
EJ - v64 - O '75 - p92
EJ - v66 - O '77 - p58
GP - v13 - Ja '75 - p2557
HB - v50 - F '74 - p56
JB - v39 - F '75 - p62
J Read - v22 - N '78 - p126
KR - v41 - O 15 '73 - p1170
LJ - v98 - O 15 '73 - p3154
NYTBR - N 4 '73 - p29
NYTBR - N 4 '73 - p52
NYTBR - D 2 '73 - p79
NYTBR - N 10 '74 - p44
Obs - D 8 '74 - p30
PW - v204 - Ag 27 '73 - p280
TES - D 9 '77 - p21

GREENE, Constance C 1924-
ConAu 61, FourBJA, SmATA 11,
TwCCW 78, WrDr 80

Beat The Turtle Drum
BL - v73 - N 15 '76 - p472
BW - N 7 '76 - pG8
CCB-B - v30 - Ap '77 - p124
Choice - v14 - N '77 - p1178
Comw - v103 - N 19 '76 - p762
HB - v52 - D '76 - p624
KR - v44 - Ag 1 '76 - p845
LA - v54 - Ap '77 - p441
NYTBR - N 14 '76 - p52
NYTBR - N 21 '76 - p62
NYTBR - Ja 27 '80 - p35
PW - v210 - Ag 9 '76 - p78
RT - v31 - O '77 - p15
SLJ - v23 - F '77 - p64
SLJ - v25 - D '78 - p33
Teacher - v94 - My '77 - p109

GREENE, Shep

The Boy Who Drank Too Much
BL - v75 - My 1 '79 - p1356
CBRS - v7 - Je '79 - p107
CCB-B - v33 - S '79 - p9
HB - v55 - Ap '79 - p198
Hi Lo - v1 - S '79 - p3
KR - v47 - Je 1 '79 - p641
PW - v215 - My 21 '79 - p69
SLJ - v25 - My '79 - p84
WLB - v54 - N '79 - p184

GREENFELD, Howard
AuBYP SUP, ConAu 81, SmATA 19

Pablo Picasso
BL - v67 - Jl 1 '71 - p905
BW - v5 - My 9 '71 - p12
CCB-B - v25 - Mr '72 - p107
Choice - v8 - Je '71 - p540
LJ - v97 - F 15 '72 - p784
PW - v200 - Jl 5 '71 - p50
TN - v28 - Ja '72 - p203

GREENWALD, Sheila 1934-
ConAu X, IlsCB 1957, SmATA 8
(also known as Green, Sheila Ellen)

The Atrocious Two
BL - v74 - Jl 1 '78 - p1678
CCB-B - v32 - S '78 - p9
KR - v46 - Mr 15 '78 - p305
SLJ - v24 - My '78 - p84

GREENYA, John

One Punch Away
Hi Lo - v1 - My '80 - p3

GREY, Elizabeth (pseud.) 1917-
Au&Wr 71, AuBYP (real name:
Hogg, Beth)

Friend Within The Gates: The Story Of Nurse Edith Cavell
BL - v57 - Jl 15 '61 - p699
CSM - My 11 '61 - p7B
HB - v37 - D '61 - p568
LJ - v86 - Je 15 '61 - p2364
NYTBR - Ag 6 '61 - p20
SR - v44 - My 13 '61 - p52
TLS - N 25 '60 - pR26

GRIESE, Bob   1945-
CelR, WhoAm 78, WhoFtbl 74

Offensive Football
BW - v6 - D 3 '72 - p10
LJ - v98 - Ja 15 '73 - p179
LJ - v98 - My 15 '73 - p1704
Nat R - v24 - Jl 21 '72 - p801

GRIPE, Maria   1923-
ConAu 29R, SmATA 2, ThrBJA,
TwCCW 78B

Pappa Pellerin's Daughter
B&B - v11 - Je '66 - p66
BS - v26 - Ag 1 '66 - p174
CCB-B - v20 - S '66 - p11
KR - v34 - My 1 '66 - p479
LJ - v91 - O 15 '66 - p5229
NYTBR - v71 - S 18 '66 - p30
Obs - Ap 10 '66 - p20
PW - v189 - Je 13 '66 - p128
Punch - v250 - Ap 20 '66 - p594
SR - v49 - Je 25 '66 - p61
Spec - Je 3 '66 - p706
TLS - My 19 '66 - p430

GRUBER, Ruth
ConAu 25R, ForWC 70, WhoWorJ
72

*Felisa Rincon De Gautier: The
Mayor Of San Juan*
BL - v69 - My 15 '73 - p907
CCB-B - v26 - Ap '73 - p124
KR - v40 - N 1 '72 - p1249
NYTBR - D 17 '72 - p8

GUESS, Edward Preston
see Preston, Edward

GUGLIOTTA, Bobette   1918-
ConAu 41R, SmATA 7

*Nolle Smith: Cowboy, Engineer,
Statesman*
BL - v68 - Ap 1 '72 - p672
LJ - v97 - Jl '72 - p2489

GUILCHER, Jean Michel

A Fern Is Born
BL - v68 - Mr 1 '72 - p563
CCB-B - v25 - F '72 - p92

CLW - v43 - Ap '72 - p479
Inst - v81 - Je '72 - p66
SR - v55 - Ja 15 '72 - p47
TLS - Jl 14 '72 - p815

GUNTHER, John   1901-1970
ConAu 9R, ConAu 25R, CurBio 61,
OxAm, SmATA 2, WhAm 6

Death Be Not Proud
BL - v45 - Mr 1 '49 - p224
Comw - v49 - F 18 '49 - p475
EJ - v62 - N '73 - p1189
HB - v25 - My '49 - p241
J Read - v22 - N '78 - p126
KR - v16 - Jl 15 '48 - p350
LJ - v74 - F 1 '49 - p197
NS - v37 - Je 18 '49 - p654
NY - v25 - F 26 '49 - p98
NYTBR - F 6 '49 - p6
SR - v32 - Mr 5 '49 - p27
Spec - v182 - My 20 '49 - p700
TLS - My 27 '49 - p348
Time - v53 - F 7 '49 - p92

GUTMAN, Bill
AuBYP SUP

Dr. J
BL - v74 - O 15 '77 - p381
SLJ - v24 - D '77 - p65

Great Baseball Stories
BL - v74 - Jl 1 '78 - p1683
BS - v38 - O '78 - p230
SLJ - v24 - My '78 - p88

Mark Fidrych
BL - v74 - O 15 '77 - p381
SLJ - v24 - D '77 - p65

Modern Baseball Superstars
Comw - v99 - N 23 '73 - p220
KR - v41 - N 1 '73 - p1210
LJ - v99 - Ap 15 '74 - p1219

Modern Football Superstars
SLJ - v21 - Ap '75 - p52

Modern Hockey Superstars
CCB-B - v30 - Ap '77 - p124
Inst - v86 - My '77 - p121
SLJ - v23 - D '76 - p71

GUTMAN, Bill (continued)

Modern Soccer Superstars
Hi Lo - v1 - Ap '80 - p3
SLJ - v26 - My '80 - p88

Modern Women Superstars
BL - v74 - Ja 15 '78 - p809
BL - v74 - Ja 15 '78 - p817
CCB-B - v31 - Je '78 - p160
SLJ - v24 - Mr '78 - p128

More Modern Baseball Superstars
SLJ - v25 - My '79 - p83

More Modern Women Superstars
BL - v76 - N 15 '79 - p496
SLJ - v26 - D '79 - p101

"My Father, The Coach" And
Other Sports Stories
KR - v44 - Ap 1 '76 - p406
SLJ - v22 - My '76 - p80

The Picture Life Of Reggie
Jackson
Teacher - v96 - My '79 - p124

GUTTMACHER, Alan F   1898-1974
ConAu 1R, ConAu 49, CurBio 65,
NewYTBS 74, WhAm 6, WhoWorJ
72

Understanding Sex
BL - v67 - N 15 '70 - p244
BL - v67 - N 15 '70 - p263
KR - v38 - My 1 '70 - p537
KR - v38 - My 15 '70 - p571
LJ - v95 - N 15 '70 - p4068
NS - v81 - Je 4 '71 - p783

GUY, Anne Welsh
ConAu 5R

Steinmetz: Wizard Of Light
KR - v33 - O 1 '65 - p1048
LJ - v90 - D 15 '65 - p5515
NYTBR - v71 - Ja 16 '66 - p36
SB - v1 - Mr '66 - p206

GUY, Rosa   1925-
BlkAW, ConAu 17R, SmATA 14,
TwCCW 78

The Disappearance
BL - v76 - O 1 '79 - p228

BOT - v2 - D '79 - p601
BW - v9 - N 11 '79 - p21
CBRS - v8 - Ja '80 - p46
CSM - v71 - O 15 '79 - pB4
HM - v259 - D '79 - p77
Inst - v89 - N '79 - p59
KR - v47 - D 1 '79 - p1380
NYTBR - N 25 '79 - p22
NYTBR - D 2 '79 - p40
PW - v216 - Ag 6 '79 - p92
SLJ - v26 - N '79 - p88
WLB - v54 - O '79 - p122

Edith Jackson
BL - v74 - Ap 15 '78 - p1339
CSM - v70 - O 23 '78 - pB13
HB - v55 - O '78 - p524
KR - v46 - My 1 '78 - p501
NYTBR - Jl 2 '78 - p11
PW - v213 - My 29 '78 - p52
SLJ - v24 - Ap '78 - p93
WLB - v52 - Ap '78 - p639

H

HAAR, Jaap Ter
  see Ter Haar, Jaap

HAAS, Ben   1926-1977
  ConAu 9R, ConAu 73

  The Troubled Summer
    BS - v26 - Ja 1 '67 - p368
    CCB-B - v20 - F '67 - p89
    CLW - v38 - F '67 - p395
    KR - v34 - O 1 '66 - p1058
    LJ - v91 - D 15 '66 - p6201
    NYTBR - v72 - Ja 22 '67 - p26
    PW - v193 - Je 10 '68 - p63

HABER, Louis   1910-
  ConAu 29R, SmATA 12, WhoE 75

  *Black Pioneers Of Science And
  Invention*
    BL - v67 - S 15 '70 - p107
    CCB-B - v24 - Ja '71 - p74
    Comw - v93 - F 26 '71 - p521
    KR - v38 - My 15 '70 - p563
    LJ - v95 - D 15 '70 - p4363
    SB - v6 - S '70 - p97

HAGERMAN, Paul Stirling

  It's An Odd World
    Par - v52 - N '77 - p112
    SLJ - v24 - Mr '78 - p128

HAGGARD, Elizabeth

  Nobody Waved Good-Bye
    NYTBR, pt.2 - N 7 '71 - p47

HALACY, Daniel Stephen, Jr.   1919-
  AuBYP, ConAu 5R

  Dive From The Sky!
    KR - v35 - S 15 '67 - p1144

Now Or Never
    BL - v68 - Mr 15 '72 - p629
    BS - v31 - F 15 '72 - p522
    CCB-B - v25 - Ap '72 - p123
    KR - v39 - N 1 '71 - p1165
    LJ - v97 - F 15 '72 - p784
    NYTBR - Ja 9 '72 - p8
    NYTBR, pt.2 - N 7 '71 - p28
    SB - v8 - My '72 - p49

*The Shipbuilders: From Clipper
Ships To Submarines To
Hovercraft*
    BL - v63 - S 15 '66 - p119
    BS - v26 - Jl 1 '66 - p142
    NYTBR - v71 - My 8 '66 - p24

HALL, Lynn   1937-
  AuBYP SUP, ConAu 21R, SmATA 2

  Captain
    SLJ - v23 - F '77 - p64

  Careers For Dog Lovers
    BB - v6 - N '78 - p2
    BL - v74 - My 15 '78 - p1485
    EJ - v67 - O '78 - p79
    KR - v46 - F 1 '78 - p113
    SLJ - v24 - Mr '78 - p129
    WCRB - v4 - Jl '78 - p46

  Flowers Of Anger
    BB - v5 - Mr '77 - p3
    BL - v73 - Ja 15 '77 - p718
    CCB-B - v30 - Ap '77 - p125
    Kliatt - v12 - Fall '78 - p9
    PW - v210 - D 6 '76 - p63

  The Secret Of Stonehouse
    BL - v65 - Ja 1 '69 - p496

  Shadows
    BL - v74 - D 15 '77 - p684
    SLJ - v24 - Ap '78 - p84

HALL, Lynn (continued)

The Siege Of Silent Henry
BL - v69 - Ja 15 '73 - p493
CCB-B - v26 - F '73 - p91
KR - v40 - D 1 '72 - p1358
LJ - v98 - My 15 '73 - p1688
NYTBR, pt.2 - N 5 '72 - p2

Sticks And Stones
BL - v68 - Jl 1 '72 - p939
CCB-B - v26 - O '72 - p25
Choice - v14 - N '77 - p1178
EJ - v62 - Mr '73 - p481
EJ - v62 - D '73 - p1300
LJ - v97 - N 15 '72 - p3813
NYTBR - My 28 '72 - p8
NYTBR, pt.2 - N 5 '72 - p26
PW - v201 - F 14 '72 - p69
TN - v29 - Ap '73 - p257
TN - v30 - Ja '74 - p203

Stray
CCB-B - v28 - F '75 - p94
KR - v42 - Ap 15 '74 - p424
LJ - v99 - S 15 '74 - p2269
NYTBR - My 4 '75 - p23
PW - v205 - Je 17 '74 - p69

HALLIBURTON, Warren   1924-
ConAu 33R, LivBAA, SelBAA,
SmATA 19

Harlem
LJ - v99 - O 15 '74 - p2746
PW - v205 - Je 3 '74 - p160
see also Katz, William Loren (co-
author)

HALLMAN, Ruth   1929-
ConAu 85

Gimme Something, Mister!
Hi Lo - v1 - S '79 - p5
SLJ - v25 - Ap '79 - p56

I Gotta Be Free
BL - v74 - N 15 '77 - p545
Cur R - v16 - D '77 - p360
KR - v46 - Ja 1 '78 - p8
SLJ - v24 - D '77 - p62

Midnight Wheels
BL - v76 - D 15 '79 - p607
Hi Lo - v1 - D '79 - p5

SLJ - v26 - S '79 - p138

Secrets Of A Silent Stranger
BL - v73 - S 15 '76 - p182
Cur R - v16 - D '77 - p360
KR - v44 - Jl 15 '76 - p794
SLJ - v23 - D '76 - p68

HALLSTEAD, William Finn, III
1924-
AuBYP SUP, ConAu 5R, SmATA
11, WhoE 77

Conqueror Of The Clouds
BL - v76 - Jl 15 '80 - p1670

HAMILTON, Virginia   1936-
BlkAW, ChLR 1, ConAu 25R,
FourBJA, SmATA 4, TwCCW 78

The House Of Dies Drear
BL - v65 - N 1 '68 - p311
BL - v65 - Ap 1 '69 - p900
BW - v2 - N 3 '68 - p12
Bl W - v20 - Ag '71 - p94
Comw - v91 - F 27 '70 - p584
HB - v44 - O '68 - p563
Inst - v78 - F '69 - p180
KR - v36 - Ag 1 '68 - p818
NYTBR - My 21 '78 - p51
NYTBR - v73 - O 13 '68 - p26
NYTBR, pt.2 - N 8 '70 - p30
NYTBR, pt.2 - F 13 '72 - p12
PW - v194 - S 30 '68 - p61
SE - v33 - My '69 - p555
SLJ - v24 - F '78 - p35
SR - v51 - N 9 '68 - p69
TN - v25 - Ap '69 - p310
Teacher - v86 - Ap '69 - p184

The Planet Of Junior Brown
A Lib - v3 - Ap '72 - p420
BL - v68 - D 1 '71 - p333
BL - v68 - Ap 1 '72 - p669
BL - v69 - My 1 '73 - p838
Bl W - v21 - Mr '72 - p70
CCB-B - v25 - D '71 - p57
CE - v48 - Ja '72 - p206
CSM - v63 - N 11 '71 - pB5
CSM - v64 - My 2 '72 - p4
Comw - v95 - N 19 '71 - p188
EJ - v63 - Ja '74 - p65
EJ - v67 - My '78 - p88
HB - v48 - F '72 - p81

HAMILTON, Virginia (continued)
>
> KR - v39 - S 1 '71 - p954
> LJ - v96 - S 15 '71 - p2928
> LJ - v96 - D 15 '71 - p4159
> NYRB - v18 - Ap 20 '72 - p13
> NYTBR - Ag 24 '71 - p8
> NYTBR - Mr 10 '74 - p35
> NYTBR - My 21 '78 - p51
> PW - v200 - Ag 23 '71 - p81
> SR - v54 - N 13 '71 - p61
> TN - v28 - Ap '72 - p309

HAMORI, Laszlo 1911-
ConAu 9R

> *Adventure In Bangkok*
> BS - v26 - Je 1 '66 - p100
> HB - v42 - Ag '66 - p438
> KR - v34 - Mr 1 '66 - p248
> LJ - v91 - My 15 '66 - p2706
> NYTBR - v71 - Je 5 '66 - p42
> TLS - N 24 '66 - p1069

> *Dangerous Journey*
> BL - v58 - My 1 '62 - p614
> CC - v79 - Je 20 '62 - p781
> CSM - My 10 '62 - p6B
> HB - v38 - Je '62 - p280
> KR - v30 - F 1 '62 - p112
> LJ - v87 - Je 15 '62 - p2431
> NYTBR - Ag 12 '62 - p26
> NYTBR - v71 - Je 5 '66 - p43

HAMRE, Leif 1914-
ConAu 5R, FourBJA, SmATA 5,
TwCCW 78B

> *Leap Into Danger*
> BL - v56 - D 15 '59 - p245
> HB - v36 - F '60 - p41
> LJ - v85 - Mr 15 '60 - p1310
> LJ - v91 - O 15 '66 - p5272

HANDELSMAN, J B
see Berger, Melvin (co-author) -
The Funny Side Of Science

HANLON, Stuart
see Meyer, Jerome S (co-author) -
Fun With The New Math

HANNAHS, Herbert

> *People Are My Profession*
> LJ - v96 - Ap 15 '71 - p1514

HANO, Arnold 1922-
AuBYP, ConAu 9R, SmATA 12,
WhoWest 76

> *Muhammad Ali: The Champion*
> BL - v74 - O 1 '77 - p303
> KR - v45 - My 15 '77 - p544
> NYTBR - Ap 30 '78 - p56
> SLJ - v24 - S '77 - p144

HARDIN, Gail

> *The Road From West Virginia*
> LJ - v97 - Mr 15 '72 - p1175

HARKER, Ronald 1909-
ConAu 77

> *Digging Up The Bible Lands*
> BL - v70 - S 1 '73 - p46
> CCB-B - v27 - O '73 - p31
> HB - v49 - O '73 - p477
> KR - v41 - Ap 1 '73 - p401
> LJ - v98 - My 15 '73 - p1581
> LJ - v98 - My 15 '73 - p1655
> LJ - v98 - My 15 '73 - p1689
> NY - v49 - D 3 '73 - p219
> Obs - Jl 16 '72 - p31
> PW - v203 - Ap 2 '73 - p65
> SB - v9 - Mr '74 - p321
> TLS - Jl 14 '72 - p810

HARKINS, Philip 1912-
ConAu 29R, MorJA, SmATA 6

> *Young Skin Diver*
> BL - v53 - S 15 '56 - p51
> HB - v32 - O '56 - p361
> KR - v24 - Je 1 '56 - p358
> NYTBR - S 9 '56 - p34
> SR   v39   N 17 '56   p71

HARMON, Lyn 1930-
ConAu 21R

> *Clyde's Clam Farm*
> LJ - v91 - Mr 15 '66 - p1700

HARRINGTON, Lyn   1911-
CaW, ConAu 5R, OxCan, OxCan
SUP, Prof, SmATA 5

China And The Chinese
BL - v63 - Mr 15 '67 - p795
BS - v26 - Ja 1 '67 - p371
CCB-B - v20 - Mr '67 - p108
LJ - v92 - Ja 15 '67 - p343
NH - v76 - N '67 - p29
NYTBR, pt.2 - v72 - My 7 '67 - p4
Pac A - v42 - Spring '69 - p83
SR - v50 - Ap 22 '67 - p100

HARRIS, Christie   1907-
ConAu 5R, ConLC 12, FourBJA,
OxCan SUP, SmATA 6, TwCCW 78

Confessions Of A Toe-Hanger
BL - v64 - S 1 '67 - p54
CCB-B - v20 - Jl '67 - p170
CLW - v39 - D '67 - p292
CSM - v59 - My 4 '67 - pB10
HB - v43 - Ap '67 - p213
KR - v35 - F 1 '67 - p144
LJ - v92 - Ap 15 '67 - p1748
TN - v24 - N '67 - p99

Let X Be Excitement
CCB-B - v22 - Jl '69 - p176
CLW - v41 - O '69 - p133
KR - v37 - F 15 '69 - p185
LJ - v94 - S 15 '69 - p3218
PW - v195 - My 12 '69 - p58
SR - v52 - My 10 '69 - p60

*You Have To Draw The Line
Somewhere*
BS - v23 - Mr 15 '64 - p442
CSM - My 7 '64 - p5B
HB - v40 - Je '64 - p290
LJ - v89 - Ap 15 '64 - p1870
NYTBR - Ag 16 '64 - p18

HARRIS, Jacqueline
see Hayden, Robert Carter (co-
author) - *Nine Black American
Doctors*

HARRIS, Janet   1932-1979
AuBYP SUP, ConAu 33R, SmATA
4, SmATA 23N

*The Long Freedom Road: The Civil
Rights Story*
CCB-B - v21 - S '67 - p7
Lis - v79 - My 16 '68 - p643
TLS - Je 6 '68 - p596

HARRIS, Leon   1926-
ConAu 9R, SmATA 4, WhoAmA 78

*Behind The Scenes In A Car
Factory*
KR - v40 - Mr 1 '72 - p261
LJ - v98 - Mr 15 '73 - p1003

*Behind The Scenes In A
Department Store*
KR - v40 - Mr 1 '72 - p262
LJ - v98 - Mr 15 '73 - p1003

*Behind The Scenes Of Television
Programs*
KR - v40 - Mr 1 '72 - p262
LJ - v98 - Mr 15 '73 - p1003

The Russian Ballet School
AB - v46 - N 23 '70 - p1570
BL - v67 - N 1 '70 - p227
BW - v4 - N 8 '70 - p25
CCB-B - v24 - Mr '71 - p107
CSM - v63 - Ja 30 '71 - p13
Comw - v93 - N 20 '70 - p206
Dance - v45 - Ja '71 - p80
Dance - v46 - Jl '72 - p90
HB - v47 - Je '71 - p299
KR - v38 - Jl 1 '70 - p683
LJ - v95 - S 15 '70 - p3048
LJ - v98 - O 15 '73 - p3123
SR - v53 - O 24 '70 - p67

HARRIS, Marilyn   1931-
ConAu X (also known as Springer,
Marilyn Harris)

The Runaway's Diary
BL - v68 - F 1 '72 - p463
BS - v31 - N 15 '71 - p386
CCB-B - v26 - S '72 - p8
KR - v39 - O 15 '71 - p1131
LJ - v97 - Mr 15 '72 - p1178
Teacher - v91 - Ap '74 - p89

HARRISON, Amelia Williams
see Compton, Margaret

HARRISON, Harry Max   1925-
ConAu 1R, ConSFA, SmATA 4,
WhoSciF, WrDr 80

The Men From P.I.G. And R.O.B.O.T.
BL - v74 - Mr 15 '78 - p1187
CCB-B - v31 - My '78 - p142
HB - v54 - Ag '78 - p395
JB - v39 - F '75 - p63
KR - v46 - Mr 15 '78 - p311
NYTBR - Ap 16 '78 - p26
Obs - F 23 '75 - p28
Obs - Jl 23 '78 - p21
SLJ - v24 - My '78 - p68
Spec - v233 - D 21 '74 - p797
TES - S 22 '78 - p23
TLS - Ap 4 '75 - p360
WLB - v52 - Ap '78 - p639

The Stainless Steel Rat Saves The World
B&B - v19 - N '73 - p129
BL - v69 - Mr 1 '73 - p620
KR - v40 - O 15 '72 - p1216
LJ - v98 - Jl '73 - p2205
PW - v202 - O 30 '72 - p50

HART, Carolyn   1936-
ConAu 13R, ForWC 70

Dangerous Summer
BS - v28 - My 1 '68 - p64
LJ - v93 - My 15 '68 - p2128

HARTER, Walter

The Phantom Hand And Other American Hauntings
KR - v44 - My 15 '76 - p596
SLJ - v23 - N '76 - p58

HASEGAWA, Sam

Stevie Wonder
SLJ - v22 - S '75 - p95

HASKINS, James   1941-
ChLR 3, ConAu 33R, SelBAA,
SmATA 9, WhoE 75, WrDr 80

Always Movin' On
BL - v73 - Ja 1 '77 - p666
BS - v36 - Ja '77 - p323
Cur R - v17 - Ag '78 - p173

SLJ - v23 - N '76 - p69

Babe Ruth And Hank Aaron: The Home Run Kings
BL - v71 - D 15 '74 - p425
KR - v42 - O 1 '74 - p1063
LJ - v99 - D 15 '74 - p3278

Barbara Jordan: Speaking Out
BL - v74 - D 1 '77 - p607
BS - v38 - Ap '78 - p18
CCB-B - v31 - F '78 - p95
Cur R - v17 - Ag '78 - p176
EJ - v67 - Ap '78 - p91
KR - v45 - D 1 '77 - p1273
SLJ - v24 - Ja '78 - p94

Dr. J: A Biography Of Julius Erving
BL - v72 - N 15 '75 - p453
KR - v43 - Jl 1 '75 - p715
SLJ - v22 - D '75 - p68

From Lew Alcindor To Kareem Abdul-Jabbar
BL - v74 - Jl 1 '78 - p1683
CCB-B - v26 - Ja '73 - p76
CSM - v64 - N 8 '72 - pB5
EJ - v62 - My '73 - p825
KR - v40 - Jl 15 '72 - p805
KR - v46 - Jl 15 '78 - p752
LJ - v97 - D 15 '72 - p4089
SLJ - v25 - S '78 - p138

The Life And Death Of Martin Luther King, Jr.
BL - v74 - O 1 '77 - p294
BW - S 11 '77 - pE6
CCB-B - v31 - Ja '78 - p78
CE - v55 - N '78 - p106
EJ - v66 - N '77 - p80
EJ - v67 - Mr '78 - p93
HB - v53 - O '77 - p553
KR - v45 - Je 1 '77 - p583
PW - v211 - Je 13 '77 - p107
SE - v42 - Ap '78 - p318
SLJ - v24 - O '77 - p112

The Story Of Stevie Wonder
BL - v73 - S 1 '76 - p38
CCB-B - v30 - Ap '77 - p125
CLW - v48 - Ap '77 - p405
KR - v44 - My 15 '76 - p604
Kliatt - v13 - Fall '79 - p30
RT - v31 - O '77 - p22

HASKINS, James (continued)
SLJ - v23 - Ja '77 - p92

Street Gangs, Yesterday And Today
BL - v71 - N 1 '74 - p284
BS - v34 - O 15 '74 - p330
BW - N 10 '74 - p8
CCB-B - v28 - Ja '75 - p78
CE - v51 - Ap '75 - p329
LJ - v99 - N 15 '74 - p3054
PW - v206 - Ag 12 '74 - p59

HASSLER, Jon Francis   1933-
ConAu 73, SmATA 19

Four Miles To Pinecone
CCB-B - v31 - O '77 - p33
HB - v53 - O '77 - p531
NYTBR - My 15 '77 - p40
PW - v211 - Je 13 '77 - p108
SLJ - v24 - S '77 - p144

HAUGAARD, Erik Christian   1923-
ConAu 5R, SmATA 4, ThrBJA,
TwCCW 78, WrDr 80

Orphans Of The Wind
BL - v63 - O 15 '66 - p265
HB - v42 - Ag '66 - p438
KR - v34 - My 1 '66 - p479
LJ - v91 - Je 15 '66 - p3266
Lis - v78 - N 16 '67 - p643
NYTBR - v71 - Jl 31 '66 - p18
Nat R - v18 - D 13 '66 - p1285
Obs - N 26 '67 - p28
PW - v189 - Je 20 '66 - p77
SR - v49 - S 17 '66 - p46
TLS - N 30 '67 - p1159

A Slave's Tale
BL - v62 - S 15 '65 - p96
CCB-B - v19 - Ap '66 - p131
Comw - v82 - My 28 '65 - p329
HB - v41 - Ag '65 - p395
KR - v33 - Ap 15 '65 - p436
LJ - v90 - Je 15 '65 - p2894
NYTBR - v70 - Ag 22 '65 - p18
Obs - D 4 '66 - p28
Punch - v251 - N 16 '66 - p754
Spec - N 11 '66 - p625
TLS - N 24 '66 - p1079

HAUTZIG, Deborah   1956-
ConAu 89

Hey, Dollface
BL - v75 - S 1 '78 - p38
CCB-B - v32 - O '78 - p30
KR - v46 - Ag 1 '78 - p811
PW - v214 - Ag 21 '78 - p60

HAUTZIG, Esther   1930-
ConAu 1R, MorBMP, SmATA 4,
ThrBJA, WrDr 80

The Endless Steppe: Growing Up In Siberia
BL - v64 - My 1 '68 - p1043
BS - v28 - My 1 '68 - p64
BW - v2 - My 5 '68 - p5
CCB-B - v21 - My '68 - p142
Comw - v88 - My 24 '68 - p302
HB - v44 - Je '68 - p311
KR - v36 - Mr 15 '68 - p343
LJ - v93 - O 15 '68 - p3982
NYTBR - v73 - My 5 '68 - p2
PW - v193 - Mr 25 '68 - p49
SR - v51 - My 11 '68 - p42
TN - v25 - N '68 - p78

HAYDEN, Naura   1942-
ConAu 73

The Hip, High-Prote, Low-Cal, Easy-Does-It Cookbook
BS - v32 - N 1 '72 - p364

HAYDEN, Robert Carter   1937-
ConAu 69, SelBAA, WrDr 80

Eight Black American Inventors
BL - v68 - Je 1 '72 - p857
BL - v68 - Je 1 '72 - p860
LJ - v98 - F 15 '73 - p654

Nine Black American Doctors
CLW - v48 - Mr '77 - p357
SB - v13 - S '77 - p86
SE - v41 - Ap '77 - p347

Seven Black American Scientists
BL - v68 - S 1 '71 - p58
LJ - v96 - N 15 '71 - p3910
SB - v7 - My '71 - p17

HAYES, William D   1913-
AuBYP, ConAu 5R, SmATA 8

HAYES, William D (continued)

Project: Scoop
KR - v34 - Ag 1 '66 - p751
LJ - v91 - S 15 '66 - p4334

HAYMAN, LeRoy 1916-
AuBYP SUP, ConAu 85

O Captain: The Death Of Abraham Lincoln
KR - v35 - D 1 '67 - p1428
LJ - v93 - My 15 '68 - p2120
PW - v193 - My 13 '68 - p59

HEAD, Ann 1915-
ConAu X (also known as Morse, Anne Christensen)

Mr. And Mrs. Bo Jo Jones
TN - v24 - N '67 - p101
TN - v24 - Ap '68 - p326
see also Morse, Charles (co-author)

HEADLEY, Elizabeth Cavanna 1909-
ConAu X, MorJA, SmATA 1, WrDr 80 (also known as Cavanna, Betty)

Diane's New Love
BL - v51 - Je 15 '55 - p434
KR - v23 - Mr 1 '55 - p175
LJ - v80 - Je 15 '55 - p1512
NYT - My 15 '55 - p28
see also Cavanna, Betty

HEALEY, Larry

The Town Is On Fire
BL - v76 - F 15 '80 - p829
CBRS - v8 - N '79 - p27
SLJ - v26 - D '79 - p99

HEAVILIN, Jay
AuBYP SUP

Fast Ball Pitcher
CCB-B - v19 - S '65 - p9

HEIDE, Florence Parry 1919-
AuBYP SUP, FourBJA

Mystery Of The Midnight Message
BL - v74 - F 15 '78 - p1013
CCB-B - v31 - Ap '78 - p128

SLJ - v24 - Ap '78 - p84

When The Sad One Comes To Stay
CCB-B - v29 - Mr '76 - p111
HB - v52 - Ap '76 - p155
KR - v43 - Ag 15 '75 - p917
Kliatt - v11 - Winter '77 - p4
NYTBR - N 16 '75 - p52
PW - v208 - Ag 25 '75 - p293
SLJ - v22 - O '75 - p99

HEINLEIN, Robert A 1907-
ConAu 1R, ConLC 8, MorJA, SmATA 9, TwCCW 78, WhoAm 78, WrDr 80

Rocket Ship Galileo
Atl - v180 - D '47 - p148
BL - v44 - D 15 '47 - p155
KR - v15 - N 1 '47 - p602
LJ - v73 - Ja 1 '48 - p49
NY - v23 - D 6 '47 - p156
NYTBR - F 22 '48 - p31

HELFMAN, Elizabeth S 1911-
ConAu 5R, ForWC 70, SmATA 3, WrDr 80

Our Fragile Earth
BL - v69 - Mr 15 '73 - p715
KR - v40 - O 15 '72 - p1196
LJ - v98 - My 15 '73 - p1682
SB - v9 - My '73 - p64

HELLER, Doris

Little Big Top
Hi Lo - v1 - D '79 - p4

HELLMAN, Harold 1927-
AuBYP SUP, ConAu 25R, SmATA 4, WrDr 80

The Lever And The Pulley
CCB-B - v26 - O '72 - p27
HB - v49 - F '73 - p73
LJ - v97 - Ap 15 '72 - p1605
SB - v8 - My '72 - p29

HEMPHILL, Paul 1936?-
AuBYP SUP, AuNews 2, ConAu 49, WrDr 80

The Nashville Sound
AB - v45 - Je 1 '70 - p1880

HEMPHILL, Paul (continued)
    Atl - v225 - Je '70 - p128
    KR - v38 - Mr 1 '70 - p294
    KR - v38 - Ap 15 '70 - p474
    LJ - v95 - Jl '70 - p2547
    LJ - v95 - O 15 '70 - p3474
    NYRB - v17 - N 4 '71 - p33
    NYT - v119 - Ap 27 '70 - p31
    NYTBR - Jl 19 '70 - p7
    New R - v162 - Je 27 '70 - p21
    PW - v197 - F 23 '70 - p155
    SR - v53 - Je 27 '70 - p57
    TN - v27 - N '70 - p93

HENDERSON, Zenna 1917-
    ConAu 1R, ConSFA, SmATA 5,
    WhoSciF

    Holding Wonder
        BL - v68 - O 1 '71 - p133
        BL - v68 - Ap 1 '72 - p664
        KR - v39 - Mr 1 '71 - p258
        KR - v39 - Ap 1 '71 - p385
        LJ - v96 - My 15 '71 - p1730
        LJ - v96 - My 15 '71 - p1830
        PW - v199 - Mr 8 '71 - p66
        TN - v28 - Ap '72 - p312

HENKEL, Stephen C 1933-
    ConAu 37R, WhoE 75, WrDr 80

    Bikes: A How-To-Do-It Guide To
    Selection, Care, Repair,
    Maintenance, Decoration, Etc.
        A Lib - v4 - F '73 - p98
        BL - v68 - Jl 15 '72 - p998
        BL - v68 - Jl 15 '72 - p1004
        CE - v49 - D '72 - p148
        Choice - v10 - O '73 - p1240
        KR - v40 - My 15 '72 - p594
        LJ - v98 - F 15 '73 - p654
        NYTBR - Je 4 '72 - p8
        PW - v202 - O 16 '72 - p51
        SA - v227 - D '72 - p117
        SB - v8 - Mr '73 - p350

HENRY, Marguerite 1902-
    ConAu 17R, JBA 51, SmATA 11,
    TwCCW 78, WhoAm 78, WrDr 80

    Album Of Dogs
        CLW - v42 - Ap '71 - p523
        LJ - v96 - Ja 15 '71 - p268

        PW - v198 - D 28 '70 - p61
        SB - v7 - My '71 - p82

    Mustang, Wild Spirit Of The West
        BL - v63 - F 1 '67 - p582
        CCB-B - v20 - Ja '67 - p74
        CE - v44 - S '67 - p54
        CLW - v39 - N '67 - p241
        KR - v34 - N 1 '66 - p1140
        LJ - v92 - My 15 '67 - p2021
        NYTBR - v72 - Ja 15 '67 - p28
        PW - v190 - N 21 '66 - p76
        SR - v49 - N 12 '66 - p51
        TN - v23 - Ap '67 - p291

HENRY, Will   (pseud.) 1912-
    AmAu&B, AuBYP SUP (real name:
    Allen, Henry Wilson)

    Maheo's Children
        BS - v28 - Ap 1 '68 - p18
        LJ - v93 - Je 15 '68 - p2547

HENTOFF, Nat   1925-
    ChLR 1, ConAu 1R, ThrBJA,
    TwCCW 78, WhoWor 74, WrDr 80

    I'm Really Dragged, But Nothing
    Gets Me Down
        BS - v28 - O 1 '68 - p277
        CCB-B - v22 - Ja '69 - p78
        EJ - v58 - My '69 - p776
        KR - v36 - S 15 '68 - p1059
        LJ - v93 - N 15 '68 - p4414
        LJ - v96 - Ja 15 '71 - p282
        NYTBR - v73 - N 3 '68 - p2
        NYTBR, pt.2 - F 15 '70 - p22
        PW - v194 - S 2 '68 - p59
        PW - v196 - S 29 '69 - p60
        SR - v51 - S 7 '68 - p34
        SR - v51 - N 9 '68 - p71
        Time - v92 - O 11 '68 - pE8

    Jazz Country
        BL - v61 - Jl 1 '65 - p1025
        BS - v25 - My 15 '65 - p98
        CCB-B - v18 - Je '65 - p150
        CSM - v57 - Je 24 '65 - p7
        Comw - v82 - My 28 '65 - p330
        HB - v41 - O '65 - p517
        KR - v33 - Mr 1 '65 - p252
        LJ - v90 - My 15 '65 - p2418
        LJ - v96 - Ja 15 '71 - p282
        NYTBR - v70 - My 9 '65 - p3

HENTOFF, Nat (continued)
NYTBR - v72 - N 5 '67 - p54
NYTBR, pt.2 - v73 - F 25 '68 - p20
Obs - Ag 7 '66 - p21
PW - v192 - Jl 10 '67 - p188
SR - v50 - Ja 28 '67 - p45
Spec - Je 3 '66 - p705
TLS - My 19 '66 - p442

Journey Into Jazz
AB - v43 - Ja 27 '69 - p280
BW - v3 - Mr 30 '69 - p16
CSM - v60 - N 7 '68 - pB4
KR - v36 - O 15 '68 - p1157
LJ - v94 - Ja 15 '69 - p300
PW - v194 - S 2 '68 - p59
RR - v86 - Mr '69 - p174
SR - v51 - N 9 '68 - p67

This School Is Driving Me Crazy
BL - v72 - O 15 '75 - p302
CCB-B - v29 - Ja '76 - p78
Inst - v85 - My '76 - p124
JB - v42 - Je '78 - p155
KR - v43 - N 15 '75 - p1296
Kliatt - v12 - Fall '78 - p9
NO - v15 - F 28 '76 - p21
Obs - D 11 '77 - p31
PW - v209 - Ja 5 '76 - p65
SLJ - v22 - F '76 - p53
TES - Ja 20 '78 - p23
TLS - Ap 7 '78 - p382

HERBERT, Frank   1920-
ConAu 53, ConLC 12, ConSFA,
SmATA 9, WhoAm 78, WrDr 80

Under Pressure
BksW - v1 - Je '77 - p17
MFSF - v53 - Jl '77 - p103
NYTBR - S 8 '74 - p40

HERMANN, Charles F

Read For The Job
Hi Lo - v2 - S '80 - p6

HERRIOT, James   (pseud.) 1916-
BioIn 10, BioIn 11, ConAu X, ConLC
12, WrDr 80 (real name: Wight,
James Alfred)

All Creatures Great And Small
Atl - v234 - Ag '74 - p91

BL - v69 - Ja 15 '73 - p464
BL - v69 - F 15 '73 - p569
BS - v32 - D 1 '72 - p410
BW - v6 - D 24 '72 - p10
CC - v92 - Ap 30 '75 - p449
CC - v92 - My 14 '75 - p500
EJ - v62 - D '73 - p1298
KR - v40 - Ag 15 '72 - p995
LJ - v97 - Ag '72 - p2575
LJ - v98 - My 15 '73 - p1657
LJ - v98 - My 15 '73 - p1713
NYT - v122 - D 14 '72 - p45
NYTBR - F 18 '73 - p10
PW - v202 - Ag 14 '72 - p42
Time - v101 - F 19 '73 - p88

HERZ, Peggy   1936-
ConAu 37R

TV Time '79
Inst - v88 - My '79 - p114

HESSELBERG, Erik
AuBYP SUP

Kon-Tiki And I
BL - v67 - O 15 '70 - p198
CCB-B - v24 - N '70 - p43
NYTBR - S 13 '70 - p42
NYTBR, pt.2 - N 8 '70 - p38
PW - v198 - Jl 20 '70 - p70

HEUMAN, William   1912-
AuBYP, ConAu 5R, SmATA 21

Famous American Indians
BL - v69 - S 15 '72 - p100
NYTBR, pt.2 - N 5 '72 - p22

Gridiron Stranger
KR - v38 - F 1 '70 - p111
LJ - v95 - My 15 '70 - p1965

Horace Higby And The Field Goal Formula
Am - v113 - N 20 '65 - p642
CSM - v57 - N 4 '65 - pB9
KR - v33 - My 15 '65 - p501
LJ - v90 - O 15 '65 - p4636

Horace Higby, Coxswain Of The Crew
LJ - v96 - D 15 '71 - p4204

HEYERDAHL, Thor   1914-
ConAu 5R, CurBio 72, IntWW 78,
SmATA 2, WhoWor 78, WrDr 80

   Kon-Tiki
     Atl - v186 - O '50 - p80
     BL - v47 - S 1 '50 - p2
     CC - v67 - S 27 '50 - p1138
     CSM - S 7 '50 - p18
     HB - v26 - N '50 - p502
     KR - v18 - Ag 15 '50 - p492
     LJ - v75 - O 1 '50 - p1664
     NS - v39 - Ap 1 '50 - p380
     NY - v26 - S 16 '50 - p117
     NYTBR - S 3 '50 - p1
     SR - v33 - S 23 '50 - p12
     Spec - v184 - Mr 31 '50 - p434
     TLS - Ap 7 '50 - p216
     Time - v56 - S 18 '50 - p112

HIBBERT, Christopher   1924-
ConAu 1R, OxCan, SmATA 4, Who
74, WrDr 80

   The Search For King Arthur
     B&B - v15 - My '70 - p40
     BL - v66 - My 1 '70 - p1100
     BS - v29 - Mr 1 '70 - p454
     BW - v4 - My 17 '70 - p26
     CCB-B - v24 - Jl '70 - p180
     CSM - v62 - My 2 '70 - p17
     LJ - v95 - Jl '70 - p2540
     NS - v79 - My 15 '70 - p706
     NYTBR - Mr 15 '70 - p49
     Obs - Jl 26 '70 - p24
     PW - v197 - Ja 26 '70 - p278
     SR - v53 - My 9 '70 - p70
     Spec - v224 - My 9 '70 - p622
     TLS - Ap 16 '70 - p424

HIBBERT, Eleanor Burford
see Holt, Victoria

HIGDON, Hal   1931-
AuBYP SUP, ConAu 9R, SmATA 4,
WrDr 80

   The Electronic Olympics
     BL - v68 - Ap 1 '72 - p660
     BL - v68 - Ap 1 '72 - p675
     CCB-B - v25 - F '72 - p92
     KR - v39 - N 1 '71 - p1155
     LJ - v96 - D 15 '71 - p4200

     SR - v55 - Ap 22 '72 - p86

HILDICK, E W   1925-
ConAu 25R, SmATA 2, TwCCW 78,
WhoChL, WrDr 80

   The Active-Enzyme Lemon-
   Freshened Junior High School
   Witch
     BL - v75 - O 1 '78 - p305
     CCB-B - v26 - Je '73 - p155
     KR - v41 - F 15 '73 - p187
     LJ - v98 - N 15 '73 - p3452
     PW - v203 - Mr 5 '73 - p83

   Manhattan Is Missing
     B&B - v18 - Ja '73 - p123
     BL - v65 - Ap 1 '69 - p894
     BS - v28 - Mr 1 '69 - p490
     BW - v3 - My 4 '69 - p30
     CCB-B - v22 - Ap '69 - p127
     HB - v45 - Je '69 - p306
     KR - v37 - Ja 15 '69 - p54
     LJ - v94 - My 15 '69 - p2073
     LJ - v94 - My 15 '69 - p2100
     LJ - v94 - D 15 '69 - p4582
     Lis - v88 - N 9 '72 - p644
     PW - v195 - F 3 '69 - p65
     PW - v198 - Ag 3 '70 - p62
     SLJ - v24 - F '78 - p35
     SR - v52 - Mr 22 '69 - p63
     Spec - v229 - N 11 '72 - p750
     TLS - D 8 '72 - p1490

   The Top-Flight Fully-Automated
   Junior High School Girl Detective
     CCB-B - v31 - D '77 - p60
     HB - v53 - D '77 - p663
     KR - v45 - Ag 1 '77 - p785
     SLJ - v23 - My '77 - p78

HILL, Douglas Arthur   1935-
ConAu 53, ConP 70, ConSFA, OxCan
SUP, WrDr 80

   Galactic Warlord
     BL - v76 - Ap 1 '80 - p1116
     BS - v40 - My '80 - p78
     GP - v18 - N '79 - p3614
     HB - v56 - Je '80 - p306
     JB - v44 - F '80 - p27
     SLJ - v26 - Ap '80 - p125

HILL, Elizabeth Starr   1925-
AuBYP SUP, ConAu 17R, SmATA
24, WrDr 80

> *Master Mike And The Miracle*
> *Maid*
> KR - v35 - O 1 '67 - p1219
> LJ - v92 - N 15 '67 - p4257

HILLARY, Louise

> *A Yak For Christmas*
> BL - v66 - S 1 '69 - p29
> GJ - v135 - Je '69 - p260
> LJ - v94 - Ap 15 '69 - p1631
> NYTBR - Je 8 '69 - p12
> PW - v195 - F 3 '69 - p64
> SR - v52 - S 13 '69 - p37

HILLER, Doris   (pseud.) 1934-
ConAu X (real name: Nussbaum,
Albert F)

> *Black Beach*
> BL - v74 - Ja 15 '78 - p809
> BL - v75 - O 15 '78 - p357

> *Little Big Top*
> SLJ - v26 - D '79 - p98

HILTON, Suzanne   1922-
AuBYP SUP, ConAu 29R, SmATA
4, WrDr 80

> *How Do They Get Rid Of It?*
> AF - v77 - Ag '71 - p54
> Am - v123 - D 5 '70 - p498
> BL - v66 - Jl 1 '70 - p1341
> BS - v30 - Je 1 '70 - p105
> Comw - v92 - My 22 '70 - p253
> KR - v38 - Mr 15 '70 - p332
> LJ - v95 - S 15 '70 - p3062
> SB - v6 - My '70 - p60

> *The Way It Was--1876*
> BL - v71 - Je 15 '75 - p1070
> CCB-B - v29 - N '75 - p46
> CLW - v47 - D '75 - p234
> HB - v51 - O '75 - p482
> KR - v43 - Je 1 '75 - p608
> NYTBR - Ag 17 '75 - p8
> NYTBR - N 16 '75 - p55
> PW - v207 - My 19 '75 - p176
> SLJ - v21 - My '75 - p64
> SLJ - v22 - D '75 - p31

HINTON, Nigel   1941-
ConAu 85

> *Collision Course*
> BL - v74 - S 15 '77 - p194
> BS - v37 - O '77 - p203
> EJ - v67 - F '78 - p79
> GP - v15 - Ap '77 - p3086
> JB - v41 - Ag '77 - p235
> KR - v45 - My 15 '77 - p543
> NYTBR - O 9 '77 - p28
> Obs - N 28 '76 - p31
> SLJ - v24 - S '77 - p144
> TLS - D 10 '76 - p1544

HINTON, S E   1950-
ChLR 3, ConAu 81, FourBJA,
SmATA 19, TwCCW 78

> *The Outsiders*
> Atl - v220 - D '67 - p136
> BL - v64 - O 1 '67 - p176
> BS - v27 - Jl 1 '67 - p144
> CCB-B - v20 - Jl '67 - p171
> CLW - v39 - D '67 - p292
> EJ - v58 - F '69 - p295
> EJ - v67 - My '78 - p88
> HB - v43 - Ag '67 - p475
> J Read - v22 - N '78 - p126
> KR - v35 - Ap 15 '67 - p506
> LJ - v92 - My 15 '67 - p2028
> NYTBR, pt.2 - F 16 '69 - p22
> NYTBR, pt.2 - My 4 '69 - p6
> NYTBR, pt.2 - My 7 '67 - p10
> PW - v191 - My 22 '67 - p64
> SR - v50 - My 13 '67 - p59
> SR - v51 - Ja 27 '68 - p34
> TLS - O 30 '70 - p1258

> *Rumble Fish*
> BL - v72 - S 1 '75 - p41
> BS - v35 - F '76 - p362
> CCB-B - v29 - D '75 - p63
> EJ - v65 - My '76 - p91
> GP - v15 - My '76 - p2891
> HB - v51 - D '75 - p601
> Inst - v85 - N '75 - p155
> JB - v40 - Ag '76 - p229
> J Read - v22 - N '78 - p127
> KR - v43 - O 15 '75 - p1193
> NS - v91 - My 21 '76 - p690
> NYT - v125 - D 20 '75 - p25
> NYTBR - D 14 '75 - p8

HINTON, S E (continued)
  Obs - N 28 '76 - p31
  PW - v208 - Jl 28 '75 - p122
  SLJ - v22 - O '75 - p106
  SLJ - v22 - D '75 - p31
  TLS - Ap 2 '76 - p388
  TN - v32 - Ap '76 - p284

  Tex
  BL - v76 - O 15 '79 - p353
  CBRS - v8 - O '79 - p17
  CCB-B - v33 - D '79 - p71
  HB - v55 - D '79 - p668
  KR - v48 - Ja 1 '80 - p9
  NYTBR - D 16 '79 - p23
  SLJ - v26 - N '79 - p88
  WLB - v54 - O '79 - p122

  That Was Then, This Is Now
  BL - v67 - Jl 15 '71 - p951
  BL - v68 - Ap 1 '72 - p664
  BS - v31 - Ag 15 '71 - p235
  BW - v5 - My 9 '71 - p5
  CCB-B - v25 - S '71 - p8
  EJ - v67 - My '78 - p88
  HB - v47 - Ag '71 - p388
  J Read - v22 - N '78 - p126
  KR - v39 - Ap 15 '71 - p442
  LJ - v96 - Je 15 '71 - p2138
  NYTBR - Ag 8 '71 - p8
  Obs - N 28 '71 - p35
  PW - v199 - My 31 '71 - p135
  SR - v54 - Je 19 '71 - p27
  TLS - O 22 '71 - p1318
  TN - v28 - Ap '72 - p312

HINTZE, Naomi A 1909-
ConAu 45, WrDr 80

  The Stone Carnation
  BL - v68 - S 15 '71 - p83
  KR - v39 - Ja 1 '71 - p20
  LJ - v96 - Mr 1 '71 - p865
  NYTBR - Mr 7 '71 - p42
  PW - v199 - Ja 18 '71 - p48

HIRSCH, S Carl 1913-
ConAu 5R, SmATA 2, ThrBJA,
WrDr 80

  Four Score...And More: The Life
  Span Of Man
  Comw - v82 - My 28 '65 - p332
  HB - v41 - Je '65 - p295

KR - v33 - Mr 15 '65 - p324
LJ - v90 - F 15 '65 - p970
SA - v213 - D '65 - p115

  The Living Community: A Venture
  Into Ecology
  BL - v62 - Je 15 '66 - p1000
  BS - v26 - My 1 '66 - p58
  CCB-B - v19 - Je '66 - p164
  KR - v34 - Mr 15 '66 - p310
  NH - v75 - N '66 - p62
  SB - v2 - S '66 - p124

HIRSHBERG, Al 1909-1973
AuBYP, ConAu 1R, ConAu 41R,
WhoAm 6, WhoE 74

  Fear Strikes Out: The Jim Piersall
  Story
  BL - v51 - Je 1 '55 - p406
  HB - v31 - D '55 - p469
  KR - v23 - Ap 15 '55 - p288
  LJ - v80 - Ap 15 '55 - p872

  The Greatest American Leaguers
  BS - v30 - Ap 1 '70 - p18
  CCB-B - v24 - S '70 - p9
  KR - v38 - F 1 '70 - p107
  LJ - v95 - My 15 '70 - p1964
  SR - v53 - Je 27 '70 - p38

  Henry Aaron: Quiet Superstar
  KR - v37 - Je 15 '69 - p633
  LJ - v94 - D 15 '69 - p4620

HITCHCOCK, Alfred 1899-1980
CurBio 60, EncMys, OxFilm, SmATA
24N, WhoWor 74, WorEFlm

  Alfred Hitchcock's Sinister Spies
  BS - v26 - O 1 '66 - p250
  LJ - v91 - N 15 '66 - p5775
  NYTBR - v71 - N 6 '66 - p58
  PW - v190 - N 7 '66 - p66
  SR - v49 - O 29 '66 - p43

HOARD, Edison 1934?-
BioIn 9

  Curse Not The Darkness
  LJ - v96 - Ap 15 '71 - p1514

HOBSON, Burton 1933-
ConAu 5R, WhoAm 74

HOBSON, Burton (continued)

Coins You Can Collect
Hob - v75 - N '70 - p141
LJ - v92 - Jl '67 - p2655

HODGE, Ken
see Awrey, Don (co-author)

HODGES, C Walter   1909-
ConAu 13R, IlsCB 1967, SmATA 2,
ThrBJA, TwCCW 78, WhoChL,
WrDr 80

The Overland Launch
B&B - v17 - My '72 - pR14
BL - v66 - Jl 15 '70 - p1407
BL - v67 - Ap 1 '71 - p660
BS - v30 - Jl 1 '70 - p145
CCB-B - v24 - O '70 - p26
HB - v46 - Ag '70 - p393
KR - v38 - Je 1 '70 - p604
LJ - v95 - O 15 '70 - p3638
NS - v78 - O 31 '69 - p623
Obs - N 30 '69 - p35
PW - v197 - Je 1 '70 - p68
SR - v53 - Ag 22 '70 - p53
Spec - v223 - N 1 '69 - p598
TLS - D 4 '69 - p1400

HOFF, Syd   1912-
ConAu 5R, IlsCB 1967, SmATA 9,
ThrBJA, TwCCW 78, WhoAm 78,
WhoWorJ 72

Irving And Me
BL - v64 - N 1 '67 - p334
BS - v27 - S 1 '67 - p223
CCB-B - v21 - O '67 - p28
CSM - v59 - N 2 '67 - pB10
Choice - v14 - N '77 - p1178
HB - v43 - O '67 - p594
KR - v35 - Je 1 '67 - p649
LJ - v92 - S 15 '67 - p3186
LJ - v95 - F 15 '70 - p742
NYTBR - v72 - O 8 '67 - p38
NYTBR - v72 - N 5 '67 - p64
SR - v50 - S 16 '67 - p49

HOFFMAN, Anne Byrne

Echoes From The Schoolyard
BL - v74 - F 15 '78 - p970
LJ - v103 - F 1 '78 - p380

Pet PM - v7 - D '78 - p107

HOFSINDE, Robert   1902-1973
ConAu 45, ConAu 73, IlsCB 1946,
SmATA 21, ThrBJA

*Indian Warriors And Their
Weapons*
BL - v61 - Je 1 '65 - p958
LJ - v90 - Ap 15 '65 - p2041
NYTBR - v70 - My 30 '65 - p20

HOGAN, Elizabeth

*The Curse Of King Tut And Other
Mystery Stories*
Hi Lo - v1 - Mr '80 - p5

HOGBEN, Lancelot   1895-1975
ConAu 61, LongCTC, TwCA, TwCA
SUP, WhAm 6

*The Wonderful World Of
Mathematics*
BS - v28 - Ja 1 '69 - p424
HB - v45 - F '69 - p75
KR - v36 - N 1 '68 - p1236
LJ - v94 - My 15 '69 - p2113
SB - v5 - My '69 - p18
TLS - O 3 '68 - p1127

HOGG, Beth Tootill
see Grey, Elizabeth

HOKE, Helen L   1903-
AuBYP, ConAu 73, SmATA 15

More Jokes, Jokes, Jokes
CC - v82 - Jl 21 '65 - p918
LJ - v90 - S 15 '65 - p3805

HOLDEN, Raymond P   1894-1972
AuBYP, ConAu 5R, ConAu 37R,
TwCA, TwCA SUP

*All About Famous Scientific
Expeditions*
NYTBR - O 19 '58 - p60

Wildlife Mysteries
KR - v40 - O 1 '72 - p1157
LJ - v98 - F 15 '73 - p644
SB - v9 - My '73 - p44

HOLLAND, Isabelle   1920-
ConAu 21R, SmATA 8, TwCCW 78,
WrDr 80

Amanda's Choice
BW - v4 - My 17 '70 - p16
CCB-B - v24 - S '70 - p9
CSM - v62 - My 7 '70 - pB6
HB - v46 - Je '70 - p297
KR - v38 - F 15 '70 - p173
LJ - v96 - Mr 15 '71 - p1116
NYTBR - My 3 '70 - p23
PW - v197 - My 18 '70 - p38
SR - v53 - My 9 '70 - p69

Heads You Win, Tails I Lose
A Lib - v5 - My '74 - p235
BL - v70 - O 15 '73 - p234
BS - v33 - S 15 '73 - p280
CCB-B - v27 - Ja '74 - p80
EJ - v63 - My '74 - p91
HB - v50 - F '74 - p56
KR - v41 - Jl 15 '73 - p759
LJ - v98 - O 15 '73 - p3155
NO - v12 - D 29 '73 - p15
NYTBR - N 25 '73 - p10
PW - v204 - S 17 '73 - p57
TN - v30 - N '73 - p81

Hitchhike
CCB-B - v31 - Ja '78 - p79
EJ - v67 - F '78 - p99
HB - v53 - D '77 - p668
KR - v45 - Ag 1 '77 - p789
Kliatt - v14 - Winter '80 - p8
NYTBR - O 30 '77 - p34
PW - v212 - S 12 '77 - p133
SLJ - v24 - S '77 - p145

The Man Without A Face
BL - v68 - My 15 '72 - p816
BS - v32 - Ap 15 '72 - p46
BW - v6 - Ag 6 '72 - p2
CCB-B - v25 - Jl '72 - p170
Comw - v97 - N 17 '72 - p157
HB - v48 - Ag '72 - p375
KR - v40 - Ja 15 '72 - p73
LJ - v97 - Jl '72 - p2489
NYTBR - Ap 9 '72 - p8
NYTBR, pt.2 - N 5 '72 - p26
Nat R - v24 - Jl 7 '72 - p754
PW - v201 - Ap 17 '72 - p59
TN - v29 - Ap '73 - p257

HOLLANDER, Phyllis
AuBYP SUP

American Women In Sports
KR - v40 - Mr 15 '72 - p329
LJ - v97 - My 15 '72 - p1932
NYTBR, pt.2 - My 7 '72 - p24
SE - v37 - D '73 - p788

HOLLANDER, Zander   1923-
AuBYP SUP, ConAu 65

Roller Hockey
BL - v72 - N 1 '75 - p366
Comw - v102 - N 21 '75 - p571
LJ - v100 - O 15 '75 - p1944
SLJ - v22 - D '75 - p70

Strange But True Football Stories
CLW - v39 - F '68 - p438
LJ - v92 - D 15 '67 - p4633

HOLM, Anne S   1922-
ConAu 17R, FourBJA, SmATA 1,
TwCCW 78B

North To Freedom
BL - v62 - S 1 '65 - p56
BS - v25 - Je 15 '65 - p145
CCB-B - v19 - S '65 - p10
HB - v41 - Ag '65 - p380
KR - v33 - Mr 1 '65 - p243
LJ - v90 - My 15 '65 - p2420
NYTBR - v70 - Jl 4 '65 - p12
SR - v48 - My 15 '65 - p46
TCR - v68 - F '67 - p451

HOLMES, Burnham   1909-
St&PR 75

Basic Training
KR - v47 - Jl 1 '79 - p746
SLJ - v25 - Ap '79 - p68

HOLMES, Marjorie   1910-
AuBYP, AuNews 1, ConAu 1R,
WhoAm 78, WrDr 80

Saturday Night
KR - v27 - F 1 '59 - p96
LJ - v84 - Ap 15 '59 - p1338
NYTBR - My 24 '59 - p38

HOLT, Victoria (pseud.) 1906-
ConAu X, EncMys, SmATA 2,
WhoAm 78, WorAu, WrDr 80 (real
name: Hibbert, Eleanor Burford)

Menfreya In The Morning
B&B - v11 - Je '66 - p45
BS - v26 - My 15 '66 - p72
HB - v42 - O '66 - p588
KR - v34 - Ja 15 '66 - p80
LJ - v91 - Mr 15 '66 - p1444
NYTBR - v71 - Ap 17 '66 - p37
PW - v189 - Ja 17 '66 - p129
PW - v191 - Mr 20 '67 - p62
Time - v87 - My 13 '66 - p114

HOLZ, Loretta 1943-
ConAu 65, SmATA 17

*The How-To Book Of
International Dolls: A
Comprehensive Guide To Making,
Costuming And Collecting Dolls*
Kliatt - v14 - Spring '80 - p52
LJ - v105 - Ap 1 '80 - p848

HONIG, Donald 1931-
ConAu 17R, IntAu&W 77, SmATA
18

Dynamite
KR - v39 - Je 1 '71 - p593
LJ - v96 - Jl '71 - p2369
PW - v200 - Jl 26 '71 - p52

Fury On Skates
BL - v71 - D 15 '74 - p425
CSM - v67 - F 5 '75 - p8
KR - v42 - S 1 '74 - p950
LJ - v99 - D 15 '74 - p3280

Going The Distance
BL - v72 - Jl 15 '76 - p1601
BS - v36 - O '76 - p239
JB - v41 - Ap '77 - p112
SLJ - v22 - My '76 - p80

Johnny Lee
CCB-B - v25 - S '71 - p8
CLW - v42 - My '71 - p581
Comw - v94 - My 21 '71 - p268
KR - v39 - Mr 1 '71 - p236
LJ - v96 - My 15 '71 - p1823
SR - v54 - Jl 17 '71 - p36

Winter Always Comes
BL - v73 - Je 1 '77 - p1490
BL - v73 - Je 1 '77 - p1498
BS - v37 - Ag '77 - p142
CCB-B - v31 - S '77 - p16
KR - v45 - Ap 1 '77 - p351
NYTBR - My 1 '77 - p41
SLJ - v23 - My '77 - p79

HOOBLER, Dorothy
ConAu 69

*Photographing History: The
Career Of Matthew Brady*
B&B - v6 - O '78 - p4
BL - v74 - Ja 15 '78 - p806
CE - v55 - O '78 - p42
KR - v45 - O 1 '77 - p1055
PW - v212 - S 19 '77 - p146
SLJ - v24 - F '78 - p65

HOOBLER, Thomas
see Hoobler, Dorothy (co-author)

HOOPER, Meredith 1939-
IntAu&W 77, WrDr 80

Everyday Inventions
BL - v73 - S 15 '76 - p137
BL - v73 - S 15 '76 - p175
LJ - v101 - O 15 '76 - p2186
LJ - v102 - Mr 1 '77 - p553
Obs - Mr 23 '75 - p27
Obs - Jl 18 '76 - p20
PW - v210 - Jl 19 '76 - p133
TLS - D 8 '72 - p1500
TLS - D 6 '74 - p1385

HOOVER, H M
ScF&FL 1

The Lost Star
BL - v75 - Ap 15 '79 - p1295
CBRS - v7 - Ap '79 - p88
CCB-B - v32 - Mr '79 - p119
CE - v56 - Ja '80 - p169
CLW - v51 - N '79 - p183
HB - v55 - Ap '79 - p199
KR - v47 - Je 1 '79 - p642
LA - v57 - F '80 - p190
SLJ - v25 - Mr '79 - p148

The Rains Of Eridan
BL - v74 - N 1 '77 - p477

HOOVER, H M (continued)
BS - v37 - D '77 - p265
CCB-B - v31 - F '78 - p96
CE - v54 - Ap '78 - p306
EJ - v67 - S '78 - p90
HB - v54 - Ap '78 - p169
KR - v45 - Ag 15 '77 - p855
SLJ - v24 - N '77 - p57

HOPKINS, Lee Bennett 1938-
AuBYP SUP, ConAu 25R, SmATA
3, WhoBlA 77, WhoE 75, WrDr 80

A-Haunting We Will Go
BL - v73 - My 1 '77 - p1343
CCB-B - v30 - Jl '77 - p175
Cur R - v17 - My '78 - p127
SLJ - v23 - My '77 - p78

*Monsters, Ghoulies And Creepy
Creatures: Fantastic Stories And
Poems*
BL - v74 - Mr 1 '78 - p1110
CCB-B - v31 - Jl '78 - p178
Cur R - v17 - My '78 - p127

Wonder Wheels
BL - v75 - Mr 15 '79 - p1145
BS - v39 - Ag '79 - p168
CBRS - v7 - Ap '79 - p89
CCB-B - v32 - Je '79 - p177
Hi Lo - v1 - Mr '80 - p3
KR - v47 - Ap 1 '79 - p392
NYTBR - Ap 8 '79 - p32
SLJ - v25 - My '79 - p86

HOPMAN, Harry

Better Tennis For Boys And Girls
BL - v68 - Je 15 '72 - p903
KR - v40 - Mr 15 '72 - p339
LJ - v97 - My 15 '72 - p1932

HORN, Daniel
see Terry, Luther (co-author)

HORNER, Dave 1934-
ConAu 17R, SmATA 12

Better Scuba Diving For Boys
Am - v115 - N 5 '66 - p556
BL - v63 - F 1 '67 - p582
LJ - v92 - Ja 15 '67 - p351

HOUSEHOLD, Geoffrey 1900-
ConAu 77, ConLC 11, ConNov 76,
SmATA 14, WhoChL, WhoWor 74,
WrDr 80

Escape Into Daylight
Am - v135 - D 11 '76 - p429
BL - v73 - D 15 '76 - p608
BS - v36 - Ja '77 - p324
CCB-B - v30 - F '77 - p91
CSM - v68 - N 3 '76 - p20
GP - v14 - Ap '76 - p2844
JB - v40 - Ag '76 - p230
KR - v44 - S 1 '76 - p974
Kliatt - v12 - Winter '78 - p8
SLJ - v23 - D '76 - p68
Spec - v236 - Ap 10 '76 - p25
TLS - Ap 2 '76 - p388
Teacher - v95 - My '78 - p109

HOUSER, Norman W
AuBYP SUP

*Drugs: Facts On Their Use And
Abuse*
BL - v66 - N 1 '69 - p347
BL - v66 - N 15 '69 - p366
BS - v29 - S 1 '69 - p211
CC - v86 - D 10 '69 - p1585
CLW - v41 - O '69 - p134
CLW - v41 - My '70 - p577
HB - v45 - D '69 - p687
KR - v37 - Je 15 '69 - p636
LJ - v94 - O 15 '69 - p3845
NYTBR - S 21 '69 - p30
NYTBR, pt.2 - N 9 '69 - p60
SB - v5 - D '69 - p267

HOUSTON, James 1921-
ChLR 3, ConAu 65, FourBJA, IlsCB
1967, OxCan SUP, SmATA 13,
TwCCW 78

Frozen Fire: A Tale Of Courage
B&B - v6 - Ap '78 - p4
BL - v74 - F 15 '78 - p1009
BS - v37 - Ja '78 - p335
CCB-B - v31 - Mr '78 - p113
CE - v54 - Mr '78 - p258
Cur R - v17 - Ag '78 - p184
HB - v54 - F '78 - p47
KR - v45 - N 15 '77 - p1197
LA - v55 - Mr '78 - p367

HOUSTON, James (continued)
RT - v32 - O '78 - p43
SE - v42 - Ap '78 - p321
SLJ - v24 - N '77 - p57

HOWARD, Don

Moving Dirt
BL - v75 - Ap 15 '79 - p1290

HOWARD, Elizabeth   1907-
AuBYP, ConAu X, MorJA, TexWr
(also known as Mizner, Elizabeth
Howard)

Out Of Step With The Dancers
BB - v6 - Ag '78 - p4
BL - v74 - Ap 1 '78 - p1255
CCB-B - v32 - S '78 - p10
KR - v46 - My 1 '78 - p501
SLJ - v24 - Ap '78 - p94

HOWE, Janet Rogers   1901-
WhoAmW 61

*The Mystery Of The Marmalade
Cat*
CSM - v61 - My 1 '69 - pB6
KR - v37 - F 1 '69 - p100
LJ - v94 - My 15 '69 - p2122

HOYT, Edwin P   1923-
AuBYP, ConAu 1R

Andrew Johnson
BS - v25 - My 15 '65 - p98
CSM - v57 - My 6 '65 - p8B
KR - v33 - Ja 15 '65 - p65
LJ - v90 - F 15 '65 - p970
NYTBR - v70 - My 9 '65 - p20

*Deadly Craft: Fire Ships To PT
Boats*
BL - v64 - Jl 1 '68 - p1234
BS - v28 - My 1 '68 - p65
KR - v36 - Ap 1 '68 - p399
LJ - v93 - My 15 '68 - p2122

HOYT, Mary Finch
AuBYP, WhoAm 78

*American Women Of The Space
Age*
BL - v62 - Jl 15 '66 - p1087
Inst - v75 - Je '66 - p139

KR - v34 - F 15 '66 - p189
LJ - v91 - Ap 15 '66 - p2226
NYTBR - v71 - Je 12 '66 - p22
SB - v2 - My '66 - p59

HUFFMAN, Suanne

Get What You Pay For
Hi Lo - v2 - S '80 - p6

HUGHES, Jill
see Cook, David (co-author)

HUGHES, Langston   1902-1967
ConAu 1R, ConAu 25R, ConLC 10,
DcLB 4, FourBJA, SmATA 4,
WhoTwCL

The Book Of Negro Humor
Bl W - v20 - F '71 - p68
LJ - v91 - F 15 '66 - p947

HUGHES, Walter Llewellyn
see Walters, Hugh

HULL, Jessie Redding

Take Care Of Millie
BL - v76 - Jl 15 '80 - p1662
Hi Lo - v2 - O '80 - p4

HULSE, Jerry

Jody
BL - v73 - Ja 1 '77 - p644
BS - v36 - F '77 - p357
KR - v44 - Ag 1 '76 - p881
Kliatt - v12 - Spring '78 - p21
LJ - v101 - N 15 '76 - p2364
PW - v210 - Ag 2 '76 - p107
PW - v212 - O 17 '77 - p82
WLB - v51 - Mr '77 - p606

HUNT, Irene   1907-
ChLR 1, ConAu 17R, SmATA 2,
ThrBJA, TwCCW 78, WrDr 80

Across Five Aprils
Am - v110 - Je 20 '64 - p850
BS - v24 - Je 15 '64 - p129
CSM - Je 11 '64 - p9
HB - v40 - Je '64 - p291
LJ - v89 - Ap 15 '64 - p1871
NYTBR, pt.2 - My 10 '64 - p8

HUNT, Irene (continued)
    Obs - N 7 '65 - p26
    Par - v40 - Ap '65 - p32
    Par - v40 - N '65 - p153
    Spec - N 12 '65 - p632
    TLS - D 9 '65 - p1147

   The Lottery Rose
    BL - v72 - My 1 '76 - p1265
    BS - v36 - Ag '76 - p149
    CCB-B - v29 - Jl '76 - p176
    CE - v53 - Ja '77 - p147
    CLW - v48 - O '76 - p138
    Comw - v103 - N 19 '76 - p762
    KR - v44 - Ap 15 '76 - p470
    LA - v54 - Ja '77 - p84
    NYTBR - My 16 '76 - p16
    PW - v209 - Mr 22 '76 - p46
    SLJ - v22 - Ap '76 - p74

   No Promises In The Wind
    BL - v66 - Je 15 '70 - p1279
    BW - v4 - My 17 '70 - p24
    CCB-B - v24 - S '70 - p11
    CE - v47 - O '70 - p29
    CSM - v62 - My 7 '70 - pB6
    HB - v46 - Je '70 - p301
    KR - v38 - Mr 15 '70 - p329
    LJ - v95 - Mr 15 '70 - p1202
    NYTBR - Ap 5 '70 - p26
    PW - v197 - Mr 16 '70 - p56
    SR - v53 - My 9 '70 - p69
    TN - v27 - Ja '71 - p209

   Up A Road Slowly
    BL - v63 - Ja 1 '67 - p490
    CCB-B - v20 - Ja '67 - p75
    CE - v44 - O '67 - p117
    HB - v43 - F '67 - p72
    KR - v34 - N 15 '66 - p1188
    LJ - v92 - F 15 '67 - p894
    NYTBR - v71 - N 6 '66 - p8
    Obs - D 3 '67 - p26
    Obs - Mr 21 '71 - p31
    PW - v190 - D 12 '66 - p56
    PW - v194 - S 2 '68 - p63
    SR - v49 - D 10 '66 - p57
    TLS - N 30 '67 - p1141
    TN - v23 - Ap '67 - p232

   William
    BL - v73 - Je 15 '77 - p1576
    CCB-B - v31 - S '77 - p17
    CLW - v49 - O '77 - p142

    HB - v53 - O '77 - p540
    KR - v45 - Je 1 '77 - p580
    SLJ - v23 - Ap '77 - p77

HUNT, Kari 1920-
AuBYP, ConAu 41R, WhoAmA 78

   Masks And Mask Makers
    BL - v57 - Je 1 '61 - p613
    HB - v37 - Ag '61 - p356
    KR - v29 - F 1 '61 - p106
    LJ - v86 - Ap 15 '61 - p1688
    NYTBR - Je 11 '61 - p34

HUNTER, Evan 1926-
ConAu 5R, ConLC 11, SmATA 24,
WorAu, WorEFlm, WrDr 80

   Me And Mr. Stenner
    B&B - v22 - Ag '77 - p54
    BL - v73 - S 15 '76 - p175
    CCB-B - v30 - F '77 - p91
    JB - v41 - Je '77 - p179
    KR - v44 - Jl 15 '76 - p795
    Kliatt - v12 - Fall '78 - p10
    LA - v54 - Ap '77 - p442
    PW - v210 - O 4 '76 - p74
    SE - v41 - Ap '77 - p348
    SLJ - v23 - O '76 - p117
    TLS - Mr 25 '77 - p359
    Teacher - v96 - O '78 - p177

HUNTER, Hilda
   see Smaridge, Norah (co-author) -
   *The Teen-Ager's Guide To
   Collecting Practically Anything*

HUNTER, Kristin Eggleston 1931-
BlkAW, ChLR 3, ConAu 13R,
FourBJA, SmATA 12, TwCCW 78

   Guests In The Promised Land
    BL - v69 - Je 1 '73 - p947
    BS - v33 - Ap 15 '73 - p45
    Bl W - v23 - S '74 - p91
    CCB-B - v26 - Je '73 - p156
    CE - v50 - O '73 - p29
    Choice - v14 - N '77 - p1178
    Comw - v99 - N 23 '73 - p216
    HB - v49 - Ag '73 - p386
    KR - v41 - My 15 '73 - p567
    LJ - v98 - S 15 '73 - p2651
    NO - v12 - Ag 11 '73 - p21

HUNTER, Kristin Eggleston (continued)
    PW - v203 - My 28 '73 - p40
    Teacher - v92 - S '74 - p130
    Teacher - v94 - O '76 - p151

    The Soul Brothers And Sister Lou
    BL - v65 - N 1 '68 - p312
    BL - v65 - Ap 1 '69 - p901
    BL - v69 - My 1 '73 - p838
    BS - v28 - O 1 '68 - p277
    BW - v2 - N 3 '68 - p20
    CE - v46 - Ap '70 - p368
    Choice - v14 - N '77 - p1178
    Comw - v91 - F 27 '70 - p585
    EJ - v64 - D '75 - p80
    EL - v31 - Ap '74 - p593
    HB - v45 - Ap '69 - p177
    KR - v36 - Jl 15 '68 - p765
    LJ - v93 - N 15 '68 - p4419
    NS - v81 - Mr 5 '71 - p312
    NYTBR - Ja 26 '69 - p26
    NYTBR, pt 2 - F 15 '70 - p22
    PW - v194 - S 30 '68 - p61
    PW - v196 - S 29 '69 - p60
    SE - v33 - My '69 - p558
    SR - v51 - O 19 '68 - p37

HUNTER, Mollie   1922-
    ConAu X, SmATA 2, ThrBJA,
    TwCCW 78, WrDr 80 (also known as
    McIlwraith, Maureen Mollie Hunter
    McVeigh)

    The Spanish Letters
    BL - v63 - Je 1 '67 - p1048
    BS - v27 - Ag 1 '67 - p183
    CCB-B - v21 - S '67 - p9
    HB - v43 - Ag '67 - p471
    KR - v35 - F 15 '67 - p208
    LJ - v92 - S 15 '67 - p3199
    LR - v20 - Spring '65 - p45
    PW - v191 - My 22 '67 - p64
    SR - v50 - My 13 '67 - p57
   see also McIlwraith, Maureen Mollie
    Hunter McVeigh

HUNTSBERRY, William E   1916-
    ConAu 1R, DrAS 78E, SmATA 5

    The Big Hang-Up
    Am - v123 - D 5 '70 - p497
    BS - v30 - My 1 '70 - p61
    CCB-B - v24 - D '70 - p60

    Comw - v92 - My 22 '70 - p248
    KR - v38 - F 15 '70 - p178

    The Big Wheels
    Am - v117 - N 4 '67 - p518
    BL - v64 - Ap 15 '68 - p983
    BS - v27 - O 1 '67 - p263
    BW - v1 - N 19 '67 - p24
    CCB-B - v21 - D '67 - p60
    CSM - v59 - N 2 '67 - pB12
    HB - v43 - O '67 - p601
    KR - v35 - Jl 15 '67 - p816
    LJ - v93 - F 15 '68 - p882
    NYTBR - v72 - O 8 '67 - p38
    SR - v50 - N 11 '67 - p50

HUSS, Barbara
    see Lubowe, Irwin I (co-author)

HUTCHINS, Ross E   1906-
    ConAu 9R, SmATA 4, ThrBJA,
    WhoAm 78

    The Last Trumpeters
    CCB-B - v21 - Mr '68 - p111
    CSM - v59 - N 2 '67 - pB11
    KR - v35 - Jl 1 '67 - p743
    Obs - O 15 '67 - p28
    PW - v192 - Ag 14 '67 - p50
    SB - v3 - Mr '68 - p322
    TLS - N 2 '67 - p1030

HYDE, Margaret Oldroyd   1917-
    ConAu 1R, SmATA 1, ThrBJA

    Exploring Earth And Space
    KR - v35 - Ag 15 '67 - p978
    LJ - v92 - D 15 '67 - p4623
    LJ - v96 - Ja 15 '71 - p276
    SB - v6 - Mr '71 - p285

    Flight For Today And Tomorrow
    BL - v67 - Mr 15 '71 - p623
    LJ - v96 - My 15 '71 - p1827
    SB - v7 - My '71 - p78

    Know Your Feelings
    ACSB - v8   Fall '75 - p17

    VD: The Silent Epidemic
    BL - v70 - O 15 '73 - p222
    CCB-B - v27 - S '73 - p10
    LJ - v98 - My 15 '73 - p1655
    LJ - v98 - My 15 '73 - p1690
    SB - v9 - Mr '74 - p312

HYNDMAN, Jane Andrews Lee
  see Wyndham, Lee

I

ILOWITE, Sheldon A

*Fury On Ice: A Canadian-
American Hockey Story*
CLW - v42 - My '71 - p581
Inst - v130 - Ap '71 - p132
LJ - v95 - D 15 '70 - p4381

INGMANSON, Dale
see Stone, A Harris (co-author) -
*Rocks And Rills: A Look At
Geology*

IRWIN, Constance Frick
see Frick, Constance H

ISH-KISHOR, Sulamith   1897?-1977
ConAu 69, ConAu 73, SmATA 17,
TwCCW 78

Our Eddie
A Lib - v1 - Ap '70 - p385
BL - v65 - My 15 '69 - p1076
BS - v29 - F 1 '70 - p423
BW - v3 - My 4 '69 - p36
CCB-B - v23 - O '69 - p25
CSM - v61 - My 1 '69 - pB6
HB - v45 - Ag '69 - p417
Inst - v79 - Ag '69 - p191
KR - v37 - Mr 15 '69 - p315
LJ - v94 - My 15 '69 - p2114
NYTBR - Jl 20 '69 - p22
PW - v195 - Je 9 '69 - p63
SR - v52 - My 10 '69 - p60

ISHMOLE, Jack   1924-
ConAu 49

Walk In The Sky
BS - v32 - My 15 '72 - p98
KR - v40 - F 1 '72 - p143
LJ - v98 - Mr 15 '73 - p1013
NYTBR, pt.2 - N 5 '72 - p7

SE - v37 - D '73 - p790

IZENBERG, Jerry
AuBYP SUP

*Great Latin Sports Figures: Proud
People*
BL - v73 - S 1 '76 - p38
Comw - v103 - N 19 '76 - p764
KR - v44 - My 15 '76 - p596

J

JABLONSKI, Edward   1922-
AuBYP, ConAu 1R, WhoAm 78

*Warriors With Wings: The Story
Of The Lafayette Escadrille*
BL - v63 - D 15 '66 - p448
BS - v26 - O 1 '66 - p250
KR - v34 - Je 15 '66 - p579
LJ - v91 - N 15 '66 - p5760
NYTBR - v71 - O 16 '66 - p38

JACKER, Corinne   1933-
ConAu 17R, WhoAmW 75, WrDr 80

*The Biological Revolution: A
Background Book On The Making
Of The New World*
BL - v68 - F 15 '72 - p502
BL - v68 - F 15 '72 - p506
CCB-B - v25 - F '72 - p92
KR - v39 - N 15 '71 - p1220
SB - v8 - My '72 - p44
SR - v55 - Ja 15 '72 - p47

JACKSON, Anita

The Actor
BL - v75 - Jl 15 '79 - p1610
Hi Lo - v2 - O '80 - p5
Kliatt - v13 - Winter '79 - p16

A Deadly Game
BL - v75 - Jl 15 '79 - p1610
Hi Lo - v2 - O '80 - p5
Kliatt - v13 - Winter '79 - p16

Dreams
BL - v75 - Jl 15 '79 - p1610
Hi Lo - v2 - O '80 - p5
Kliatt - v13 - Winter '79 - p16

The Ear
BL - v75 - Jl 15 '79 - p1610
Hi Lo - v2 - O '80 - p5

Kliatt - v13 - Winter '79 - p16
TN - v36 - Winter '80 - p198

'57 T-Bird
BL - v75 - Jl 15 '79 - p1610
Hi Lo - v2 - O '80 - p5
Kliatt - v13 - Winter '79 - p16

Homecoming
BL - v75 - Jl 15 '79 - p1610
Hi Lo - v2 - O '80 - p5
Kliatt - v13 - Winter '79 - p16

No Rent To Pay
BL - v75 - Jl 15 '79 - p1610
Hi Lo - v2 - O '80 - p5
Kliatt - v13 - Winter '79 - p16

Z B-4
BL - v75 - Jl 15 '79 - p1610
Hi Lo - v2 - O '80 - p5
Kliatt - v13 - Winter '79 - p16

JACKSON, Caary Paul   1902-
AuBYP, ConAu 5R, SmATA 6

No Talent Letterman
KR - v34 - F 15 '66 - p186
LJ - v91 - Jl '66 - p3551
PW - v190 - O 3 '66 - p84

JACKSON, Jesse   1908-
ConAu 25R, ConLC 12, SelBAA,
SmATA 2, TwCCW 78, WrDr 80

*Make A Joyful Noise Unto The
Lord!: The Life Of Mahalia
Jackson*
CCB-B - v28 - N '74 - p44
HB - v50 - D '74 - p700
SLJ - v21 - Ja '75 - p43

Tessie
BL - v65 - S 15 '68 - p122

121

JACKSON, Jesse (continued)
BS - v28 - Jl 1 '68 - p154
BW - v2 - My 5 '68 - p34
CCB-B - v22 - S '68 - p9
CSM - v60 - Je 13 '68 - p5
Comw - v88 - My 24 '68 - p306
HB - v44 - Ag '68 - p430
KR - v36 - My 1 '68 - p518
LJ - v93 - O 15 '68 - p3983
NYTBR - v73 - My 26 '68 - p30
SR - v51 - Je 15 '68 - p33

JACKSON, Orpha B
see Jackson, Caary Paul (co-author)

JACKSON, Robert   1941-

Fighter Pilots Of World War I
BL - v74 - F 1 '78 - p903
BS - v37 - F '78 - p358
LR - v26 - Autumn '77 - p264

Fighter Pilots Of World War II
BL - v73 - My 1 '77 - p1339
LJ - v101 - D 1 '76 - p2485

JACKSON, Robert Blake   1926-
AuBYP, ConAu 5R, SmATA 8

Behind The Wheel
KR - v39 - My 15 '71 - p556
LJ - v96 - My 15 '71 - p1822

Earl The Pearl: The Story Of Baltimore's Earl Monroe
KR - v37 - D 1 '69 - p1262
LJ - v95 - My 15 '70 - p1965

Fisk Of Fenway Park: New England's Favorite Catcher
BL - v72 - Jl 15 '76 - p1596
KR - v44 - My 15 '76 - p597
SLJ - v23 - S '76 - p118

Grand Prix At The Glen
BL - v62 - D 1 '65 - p363
KR - v33 - S 1 '65 - p913
LJ - v90 - O 15 '65 - p4636

Here Comes Bobby Orr
BL - v68 - Ap 1 '72 - p676
KR - v39 - N 1 '71 - p1161
LJ - v96 - D 15 '71 - p4202

Road Race Round The World: New York To Paris, 1908
SLJ - v24 - S '77 - p130

Sports Cars
BL - v69 - My 1 '73 - p863
LJ - v98 - My 15 '73 - p1705

Stock Car Racing: Grand National Competition
BL - v64 - Ap 15 '68 - p995
KR - v36 - Ja 15 '68 - p60
LJ - v93 - My 15 '68 - p2130

Supermex: The Lee Trevino Story
KR - v41 - My 15 '73 - p563
LJ - v98 - D 15 '73 - p3724
PW - v203 - My 14 '73 - p47

JACKSON, Shirley   1919-1965
ConAu 1R, ConAu 25R, ConLC 11,
OxAm, SmATA 2, WhAm 4

The Witchcraft Of Salem Village
Kliatt - v11 - Winter '77 - p27
NYTBR - N 25 '56 - p56

JACOBS, David   1939-
AmM&WS 78S

Beethoven
BL - v66 - Je 1 '70 - p1214
BS - v30 - Ap 1 '70 - p18
CCB-B - v24 - Jl '70 - p180
CSM - v62 - My 7 '70 - pB7
KR - v38 - F 1 '70 - p115
LJ - v96 - Jl '71 - p2373
PW - v197 - Mr 30 '70 - p65
SR - v53 - My 9 '70 - p70
TLS - O 30 '70 - p1268

JACOBS, Emma Atkins

A Chance To Belong
BL - v50 - D 1 '53 - p151
KR - v21 - Ag 1 '53 - p489
LJ - v78 - N 1 '53 - p1943
SR - v36 - N 14 '53 - p68

JACOBS, Karen Folger   1940-
AmM&WS 78S

Girl Sports
LJ - v103 - My 15 '78 - p1075
SLJ - v24 - My '78 - p86

JACOBS, Karen Folger (continued)
WLB - v52 - Ap '78 - p639

JACOBS, Lou, Jr.   1921-
AuBYP SUP, ConAu 21R, SmATA
2, WhoWest 78

Jumbo Jets
BL - v66 - Mr 1 '70 - p847
CCB-B - v24 - S '70 - p12
SB - v6 - My '70 - p63

JACOBSON, Ethel
ConAu 37R, WrDr 80

The Cats Of Sea-Cliff Castle
LJ - v97 - S 15 '72 - p2936
PW - v201 - My 22 '72 - p51

JAGENDORF, Moritz   1888-1981
ConAu 5R, MorJA, SmATA 2,
SmATA 24N, WrDr 80

The First Book Of Puppets
BL - v49 - F 1 '53 - p192
KR - v20 - O 1 '52 - p659
LJ - v78 - F 1 '53 - p226
WLB - v49 - Mr '53 - p87

JAMES, Charles L   1934-
ConAu 29R, DrAS 74E, LivBAA,
SelBAA

*From The Roots: Short Stories By
Black Americans*
Bl W - v19 - S '70 - p97

JAMES, Stuart

The Firefighters
Hi Lo - v2 - N '80 - p5

JAMES, T G H

The Archaeology Of Ancient Egypt
BL - v70 - S 1 '73 - p46
CCB-B - v27 - O '73 - p31
CLW - v45 - N '73 - p185
HB - v49 - O '73 - p478
KR - v41 - Ap 1 '73 - p401
LJ - v98 - My 15 '73 - p1581
LJ - v98 - My 15 '73 - p1655
LJ - v98 - My 15 '73 - p1689
NY - v49 - D 3 '73 - p219
Obs - Jl 16 '72 - p31

PW - v203 - Ap 2 '73 - p65
SLJ - v25 - S '78 - p43
TLS - Jl 14 '72 - p810

JAMESON, Jon

The Picture Life Of O. J. Simpson
Comw - v104 - N 11 '77 - p734
SLJ - v23 - My '77 - p80

JANE, Mary C   1909-
AuBYP, ConAu 1R, ForWC 70,
SmATA 6

Mystery On Nine-Mile Marsh
KR - v35 - Jl 1 '67 - p740
LJ - v92 - N 15 '67 - p4269
PW - v193 - Ja 8 '68 - p67

JANECZKO, Paul

*The Crystal Image: A Poetry
Anthology*
Kliatt - v11 - Fall '77 - p15

JARUNKOVA, Klara

Don't Cry For Me
BL - v65 - O 15 '68 - p234
BS - v28 - Ag 1 '68 - p195
CCB-B - v22 - O '68 - p30
EJ - v58 - F '69 - p295
LJ - v93 - My 15 '68 - p2123
NYTBR - v73 - S 22 '68 - p28

JEFFRIES, Roderic Graeme   1926-
AuBYP, ConAu 17R, EncMys,
SmATA 4

Patrol Car
BL - v63 - Jl 15 '67 - p1193
CCB-B - v21 - S '67 - p10
HB - v43 - Je '67 - p354
KR - v35 - F 1 '67 - p138
LJ - v92 - My 15 '67 - p2039
PW - v191 - Je 12 '67 - p59

Trapped
CCB-B - v25 - Ap '72 - p124
HB - v48 - Je '72 - p269
KR - v40 - F 1 '72 - p136
LJ - v97 - Je 15 '72 - p2243
see also Ashford, Jeffrey

JOFFO, Joseph

A Bag Of Marbles
BL - v71 - N 1 '74 - p264
CSM - v66 - O 2 '74 - p13
GP - v14 - Jl '75 - p2676
KR - v42 - Ag 1 '74 - p851
KR - v42 - Ag 15 '74 - p886
LJ - v99 - Ag '74 - p1937
NO - v13 - N 2 '74 - p23
PW - v206 - Ag 5 '74 - p57

JOHNSON, Annabel   1921-
ConAu 9R, SmATA 2, ThrBJA,
TwCCW 78, WrDr 80

The Burning Glass
BL - v63 - D 1 '66 - p418
BS - v26 - N 1 '66 - p294
CCB-B - v20 - D '66 - p60
CLW - v38 - Ja '67 - p340
CSM - v58 - N 3 '66 - pB11
HB - v42 - D '66 - p719
KR - v34 - S 1 '66 - p913
LJ - v91 - N 15 '66 - p5760

Count Me Gone
BL - v64 - Jl 15 '68 - p1281
BW - v2 - O 13 '68 - p14
CCB-B - v21 - Jl '68 - p176
CSM - v60 - Je 13 '68 - p5
HB - v44 - Ag '68 - p431
LJ - v93 - O 15 '68 - p3983
NYTBR - v73 - My 5 '68 - p8

A Golden Touch
BS - v23 - Ap 15 '63 - p41
CSM - My 9 '63 - p5B
Comw - v78 - My 24 '63 - p257
HB - v39 - Ap '63 - p177
LJ - v88 - Je 15 '63 - p2561
NYTBR - O 25 '64 - p36
NYTBR, pt.2 - My 12 '63 - p26

The Grizzly
Am - v111 - N 21 '64 - p667
CSM - N 5 '64 - p5B
Comw - v81 - N 6 '64 - p206
HB - v40 - D '64 - p616
LJ - v89 - D 15 '64 - p5018
NYTBR - O 25 '64 - p36
Par - v40 - O '65 - p108

JOHNSON, Corinne Benson
AuBYP SUP

Love And Sex And Growing Up
SLJ - v24 - Mr '78 - p130

JOHNSON, Edgar Raymond
see Johnson, Annabel (co-author)

JOHNSON, Eric Warner   1918-
AuBYP SUP, ConAu 5R, SmATA 8,
WhoE 77, WrDr 80

Sex: Telling It Straight
BL - v67 - D 1 '70 - p303
Comw - v93 - N 20 '70 - p205
KR - v38 - N 15 '70 - p1257
NYTBR, pt.2 - N 7 '71 - p47
Par - v46 - F '71 - p42
SB - v6 - Mr '71 - p331
see also Johnson, Corinne Benson (co-author)

JOHNSON, Gerald W   1890-
ConAu 85, OxAm, SmATA 19,
ThrBJA, WhoAm 78

Franklin D. Roosevelt: Portrait Of A Great Man
BL - v63 - Jl 15 '67 - p1194
BS - v27 - Jl 1 '67 - p145
CCB-B - v20 - Jl '67 - p171
CE - v44 - Ja '68 - p324
EJ - v56 - N '67 - p1221
Inst - v76 - Je '67 - p142
KR - v35 - Mr 15 '67 - p346
LJ - v92 - S 15 '67 - p3200
NY - v43 - D 16 '67 - p182
NYTBR - v72 - N 5 '67 - p65
NYTBR, pt.2 - v72 - My 7 '67 - p36
PW - v191 - Ap 10 '67 - p82
SR - v50 - My 13 '67 - p56

JOHNSON, Pat

Horse Talk
Am - v117 - N 4 '67 - p520
CSM - v60 - N 30 '67 - pB5
LJ - v93 - Ja 15 '68 - p292
PW - v192 - O 16 '67 - p58

JOHNSTON, Johanna
ConAu 57, FourBJA, SmATA 12

JOHNSTON, Johanna (continued)

Paul Cuffee: America's First Black Captain
BL - v67 - Mr 1 '71 - p560
KR - v38 - N 15 '70 - p1251
LJ - v96 - Je 15 '71 - p2131

Together In America: The Story Of Two Races And One Nation
BL - v62 - S 1 '65 - p56
BS - v25 - Ap 15 '65 - p52
CC - v82 - Je 30 '65 - p838
CCB-B - v18 - Ap '65 - p119
CLW - v36 - My '65 - p639
Comw - v82 - My 28 '65 - p331
KR - v33 - F 1 '65 - p113
LJ - v90 - F 15 '65 - p972

JONES, Adrienne   1915-
ConAu 33R, SmATA 7, WhoAmW 77, WrDr 80

Another Place, Another Spring
BL - v68 - Ap 15 '72 - p717
BL - v68 - Ap 15 '72 - p724
CLW - v43 - Ap '72 - p470
CLW - v43 - Ap '72 - p481
HB - v48 - F '72 - p57
KR - v39 - N 1 '71 - p1164
LJ - v96 - D 15 '71 - p4190
PW - v200 - N 22 '71 - p41

JONES, Claire
WhoAmA 78

Pollution: The Noise We Hear
B&B - v18 - Jl '73 - p141

JONES, Cordelia

A Cat Called Camouflage
Am - v125 - D 4 '71 - p488
BL - v68 - Ja 15 '72 - p433
BS - v31 - O 15 '71 - p335
CE - v49 - O '72 - p28
EJ - v61 - Mr '72 - p433
KR - v39 - S 15 '71 - p1013
LJ - v96 - D 15 '71 - p4184
PW - v200 - S 6 '71 - p51
SR - v54 - O 16 '71 - p57

JONES, Hettie   1934-
AuBYP SUP, ConAu 81

Big Star Fallin' Mama: Five Black Women In Music
BL - v70 - Mr 1 '74 - p741
BS - v34 - Ap 15 '74 - p53
Bl W - v24 - Jl '75 - p62
CCB-B - v27 - My '74 - p145
Inst - v83 - N '73 - p125
KR - v41 - O 15 '73 - p1173
KR - v41 - D 15 '73 - p1359
LJ - v99 - My 15 '74 - p1483
NYTBR - D 30 '73 - p10
PW - v205 - Ja 28 '74 - p301

JONES, Ron

The Acorn People
BL - v73 - My 1 '77 - p1331
BksW - v1 - Ap '77 - p38

JONES, Weyman B   1928-
ConAu 17R, FourBJA, SmATA 4

Computer
BL - v66 - My 1 '70 - p1092
BS - v30 - Ap 1 '70 - p18
KR - v37 - D 1 '69 - p1271
LJ - v95 - Ap 15 '70 - p1651
SB - v6 - My '70 - p18

Edge Of Two Worlds
BL - v64 - Jl 15 '68 - p1286
BW - v2 - S 29 '68 - p18
KR - v36 - Ap 15 '68 - p466
LJ - v93 - Ap 15 '68 - p1812
NYTBR - v73 - My 5 '68 - p32
PW - v193 - Ap 29 '68 - p78
SR - v51 - N 9 '68 - p68

JORDAN, Ben

Sky Jumpers: A Novel About Free Fall Parachuting
KR - v33 - Mr 1 '65 - p249
LJ - v90 - Jl '65 - p3133

JORDAN, Hope Dahle   1905-
ConAu 77, SmATA 15

The Fortune Cake
BL - v68 - Jl 1 '72 - p942
HB - v48 - O '72 - p467
KR - v40 - Ja 15 '72 - p68
LJ - v97 - Ap 15 '72 - p1606

JORDAN, Hope Dahle (continued)

Haunted Summer
CCB-B - v21 - S '67 - p10
HB - v43 - Ag '67 - p475
KR - v35 - My 15 '67 - p608
LJ - v92 - S 15 '67 - p3200
NYTBR - v72 - N 5 '67 - p64
NYTBR, pt.2 - v72 - My 7 '67 - p12
TN - v24 - N '67 - p99

JORDAN, June 1936-
ConAu 33R, ConLC 11, FourBJA,
SelBAA, SmATA 4, TwCCW 78

Dry Victories
BL - v69 - Ja 1 '73 - p449
CCB-B - v26 - Ap '73 - p125
EJ - v63 - Ja '74 - p67
KR - v40 - Jl 15 '72 - p809
KR - v40 - D 15 '72 - p1424
LJ - v97 - N 15 '72 - p3806
NYTBR, pt.1 - F 11 '73 - p8
SE - v37 - D '73 - p785
Teacher - v93 - Ap '76 - p122

His Own Where
BL - v68 - Ja 1 '72 - p391
BL - v68 - Ja 1 '72 - p394
BL - v68 - Ap 1 '72 - p664
CCB-B - v25 - D '71 - p58
CSM - v63 - N 11 '71 - pB6
CSM - v64 - F 24 '72 - p7
Comw - v95 - N 19 '71 - p188
EJ - v63 - Ja '74 - p65
EJ - v67 - My '78 - p88
HB - v47 - D '71 - p620
KR - v39 - S 15 '71 - p1021
LJ - v96 - D 15 '71 - p4159
LJ - v96 - D 15 '71 - p4190
NYRB - v18 - Ap 20 '72 - p13
NYT - v121 - D 16 '71 - p67
NYTBR, pt.2 - N 7 '71 - p6
NYTBR, pt.2 - N 7 '71 - p28
NYTBR, pt.2 - My 6 '73 - p28
PW - v200 - O 18 '71 - p50
TN - v28 - Ap '72 - p312

Soulscript
BL - v67 - O 15 '70 - p165
BL - v67 - Ap 1 '71 - p654
Bl W - v20 - Ja '71 - p95
KR - v38 - Ap 1 '70 - p425
KR - v38 - My 1 '70 - p519

LJ - v95 - Jl '70 - p2540
PW - v197 - My 18 '70 - p36
TN - v27 - Ap '71 - p309
VQR - v47 - Winter '71 - pR20

JORGENSEN, Mary Venn
see Adrian, Mary

K

KAATZ, Evelyn

Motorcycle Road Racer
KR - v45 - D 1 '77 - p1268
SLJ - v24 - F '78 - p59

KADESCH, Robert R 1922-
AmM&WS 76P, AuBYP SUP,
ConAu 57, WhoAm 78

Math Menagerie
BL - v67 - F 15 '71 - p490
BL - v67 - Ap 1 '71 - p660
BS - v30 - Ja 15 '71 - p452
CCB-B - v24 - Jl '71 - p173
Comw - v93 - N 20 '70 - p205
KR - v38 - O 15 '70 - p1169
LJ - v96 - Ja 15 '71 - p277
NY - v46 - D 5 '70 - p208
SB - v6 - Mr '71 - p293

KAHN, Albert E 1912-1979
ConAu 89, NewYTBS 79, WhoWest
78

*Days With Ulanova: An Intimate
Portrait Of The Legendary Russian
Ballerina*
BW - v9 - S 9 '79 - p13
Dance - v54 - Je '80 - p117
Kliatt - v14 - Winter '80 - p61
NYTBR - N 11 '79 - p43

KAHN, Ely Jacques 1916-
ConAu 65, TwCA SUP, WhoAm 78

A Building Goes Up
BL - v65 - Je 15 '69 - p1176
CCB-B - v22 - Je '69 - p160
KR - v37 - Mr 15 '69 - p310
LJ - v95 - My 15 '70 - p1944
SB - v5 - My '69 - p84
SR - v52 - My 10 '69 - p59

KAHN, Joan 1914-
AuBYP SUP, ConAu 77

Some Things Fierce And Fatal
BL - v68 - N 1 '71 - p242
BS - v31 - N 15 '71 - p386
BW - v5 - N 7 '71 - p11
CCB-B - v25 - D '71 - p58
CE - v49 - N '72 - p85
CLW - v43 - F '72 - p361
KR - v39 - Ag 15 '71 - p886
LJ - v96 - D 15 '71 - p4200
NY - v47 - D 4 '71 - p199
NYTBR, pt.1 - F 13 '72 - p8
PW - v200 - O 18 '71 - p51
TLS - Ap 28 '72 - p484

KAISER, Ernest
see Halliburton, Warren J (co-
author)

KAMM, Herbert 1917-
ConAu 69, WhoAm 78

*The Junior Illustrated
Encyclopedia Of Sports*
SLJ - v22 - N '75 - p92

KANTOR, MacKinlay 1904-1977
ConAu 61, ConAu 73, ConLC 7,
ConNov 76, OxAm, WhoAm 78

The Daughter Of Bugle Ann
KR - v21 - Ja 15 '53 - p54
LJ - v78 - Ap 15 '53 - p729
LJ - v78 - Je 15 '53 - p1164
NYT - Ap 19 '53 - p4

The Voice Of Bugle Ann
BL - v32 - S '35 - p15
CSM - Ag 27 '35 - p13
Cu H - v43 - O '35 - pR12
LJ - v60 - N 1 '35 - p828

KANTOR, MacKinlay (continued)
  NAR - v240 - D '35 - p550
  NYT - Ag 25 '35 - p7
  Nat - v141 - S 4 '35 - p279
  New R - v84 - O 23 '35 - p312
  SR - v12 - Ag 31 '35 - p4
  TLS - D 7 '35 - p841

KARK, Nina Mary
  see Bawden, Nina

KASTNER, Erich   1899-1974
  OxGer, SmATA 14, ThrBJA,
  TwCCW 78B, WhoChL, WorAu

  Lisa And Lottie
    BL - v65 - Jl 1 '69 - p1229
    CCB-B - v24 - Jl '70 - p181
    KR - v37 - Ap 15 '69 - p443
    LJ - v94 - S 15 '69 - p3206

KATZ, Bobbi   1933-
  ConAu 37R, SmATA 12, WrDr 80

  Volleyball Jinx
    BL - v74 - F 15 '78 - p1013
    CCB-B - v31 - My '78 - p143
    SLJ - v24 - Ap '78 - p86

KATZ, Susan

  Kristy And Jimmy
    SLJ - v25 - Mr '79 - p140

KATZ, William Loren   1927-
  AuBYP SUP, ConAu 21R, SmATA
  13, WhoAm 78, WrDr 80

  A History Of Black Americans
    SS - v65 - O '74 - p231

KAUFMAN, Bel
  ConAu 13R, WhoAm 78, WrDr 80

  Up The Down Staircase
    Am - v112 - F 6 '65 - p198
    Am - v112 - My 8 '65 - p677
    BL - v61 - Ja 1 '65 - p424
    BS - v24 - F 1 '65 - p416
    CC - v82 - Ja 27 '65 - p113
    CSM - Mr 6 '65 - p9
    Choice - v2 - Mr '65 - p22
    Comw - v82 - My 14 '65 - p260
    Cres - v28 - S '65 - p24

    LJ - v90 - Ja 1 '65 - p135
    NYRB - v6 - Jl 7 '66 - p20
    NYT - v114 - F 9 '65 - p39M
    NYTBR - v70 - F 14 '65 - p42
    Nat R - v17 - Je 1 '65 - p476
    PW - v191 - Mr 27 '67 - p62
    SE - v30 - F '66 - p143
    SR - v48 - Mr 20 '65 - p71
    TCR - v66 - My '65 - p777
    TCR - v66 - My '65 - p778
    Time - v85 - F 12 '65 - p96

KAULA, Edna Mason   1906-
  AuBYP, ConAu 5R, SmATA 13

  African Village Folktales
    KR - v36 - Je 1 '68 - p599
    LJ - v93 - Jl '68 - p2734
    NYTBR - v73 - My 5 '68 - p30
    PW - v193 - Je 3 '68 - p129

KAVALER, Lucy   1930-
  AuBYP, ConAu 57, SmATA 23

  *Freezing Point: Cold As A Matter
  Of Life And Death*
    BL - v67 - Ja 1 '71 - p350
    BL - v67 - Ja 1 '71 - p654
    BS - v30 - O 15 '70 - p286
    BW - v4 - Ag 30 '70 - p3
    KR - v38 - Ap 1 '70 - p426
    KR - v38 - Ap 15 '70 - p475
    KR - v38 - Jl 1 '70 - p726
    LJ - v95 - Je 1 '70 - p2170
    LJ - v96 - Mr 1 '71 - p788
    NYTBR - S 27 '70 - p10
    PW - v198 - Jl 20 '70 - p61
    SA - v224 - Je '71 - p132
    SB - v6 - D '70 - p221
    TN - v27 - Ap '71 - p309
    WSJ - v176 - S 28 '70 - p14

KAY, Eleanor

  Nurses And What They Do
    BL - v64 - My 1 '68 - p1045
    KR - v36 - F 15 '68 - p194
    Obs - My 19 '68 - p1322
    SB - v4 - My '68 - p53

KEEFE, John E   1942-
  DrAS 74F

KEEFE, John E (continued)

Aim For A Job In Appliance Service
BL - v66 - S 1 '69 - p46

KELLER, Roseanne

Five Dog Night And Other Tales
BL - v76 - Ap 15 '80 - p1184
Hi Lo - v1 - D '79 - p3

Two For The Road
Hi Lo - v1 - D '79 - p3

KELLEY, Leo P 1928-
ConSFA, EncSF, ScF&FL 1,
ScF&FL 2

Backward In Time
BL - v76 - Ja 15 '80 - p715
Hi Lo - v1 - Ja '80 - p5

Dead Moon
BL - v75 - Jl 15 '79 - p1632
Hi Lo - v2 - O '80 - p4

Death Sentence
BL - v76 - Ja 15 '80 - p715
Hi Lo - v1 - Ja '80 - p5

Earth Two
BL - v76 - Ja 15 '80 - p715
Hi Lo - v1 - Ja '80 - p5

Good-Bye To Earth
BL - v75 - Jl 15 '79 - p1632
Hi Lo - v2 - O '80 - p4

King Of The Stars
BL - v75 - Jl 15 '79 - p1632
Hi Lo - v2 - O '80 - p4

Night Of Fire And Blood
Hi Lo - v1 - O '79 - p3
SLJ - v26 - D '79 - p82

On The Red World
BL - v75 - Jl 15 '79 - p1632
Hi Lo - v2 - O '80 - p4

Prison Satellite
BL - v76 - Ja 15 '80 - p715
Hi Lo - v1 - Ja '80 - p5

Star Gold
BL - v76 - Ap 15 '80 - p1184

Hi Lo - v1 - O '79 - p3
SLJ - v26 - D '79 - p82

Sunworld
Hi Lo - v1 - Ja '80 - p5

Vacation In Space
BL - v75 - Jl 15 '79 - p1632
Hi Lo - v2 - O '80 - p4

Where No Sun Shines
BL - v75 - Jl 15 '79 - p1633
Hi Lo - v2 - O '80 - p4

Worlds Apart
BL - v76 - Ja 15 '80 - p715
Hi Lo - v1 - Ja '80 - p5

KEMPF, Sharon
see Chandler, Caroline A (co-author)

KENDAL, Wallis 1937-
Prof

Just Gin
KR - v41 - Ap 1 '73 - p384
LJ - v98 - S 15 '73 - p2665

KENDALL, Lace (pseud.) 1916-
ConAu X, SmATA 3, ThrBJA,
WhoAm 78 (real name: Stoutenburg,
Adrien Pearl)

Houdini: Master Of Escape
BL - v57 - Ap 1 '61 - p500
KR - v28 - Jl 1 '60 - p509
LJ - v85 - D 15 '60 - p4567

Masters Of Magic
BL - v63 - O 1 '66 - p188
BS - v26 - My 1 '66 - p58
KR - v34 - Ja 1 '66 - p12
LJ - v91 - My 15 '66 - p2708
see also Stoutenburg, Adrien Pearl

KENEALY, James P 1927-
ConAu 93

Better Camping For Boys
BL - v70 - Mr 15 '74 - p821
CCB-B - v27 - Je '74 - p159
CLW - v45 - My '74 - p503
KR - v42 - Ja 15 '74 - p57
LJ - v99 - Ap 15 '74 - p1220
NYTBR - My 5 '74 - p44

KENT, Deborah

> *Belonging*
> CLW - v50 - O '78 - p109
> Kliatt - v14 - Spring '80 - p6

KERR, M E   (pseud.) 1927-
ConLC 12, FourBJA, SmATA 20,
TwCCW 78, WrDr 80 (real name:
Meaker, Marijane)

> *Dinky Hocker Shoots Smack*
> BL - v69 - D 1 '72 - p351
> BL - v69 - D 1 '72 - p357
> BS - v32 - O 15 '72 - p339
> BS - v33 - N 1 '73 - p355
> CCB-B - v26 - D '72 - p59
> EJ - v62 - D '73 - p1298
> EJ - v63 - My '74 - p91
> Econ - v249 - D 29 '73 - p59
> HB - v49 - F '73 - p56
> KR - v40 - O 1 '72 - p1152
> KR - v40 - D 15 '72 - p1420
> LJ - v97 - D 15 '72 - p4056
> LJ - v97 - D 15 '72 - p4079
> NS - v86 - N 9 '73 - p700
> NY - v48 - D 2 '72 - p190
> NYTBR, pt.1 - F 11 '73 - p8
> PW - v203 - Ja 1 '73 - p57
> Spec - v231 - O 20 '73 - pR10
> TLS - N 23 '73 - p1433
> TN - v29 - Ap '73 - p253
> TN - v30 - Ja '74 - p203
> Teacher - v90 - Mr '73 - p80

> *Gentlehands*
> BL - v74 - Mr 15 '78 - p1175
> BS - v38 - S '78 - p180
> BW - Jl 9 '78 - pE4
> CCB-B - v31 - Ap '78 - p129
> Comw - v105 - N 10 '78 - p733
> EJ - v67 - S '78 - p90
> HB - v54 - Je '78 - p284
> J Read - v22 - N '78 - p183
> KR - v46 - F 15 '78 - p183
> NYTBR - Ap 30 '78 - p30
> PW - v213 - Ja 9 '78 - p81
> SLJ - v24 - Mr '78 - p138
> SLJ - v24 - My '78 - p36

> *If I Love You, Am I Trapped Forever?*
> BL - v69 - Je 15 '73 - p984
> BS - v33 - My 15 '73 - p98
> CCB-B - v26 - Je '73 - p157
> CSM - v65 - My 5 '73 - p10
> EJ - v66 - O '77 - p57
> HB - v49 - Je '73 - p276
> KR - v41 - F 1 '73 - p123
> LJ - v98 - Ap 15 '73 - p1395
> NYTBR - S 16 '73 - p8
> NYTBR - N 4 '73 - p52
> NYTBR - My 12 '74 - p39
> PT - v7 - D '73 - p126
> PW - v203 - F 12 '73 - p68

> *I'll Love You When You're More Like Me*
> BB - v5 - Ja '78 - p3
> BL - v74 - S 1 '77 - p32
> BL - v74 - S 1 '77 - p42
> BS - v37 - D '77 - p294
> CCB-B - v31 - S '77 - p18
> EJ - v67 - F '78 - p99
> HB - v53 - D '77 - p668
> KR - v45 - Jl 1 '77 - p673
> Kliatt - v13 - Spring '79 - p9
> NYTBR - N 13 '77 - p50
> PW - v211 - Je 27 '77 - p111
> SLJ - v24 - O '77 - p124
> WCRB - v3 - N '77 - p48

> *Love Is A Missing Person*
> BB - v3 - O '75 - p4
> BL - v72 - S 1 '75 - p34
> BS - v35 - D '75 - p299
> CCB-B - v29 - N '75 - p48
> EJ - v65 - Mr '76 - p90
> EJ - v68 - O '79 - p102
> J Read - v20 - O '76 - p79
> KR - v43 - Jl 1 '75 - p717
> Kliatt - v11 - Spring '77 - p6
> NYTBR - O 19 '75 - p10
> PW - v207 - Je 30 '75 - p58
> SLJ - v22 - N '75 - p92

KESTER, Ellen Skinner

> *The Climbing Rope*
> SLJ - v25 - Ja '79 - p51

KETCHAM, Hank   1920-
ArtCS, BioIn 3, BioIn 11, CurBio 56

KETCHAM, Hank (continued)

I Wanna Go Home!
BS - v25 - F 15 '66 - p433
KR - v33 - S 15 '65 - p1024
LJ - v90 - D 1 '65 - p5277
Trav - v125 - F '66 - p61

KEY, Alexander   1904-1979
AuBYP, ConAu 5R, SmATA 8,
SmATA 23N, WrDr 80

Escape To Witch Mountain
BL - v64 - Ap 15 '68 - p996
BW - v2 - S 29 '68 - p18
CSM - v60 - My 2 '68 - pB8
KR - v36 - Mr 15 '68 - p344
PW - v193 - My 13 '68 - p58
Teacher - v92 - My '75 - p92

The Golden Enemy
BW - v3 - My 4 '69 - p20
KR - v37 - Mr 15 '69 - p316
LJ - v94 - Ap 15 '69 - p1782

KILLENS, John Oliver   1916-
ConAu 77, ConLC 10, ConNov 76,
SelBAA, WhoBlA 77, WrDr 80

Great Gittin' Up Morning: A
Biography Of Denmark Vesey
BL - v68 - Je 1 '72 - p862
BL - v69 - My 1 '73 - p838
BS - v31 - Mr 15 '72 - p566
CCB-B - v26 - Mr '73 - p108
CSM - v64 - My 4 '72 - pB5
KR - v40 - Ja 1 '72 - p11
LJ - v97 - S 15 '72 - p2962
NYRB - v18 - Ap 20 '72 - p39
NYTBR - Ap 30 '72 - p8
PW - v201 - Ap 10 '72 - p58

KILLILEA, Marie   1913-
ConAu 5R, SmATA 2, WhoE 74

Karen
A Lead - v17 - F '69 - p366
BL - v49 - O 1 '52 - p44
KR - v20 - Ag 1 '52 - p484
LJ - v77 - S 15 '52 - p1499
NYTBR - S 28 '52 - p10
SR - v35 - S 20 '52 - p15

KINGMAN, Lee   1919-
ConAu 5R, MorJA, SmATA 1,
TwCCW 78, WrDr 80

Break A Leg, Betsy Maybe!
BL - v73 - N 15 '76 - p466
BL - v73 - N 15 '76 - p474
CCB-B - v30 - My '77 - p144
EJ - v69 - Ja '80 - p78
HB - v53 - F '77 - p56
KR - v44 - O 1 '76 - p1101
SLJ - v23 - O '76 - p118

Head Over Wheels
SLJ - v25 - O '78 - p156

The Peter Pan Bag
BL - v67 - S 15 '70 - p96
CCB-B - v24 - O '70 - p29
CSM - v62 - My 7 '70 - pB6
Comw - v92 - My 22 '70 - p250
HB - v46 - Ag '70 - p394
KR - v38 - Ap 15 '70 - p465
LJ - v96 - Ap 15 '71 - p1516
NYTBR - Jl 12 '70 - p26
NYTBR, pt.2 - N 7 '71 - p47
SR - v53 - Je 27 '70 - p56

KINNEY, Cle
see Kinney, Jean (co-author)

KINNEY, Jean   1912-
AuBYP SUP, ConAu 9R, ForWC 70,
SmATA 12

21 Kinds Of American Folk Art
And How To Make Each One
BL - v69 - O 1 '72 - p149
CLW - v44 - N '72 - p248
HB - v48 - Ag '72 - p387
NYTBR - Jl 2 '72 - p8
NYTBR, pt.2 - N 5 '72 - p28

KINNICK, B J
WhoAmW 72

Voices of Man/I Have A Dream
EJ - v58 - Ja '69 - p145

Voices of Man/Let Us Be Men
EJ - v58 - Ja '69 - p145

KJELGAARD, Jim   1910-1959
JBA 51, SmATA 17, TwCCW 78

KJELGAARD, Jim (continued)

Big Red
BL - v42 - D 15 '45 - p132
KR - v13 - O 1 '45 - p437
Kliatt - v11 - Winter '77 - p5
LJ - v71 - Ja 1 '46 - p58
NYTBR - N 11 '45 - p26

Dave And His Dog, Mulligan
BS - v26 - Ag 1 '66 - p175
LJ - v91 - Jl '66 - p3543

Hidden Trail
HB - v38 - Ag '62 - p377
LJ - v87 - My 15 '62 - p2034
NYTBR - Ap 29 '62 - p42

Outlaw Red
BL - v50 - N 15 '53 - p125
KR - v21 - S 1 '53 - p587
LJ - v78 - N 15 '53 - p2046
NYTBR - D 20 '53 - p16

KLAGSBRUN, Francine Lifton
ConAu 21R, ForWC 70, WhoAmW
77

Psychiatry
LJ - v95 - My 15 '70 - p1954

KLEIN, Aaron
see Pearce, W E (co-author)

KLEIN, Dave   1940-
ConAu 89

*On The Way Up: What It's Like To
Be In The Minor Leagues*
BL - v74 - O 1 '77 - p303
KR - v45 - S 1 '77 - p940
SLJ - v24 - D '77 - p63

Pro Basketball's Big Men
KR - v41 - S 15 '73 - p1042
LJ - v98 - D 15 '73 - p3721

KLEIN, H Arthur
AuBYP, ConAu 13R, SmATA 8

*Surf's Up!: An Anthology Of
Surfing*
BL - v63 - D 1 '66 - p414
CE - v43 - F '67 - p355
LJ - v92 - Ja 15 '67 - p352

SA - v215 - D '66 - p148

KLEIN, Mina Cooper
see Klein, H Arthur (co-author)

KLEIN, Norma   1938-
ChLR 2, ConAu 41R, SmATA 7,
TwCCW 78, WrDr 80

It's Not What You Expect
BL - v70 - S 15 '73 - p122
BS - v33 - My 15 '73 - p98
BS - v34 - Je 1 '74 - p127
BW - v7 - My 13 '73 - p7
CCB-B - v26 - Jl '73 - p172
Choice - v14 - N '77 - p1178
KR - v41 - F 15 '73 - p194
NYTBR - Je 3 '73 - p8
PW - v203 - Mr 5 '73 - p82
TN - v30 - Ja '74 - p199

Mom, The Wolf Man And Me
BL - v69 - Ja 1 '73 - p449
CCB-B - v26 - F '73 - p93
Comw - v97 - N 17 '72 - p158
HB - v49 - F '73 - p56
KR - v40 - S 1 '72 - p1027
LJ - v97 - D 15 '72 - p4057
LJ - v97 - D 15 '72 - p4072
NW - v83 - Mr 4 '74 - p83
NYTBR - S 24 '72 - p8
NYTBR - F 10 '74 - p30
NYTBR, pt.2 - N 5 '72 - p28
PW - v202 - N 13 '72 - p46
TN - v30 - Ja '74 - p203
Teacher - v90 - Ja '73 - p92

Sunshine
BL - v71 - O 15 '74 - p238
CLW - v49 - O '77 - p109
EJ - v65 - Ja '76 - p98
EJ - v65 - My '76 - p91
KR - v43 - S 15 '75 - p1083
LJ - v99 - S 15 '74 - p2176
LJ - v99 - N 15 '74 - p3061
PW - v206 - Ag 12 '74 - p58

Taking Sides
BL - v70 - Jl 15 '74 - p1254
CCB-B - v28 - N '74 - p46
KR - v42 - Jl 1 '74 - p688
LJ - v99 - O 15 '74 - p2747
NYTBR - S 29 '74 - p8
PW - v205 - Jl 22 '74 - p70

KLUGER, Ruth

The Secret Ship
Hi Lo - v1 - S '79 - p3
J Read - v22 - F '79 - p477

KNAPP, Ron

Tutankhamun And The Mysteries Of Ancient Egypt
Hi Lo - v1 - D '79 - p6
SLJ - v26 - F '80 - p57

KNIGHT, Damon   1922-
ConAu 49, ConSFA, SmATA 9, WhoSciF, WorAu, WrDr 80

A Pocketful Of Stars
KR - v39 - Ag 1 '71 - p836
LJ - v96 - S 1 '71 - p2673
PW - v200 - Ag 23 '71 - p76
TLS - O 13 '72 - p1235

Toward Infinity
KR - v36 - S 1 '68 - p991

KNIGHT, David C   1925-
AuBYP, ConAu 73, SmATA 14

Harnessing The Sun: The Story Of Solar Energy
ACSB - v10 - Winter '77 - p27
BL - v72 - Je 1 '76 - p1407
KR - v44 - My 15 '76 - p605
SB - v12 - D '76 - p133
SLJ - v23 - S '76 - p134

Poltergeists
BL - v69 - Mr 1 '73 - p649
CE - v50 - O '73 - p32
KR - v40 - O 15 '72 - p1207
SR - v55 - N 11 '72 - p78

The Spy Who Never Was And Other True Spy Stories
BL - v75 - D 15 '78 - p681
Par - v54 - Ap '79 - p24
SLJ - v25 - D '78 - p54

KNIGHT, Eric   1897-1943
CurBio 42, CurBio 43, FourBJA, SmATA 18, WhAm 2, WhoChL

Lassie Come-Home
BL - v68 - F 1 '72 - p468
BL - v74 - Jl 15 '78 - p1734
LJ - v97 - Ap 15 '72 - p1606
NYTBR, pt.2 - F 13 '72 - p12
PW - v200 - N 22 '71 - p41
Teacher - v90 - F '73 - p125

KNIGHT, Frank   1905-
ConAu 73, SmATA 14, TwCCW 78, WhoChL, WrDr 80

Ships: From Noah's Ark To Nuclear Submarine
BL - v67 - Je 1 '71 - p834
KR - v39 - Ja 15 '71 - p62
LJ - v96 - My 15 '71 - p1805

Stories Of Famous Explorers By Land
LJ - v92 - Ja 15 '67 - p336

KNIGHTLEY, Phillip   1929-
ConAu 25R, WhoWor 74, WrDr 80

Lawrence Of Arabia
BB - v5 - Je '77 - p3
B&B - v21 - Jl '76 - p40
BS - v37 - Jl '77 - p126
CE - v54 - Ja '78 - p142
GP - v14 - Ap '76 - p2836
KR - v44 - S 15 '76 - p1041
LJ - v94 - D 15 '69 - p4520
SLJ - v23 - D '76 - p55

KNOTT, Bill   1927-
AuBYP SUP, ConAu 5R, SmATA 3, WrDr 80

The Secret Of The Old Brownstone
LJ - v94 - My 15 '69 - p2122
PW - v195 - Ap 7 '69 - p56

KNUDSON, R R   1932-
ConAu 33R, SmATA 7, WhoAmW 74, WrDr 80 (also known as Knudson, Rozanne)

Fox Running
BL - v72 - S 15 '75 - p166
BS - v36 - Ap '76 - p30
CCB-B - v29 - My '76 - p147
HB - v52 - F '76 - p56
KR - v43 - N 1 '75 - p1239

KNUDSON, R R (continued)
SLJ - v22 - D '75 - p69

You Are The Rain
KR - v42 - Mr 15 '74 - p308
LJ - v99 - O 15 '74 - p2747
PW - v205 - Ja 21 '74 - p85

Zanballer
BL - v69 - Ap 1 '73 - p764
CCB-B - v26 - Ap '73 - p127
EJ - v62 - Ap '73 - p649
EJ - v64 - S '75 - p80
KR - v40 - O 15 '72 - p1201
LJ - v97 - D 15 '72 - p4089
SLJ - v24 - My '78 - p39

KOCH, Charlotte
see Raymond, Charles

KOCH, Raymond
see Raymond, Charles

KOMAROFF, Katherine

Sky Gods: The Sun And Moon In Art And Myth
BL - v71 - S 1 '74 - p43
CSM - v67 - F 5 '75 - p8
KR - v42 - D 15 '74 - p1308

KOMROFF, Manuel   1890-1974
ConAu 1R, ConAu 53, DcLB 4,
OxAm, SmATA 2, SmATA 20N,
WhAm 6

Napoleon
B&B - v18 - Je '73 - p133
BL - v51 - D 15 '54 - p180
HB - v30 - O '54 - p341
KR - v22 - Jl 1 '54 - p397
LJ - v79 - N 15 '54 - p2257
NY - v30 - N 27 '54 - p221

True Adventures Of Spies
KR - v22 - Ja 15 '54 - p36
LJ - v79 - S 15 '54 - p1672
NYTBR - Je 27 '54 - p18

KONIGSBURG, E L   1930-
ChLR 1, ConAu 21R, SmATA 4,
ThrBJA, TwCCW 78, WrDr 80

About The B'nai Bagels
BL - v65 - Je 15 '69 - p1176

CCB-B - v23 - S '69 - p12
CE - v46 - F '70 - p263
CLW - v41 - D '69 - p262
CLW - v41 - Ja '70 - p318
CLW - v43 - F '72 - p330
CLW - v48 - F '77 - p281
Comw - v90 - My 23 '69 - p297
Comw - v91 - N 21 '69 - p256
HB - v45 - Je '69 - p307
HB - v49 - Ap '73 - p173
KR - v37 - F 15 '69 - p179
LJ - v94 - Mr 15 '69 - p1329
LJ - v95 - F 15 '70 - p742
NCW - v216 - Mr '73 - p93
NO - v8 - S 1 '69 - p17
NYTBR - Mr 30 '69 - p28
NYTBR - Je 8 '69 - p44
NYTBR, pt.2 - N 9 '69 - p61
PW - v195 - Mr 31 '69 - p57
RR - v28 - Jl '69 - p700
SLJ - v24 - My '78 - p39
SR - v52 - Mr 22 '69 - p63

From The Mixed-Up Files Of Mrs. Basil E. Frankweiler
Am - v117 - N 4 '67 - p516
B&B - v14 - Jl '69 - p36
BL - v64 - O 1 '67 - p199
BW - v1 - N 5 '67 - p20
CCB-B - v21 - Mr '68 - p112
CLW - v39 - Ja '68 - p371
CLW - v39 - F '68 - p438
CSM - v59 - N 2 '67 - pB10
HB - v43 - O '67 - p595
KR - v35 - Jl 1 '67 - p740
LJ - v92 - O 15 '67 - p3851
Lis - v82 - N 6 '69 - p638
NYTBR - v72 - N 5 '67 - p44
NYTBR, pt.2 - N 5 '72 - p42
Obs - Ap 6 '69 - p26
Obs - Je 2 '74 - p29
Par - v43 - Je '68 - p68
PW - v192 - Ag 7 '67 - p54
SR - v50 - O 21 '67 - p43
Spec - v222 - My 16 '69 - p657
TLS - Ap 3 '69 - p355
TN - v24 - Ja '68 - p223
Teacher - v90 - Ja '73 - p90

A Proud Taste For Scarlet And Miniver
Am - v129 - D 1 '73 - p431
BL - v70 - N 1 '73 - p287

KONIGSBURG, E L (continued)
BL - v70 - N 1 '73 - p292
BL - v70 - Mr 15 '74 - p827
CCB-B - v27 - S '73 - p10
CSM - v66 - My 1 '74 - pF1
Choice - v12 - N '75 - p1133
Comw - v99 - N 23 '73 - p216
GP - v14 - My '75 - p2652
HB - v49 - O '73 - p466
JB - v39 - Ap '75 - p119
KR - v41 - Jl 1 '73 - p685
Kliatt - v11 - Spring '77 - p6
LJ - v98 - O 15 '73 - p3147
NYTBR - O 14 '73 - p8
NYTBR - N 4 '73 - p52
PW - v204 - Ag 6 '73 - p65
TLS - Ap 4 '75 - p370
Teacher - v91 - N '73 - p130

The Second Mrs. Giaconda
BB - v3 - O '75 - p2
BL - v72 - S 1 '75 - p42
BS - v35 - N '75 - p259
CCB-B - v29 - Ja '76 - p80
HB - v51 - O '75 - p470
JB - v41 - F '77 - p39
J Read - v20 - O '76 - p80
KR - v43 - Jl 1 '75 - p718
LA - v53 - F '76 - p202
NYTBR - O 5 '75 - p8
PW - v208 - D 1 '75 - p66
SLJ - v22 - S '75 - p121
TLS - O 1 '76 - p1249
Teacher - v93 - Ap '76 - p117

KOOB, Theodora 1918-
AuBYP, ConAu 5R, SmATA 23

The Deep Search
BS - v29 - Ap 1 '69 - p21
CCB-B - v23 - S '69 - p12
KR - v37 - F 15 '69 - p185
LJ - v94 - N 15 '69 - p4298

This Side Of Victory
BS - v27 - D 1 '67 - p362
KR - v35 - Ag 15 '67 - p967
LJ - v92 - S 15 '67 - p3200

KOTZWINKLE, William 1938-
ConAu 45, ConLC 5, SmATA 24

The Leopard's Tooth
BB - v4 - Ag '76 - p4

CCB-B - v30 - S '76 - p12
KR - v44 - Ap 1 '76 - p390
SLJ - v22 - My '76 - p60

KOUFAX, Sandy 1935-
ConAu 89, CurBio 64, CelR, WhoAm
76, WhoProB 73 (also known as
Koufax, Sanford)

Koufax
BL - v63 - O 1 '66 - p148
BS - v26 - O 1 '66 - p251
CLW - v38 - N '66 - p209
Comt - v42 - N '66 - p87
LJ - v91 - O 1 '66 - p4691
LJ - v91 - D 15 '66 - p6220
NYTBR - v71 - S 18 '66 - p46
Nat - v204 - Ja 30 '67 - p149

KOVALIK, Nada
see Kovalik, Vladimir (co-author)

KOVALIK, Vladimir 1928-
ConAu 25R

The Ocean World
Am - v115 - Jl 2 '66 - p15
BL - v62 - Jl 15 '66 - p1083
BS - v26 - Jl 1 '66 - p142
KR - v34 - Ap 1 '66 - p379
LJ - v91 - My 15 '66 - p2718
NH - v75 - N '66 - p76
NYTBR - v71 - My 8 '66 - p16
PW - v189 - My 30 '66 - p89
SB - v2 - S '66 - p117
SR - v49 - Je 25 '66 - p61

KOWET, Don 1937-
AuBYP SUP, ConAu 57

Vida Blue: Coming Up Again
LJ - v99 - D 15 '74 - p3279

KRAKOWSKI, Lili 1930-
ConAu 85, ForWC 70

*Starting Out: The Guide I Wish
I'd Had When I Left Home*
BL - v70 - F 15 '74 - p616
BL - v70 - F 15 '74 - p650
KR - v41 - Ag 15 '73 - p938
LJ - v98 - O 1 '73 - p2859
LJ - v98 - D 15 '73 - p3728
RSR - v2 - Ja '74 - p32

KRASKE, Robert

> *Harry Houdini*
> Teacher - v91 - S '73 - p143

> *The Twelve Million Dollar Note*
> KR - v45 - O 1 '77 - p1056
> SA - v239 - D '78 - p34
> SLJ - v24 - S '77 - p131

KROLL, Francis Lynde   1904-1973
ConAu P-1, SmATA 10

> *Top Hand*
> KR - v33 - F 1 '65 - p112

KROPP, Paul

> *Burn Out*
> BIC - v9 - Mr '80 - p23
> Hi Lo - v2 - N '80 - p4

> *Hot Cars*
> BIC - v9 - Mr '80 - p23
> Hi Lo - v2 - N '80 - p4

KUGELMASS, J Alvin   1910-1972
AuBYP, ConAu 5R, ConAu 33R,
WhoAm 76

> *Ralph J. Bunche: Fighter For Peace*
> NYTBR - N 16 '52 - p20

KURLAND, Michael   1938-
ConAu 61, ConSFA, EncSF,
ScF&FL 1, ScF&FL 2

> *The Princes Of Earth*
> BL - v74 - Ap 1 '78 - p1249
> KR - v46 - F 15 '78 - p205
> SLJ - v25 - N '78 - p76

KUSAN, Ivan   1933-
AuBYP, ConAu 9R

> *Mystery Of Green Hill*
> CSM - My 10 '62 - p6B
> HB - v38 - Ap '62 - p173
> KR - v30 - Ja 1 '62 - p13
> LJ - v87 - Je 15 '62 - p2420
> NYTBR, pt.2 - My 13 '62 - p31

KWOLEK, Constance   1933-
ConAu X, WrDr 80 (also known as
Porcari, Constance Kwolek)

> *Loner*
> CCB-B - v24 - Mr '71 - p108
> KR - v38 - Jl 1 '70 - p689
> LJ - v95 - O 15 '70 - p3638

KYLE, Elisabeth   (pseud.)
ConAu X, MorJA, SmATA 3,
TwCCW 78, WhoChL, WrDr 80 (real
name: Dunlop, Agnes Mary Robinson)

> *Girl With A Pen, Charlotte Bronte*
> BS - v24 - Ap 15 '64 - p42
> CSM - My 7 '64 - p6B
> HB - v40 - Ap '64 - p186
> LJ - v89 - My 15 '64 - p2230
> NYTBR, pt.2 - My 10 '64 - p10
> SR - v47 - My 16 '64 - p91

L

LAGUMINA, Salvatore J   1928-
ConAu 77, DrAS 78H

*An Album Of The Italian-
American*
BL - v69 - My 1 '73 - p859
LJ - v98 - My 15 '73 - p1690

LAKLAN, Carli   (pseud.) 1907-
AuBYP SUP, ConAu X, SmATA 5
(real name: Laughlin, Virginia Carli)

Migrant Girl
BL - v68 - Je 15 '72 - p895
CCB-B - v24 - Jl '71 - p173
EJ - v60 - My '71 - p667
KR - v38 - Ag 15 '70 - p886
LJ - v95 - N 15 '70 - p4055
NYTBR, pt.2 - N 8 '70 - p2

Nurse In Training
CCB-B - v19 - S '65 - p12

Ski Bum
LJ - v98 - D 15 '73 - p3720
see also Clarke, John

LAMBERT, Eloise

*Our Names: Where They Came
From And What They Mean*
BL - v57 - F 1 '61 - p329
CSM - F 2 '61 - p7
KR - v28 - Ag 15 '60 - p689
LJ - v85 - D 15 '60 - p4576
NYTBR - Ap 9 '61 - p34
SR - v43 - D 17 '60 - p35

L'AMOUR, Louis   1908-
AuNews 1, AuNews 2, ConAu 1R,
WhoAm 78, WhoWor 78

The Proving Trail
Esq - v91 - Mr 13 '79 - p22

Kliatt - v13 - Spring '79 - p9

LAMPEL, Rusia

That Summer With Ora
BL - v64 - Ap 1 '68 - p931
CCB-B - v21 - F '68 - p96
CSM - v60 - My 2 '68 - pB11
KR - v35 - D 1 '67 - p1425
LJ - v93 - F 15 '68 - p883

LAMPMAN, Evelyn Sibley   1907-
ConAu 13R, MorJA, SmATA 4,
SmATA 23N, TwCCW 78,
WhoAmW 77, WrDr 80

Once Upon The Little Big Horn
EJ - v60 - D '71 - p1260
KR - v39 - Je 1 '71 - p591
LJ - v96 - S 15 '71 - p2918
NYTBR - Jl 11 '71 - p8
NYTBR, pt.2 - N 7 '71 - p30

The Year Of Small Shadow
BL - v68 - O 1 '71 - p152
BL - v69 - O 15 '72 - p177
BW - v5 - N 7 '71 - p13
CCB-B - v25 - D '71 - p59
CE - v48 - F '72 - p258
Comw - v97 - F 23 '73 - p474
EJ - v61 - F '72 - p304
HB - v47 - D '71 - p611
KR - v39 - Je 15 '71 - p642
LJ - v96 - S 15 '71 - p2918
PW - v200 - Ag 2 '71 - p64

LAND, Charles

Calling Earth
Hi Lo - v1 - Mr '80 - p4

LANDAU, Elaine   1948-
AuBYP SUP, ConAu 53, SmATA 10,
WhoAmW 77

    Death: Everyone's Heritage
      CCB-B - v30 - D '76 - p59
      SB - v13 - D '77 - p127

    Yoga For You
      BL - v74 - Ja 15 '78 - p807
      KR - v45 - D 1 '77 - p1274
      SLJ - v24 - Ja '78 - p95

LANE, Rose Wilder   1887-1968
AuBYP SUP, REnAL, TwCA, TwCA
SUP, WhAm 5

    Let The Hurricane Roar
      BL - v29 - Mr '33 - p206
      CSM - Mr 4 '33 - p8
      NYTBR - F 26 '33 - p7
      New R - v75 - Ag 2 '33 - p324
      SR - v9 - Mr 4 '33 - p465
      TLS - O 5 '33 - p662

    Young Pioneers
      BL - v72 - Je 1 '76 - p1387
      BL - v72 - Je 1 '76 - p1407

LANGE, Suzanne   1945-
ConAu 29R, SmATA 5

    *The Year: Life On An Israeli
    Kibbutz*
      CCB-B - v24 - Ja '71 - p76
      EJ - v60 - S '71 - p827
      LJ - v95 - N 15 '70 - p4056

LANGER, Richard W

    The Joy Of Camping
      BL - v70 - O 15 '73 - p202
      KR - v41 - Ap 1 '73 - p449
      LJ - v98 - Je 15 '73 - p1932
      NYTBR - Jl 14 '74 - p12

LANGTON, Jane   1922-
ConAu 1R, SmATA 3, TwCCW 78,
WrDr 80

    The Boyhood Of Grace Jones
      BL - v69 - F 1 '73 - p529
      BW - v6 - N 5 '72 - p5
      CCB-B - v27 - O '73 - p30
      CE - v49 - Mr '73 - p320

    CSM - v66 - D 5 '73 - pB12
    CSM - v67 - Je 10 '75 - p16
    HB - v49 - F '73 - p49
    KR - v40 - N 15 '72 - p1306
    TN - v29 - Je '73 - p357
    Teacher - v93 - N '75 - p117

LARRANAGA, Robert D   1940-
ConAu 49

    Famous Crimefighters
      LJ - v96 - F 15 '71 - p741

    Pirates And Buccaneers
      LJ - v96 - F 15 '71 - p741

LARRICK, Nancy   1910-
ConAu 1R, MorBMP, SmATA 4,
WhoAmW 77, WrDr 80

    On City Streets
      BL - v65 - Ja 1 '69 - p491
      BL - v65 - Ja 1 '69 - p497
      CCB-B - v22 - F '69 - p97
      CE - v45 - My '69 - p532
      EJ - v58 - F '69 - p292
      HB - v45 - Ap '69 - p181
      NYTBR, pt.2 - F 15 '70 - p22
      Teacher - v93 - F '76 - p29

LATHAM, Frank B   1910-
AuBYP SUP, ConAu 49, SmATA 6

    *FDR And The Supreme Court
    Fight 1937: A President Tries To
    Reorganize The Federal Judiciary*
      BL - v68 - Je 15 '72 - p909
      BS - v32 - Ap 15 '72 - p45

LATHAM, Jean Lee   1902-
ConAu 5R, ConLC 12, MorBMP,
MorJA, SmATA 2, TwCCW 78

    *Elizabeth Blackwell: Pioneer
    Woman Doctor*
      BL - v72 - D 15 '75 - p579
      Inst - v85 - My '76 - p113
      SB - v12 - My '76 - p43
      SLJ - v22 - F '76 - p40

LAUBER, Patricia   1924-
ConAu 9R, SmATA 1, ThrBJA

    Look-It-Up Book Of Mammals
      CLW - v39 - F '68 - p436

LAUBER, Patricia (continued)
    CSM - v59 - N 2 '67 - pB11
    Inst - v77 - Ja '68 - p152
    KR - v35 - S 1 '67 - p1051
    Obs - My 19 '68 - p1312
    PW - v192 - N 13 '67 - p79
    SB - v3 - My '68 - p325

    Look-It-Up Book Of Stars And
    Planets
    CSM - v59 - N 2 '67 - pB8
    PW - v192 - N 13 '67 - p80

LAUGHLIN, Virginia Carli
see Clarke, John
    Laklan, Carli

LAWICK-GOODALL, Jane Van
ASpks, ConAu 45, CurBio 67 (listed
under Van Lawick-Goodall, Jane)

    In The Shadow Of Man
    BL - v68 - Ja 1 '72 - p374
    BL - v68 - Ja 1 '72 - p391
    BL - v68 - Ap 1 '72 - p664
    BS - v31 - N 15 '71 - p376
    BS - v32 - F 1 '73 - p503
    BS - v34 - Jl 1 '74 - p179
    BW - v5 - O 17 '71 - p6
    CSM - v63 - O 13 '71 - p9
    Choice - v8 - Ja '72 - p1471
    EJ - v64 - O '75 - p90
    Econ - v241 - O 30 '71 - p61
    HB - v47 - D '71 - p629
    KR - v39 - Ag 15 '71 - p914
    LJ - v96 - D 1 '71 - p4023
    LJ - v97 - Mr 1 '72 - p831
    Lis - v86 - N 25 '71 - p728
    NS - v82 - D 3 '71 - p790
    NW - v78 - N 15 '71 - p122A
    NYT - v121 - N 26 '71 - p34
    NYTBR - D 3 '72 - p6
    Nat - v214 - Ja 17 '72 - p89
    Obs - O 24 '71 - p36
    PW - v200 - Ag 9 '71 - p45
    PW - v202 - O 2 '72 - p56
    SA - v225 - D '71 - p106
    SB - v7 - Mr '72 - p318
    TLS - N 19 '71 - p1440
    TN - v28 - Ap '72 - p313
    Time - v98 - N 8 '71 - p104

LAWRENCE, Mildred   1907-
ConAu 1R, MorJA, SmATA 3,
TwCCW 78, WhoAmW 75

    Along Comes Spring
    BL - v55 - N 1 '58 - p132
    HB - v34 - O '58 - p398
    LJ - v83 - S 15 '58 - p2509

    Good Morning, My Heart
    BL - v54 - O 15 '57 - p108
    CSM - O 10 '57 - p11
    KR - v25 - Ag 1 '58 - p531
    LJ - v82 - O 15 '57 - p2707
    NYT - S 22 '57 - p36

    Inside The Gate
    BW - v2 - N 3 '68 - p26
    CCB-B - v23 - S '69 - p12
    CSM - v60 - N 7 '68 - pB11
    EJ - v58 - F '69 - p294
    HB - v44 - O '68 - p564
    KR - v36 - Je 15 '68 - p649

    The Questing Heart
    BL - v56 - O 1 '59 - p85
    CSM - N 5 '59 - p6B
    HB - v36 - F '60 - p41
    KR - v27 - Ag 1 '59 - p554
    LJ - v84 - N 15 '59 - p3640

    Walk A Rocky Road
    EJ - v61 - Mr '72 - p434
    KR - v39 - S 15 '71 - p1022
    LJ - v96 - D 15 '71 - p4191

LAWSON, Donald Elmer   1917-
AuBYP, ConAu 1R, SmATA 9,
WhoAm 78

    The United States In The Civil
    War
    BL - v74 - N 15 '77 - p552
    KR - v45 - Jl 1 '77 - p670
    SLJ - v24 - O '77 - p125

    The United States In The Spanish-
    American War
    BL - v73 - S 15 '76 - p178
    Inst - v86 - N '76 - p157
    KR - v44 - My 1 '76 - p538
    SLJ - v22 - Ap '76 - p90

LAWSON, Donna   1937-
ConAu 41R

LAWSON, Donna (continued)

*Beauty Is No Big Deal: The
Common Sense Beauty Book*
KR - v39 - Ap 1 '71 - p414
KR - v39 - My 1 '71 - p520
LJ - v96 - Je 1 '71 - p1978
LJ - v96 - D 15 '71 - p4209

LAWSON, Robert   1892-1957
ChLR 2, IlsCB 1946, JBA 51,
TwCCW 78, WhAm 3, YABC 2

Mr. Revere And I
CSM - v66 - Ja 9 '74 - pF4
Teacher - v91 - Mr '74 - p110
Teacher - v92 - Ap '75 - p112

LAYCOCK, George   1921-
AuBYP, ConAu 5R, SmATA 5,
WhoMW 76

Air Pollution
KR - v40 - Mr 15 '72 - p330
LJ - v98 - Mr 15 '73 - p1005
LJ - v98 - My 1 '73 - p1441
NYTBR, pt.2 - My 7 '72 - p8
SB - v8 - S '72 - p171

King Gator
BS - v28 - My 1 '68 - p65
LJ - v93 - Ap 15 '68 - p1800
PW - v193 - Ap 15 '68 - p98

Water Pollution
CCB-B - v26 - Mr '73 - p108
KR - v40 - Ap 15 '72 - p482
LJ - v97 - O 15 '72 - p3453
LJ - v98 - My 1 '73 - p1441
NYTBR, pt.2 - My 7 '72 - p8

LAZARUS, Keo   1913-
AuBYP SUP, ConAu 41R, SmATA
21, WrDr 80

Rattlesnake Run
BL - v64 - Jl 15 '68 - p1286
BW - v2 - My 5 '68 - p22
KR - v36 - Ja 15 '68 - p57
LJ - v93 - Ap 15 '68 - p1800

LEACH, Christopher

Free, Alone And Going
BL - v69 - My 1 '73 - p859

KR - v41 - F 15 '73 - p194
LJ - v98 - S 15 '73 - p2666
PW - v203 - Mr 26 '73 - p71

Rosalinda
B&B - v23 - Je '78 - p72
BL - v74 - Je 1 '78 - p1552
CCB-B - v32 - S '78 - p12
CR - v233 - O '78 - p216
EJ - v67 - N '78 - p83
GP - v17 - S '78 - p3387
LA - v55 - S '78 - p740
SLJ - v25 - S '78 - p142
TES - Je 16 '78 - p46
TLS - Jl 7 '78 - p765

LEACH, Maria   1892-1977
ConAu 53, ConAu 69, FourBJA

Noodles, Nitwits, And Numskulls
LA - v55 - N '78 - p962

Whistle In The Graveyard
BL - v71 - S 1 '74 - p44
CCB-B - v28 - Ja '75 - p81
HB - v50 - D '74 - p689
KR - v42 - Je 1 '74 - p584
LJ - v99 - S 15 '74 - p2273
NYTBR - Jl 28 '74 - p8

LECKIE, Robert   1920-
AuBYP, ConAu 13R

Helmet For My Pillow
BS - v32 - Ag 15 '72 - p244

LEDERER, William   1912-
ConAu 1R, WhoAm 78, WhoSpyF,
WorAu

The Ugly American
BL - v55 - O 15 '58 - p99
CSM - N 26 '58 - p15
KR - v26 - Ag 15 '58 - p615
LJ - v83 - O 15 '58 - p2842
NYT - O 5 '58 - p5
NYTBR - O 5 '58 - p5
Nat - v187 - O 4 '58 - p199
SR - v41 - O 4 '58 - p32
Time - v72 - O 6 '58 - p92

LEE, C Y   1917-
ConAu 9R, NatPD, WorAu

LEE, C Y (continued)

The Land Of The Golden Mountain
BL - v64 - O 1 '67 - p169
BS - v27 - Jl 1 '67 - p138
HB - v43 - O '67 - p601
KR - v35 - Ap 1 '67 - p439
KR - v35 - Je 1 '67 - p655
LJ - v92 - S 15 '67 - p3201

LEE, Essie E 1920-
ConAu 49

Alcohol--Proof Of What?
ACSB - v10 - Winter '77 - p28
BL - v72 - My 15 '76 - p1330
BL - v72 - My 15 '76 - p1337
BS - v36 - Ag '76 - p151
Cur R - v16 - Ag '77 - p176
KR - v44 - Mr 15 '76 - p334
SB - v12 - D '76 - p129

LEE, H Alton 1942-
ConAu 81

Seven Feet Four And Growing
BL - v74 - F 15 '78 - p997
SLJ - v25 - S '78 - p142

LEE, Mildred 1908-
ConAu X, SmATA 6, ThrBJA,
TwCCW 78, WrDr 80 (also known as
Scudder, Mildred Lee)

Fog
BL - v69 - D 1 '72 - p351
BS - v6 - N 5 '72 - p8
BS - v32 - N 15 '72 - p395
CCB-B - v26 - D '72 - p59
CE - v49 - Mr '73 - p320
HB - v49 - F '73 - p57
KR - v40 - O 15 '72 - p1202
KR - v40 - D 15 '72 - p1420
LJ - v97 - N 15 '72 - p3814
LJ - v97 - D 15 '72 - p4057
NO - v11 - N 18 '72 - p28
NYTBR - D 3 '72 - p80
NYTBR, pt.2 - N 5 '72 - p2
PW - v202 - S 4 '72 - p51
TN - v29 - Ap '73 - p257
Teacher - v90 - F '73 - p126

The Skating Rink
Am - v121 - D 13 '69 - p595
BL - v65 - Je 1 '69 - p1120
BW - v3 - My 4 '69 - p5
CCB-B - v23 - N '69 - p48
HB - v45 - Ap '69 - p178
KR - v37 - F 15 '69 - p185
LJ - v94 - Ap 15 '69 - p1798
LJ - v94 - My 15 '69 - p2073
NYTBR - Je 29 '69 - p26
NYTBR, pt.2 - N 9 '69 - p60
PW - v195 - My 12 '69 - p57
SR - v52 - My 10 '69 - p60

Sycamore Year
B&B - v3 - F '75 - p4
BL - v71 - O 1 '74 - p173
BW - D 15 '74 - p6
CCB-B - v28 - F '75 - p95
HB - v51 - F '75 - p55
KR - v42 - Jl 1 '74 - p688
LJ - v99 - S 15 '74 - p2293
NYTBR - Ja 26 '75 - p8

LEECH, Jay
see Spencer, Zane (co-author)

LEEN, Nina
BioIn 4

Snakes
BB - v6 - Ag '78 - p2
BL - v74 - My 15 '78 - p1495
CCB-B - v32 - O '78 - p32
Comw - v105 - N 10 '78 - p734
EJ - v67 - O '78 - p80
HB - v55 - O '78 - p541
KR - v46 - My 1 '78 - p499
NYTBR - Ap 30 '78 - p47
PW - v213 - Mr 27 '78 - p72
SLJ - v24 - My '78 - p69

LEETE, Harley M 1918-
St&PR 75, WhoAdv 12

The Best Of Bicycling
CM - v13 - Spring '73 - p175
KR - v38 - Ag 1 '70 - p848
LJ - v96 - F 15 '71 - p651
NYTBR - Je 4 '72 - p8

LEFKOWITZ, R J
see Bendick, Jeanne (co-author) -
Electronics For Young People

LEGUIN, Ursula Kroeber   1929-
ChLR 3, ConAu 21R, ConLC 13,
FourBJA, SmATA 4, TwCCW 78,
WhoAm 78

> ***Very Far Away From Anywhere
> Else***
> BB - v5 - Mr '77 - p4
> BL - v73 - S 15 '76 - p138
> BL - v73 - S 15 '76 - p178
> BW - O 10 '76 - pE6
> CCB-B - v30 - Ja '77 - p77
> CE - v53 - F '77 - p213
> CLW - v49 - D '77 - p199
> CSM - v68 - N 3 '76 - p20
> Comw - v103 - N 19 '76 - p763
> EJ - v66 - S '77 - p84
> EJ - v67 - My '78 - p89
> HB - v53 - F '77 - p57
> KR - v44 - Jl 1 '76 - p739
> LA - v54 - Ap '77 - p442
> NO - v15 - D 25 '76 - p15
> NYTBR - N 14 '76 - p29
> NYTBR - Mr 5 '78 - p41
> SLJ - v23 - O '76 - p118

LEHRMAN, Steve
see Shapiro, Neal (co-author)

LEMBECK, Ruth

> ***Teenage Jobs***
> BL - v67 - Je 1 '71 - p831
> LJ - v96 - My 15 '71 - p1834

L'ENGLE, Madeleine   1918-
ChLR 1, ConAu 1R, ConLC 12,
MorJA, SmATA 1, TwCCW 78,
WhoAm 78

> ***The Journey With Jonah***
> BL - v64 - D 15 '67 - p502
> BS - v27 - O 1 '67 - p263
> BW - v1 - N 5 '67 - p34
> CCB-B - v21 - D '67 - p62
> CLW - v39 - D '67 - p298
> CSM - v59 - N 2 '67 - pB7
> EJ - v57 - My '68 - p752
> HB - v44 - Ap '68 - p184

> KR - v35 - Ag 15 '67 - p975
> LJ - v93 - Ja 15 '68 - p307
> NYTBR - v73 - Ja 21 '68 - p28
> SR - v50 - N 11 '67 - p48

> ***A Wind In The Door***
> BL - v69 - Je 1 '73 - p944
> BL - v69 - Je 1 '73 - p948
> BS - v33 - My 15 '73 - p98
> CCB-B - v27 - S '73 - p12
> CE - v50 - O '73 - p30
> Comw - v99 - N 23 '73 - p215
> HB - v49 - Ag '73 - p379
> Inst - v83 - Ag '73 - p74
> KR - v41 - Ap 15 '73 - p463
> LJ - v98 - My 15 '73 - p1655
> LJ - v98 - My 15 '73 - p1691
> NYTBR - Jl 8 '73 - p8
> PW - v203 - Ap 16 '73 - p54
> TLS - Ap 4 '75 - p360
> TN - v30 - N '73 - p81
> TN - v34 - Spring '78 - p265
> Teacher - v91 - D '73 - p73

> ***The Young Unicorns***
> B&B - v15 - N '69 - p41
> BS - v28 - Jl 1 '68 - p154
> BW - v2 - My 5 '68 - p5
> CCB-B - v21 - Je '68 - p161
> CSM - v60 - Je 13 '68 - p5
> EJ - v58 - F '69 - p296
> HB - v44 - Je '68 - p329
> KR - v36 - My 15 '68 - p555
> NYTBR - v73 - My 26 '68 - p30
> Obs - Ag 24 '69 - p20
> PW - v193 - Ap 15 '68 - p97
> SR - v51 - My 11 '68 - p42
> TLS - O 16 '69 - p1190

LENSKI, Lois   1893-1974
ConAu 53, ConAu P-1, IlsCB 1967,
JBA 51, SmATA 1, TwCCW 78,
WhAm 6

> ***Deer Valley Girl***
> KR - v36 - F 15 '68 - p183
> Obs - My 19 '68 - p1312

LENT, Henry B   1901-1973
ConAu 73, JBA 51, SmATA 17

> ***The Look Of Cars: Yesterday,
> Today, Tomorrow***
> KR - v34 - Ap 15 '66 - p433

LENT, Henry B (continued)
    LJ - v91 - Jl '66 - p3552
    PW - v189 - My 30 '66 - p89

LESKOWITZ, Irving
see Stone, A Harris (co-author)

LESLIE-MELVILLE, Betty   1929-
ConAu 81

    Raising Daisy Rothschild
    BL - v74 - Ja 1 '78 - p742
    GW - v119 - D 10 '78 - p22
    KR - v45 - Ag 1 '77 - p831
    Kliatt - v13 - Spring '79 - p55
    LJ - v103 - Ja 15 '78 - p180
    NYTBR - N 13 '77 - p18
    NYTBR - F 11 '79 - p37
    PW - v212 - S 5 '77 - p64

LESLIE-MELVILLE, Jock
see Leslie-Melville, Betty (co-author)

LESTER, Julius   1939-
ChLR 2, ConAu 17R, FourBJA,
SelBAA, SmATA 12, WhoBlA 77

    Long Journey Home
    BL - v69 - O 15 '72 - p190
    BL - v69 - My 1 '73 - p838
    BW - v6 - S 3 '72 - p9
    CCB-B - v26 - O '72 - p28
    CSM - v64 - Ag 2 '72 - p11
    EJ - v63 - Ja '74 - p66
    HB - v49 - Ap '73 - p146
    HT - v23 - D '73 - p885
    JNE - v43 - Summer '74 - p395
    KR - v40 - Je 1 '72 - p629
    KR - v40 - D 15 '72 - p1420
    LJ - v97 - Jl '72 - p2490
    LJ - v97 - D 15 '72 - p4057
    NYRB - v18 - Ap 20 '72 - p39
    NYTBR - Je 4 '72 - p28
    NYTBR - Jl 23 '72 - p8
    NYTBR, pt.2 - N 5 '72 - p26
    Obs - Jl 22 '79 - p37
    PW - v201 - Je 5 '72 - p140
    TLS - S 28 '73 - p1118
    TN - v29 - Je '73 - p357

    To Be A Slave
    BL - v65 - F 15 '69 - p648
    BL - v65 - Ap 1 '69 - p901

    BL - v69 - My 1 '73 - p838
    BW - v3 - Mr 16 '69 - p12
    CCB-B - v22 - Ap '69 - p129
    CE - v46 - F '70 - p267
    CE - v46 - Ap '70 - p368
    CLW - v41 - D '69 - p262
    CSM - v61 - My 1 '69 - pB7
    EJ - v63 - Ja '74 - p67
    Econ - v237 - D 26 '70 - p40
    HB - v45 - F '69 - p65
    KR - v36 - N 1 '68 - p1233
    ND - v18 - Je '69 - p51
    NYRB - v18 - Ap 20 '72 - p39
    NYTBR - v73 - N 3 '68 - p7
    NYTBR, pt.2 - N 8 '70 - p30
    NYTBR, pt.2 - F 13 '72 - p14
    Obs - N 29 '70 - p31
    PW - v197 - Ja 19 '70 - p83
    SE - v33 - Je 5 '95 - p63
    SR - v52 - Mr 22 '69 - p63
    Spec - v231 - O 20 '73 - pR21
    TLS - D 11 '70 - p1456
    Teacher - v86 - My '69 - p129
    Teacher - v93 - Ap '76 - p121

LEVIN, Jane Whitbread

    Star Of Danger
    BL - v63 - Ja 15 '67 - p538
    CCB-B - v20 - Ja '67 - p75
    CSM - v58 - N 3 '66 - pB11
    Comw - v85 - N 11 '66 - p176
    KR - v34 - Jl 15 '66 - p691
    LJ - v92 - Ja 15 '67 - p344
    NYTBR - v72 - Ja 8 '67 - p30

LEVINE, Joseph
see Pine, Tillie S (co-author)

LEVINGER, Elma Ehrlich   1887-1958
AuBYP, OhA&B, REnAL, WhAm 3

    Albert Einstein
    BL - v45 - Ap 1 '49 - p264
    BOT   v17   F 15 '49 - p87
    CSM - My 26 '49 - p12
    HB - v25 - My '49 - p218
    LJ - v74 - Ap 15 '49 - p669
    NY - v25 - D 3 '49 - p186
    NYTBR - My 29 '49 - p14
    SR - v32 - Ag 13 '49 - p35

LEVITIN, Sonia   1934-
AuBYP SUP, ConAu 29R, SmATA 4

The Mark Of Conte
BB - v4 - Jl '76 - p3
BL - v72 - Ap 15 '76 - p1186
BL - v73 - My 15 '77 - p1426
BS - v36 - Ag '76 - p151
BW - D 12 '76 - pH4
CCB-B - v29 - Jl '76 - p177
HB - v52 - Je '76 - p289
J Read - v21 - O '77 - p86
KR - v44 - Mr 15 '76 - p331
LJ - v53 - S '76 - p700
SLJ - v22 - Ap '76 - p90

The No-Return Trail
BL - v74 - Je 15 '78 - p1618
BS - v38 - O '78 - p230
KR - v46 - Je 1 '78 - p600
SLJ - v24 - Ap '78 - p94

LEVOY, Myron
AuBYP SUP

*The Witch Of Fourth Street And
Other Stories*
BL - v68 - Je 1 '72 - p862
BW - v6 - My 7 '72 - p4
CCB-B - v26 - Ja '73 - p78
HB - v48 - Ag '72 - p372
KR - v40 - F 1 '72 - p136
LJ - v97 - My 15 '72 - p1915
NYTBR - Je 18 '72 - p8
PW - v201 - Ap 3 '72 - p72
TLS - D 8 '72 - p1491
Teacher - v92 - Ap '75 - p112
VV - v19 - D 16 '74 - p51

LEWIS, Alfred   1912-1968
AuBYP

The New World Of Computers
KR - v33 - Ja 15 '65 - p64
LJ - v90 - F 15 '65 - p974

LEWIS, Claude   1934-
ConAu 9R

*Benjamin Banneker: The Man
Who Saved Washington*
BL - v67 - S 1 '70 - p58
CCB-B - v24 - O '70 - p30
KR - v38 - Ap 1 '70 - p392

LJ - v96 - Mr 15 '71 - p1134
NHB - v34 - Mr '71 - p70

LEWIS, Richard   1935-
BkP, ConAu 9R, OxCan SUP,
SmATA 3

*Miracles: Poems By Children Of
The English-Speaking World*
BL - v63 - D 1 '66 - p400
CCB-B - v20 - Mr '67 - p111
CE - v44 - My '68 - p561
CSM - v59 - N 23 '66 - p15
Choice - v4 - S '67 - p730
HB - v42 - D '66 - p726
HR - v20 - Spring '67 - p137
Inst - v77 - Ag '67 - p208
KR - v34 - Jl 15 '66 - p744
LJ - v91 - O 1 '66 - p4671
NYRB - v7 - O 20 '66 - p25
NYTBR - v71 - N 6 '66 - p1
PW - v190 - Jl 18 '66 - p76
PW - v190 - N 28 '66 - p61
SR - v50 - F 18 '67 - p42
TLS - N 30 '67 - p1132
Time - v89 - Ja 6 '67 - p101

*Out Of The Earth I Sing: Poetry
And Songs Of Primitive Peoples Of
The World*
BL - v64 - Ap 1 '68 - p931
BW - v1 - N 5 '67 - p26
BW - v2 - My 5 '68 - p5
CCB-B - v21 - Jl '68 - p176
HB - v44 - Ap '68 - p187
Inst - v77 - Je '68 - p142
KR - v36 - Ja 1 '68 - p11
LJ - v93 - F 15 '68 - p883

LEWITON, Mina   1904-1970
ConAu 29R, ConAu P-2, MorJA,
SmATA 2

Especially Humphrey
CLW - v39 - F '68 - p439
LJ - v93 - Ja 15 '68 - p293

LIBBY, Bill   1927-
AuBYP SUP, ConAu 25R, SmATA
5, WrDr 80

Baseball's Greatest Sluggers
Inst - v82 - My '73 - p69
KR - v41 - Ap 1 '73 - p395

LIBBY, Bill (continued)
LJ - v98 - My 15 '73 - p1703
LJ - v98 - D 15 '73 - p3721

Rocky
BS - v31 - My 15 '71 - p99
KR - v39 - F 15 '71 - p183
LJ - v96 - My 15 '71 - p1825

LIEBERMAN, Mark   1942-
ConAu 29R

The Dope Book: All About Drugs
BL - v68 - N 1 '71 - p242
Inst - v81 - N '71 - p133
KR - v39 - Ap 1 '71 - p383
LJ - v96 - Je 15 '71 - p2139
LJ - v96 - Jl '71 - p2291
NYTBR, pt.2 - My 2 '71 - p32
NYTBR, pt.2 - N 7 '71 - p28
SB - v7 - D '71 - p256

LIEBERS, Arthur   1913-
ConAu 5R, SmATA 12, WrDr 80

You Can Be A Carpenter
BL - v70 - N 1 '73 - p293
CCB-B - v27 - Ap '74 - p131
CLW - v45 - N '73 - p190
KR - v41 - My 15 '73 - p570
LJ - v99 - F 15 '74 - p581

You Can Be A Mechanic
BL - v72 - S 1 '75 - p43
KR - v43 - Je 1 '75 - p617
SLJ - v22 - S '75 - p107

You Can Be A Plumber
BL - v70 - Jl 1 '74 - p1201
KR - v42 - Ap 1 '74 - p376
LJ - v99 - O 15 '74 - p2747

You Can Be A Professional Driver
BL - v73 - S 1 '76 - p40
KR - v44 - My 1 '76 - p548
SLJ - v23 - S '76 - p120

LIGHTBODY, Donna M

Hooks And Loops
BL - v72 - N 15 '75 - p455
SLJ - v22 - Ja '76 - p54

LINDGREN, Astrid   1907-
ChLR 1, ConAu 13R, MorJA,
SmATA 2, TwCCW 78B, WhoAmW
77

Rasmus And The Vagabond
BL - v56 - Je 1 '60 - p608
CSM - My 12 '60 - p3B
Comw - v72 - My 27 '60 - p233
HB - v36 - Ap '60 - p133
KR - v28 - F 1 '60 - p90
LJ - v85 - My 15 '60 - p2040
NYTBR, pt.2 - My 8 '60 - p18
PW - v193 - My 20 '68 - p63
SR - v43 - N 12 '60 - p94
TLS - D 1 '61 - pR18

LINEHAM, Don

Soft Touch: A Sport That Lets You Touch Life
LJ - v101 - N 15 '76 - p2391
WLB - v51 - Mr '77 - p606

LINGARD, Joan   1932-
ConAu 41R, SmATA 8, TwCCW 78,
WrDr 80

Into Exile
BL - v70 - Ja 1 '74 - p489
BS - v33 - N 15 '73 - p382
CCB-B - v27 - Mr '74 - p113
Comw - v99 - N 23 '73 - p216
LJ - v99 - F 15 '74 - p581
Spec - v231 - O 20 '73 - pR10
TLS - S 28 '73 - p1118

LINN, Ed   1922-
ConAu 97, WhoAm 78

Koufax
BS - v26 - O 1 '66 - p251
CLW - v38 - N '66 - p87
Comt - v42 - N '66 - p87
LJ - v91 - O 1 '66 - p4691
LJ - v91 - D 15 '66 - p6220
NO - v5-7 - N '66 - p23
NYTBR - S 18 '66 - p46
Nat - v204 - Ja 30 '67 - p149

LIPMAN, David   1931-
AuBYP SUP, ConAu 21R, SmATA
21, WhoAm 78, WrDr 80

LIPMAN, David (continued)

Jim Hart: Underrated Quarterback
BL - v73 - Je 1 '77 - p1499
KR - v45 - Mr 15 '77 - p293
SLJ - v23 - My '77 - p80

LIPMAN, Marilyn
see Lipman, David (co-author)

LIPSYTE, Robert 1938-
AuBYP SUP, ConAu 17R, SmATA 5

The Contender
BL - v64 - D 15 '67 - p497
BW - v1 - N 5 '67 - p38
CCB-B - v21 - My '68 - p145
CE - v46 - Ap '70 - p368
CSM - v59 - N 2 '67 - pB13
Comw - v87 - N 10 '67 - p181
EJ - v59 - Ap '70 - p591
HB - v43 - D '67 - p759
J Read - v22 - N '78 - p128
KR - v35 - S 15 '67 - p1146
LJ - v92 - N 15 '67 - p4262
NYTBR - v72 - N 5 '67 - p64
NYTBR - v72 - N 12 '67 - p42
SR - v51 - Mr 16 '68 - p39
TN - v24 - Ap '68 - p323

LISS, Howard 1922-
AuBYP, ConAu 25R, SmATA 4

Bobby Orr: Lightning On Ice
SLJ - v22 - D '75 - p69

Football Talk For Beginners
BL - v66 - Je 15 '70 - p1280
CCB-B - v24 - O '70 - p30
KR - v38 - Mr 1 '70 - p247
LJ - v95 - My 15 '70 - p1965
PW - v197 - Je 15 '70 - p66

The Front 4: Let's Meet At The Quarterback
BL - v68 - Ap 15 '72 - p718
BL - v68 - Ap 15 '72 - p725
CCB-B - v25 - Mr '72 - p111
LJ - v96 - D '71 - p4200

Hockey's Greatest All-Stars
KR - v40 - Ag 1 '72 - p862
LJ - v98 - My 15 '73 - p1705

More Strange But True Baseball Stories
KR - v40 - Ap 15 '72 - p482
LJ - v97 - My 15 '72 - p1930
NY - v48 - D 2 '72 - p190

Triple Crown Winners
LJ - v94 - D 15 '69 - p4620
PW - v196 - N 3 '69 - p49
SR - v53 - Je 27 '70 - p38

LISTON, Robert A 1927-
AuBYP, ConAu 17R, SmATA 5

Your Career in Civil Service
BL - v62 - Je 15 '66 - p997
BS - v26 - Jl 1 '66 - p141
LJ - v91 - My 15 '66 - p2710

LITSKY, Frank

Winners In Gymnastics
BL - v74 - Ap 15 '78 - p1357
JB - v43 - F '79 - p36
SLJ - v24 - My '78 - p87

The Winter Olympics
BL - v76 - O 1 '79 - p283
SLJ - v26 - D '79 - p101

LITTKE, Lael J 1929-
ConAu 85

Tell Me When I Can Go
BL - v75 - F 15 '79 - p927
Hi Lo - v1 - O '79 - p4

LITTLE, Jean 1932-
ConAu 21R, FourBJA, OxCan SUP,
SmATA 2, TwCCW 78, WrDr 80

Kate
BL - v68 - N 15 '71 - p292
BW - v5 - N 7 '71 - p14
CCB-B - v25 - D '71 - p59
CLW - v43 - F '72 - p361
CSM - v63 - N 11 '71 - pB5
EJ - v61 - Mr '72 - p434
HB - v48 - F '72 - p49
KR - v39 - O 1 '71 - p1070

LITTLE, Jean (continued)
LJ - v96 - D 15 '71 - p4185
NYTBR - Ja 16 '72 - p8
PW - v200 - O 18 '71 - p50
SR - v54 - O 16 '71 - p57

Look Through My Window
BL - v67 - S 15 '70 - p108
CCB-B - v24 - Ja '71 - p76
HB - v46 - D '70 - p620
KR - v38 - Je 1 '70 - p599
PW - v197 - Je 29 '70 - p104
SR - v53 - O 24 '70 - p67
Spec - v47 - Mr '71 - p43

LIVINGSTON, Myra Cohn 1926-
BkP, ConAu 1R, FourBJA, SmATA
5, TwCCW 78, WhoAmW 77

The Malibu And Other Poems
CCB-B - v26 - Ja '73 - p79
CSM - v64 - N 8 '72 - pB2
Inst - v82 - N '72 - p128
KR - v40 - Jl 1 '72 - p726
LJ - v97 - O 15 '72 - p3453
NYTBR, pt.2 - N 5 '72 - p32

LIVINGSTON, Peter
AuBYP SUP

On Astrology
KR - v43 - Mr 15 '75 - p313
SLJ - v21 - My '75 - p57

LLOYD-JONES, Buster
IntAu&W 77

Animals Came In One By One
BL - v63 - Ap 1 '67 - p824
CCB-B - v20 - My '67 - p142
KR - v34 - D 1 '66 - p1264
LJ - v92 - Mr 15 '67 - p1170
LJ - v92 - Mr 15 '67 - p1336
PW - v190 - N 28 '66 - p57
Punch - v251 - O 12 '66 - p567
SR - v50 - My 13 '67 - p58

LOCKWOOD, Charles A 1890-1968
ConAu 1R, NatCAB 53, WhAm 4

Down To The Sea In Subs: My Life In The U.S. Navy
BL - v63 - Ap 15 '67 - p882
KR - v34 - D 15 '66 - p1332

LJ - v92 - Mr 1 '67 - p1007
PW - v190 - N 28 '66 - p57
TN - v24 - N '67 - p102
Yacht - v121 - Je '67 - p102

LOGAN, Rayford Wittingham
see Sterling, Philip (co-author) -
Four Took Freedom

LOMASK, Milton 1909-
ConAu 1R, DrAS 74H, SmATA 20

This Slender Reed: A Life Of James K. Polk
BS - v26 - N 1 '66 - p295
CLW - v38 - N '66 - p213
Comw - v85 - N 11 '66 - p176
HB - v43 - F '67 - p88
KR - v34 - Jl 1 '66 - p632
LJ - v91 - O 15 '66 - p5252

LONDON, Jack 1876-1916
JBA 34, OxAm, SmATA 18, TwCA,
TwCA SUP, WhAm 1, WhoTwCL

The Call Of The Wild
BB - v6 - My '78 - p4
B&B - v22 - Je '77 - p68
BL - v65 - F 1 '69 - p597
LA - v55 - S '78 - p742
SLJ - v24 - F '78 - p72
TLS - Mr 14 '68 - p263

LONG, Judy 1953-
ConAu 65, SmATA 20

Volunteer Spring
BW - Ap 11 '76 - p4
CCB-B - v30 - N '76 - p45
PW - v209 - Mr 15 '76 - p58
SLJ - v22 - My '76 - p71
Teacher - v95 - O '77 - p171

LONGMAN, Harold S 1919-
ConAu 25R, SmATA 5

Would You Put Your Money In A Sand Bank?: Fun With Words
BL - v64 - Je 15 '68 - p1187
CSM - v60 - My 2 '68 - pB4
Inst - v78 - Ag '68 - p192
LJ - v93 - Je 15 '68 - p2540
LJ - v98 - O 15 '73 - p3163
NYTBR - Ap 13 '69 - p30

LONGMAN, Harold S (continued)
    RT - v32 - N '78 - p148
    TN - v25 - N '68 - p78

LORD, Beman   1924-
    ConAu 33R, FourBJA, SmATA 5

    Guards For Matt
        Inst - v78 - Ap '69 - p148
        NYTBR - N 12 '61 - p46

    Look At Cars
        BL - v67 - Mr 15 '71 - p623
        LJ - v96 - F 15 '71 - p744

    Mystery Guest At Left End
        CCB-B - v18 - Jl '65 - p165
        NYTBR - N 1 '64 - p46

    Quarterback's Aim
        BL - v57 - F 1 '61 - p330
        HB - v36 - O '60 - p402
        KR - v28 - Ag 1 '60 - p621
        LJ - v85 - S 15 '60 - p3224
        NYTBR - D 11 '60 - p44
        SR - v43 - D 17 '60 - p35

    Rough Ice
        NYTBR - N 10 '63 - p49

    Shot-Put Challenge
        KR - v37 - My 1 '69 - p505
        LJ - v94 - D 15 '69 - p4620
        PW - v195 - Ap 21 '69 - p66

    Shrimp's Soccer Goal
        CCB-B - v24 - Mr '71 - p109
        KR - v38 - S 15 '70 - p1038
        LJ - v95 - D 15 '70 - p4381
        SR - v53 - N 14 '70 - p35

    The Trouble With Francis
        BL - v55 - O 1 '58 - p80
        LJ - v84 - Ja 15 '59 - p244
        NYTBR - Ja 18 '59 - p28
        SR - v42 - Ja 24 '59 - p37

LORD, Walter   1917-
    ConAu 1R, CurBio 72, SmATA 3,
    WhoAm 78, WorAu

    A Night To Remember
        BL - v73 - Ap 1 '77 - p1139
        BL - v73 - Ap 1 '77 - p1170
        NYTBR - F 5 '78 - p41
        SLJ - v23 - Mr '77 - p158

    Spec - v237 - N 20 '76 - p20
    TLS - N 26 '76 - p1472
    VV - v21 - D 13 '76 - p77
    Yacht - v141 - My '77 - p122

LOVE, Sandra   1940-
    ConAu 69

    Melissa's Medley
        BL - v74 - Ap 15 '78 - p1352
        CCB-B - v32 - S '78 - p13
        SLJ - v24 - My '78 - p87

LOWRY, Lois   1937-
    AuBYP SUP, ConAu 69, SmATA 23

    Find A Stranger, Say Goodbye
        B&B - v6 - S '78 - p2
        BL - v74 - Ap 15 '78 - p1341
        CCB-B - v32 - O '78 - p33
        Comw - v105 - N 10 '78 - p733
        HB - v54 - Je '78 - p285
        KR - v46 - Mr 1 '78 - p248
        PW - v213 - My 15 '78 - p104
        SLJ - v24 - My '78 - p77

LUBOWE, Irwin Irville   1905-
    ConAu 53

    A Teen-Age Guide To Healthy
    Skin And Hair
        BL - v62 - Je 12 '65 - p24
        BL - v69 - F 1 '73 - p525
        KR - v33 - O 1 '65 - p1052
        LJ - v91 - Ja 15 '66 - p437
        Par - v41 - D '66 - p10

LUGER, H C

    The Elephant Tree
        BL - v74 - My 15 '78 - p1496
        KR - v46 - Je 1 '78 - p600
        NYTBR - Ap 30 '78 - p45
        SLJ - v24 - My '78 - p78

LUIS, Earlene W   1929-
    ConAu 61, SmATA 11

    Wheels For Ginny's Chariot
        Am - v115 - Jl 2 '66 - p14
        Am - v115 - Jl 2 '66 - p14
        BL - v63 - S 15 '66 - p120
        BS - v26 - Ja 5 '66 - p58
        CCB-B - v20 - S '66 - p14

LUIS, Earlene W (continued)
   LJ - v91 - Je 15 '66 - p3268

LYLE, Katie Letcher   1938-
   ConAu 49, SmATA 8

   Fair Day, And Another Step Begun
      A Lib - v5 - Jl '74 - p360
      BL - v70 - Ap 1 '74 - p870
      BS - v34 - Ap 15 '74 - p54
      CCB-B - v28 - S '74 - p12
      KR - v42 - Ap 15 '74 - p433
      LJ - v99 - S 15 '74 - p2294
      NY - v50 - D 2 '74 - p182
      NYTBR - My 19 '74 - p8
      NYTBR - N 3 '74 - p52
      PW - v205 - Mr 4 '74 - p76
      VQR - v50 - Autumn '74 - pR120

   I Will Go Barefoot All Summer
   For You
      A Lib - v5 - Jl '74 - p360
      BL - v69 - Je 15 '73 - p990
      BW - v7 - My 13 '73 - p7
      KR - v41 - F 1 '73 - p124
      LJ - v98 - My 15 '73 - p1682
      NYTBR - Ap 29 '73 - p8
      PW - v203 - My 7 '73 - p66
      Teacher - v92 - S '74 - p130

LYON, Elinor   1921-
   ConAu 25R, SmATA 6, WrDr 80
   (also known as Wright, Elinor Bruce)

   Cathie Runs Wild
      CCB-B - v22 - F '69 - p98
      LJ - v93 - Jl '68 - p2734

   Rider's Rock
      BL - v65 - Ja 15 '69 - p547
      LJ - v93 - My 15 '68 - p2127
      PW - v194 - O 7 '68 - p54

LYON, Nancy

   Totem Poles And Tribes
      SLJ - v25 - N '78 - p64

LYTTLE, Richard Bard   1927-
   AuBYP SUP, ConAu 33R, SmATA
   23

   Getting Into Pro Basketball
      SLJ - v25 - My '79 - p86

see also Dolan, Edward F, Jr. (co-
   author) -
   Archie Griffin
   Bobby Clarke
   Fred Lynn
   Janet Guthrie
   Jimmy Young
   Kyle Rote, Jr.
   Martina Navratilova
   Scott May

M

MACCRACKEN, Mary 1926-
ConAu 49, WrDr 80

Lovey: A Very Special Child
BL - v73 - O 1 '76 - p223
BS - v36 - D '76 - p295
HB - v53 - F '77 - p82
KR - v44 - Jl 1 '76 - p775
LJ - v101 - S 1 '76 - p1782
NYTBR - O 17 '76 - p8
NYTBR - O 23 '77 - p51
PW - v210 - Jl 12 '76 - p67
PW - v212 - S 5 '77 - p71
SLJ - v23 - Ja '77 - p108

MACDONALD, Zillah 1885-
AuBYP, ConAu P-1, SmATA 11,
WhoAmW 77

Marcia, Private Secretary
CSM - Jl 14 '49 - p7
KR - v17 - F 15 '49 - p86
LJ - v74 - Ap 15 '49 - p669
NYTBR - Mr 13 '49 - p24

MACHOL, Libby 1916-
ConAu 21R

Giana
BL - v64 - F 15 '68 - p682
CCB-B - v21 - Ja '68 - p79
KR - v35 - Ag 15 '67 - p1013
LJ - v92 - O 1 '67 - p3414
LJ - v93 - Ap 15 '68 - p1824
NYTBR - v72 - D 10 '67 - p26
SR - v50 - D 16 '67 - p36

MACK, John 1935-
BioIn 9

Nobody Promised Me
LJ - v96 - Ap 15 '71 - p1514

MACKELLAR, William 1914-
AuBYP, ConAu 33R, SmATA 4

*Score!: A Baker's Dozen Sports
Stories*
KR - v35 - S 1 '67 - p1057
LJ - v92 - D 15 '67 - p4634

MACLEOD, Charlotte 1922-
ConAu 21R

The Fat Lady's Ghost
LJ - v93 - S 15 '68 - p3319

MACPHERSON, Margaret 1908-
BrCA, ConAu 49, FourBJA, SmATA
9, TwCCW 78

The Rough Road
BL - v62 - Jl 15 '66 - p1088
CCB-B - v20 - Mr '67 - p112
CSM - v58 - Je 30 '66 - p11
HB - v42 - Je '66 - p316
KR - v33 - D 15 '65 - p1230
LJ - v91 - Mr 15 '66 - p1720
PW - v189 - F 14 '66 - p144
Punch - v249 - D 15 '65 - p897
TLS - D 9 '65 - p1134

MADDEN, Betsy

The All-America Coeds
CCB-B - v24 - Je '71 - p159
KR - v39 - My 1 '71 - p501
LJ - v96 - My 15 '71 - p1823

MADDOCK, Reginald 1912-
ConAu 81, SmATA 15, TwCCW 78,
WrDr 80

The Pit
B&B - v11 - Je '66 - p67
BL - v64 - Ap 1 '68 - p932
BS - v28 - Ap 1 '68 - p18

MADDOCK, Reginald (continued)
    BW - v2 - My 5 '68 - p5
    CCB-B - v21 - Mr '68 - p113
    CSM - v60 - My 9 '68 - p15
    HB - v44 - Je '68 - p330
    KR - v36 - F 1 '68 - p123
    NS - v71 - My 20 '66 - p742
    SR - v51 - F 24 '68 - p51
    TLS - My 19 '66 - p439

MADISON, Arnold   1937-
AuBYP SUP, ConAu 21R, SmATA 6

    Great Unsolved Cases
        BL - v75 - O 15 '78 - p370
        Hi Lo - v1 - O '79 - p5
        TES - Ja 11 '80 - p26
        TN - v36 - Winter '80 - p198

    Lost Treasures Of America
        BB - v6 - Je '78 - p3
        BL - v74 - Ja 15 '78 - p813
        SE - v42 - Ap '78 - p318
        SLJ - v25 - S '78 - p161

MADISON, Winifred
ConAu 37R, SmATA 5

    Max's Wonderful Delicatessen
        BS - v32 - D 15 '72 - p446
        KR - v40 - O 15 '72 - p1202
        LJ - v98 - Ap 15 '73 - p1396
        NO - v11 - N 18 '72 - p28
        PW - v202 - O 16 '72 - p50

MAGNUSSON, Magnus   1929-
IntAu&W 77, WrDr 80

    Introducing Archaeology
        BL - v70 - S 1 '73 - p47
        CCB-B - v27 - O '73 - p31
        CLW - v45 - N '73 - p185
        HB - v49 - Ag '73 - p391
        KR - v41 - Ap 1 '73 - p401
        LJ - v98 - My 15 '73 - p1581
        LJ - v98 - My 15 '73 - p1655
        LJ - v98 - My 15 '73 - p1689
        LR - v23 - Autumn '72 - p300
        NY - v49 - D 3 '73 - p219
        Obs - Jl 16 '72 - p31
        PW - v203 - Ap 2 '73 - p65
        SB - v9 - Mr '74 - p321
        TLS - Jl 14 '72 - p810

MAHONY, Elizabeth Winthrop
    see Winthrop, Elizabeth

MAJOR, Kevin   1949-
ConAu 97

    Hold Fast
        BIC - v8 - Ap '79 - p3
        SN - v93 - O '78 - p14

MALONE, Robert

    Rocketship: An Incredible Journey
    Through Science Fiction And
    Science Fact
        Kliatt - v12 - Winter '78 - p13
        S&T - v54 - D '77 - p519
        SLJ - v24 - Mr '78 - p146

MANN, Peggy
ConAu 25R, IntAu&W 77, SmATA
6, WrDr 80

    The Drop-In
        BL - v75 - Je 15 '79 - p1533
        Hi Lo - v1 - S '79 - p2

    Luis Munoz Marin: The Man Who
    Remade Puerto Rico
        BL - v73 - N 1 '76 - p410
        KR - v44 - Jl 1 '76 - p741
        SE - v41 - Ap '77 - p350
        SLJ - v23 - O '76 - p109

    There Are Two Kinds Of Terrible
        Am - v137 - D 3 '77 - p406
        BL - v73 - F 1 '77 - p836
        BS - v37 - O '77 - p203
        CCB-B - v31 - S '77 - p21
        KR - v45 - Je 15 '77 - p626
        PW - v211 - My 2 '77 - p60
        RT - v31 - Ap '78 - p840
        SLJ - v23 - Ja '77 - p94
        Teacher - v95 - My '78 - p103
    see also Kluger, Ruth (co-author)

MANNING-SANDERS, Ruth   1895-
ConAu 73, SmATA 15, ThrBJA,
TwCCW 78, WrDr 80

    A Book Of Witches
        BL - v63 - O 15 '66 - p267
        CCB-B - v20 - D '66 - p60
        CSM - v67 - Je 10 '75 - p17
        HB - v42 - O '66 - p564

MANNING-SANDERS, Ruth
(continued)
    LJ - v91 - S 15 '66 - p4339
    NYTBR - v72 - Ja 15 '67 - p28
    PW - v190 - O 3 '66 - p84
    SR - v49 - N 12 '66 - p50
    Spec - N 12 '65 - p631

MANNIX, Daniel 1911-
AuBYP SUP, BioIn 1, BioIn 2

   The Outcasts
    BL - v62 - O 1 '65 - p162
    CCB-B - v18 - Jl '65 - p166
    HB - v41 - Ag '65 - p387
    Inst - v75 - N '65 - p94
    KR - v33 - Ja 15 '65 - p58
    LJ - v90 - Mr 15 '65 - p1550
    NYTBR - v70 - Je 13 '65 - p24

MANTLE, Mickey 1931-
BioNews 74, ConAu 89, CurBio 53,
NewYTBS 74, WhoAm 78, WhoProB
73

   The Education Of A Baseball
   Player
    BL - v64 - Ja 1 '68 - p526
    BS - v27 - O 15 '67 - p268
    KR - v35 - Jl 1 '67 - p784
    KR - v35 - Ag 15 '67 - p980
    LJ - v92 - Ag '67 - p2800
    LJ - v92 - O 15 '67 - p3876
    NYTBR - v72 - O 1 '67 - p8
    NYTBR - v72 - D 3 '67 - p64
    PW - v192 - Jl 10 '67 - p179
    PW - v195 - F 24 '69 - p68

MARR, John S 1940-
ConAu 81

   A Breath Of Air And A Breath Of
   Smoke
    CCB-B - v25 - Jl '72 - p173
    CLW - v43 - My '72 - p536
    LJ - v97 - Jl '72 - p2485
    SB - v8 - S '72 - p160
    Spec - v226 - My 29 '71 - p1260

MARRIOTT, Alice 1910-
BioIn 2, BioIn 8, ConAu 57

   The Black Stone Knife
    PW - v193 - Ja 8 '68 - p69

MARSHALL, Anthony D 1924-
ConAu 29R, SmATA 18, WhoAm 78,
WhoGov 77

   Africa's Living Arts
    LJ - v95 - Jl '70 - p2541

MARTIN, Albert (pseud.) 1934-
ConAu X (real name: Nussbaum,
Albert F)

   Secret Spy
    BL - v75 - Jl 15 '79 - p1622
    Hi Lo - v1 - D '79 - p4
    SLJ - v26 - D '79 - p98

MARTIN, Joseph Plumb 1760-1850
BioIn 7, BioIn 10, BioIn 11

   Yankee Doodle Boy
    BL - v61 - F '65 - p526
    CE - v42 - O '65 - p116
    HB - v41 - F '65 - p65
    LJ - v89 - D 15 '64 - p5019
    NYTBR, pt.2 - N 1 '64 - p56

MARX, Robert F 1934?-
AuBYP, ConAu 9R, SmATA 24,
WrDr 80

   They Dared The Deep: A History
   Of Diving
    BL - v64 - O 1 '67 - p178
    BS - v27 - Jl 1 '67 - p145
    KR - v35 - My 15 '67 - p612
    LJ - v93 - F 15 '68 - p884
    NYTBR - v72 - Ag 6 '67 - p26

MASIN, Herman L 1913-

   How To Star In Basketball
    BL - v63 - Mr 15 '67 - p796
    LJ - v92 - Ja 15 '67 - p351
    Teacher - v92 - Mr '75 - p41

   How To Star In Football
    BL - v63 - Mr 15 '67 - p796
    LJ - v92 - Ja 15 '67 - p352
    Teacher - v92 - Mr '75 - p41

MASON, Herbert Molloy, Jr. 1927-
ConAu 13R, WrDr 80

   Secrets Of The Supernatural
    BL - v72 - N 1 '75 - p359

MASON, Herbert Molloy, Jr.
(continued)
BS - v35 - Ja '76 - p325
KR - v43 - D 1 '75 - p1341
SLJ - v22 - Ja '76 - p55

MASSIE, Diane Redfield   1930-
ConAu 81, IlsCB 1967, SmATA 16

Cockle Stew And Other Rhymes
KR - v35 - Ag 15 '67 - p956
LJ - v92 - N 15 '67 - p4245
NYTBR - v72 - N 5 '67 - p61

MATHER, Melissa

One Summer In Between
BL - v63 - Je 15 '67 - p1088
BS - v27 - Ap 1 '67 - p17
HB - v43 - D '67 - p770
KR - v35 - Ja 15 '67 - p80
LJ - v92 - F 15 '67 - p795
LJ - v92 - My 15 '67 - p2048
NYTBR - v72 - Mr 19 '67 - p46
PW - v190 - N 7 '66 - p62
PW - v193 - Mr 4 '68 - p66
SR - v50 - Ap 22 '67 - p101
TN - v24 - N '67 - p102
TN - v24 - Ap '68 - p327

MATHEWS, William H
see Brownmiller, Susan (co-author)

MATHIS, Sharon Bell   1937-
ChLR 3, ConAu 41R, FourBJA,
SelBAA, SmATA 7, TwCCW 78,
WhoBlA 77

Listen For The Fig Tree
BL - v70 - My 15 '74 - p1052
BL - v70 - My 15 '74 - p1057
BL - v71 - Mr 15 '75 - p748
BS - v34 - Jl 15 '74 - p202
CCB-B - v27 - Jl '74 - p182
Choice - v14 - N '77 - p1178
Comw - v101 - N 22 '74 - p192
EJ - v64 - D '75 - p80
HB - v50 - Je '74 - p287
KR - v42 - F 1 '74 - p121
LJ - v99 - Mr 15 '74 - p904
NYTBR - Ap 7 '74 - p8
PW - v205 - Ja 21 '74 - p85

Teacup Full Of Roses
BL - v69 - O 1 '72 - p139
BL - v69 - O 1 '72 - p150
BW - v6 - Ag 6 '72 - p2
Bl W - v22 - Ag '73 - p86
CCB-B - v26 - O '72 - p29
CE - v49 - My '73 - p422
Choice - v14 - N '77 - p1178
EJ - v62 - D '73 - p1300
EJ - v63 - Ja '74 - p66
EJ - v63 - F '74 - p92
EJ - v64 - D '75 - p80
HB - v49 - F '73 - p58
KR - v40 - Je 1 '72 - p629
LJ - v97 - N 15 '72 - p3814
NHB - v36 - Mr '73 - p69
NYTBR - Je 4 '72 - p28
NYTBR - S 10 '72 - p8
NYTBR, pt.2 - N 5 '72 - p28
PW - v202 - Jl 17 '72 - p122
SE - v37 - D '73 - p787
TN - v29 - Ap '73 - p257
Teacher - v91 - F '74 - p98

MATTHEWS, Clayton
see Brisco, Patty

MATTHEWS, Patricia
see Brisco, Patty

MATTHEWS, William H, III   1919-
AmM&WS 76P, AuBYP SUP,
ConAu 9R, WhoS&SW 78

Introducing The Earth
BL - v69 - O 15 '72 - p192
KR - v40 - Je 1 '72 - p633
LJ - v97 - O 15 '72 - p3462

Wonders Of Fossils
BL - v64 - Jl 15 '68 - p1287
Comw - v88 - My 24 '68 - p308
KR - v36 - Mr 15 '68 - p349
LJ - v93 - My 15 '68 - p2114
SB - v4 - My '68 - p34

MAXWELL, Edith   1923-
AuBYP SUP, ConAu 49, SmATA 7,
WhoAmW 77

Just Dial A Number
BS - v31 - Ap 15 '71 - p47
KR - v38 - D 15 '70 - p1348

MAXWELL, Edith (continued)
  LJ - v96 - My 15 '71 - p1815
  NYTBR - Ap 18 '71 - p40
  PW - v199 - F 8 '71 - p81

MAY, Julian 1931-
AuBYP, ConAu 1R, SmATA 11

  Hank Aaron Clinches The Pennant
    CCB-B - v26 - O '72 - p29

MAYER, Ann M 1938-
ConAu 57, SmATA 14

  Who's Out There? UFO
  Encounters
    Hi Lo - v1 - Ja '80 - p3
    SLJ - v26 - Ja '80 - p73

MAYERSON, Charlotte Leon
ConAu 13R, ForWC 70

  Two Blocks Apart: Juan Gonzales
  And Peter Quinn
    BL - v62 - S 1 '65 - p14
    CC - v82 - Jl 7 '65 - p871
    Crit - v24 - O '65 - p86
    EJ - v56 - N '67 - p1215
    HB - v41 - D '65 - p650
    HM - v231 - S '65 - p141
    KR - v33 - My 1 '65 - p494
    KR - v33 - Je 1 '65 - p536
    LJ - v90 - Jl '65 - p3064
    LJ - v90 - S 15 '65 - p3818
    NYTBR, pt.2 - v72 - F 26 '67 - p32
    PW - v190 - S 26 '66 - p135

MAZER, Harry 1925-
ConAu 97

  Guy Lenny
    KR - v39 - O 15 '71 - p1121
    Kliatt - v11 - Fall '77 - p7
    LJ - v96 - O 15 '71 - p3478
    Teacher - v90 - F '73 - p125

  The Last Mission
    BB - v7 - Ja '80 - p3
    BOT - v2 - D '79 - p601
    CBRS - v8 - O '79 - p18
    KR - v48 - Ja 1 '80 - p10
    NYTBR - N 25 '79 - p22
    NYTBR - D 2 '79 - p41
    PW - v216 - D 10 '79 - p70

  SLJ - v26 - N '79 - p91
  WLB - v54 - O '79 - p123

  Snow Bound
    BL - v70 - S 15 '73 - p123
    J Read - v22 - N '78 - p128
    KR - v41 - Ap 1 '73 - p384
    LJ - v98 - Jl '73 - p2202
    NYTBR - Ag 12 '73 - p8
    PW - v203 - Mr 26 '73 - p70

  The War On Villa Street
    BL - v75 - N 15 '78 - p547
    CBRS - v7 - F '79 - p69
    CCB-B - v32 - Ja '79 - p84
    KR - v46 - D 1 '78 - p1311
    Kliatt - v14 - Winter '80 - p12
    PW - v214 - D 25 '78 - p60
    SLJ - v25 - D '78 - p62
    TN - v36 - Winter '80 - p209
    WLB - v53 - Ja '79 - p380
  see also Mazer, Norma Fox (co-
  author) - *The Solid Gold Kid*

MAZER, Norma Fox 1931-
ConAu 69, SmATA 24

  Dear Bill, Remember Me?
    NYTBR - F 26 '78 - p41

  A Figure Of Speech
    BL - v70 - Ja 15 '74 - p544
    BS - v33 - N 15 '73 - p382
    CCB-B - v27 - Ja '74 - p82
    CE - v54 - Ja '78 - p124
    Choice - v14 - N '77 - p1178
    HB - v50 - Ap '74 - p152
    KR - v41 - S 15 '73 - p1043
    LJ - v99 - F 15 '74 - p582
    NYTBR - Mr 17 '74 - p8
    PW - v204 - S 17 '73 - p57

  The Solid Gold Kid
    BB - v6 - Je '78 - p3
    BL - v73 - Je 1 '77 - p1499
    BS - v37 - O '77 - p204
    BW - Jl 10 '77 - pH10
    CCB-B - v30 - Jl '77 - p178
    EJ - v67 - F '78 - p79
    HB - v53 - Ag '77 - p451
    KR - v45 - Ap 1 '77 - p360
    PW - v211 - Mr 28 '77 - p78
    RT - v32 - O '78 - p44

MAZER, Norma Fox (continued)
SLJ - v24 - S '77 - p147

Up In Seth's Room
BL - v76 - N 1 '79 - p440
CBRS - v8 - D '79 - p39
KR - v47 - D 1 '79 - p1380
NYTBR - Ja 20 '80 - p30
PW - v216 - S 10 '79 - p74
WLB - v54 - O '79 - p123

MCCAGUE, James 1909-
ConAu 1R

Tecumseh
CE - v47 - D '70 - p160
LJ - v95 - N 15 '70 - p4062

MCCALL, Joseph R
see McCall, Virginia Nielsen (co-author)

MCCALL, Virginia Nielsen 1909-
AuBYP SUP, ConAu 1R, SmATA 13, WhoAmW 75 (also known as Nielsen, Virginia)

Your Career In Parks And Recreation
BL - v67 - S 15 '70 - p97
BS - v30 - My 1 '70 - p62
Choice - v7 - S '70 - p822
LJ - v96 - F 15 '71 - p744
see also Nielsen, Virginia

MCCALLUM, John Dennis 1924-
ConAu 53, IntAu&W 77

Getting Into Pro Football
BL - v75 - Jl 1 '79 - p1583
SLJ - v25 - My '79 - p86

MCCANNON, Dindga
AfroAA

Peaches
BL - v71 - Ja 15 '75 - p508
BW - N 10 '74 - p5
KR - v42 - N 1 '74 - p1151
SLJ - v21 - Ja '75 - p55

MCCARTHY, Pat

True Ghost Stories: Tales Of The Supernatural Based On Actual Reports
Hi Lo - v1 - Ap '80 - p3

MCCONNELL, James Douglas Rutherford
see Rutherford, Douglas

MCDONALD, Gerald 1905-1970
BioIn 8, BioIn 9, ConAu P-1, SmATA 3

A Way Of Knowing: A Collection Of Poems For Boys
BL - v55 - Jl 15 '59 - p634
HB - v35 - Ag '59 - p302
KR - v27 - Mr 15 '59 - p227
LJ - v84 - My 15 '59 - p1705
NYTBR - S 13 '59 - p58
SR - v42 - Jl 18 '59 - p38

MCDONNELL, Virginia B 1917-
AuBYP SUP, ConAu 21R, WhoAmW 77, WhoE 77

Trouble At Mercy Hospital
CCB-B - v22 - Ja '69 - p82
LJ - v94 - F 15 '69 - p875

MCFALL, Karen

Pat King's Family
BL - v74 - Jl 15 '78 - p1722

MCFARLAND, Kenton Dean 1920-
AuBYP SUP, ConAu 61, SmATA 11

Airplanes: How They Work
BL - v63 - O 15 '66 - p266

MCFARLAND, Kevin

More Incredible!
Kliatt - v13 - Winter '79 - p63

MCGIVERN, Maureen Daly
see Daly, Maureen

MCGONAGLE, Bob

Careers In Sports
BL - v72 - N 1 '75 - p370
CLW - v47 - Ap '76 - p408

MCGONAGLE, Bob (continued)
SLJ - v22 - D '75 - p68

MCGONAGLE, Marquita
see McGonagle, Bob (co-author)

MCGRAW, Eloise Jarvis 1915-
BioIn 3, BioIn 4, ConAu 5R, MorJA,
SmATA 1, TwCCW 78

Greensleeves
BW - v2 - N 3 '68 - p26
CSM - v60 - N 7 '68 - pB11
KR - v36 - S 15 '68 - p1060
LJ - v93 - O 15 '68 - p3984

MCHARGUE, Georgess 1941-
AuBYP SUP, ChLR 2, ConAu 25R,
SmATA 4

*Little Victories, Big Defeats: War
As The Ultimate Pollution*
EJ - v68 - F '79 - p94

Mummies
BL - v69 - Mr 15 '73 - p698
CE - v50 - O '73 - p34
HB - v49 - Ap '73 - p152
KR - v40 - O 1 '72 - p1158
LJ - v98 - My 15 '73 - p1683
PW - v202 - D 18 '72 - p40
TN - v29 - Je '73 - p357
Teacher - v90 - Ap '73 - p90

**MCILWRAITH, Maureen Mollie
Hunter McVeigh** 1922-
ConAu 29R, SmATA 2, ThrBJA,
WrDr 80 (also known as Hunter,
Mollie)

*The Walking Stones: A Story Of
Suspense*
Am - v123 - D 5 '70 - p496
BL - v67 - N 1 '70 - p228
BW - v4 - N 8 '70 - p8
CCB-B - v24 - Je '71 - p157
CSM - v62 - N 12 '70 - pB7
HB - v47 - F '71 - p51
KR - v38 - Ag 1 '70 - p800
LJ - v95 - D 15 '70 - p4375
NYTBR, pt.2 - N 8 '70 - p24
TN - v27 - Ap '71 - p305
see also Hunter, Mollie

MCKAY, Robert W 1921-
AuBYP SUP, ConAu 13R, SmATA
15

Canary Red
BL - v65 - O 15 '68 - p234
BS - v28 - S 1 '68 - p227
KR - v36 - Je 15 '68 - p649
LJ - v93 - O 15 '68 - p3984

Dave's Song
BL - v66 - Ap 1 '70 - p968
CCB-B - v24 - O '70 - p30
EJ - v59 - My '70 - p735
KR - v37 - N 15 '69 - p1203
SR - v53 - My 9 '70 - p69

The Running Back
BL - v76 - N 15 '79 - p494
KR - v48 - F 1 '80 - p134
SLJ - v26 - D '79 - p100

The Troublemaker
BL - v68 - My 1 '72 - p766
BS - v31 - F 15 '72 - p523
EJ - v61 - My '72 - p769
LJ - v97 - My 15 '72 - p1923

MCKIMMEY, James 1923-
ConAu 85

Buckaroo
Hi Lo - v2 - N '80 - p5

MCKOWN, Robin 1907-
ConAu 1R, SmATA 6, ThrBJA,
WhoE 75

Patriot Of The Underground
CCB-B - v19 - D '65 - p65
NYTBR - Je 7 '64 - p28

MCPHEE, Richard B

Rounds With A Country Vet
BL - v74 - F 15 '78 - p1009
CCB-B - v31 - Je '78 - p164
Comw - v105 - N 10 '78 - p734
Inst - v87 - My '78 - p115
KR - v46 - Ja 15 '78 - p51
PW - v213 - Ja 2 '78 - p65
SLJ - v24 - Mr '78 - p131
SR - v5 - My 27 '78 - p58

MCWHIRTER, Alan Ross
see McWhirter, Norris Dewar (co-
author)

MCWHIRTER, Norris Dewar   1925-
BioIn 8, ConAu 13R

    *Guinness Book Of Amazing
    Achievements*
       EJ - v65 - My '76 - p91
       Inst - v85 - My '76 - p112
       SLJ - v22 - Mr '76 - p105

    *Guinness Book Of Astounding
    Feats And Events*
       Inst - v85 - My '76 - p112
       SLJ - v22 - Mr '76 - p105

    *Guinness Book Of Phenomenal
    Happenings*
       BL - v72 - My 1 '76 - p1268
       SLJ - v23 - S '76 - p122

    *Guinness Book Of Young
    Recordbreakers*
       ARBA - v8 - '77 - p61
       BL - v72 - My 1 '76 - p1268
       SLJ - v23 - D '76 - p72

MEADER, Stephen W   1892-
ConAu 5R, JBA 51, SmATA 1,
TwCCW 78, WhoAm 78

    Lonesome End
       BS - v28 - N 1 '68 - p325
       CSM - v60 - N 7 '68 - pB12
       KR - v36 - O 1 '68 - p1121
       PW - v194 - O 7 '68 - p55

    River Of The Wolves
       BL - v45 - N 1 '48 - p92
       CSM - Ja 27 '49 - p7
       Comw - v49 - D 3 '48 - p214
       HB - v25 - Ja '49 - p41
       KR - v16 - O 1 '48 - p530
       LJ - v73 - D 1 '48 - p1747
       NY - v24 - D 11 '48 - p132
       NYTBR - Ja 30 '49 - p28
       SR - v31 - N 13 '48 - p32

MEADOWCROFT, Enid LaMonte
1898-1966
    BioIn 2, BioIn 7, ConAu X, JBA 51,
    SmATA 3 (also known as Wright,
    Enid Meadowcroft)

    By Secret Railway
       BL - v45 - N 1 '48 - p92
       CSM - O 28 '48 - p11
       KR - v16 - Ag 15 '48 - p400
       NY - v24 - D 11 '48 - p131
       NYTBR - N 14 '48 - p58
       SR - v31 - N 13 '48 - p28

    Scarab For Luck
       Comw - v80 - My 22 '64 - p268
       HB - v40 - Ap '64 - p179
       LJ - v89 - Mr 15 '64 - p1452
       NYTBR - Ag 2 '64 - p20

    *When Nantucket Men Went
    Whaling*
       LJ - v92 - Ja 15 '67 - p336

MEAKER, Marijane
see Kerr, M E

MEANS, Florence Crannell   1891-
ConAu 1R, JBA 51, SmATA 1,
TwCCW 78, WhoAm 78

    Candle In The Mist
       NYTBR - Ja 24 '32 - p19

    Shuttered Windows
       BL - v35 - S 15 '38 - p31
       Comw - v29 - D 2 '38 - p157
       HB - v14 - S '38 - p290
       LJ - v63 - O 15 '38 - p799
       LJ - v63 - N 1 '38 - p825
       NYTBR - Ag 28 '38 - p10

MEDEARIS, Mary   1915-
ConAu 69, SmATA 5

    Big Doc's Girl
       NYTBR - S 13 '42 - p7

MEEK, Jacklyn O'Hanlon
see O'Hanlon, Jacklyn

MEHTA, Rama
see Galbraith, Catherine Atwater
(co-author)

MEIGS, Cornelia   1884-1973
ConAu 9R, ConAu 45, JBA 51,
SmATA 6, TwCCW 78, WhAm 6

MEIGS, Cornelia (continued)

*Invincible Louisa: The Story Of
The Author Of Little Women*
BS - v28 - O 1 '68 - p274
BW - v2 - N 3 '68 - p1
NYTBR - v73 - S 29 '68 - p46
PW - v194 - S 2 '68 - p29

MELTZER, Milton 1915-
ConAu 13R, DrAS 78H, MorBMP,
SmATA 1, ThrBJA, WhoAm 78

Langston Hughes
AL - v41 - Mr '69 - p142
BL - v65 - Ja 1 '69 - p498
BL - v65 - Ap 1 '69 - p901
BS - v28 - Ja 1 '69 - p423
BW - v3 - F 2 '69 - p12
CSM - v61 - My 1 '69 - pB7
Cres - v33 - D '69 - p23
EJ - v58 - My '69 - p783
HB - v45 - Ap '69 - p183
Inst - v79 - Ag '69 - p191
LJ - v94 - Ja 15 '69 - p313
SE - v33 - My '69 - p562

Underground Man
BL - v69 - Ja 1 '73 - p446
CCB-B - v27 - S '73 - p14
CE - v49 - Ap '73 - p374
KR - v40 - N 15 '72 - p1313
LJ - v98 - Ap 15 '73 - p1397
NYTBR - Mr 18 '73 - p12
SE - v37 - D '73 - p786
TN - v29 - Ap '73 - p253
Teacher - v92 - Ap '75 - p113

MENNINGER, William C 1899-1966
ConAu 25R, CurBio 45, CurBio 66,
REnAL, WhAm 4

How To Be A Successful Teenager
LJ - v92 - F 15 '67 - p896
NYTBR - v72 - Mr 5 '67 - p30

MERCER, Charles Edward 1917-
AuBYP SUP, ConAu 1R, SmATA
16, WhoAm 78

Miracle At Midway
KR - v46 - Ja 1 '78 - p9
PW - v212 - O 31 '77 - p59
SLJ - v24 - F '78 - p66

MERGENDAHL, T E, Jr.

What Does A Photographer Do?
LJ - v90 - Ap 15 '65 - p2023

MERIWETHER, Louise 1923?-
ConAu 77, SelBAA, WhoBlA 77

Daddy Was A Number Runner
A Lib - v1 - D '70 - p1088
BL - v67 - Ap 1 '71 - p654
BW - v5 - Je 20 '71 - p11
Bl W - v19 - My '70 - p51
Bl W - v19 - Jl '70 - p85
EJ - v60 - My '71 - p657
EJ - v63 - Ja '74 - p66
EJ - v64 - D '75 - p80
KR - v38 - Ja 1 '70 - p22
KR - v38 - F 1 '70 - p119
LJ - v95 - F 15 '70 - p685
LJ - v95 - S 15 '70 - p3080
LJ - v95 - D 15 '70 - p4328
NS - v83 - Ja 7 '72 - p23
NY - v46 - Jl 11 '70 - p77
NYTBR - Je 28 '70 - p31
NYTBR - D 6 '70 - p100
Obs - Ja 9 '72 - p31
PW - v197 - Ja 19 '70 - p78
PW - v199 - My 3 '71 - p58
SR - v53 - My 23 '70 - p51
SR - v54 - Jl 24 '71 - p42
TLS - Ja 21 '72 - p57
TN - v27 - Ap '71 - p309

MERRIAM, Eve 1916-
BkP, ConAu 5R, SmATA 3, ThrBJA,
TwCCW 78, WhoAm 78

Out Loud
CCB-B - v27 - O '73 - p32
HB - v49 - O '73 - p475
KR - v41 - Ap 15 '73 - p460
LJ - v98 - S 15 '73 - p2642
PW - v203 - Je 25 '73 - p74

MERTZ, Barbara Gross
see Peters, Elizabeth

MEYER, Carolyn 1935-
AuBYP SUP, ConAu 49, SmATA 9

C. C. Poindexter
BL - v75 - S 1 '78 - p40
KR - v46 - O 15 '78 - p1142

MEYER, Carolyn (continued)
    SLJ - v25 - O '78 - p157
    WLB - v53 - O '78 - p180

MEYER, Jerome Sydney   1895-1975
AuBYP, ConAu 1R, ConAu 57,
SmATA 3, WhoWorJ 72

   Fun With The New Math
       BL - v62 - Jl 15 '66 - p1070
       CCB-B - v20 - D '66 - p60
       HB - v42 - D '66 - p732
       LJ - v91 - S 15 '66 - p4340
       NYTBR - v71 - Mr 6 '66 - p46
       SB - v2 - D '66 - p176

   *Great Accidents In Science That
   Changed The World*
       LJ - v93 - F 15 '68 - p885
       SB - v3 - Mr '68 - p325

MEYERS, James

   Incredible Animals
       BS - v36 - Je '76 - p103

MICHENER, James A   1907-
ConAu 5R, ConLC 11, Conv 3,
CurBio 75, OxAm, TwCA SUP

   The Bridges At Toko-Ri
       Atl - v192 - S '53 - p78
       BL - v50 - S 1 '53 - p13
       CSM - Jl 9 '53 - p7
       Comw - v58 - Jl 31 '53 - p426
       HB - v29 - D '53 - p469
       KR - v21 - Jl 1 '53 - p395
       LJ - v78 - Jl '53 - p1232
       NY - v29 - Ag 1 '53 - p59
       NYTBR - Jl 12 '53 - p5
       New R - v129 - Ag 17 '53 - p20
       SR - v36 - Jl 11 '53 - p22
       Time - v62 - Jl 13 '53 - p102

MIKLOWITZ, Gloria D   1927-
AuBYP SUP, ConAu 25R, SmATA
4, WrDr 80

   *Did You Hear What Happened To
   Andrea?*
       BL - v75 - Jl 1 '79 - p1576
       BS - v39 - D '79 - p354
       CBRS - v8 - S '79 - p9
       CCB-B - v33 - D '79 - p75

   Hi Lo - v1 - Mr '80 - p4
   J Read - v23 - Ap '80 - p662
   KR - v47 - S 1 '79 - p1005
   PW - v215 - Je 11 '79 - p103
   SLJ - v26 - S '79 - p159
   WLB - v54 - N '79 - p184

   Dr. Martin Luther King, Jr.
       BL - v74 - Je 15 '78 - p1621

   Paramedic Emergency!
       BL - v74 - O 1 '77 - p283
       BL - v74 - O 1 '77 - p299
       Cur R - v16 - D '77 - p361

   Steve Cauthen
       BL - v75 - Mr 15 '79 - p1162
       Hi Lo - v1 - N '79 - p6
       SLJ - v26 - O '79 - p152

MILES, Betty   1928-
AuBYP, ConAu 1R, SmATA 8,
WrDr 80

   All It Takes Is Practice
       BL - v73 - Ja 1 '77 - p667
       BW - Je 10 '79 - pE2
       CCB-B - v30 - F '77 - p95
       HB - v53 - F '77 - p54
       KR - v44 - O 15 '76 - p1138
       RT - v31 - My '78 - p915
       SE - v41 - Ap '77 - p350
       SLJ - v23 - D '76 - p70

   Looking On
       BL - v74 - My 1 '78 - p1436
       CCB-B - v32 - S '78 - p14
       HB - v54 - Je '78 - p278
       KR - v46 - My 15 '78 - p552
       PW - v213 - My 29 '78 - p52
       SLJ - v24 - Mr '78 - p139

MILGROM, Harry   1912-
AmM&WS 76P, AuBYP SUP,
ConAu 1R, WhoE 77

   ABC Of Ecology
       CCB-B - v26 - O '72 - p30
       KR - v40 - F 15 '72 - p198
       LJ - v98 - F 15 '73 - p638
       SB - v8 - S '72 - p139

MILLAR, Barbara
see Luis, Earlene W (co-author)

MILLARD, Adele

   Cats In Fact And Legend
     ACSB - v10 - Spring '77 - p38

MILLER, Joan Block
   see Armstrong, Fiona (co-author)

MILLER, Melba 1909-
   AmM&WS 73S, LEduc 74,
   WhoAmW 72

   The Black Is Beautiful Beauty
   Book
     CCB-B - v28 - Je '75 - p164
     KR - v43 - Mr 15 '75 - p319
     SLJ - v21 - My '75 - p66

MILLS, Donia Whiteley

   A Long Way Home From Troy
     BL - v68 - F 15 '72 - p503
     BL - v68 - F 15 '72 - p507
     LJ - v97 - F 15 '72 - p786

MILTON, Hilary 1920-
   ConAu 57, SmATA 23

   Mayday! Mayday!
     BL - v75 - Je 15 '79 - p1537
     CBRS - v7 - Je '79 - p108
     CCB-B - v33 - S '79 - p12
     NYTBR - Je 3 '79 - p44
     SLJ - v25 - My '79 - p74

MINAHAN, John 1933-
   ConAu 45

   Jeremy
     BW - v7 - D 16 '73 - p6
     J Read - v22 - N '78 - p128

MINTONYE, Grace
   see Seidelman, James E (co-author) -
     Creating With Clay
     Creating With Paint
     Creating With Paper

MIZNER, Elizabeth Howard
   see Howard, Elizabeth

MOHN, Peter B

   The Golden Knights
     BL - v74 - D 15 '77 - p684
     SLJ - v25 - S '78 - p144

MOHR, Nicholasa 1935-
   AfroAA, ConAu 49, ConLC 12,
   SmATA 8

   Nilda
     BL - v70 - Ja 15 '74 - p544
     BL - v70 - F 1 '74 - p593
     BW - F 10 '74 - p4
     CCB-B - v27 - Mr '74 - p115
     Choice - v12 - N '75 - p1133
     Comw - v99 - N 23 '73 - p216
     HB - v50 - Ap '74 - p153
     KR - v41 - O 1 '73 - p1097
     KR - v41 - D 15 '73 - p1350
     LJ - v98 - D 15 '73 - p3690
     LJ - v98 - D 15 '73 - p3713
     NW - v83 - Mr 4 '74 - p83
     NYTBR - N 4 '73 - p27
     NYTBR - N 4 '73 - p52
     NYTBR - D 2 '73 - p79
     NYTBR - N 10 '74 - p43
     PW - v204 - Ag 27 '73 - p280
     Teacher - v96 - Ja '79 - p64

MOLLOY, Anne S 1907-
   AuBYP, ConAu 13R, ForWC 70

   Girl From Two Miles High
     BL - v64 - F 1 '68 - p640
     CCB-B - v21 - F '68 - p97
     KR - v35 - Jl 15 '67 - p808
     LJ - v92 - O 15 '67 - p3866
     SR - v50 - O 21 '67 - p43

MONJO, F N 1924-1978
   ChLR 2, ConAu 81, SmATA 16,
   TwCCW 78

   Grand Papa And Ellen Aroon
     BB - v3 - Ap '75 - p2
     CCB-B - v28 - My '75 - p151
     KR - v43 - Ja 1 '75 - p23
     NY - v50 - D 2 '74 - p198
     PW - v206 - O 21 '74 - p51
     Teacher - v94 - O '76 - p146

MONTGOMERY, Elizabeth Rider
1902-
ConAu 1R, SmATA 3, WhoAmW 77,
WhoPNW

   Duke Ellington
      CCB-B - v25 - Jl '72 - p174
      JLD - v11 - Ap '78 - p44
      LJ - v97 - S 15 '72 - p2952

   Walt Disney
      BL - v68 - Ap 1 '72 - p676
      JLD - v11 - Ap '78 - p44
      LJ - v97 - Jl '72 - p2485

   Will Rogers: Cowboy Philosopher
      JLD - v11 - Ap '78 - p44

MONTGOMERY, Rutherford George
1894-
ConAu 9R, MorJA, SmATA 3,
TwCCW 78, WhoAm 78

   Kildee House
      Atl - v184 - D '49 - p103
      Atl - v184 - D '49 - p103
      BL - v46 - O 15 '49 - p70
      CSM - N 17 '49 - p10
      KR - v17 - S 1 '49 - p470
      LJ - v74 - O 15 '49 - p1540
      LJ - v74 - N 15 '49 - p1761
      NYT - N 13 '49 - p28

MOON, Sheila   1910-
AuBYP SUP, ConAu 25R, SmATA 5

   Knee-Deep In Thunder
      BL - v64 - D 15 '67 - p503
      BW - v1 - O 1 '67 - p24
      CCB-B - v21 - F '68 - p98
      CLW - v39 - D '67 - p293
      HB - v43 - O '67 - p589
      KR - v35 - Ag 15 '67 - p968
      LJ - v92 - O 15 '67 - p3853
      NYTBR - v72 - O 22 '67 - p62
      TN - v24 - Ap '68 - p324

MOONEY, Thomas J

   One Cool Sister And Other
   Modern Stories
      Hi Lo - v1 - Ap '80 - p4

MOORE, Chuck
 see Stone, Willie

MOORE, Patrick   1923-
ConAu 13R, DcLEL 1940, FourBJA,
WhoSciF, WrDr 80

   Seeing Stars
      BL - v68 - Ap 1 '72 - p676
      KR - v39 - N 1 '71 - p1161
      LJ - v97 - My 15 '72 - p1915

MORAN, Lyn

   The Young Gymnasts
      SLJ - v25 - My '79 - p88

MORAY, Ann

   The Rising Of The Lark
      Am - v110 - Mr 28 '64 - p452
      Crit - v22 - Je '64 - p74
      HB - v40 - Je '64 - p306
      LJ - v89 - F 1 '64 - p656
      NYTBR - F 2 '64 - p34
      SR - v47 - Mr 14 '64 - p30

MOREY, Walter Nelson   1907-
ConAu 29R, SmATA 3, ThrBJA,
TwCCW 78, WrDr 80

   Canyon Winter
      BL - v69 - F 1 '73 - p530
      KR - v40 - N 1 '72 - p1246
      LJ - v98 - Ja 15 '73 - p262
      Obs - Ag 4 '74 - p28
      TLS - S 20 '74 - p1010

   Gentle Ben
      Obs - D 6 '70 - p27

   Sandy And The Rock Star
      BL - v75 - Jl 1 '79 - p1581
      CLW - v51 - D '79 - p234
      HB - v55 - Ag '79 - p416
      J Read - v23 - F '80 - p472
      KR - v47 - Jl 1 '79 - p745
      LJ - v57 - My '80 - p557
      NYTBR - Je 3 '79 - p44
      PW - v215 - Mr 19 '79 - p94
      SLJ - v26 - S '79 - p145

   Scrub Dog Of Alaska
      BL - v68 - Ja 1 '72 - p394
      CCB-B - v25 - My '72 - p143
      GP - v13 - Ap '75 - p2601
      HB - v48 - F '72 - p50
      JB - v39 - Ap '75 - p125

MOREY, Walter Nelson (continued)
  KR - v39 - O 15 '71 - p1132
  LJ - v96 - N 15 '71 - p3902
  PW - v200 - Ag 16 '71 - p57

  Year Of The Black Pony
  BB - v4 - N '76 - p2
  BL - v72 - Jl 1 '76 - p1528
  BW - Ap 11 '76 - p4
  CCB-B - v29 - Jl '76 - p179
  CLW - v48 - O '76 - p138
  HB - v52 - Ag '76 - p399
  JB - v42 - Je '78 - p158
  KR - v44 - Mr 1 '76 - p257
  LA - v54 - Ja '77 - p83
  SLJ - v22 - Ap '76 - p77

MORGAN, Barbara Ellen   1944-
  WhoMW 78

  Journey For Tobiyah
  CCB-B - v20 - N '66 - p46
  CE - v43 - My '67 - p537
  HB - v42 - D '66 - p720
  Inst - v76 - N '66 - p51
  KR - v34 - S 1 '66 - p909
  LJ - v91 - D 15 '66 - p6195

MORGAN, Joe   1943-
  WhoAm 78, WhoBlA 77, WhoProB
  73

  Baseball My Way
  BL - v73 - N 15 '76 - p468
  BL - v73 - N 15 '76 - p476
  CLW - v48 - Mr '77 - p358
  SLJ - v23 - D '76 - p70

MORIN, Relman   1907-1973
  ConAu 1R, ConAu 41R, CurBio 58,
  NewYTBE 73, WhoAm 6

  *Dwight D. Eisenhower: A Gauge Of
  Greatness*
  BL - v66 - N 15 '69 - p381
  Choice - v6 - O '69 - p1106
  LJ - v94 - S 15 '69 - p3045

MORRIS, Jeannie

  Brian Piccolo: A Short Season
  BL - v68 - Ap 1 '72 - p644
  BW - v6 - Jl 16 '72 - p10
  KR - v39 - S 1 '71 - p990

  LJ - v96 - O 15 '71 - p3342
  NYTBR - N 21 '71 - p34
  NYTBR - D 5 '71 - p44
  PW - v201 - My 29 '72 - p34
  SR - v54 - D 11 '71 - p46
  WLB - v46 - Ap '72 - p704

MORRIS, Rosamund
  ScF&FL

  Masterpieces Of Horror
  NYTBR - v71 - Jl 24 '66 - p29

  *Masterpieces Of Mystery And
  Detection*
  NYTBR - v71 - Jl 24 '66 - p29

  Masterpieces Of Suspense
  NYTBR - v71 - Jl 24 '66 - p29

MORRIS, Terry   1914-
  ConAu 9R, WhoAmW 77, WhoE 77

  Shalom, Golda
  BL - v68 - F 15 '72 - p503
  BS - v31 - O 15 '71 - p335
  KR - v39 - Jl 1 '71 - p723
  LJ - v97 - Jl '72 - p2490
  PW - v200 - N 15 '71 - p73
  SE - v39 - Mr '75 - p145

MORRIS, Wright   1910-
  ConAu 9R, ConLC 7, DcLB, OxAm,
  WhoTwCL

  In Orbit
  Atl - v219 - Ap '67 - p144
  BS - v26 - F 15 '67 - p409
  BW - v2 - Je 23 '68 - p13
  Comw - v86 - Ap 7 '67 - p98
  HM - v234 - Mr '67 - p139
  KR - v34 - D 15 '66 - p1298
  LJ - v92 - F 1 '67 - p196
  NO - v6 - Mr 20 '67 - p21
  NYRB - v8 - My 4 '67 - p35
  NYT - v116 - F 23 '67 - p37M
  NYTBR - v72 - F 5 '67 - p44
  PR - v35 - Winter '68 - p141
  PW - v190 - D 12 '67 - p48
  PW - v193 - My 13 '68 - p61
  SR - v50 - F 18 '67 - p29
  SR - v50 - D 30 '67 - p19
  Time - v89 - F 17 '67 - p104

MORRISON, Lillian 1917-
BkP, ConAu 9R, SmATA 3

Best Wishes, Amen
BL - v71 - F 1 '75 - p572
CCB-B - v28 - Ap '75 - p135
HB - v51 - F '75 - p63
KR - v42 - D 1 '74 - p1257
NY - v51 - D 1 '75 - p185
PW - v206 - N 11 '74 - p49
SLJ - v21 - Mr '75 - p100
Teacher - v92 - Ap '75 - p32

The Sidewalk Racer And Other Poems Of Sports And Motion
BW - N 13 '77 - pE4
CCB-B - v31 - D '77 - p64
CE - v54 - N '77 - p90
EJ - v67 - F '78 - p99
HB - v53 - O '77 - p548
KR - v45 - Je 1 '77 - p584
LA - v54 - N '77 - p951
NYTBR - N 13 '77 - p47
PW - v211 - My 23 '77 - p246
SLJ - v24 - S '77 - p133

Sprints And Distances: Sports In Poetry
BL - v62 - Ja 15 '66 - p482
CCB-B - v20 - S '66 - p15
CE - v42 - My '66 - p564
HB - v41 - D '65 - p641
KR - v33 - S 1 '65 - p916
LJ - v90 - O 15 '65 - p4636
NYTBR - v70 - N 7 '65 - p6
Poet - v108 - Ag '66 - p343
SR - v48 - N 13 '65 - p62

Touch Blue
NYTBR - Jl 6 '58 - p13

MORSE, Ann Christensen
see Head, Ann
Morse, Charles (co-author)

MORSE, Charles

Jackson Five
RT - v29 - Ja '76 - p415
SLJ - v22 - S '75 - p95

Roberta Flack
CCB-B - v28 - Jl '75 - p181
SLJ - v22 - S '75 - p95

MORSE, Evangeline 1914-
LivBAA

Brown Rabbit: Her Story
BW - v1 - O 8 '67 - p24
CCB-B - v21 - O '67 - p30
HB - v43 - D '67 - p754
KR - v35 - Mr 15 '67 - p342
LJ - v93 - Ja 15 '68 - p293
NYTBR - v72 - Ag 13 '67 - p26

MORTON, Jane

Running Scared
SLJ - v25 - My '79 - p65

MOSKIN, Marietta D 1928-
ConAu 73, SmATA 23

A Paper Dragon
KR - v36 - Ja 1 '68 - p13
LJ - v93 - My 15 '68 - p2124

MOTT, Michael 1930-
ConAu 5R, DcLEL 1940

Master Entrick: An Adventure, 1754-1756
Am - v115 - N 5 '66 - p553
BS - v26 - D 1 '66 - p340
HB - v43 - F '67 - p73
KR - v34 - S 1 '66 - p906
LJ - v91 - N 15 '66 - p5762
TLS - D 9 '65 - p1147

MOWAT, Farley 1921-
CanWW 79, ConAu 1R, OxCan,
OxCan SUP, SmATA 3, ThrBJA,
TwCCW 78

The Curse Of The Viking Grave
CCB-B - v20 - D '66 - p61
CLW - v39 - O '67 - p157
KR - v34 - Jl 1 '66 - p635
LJ - v92 - Ja 15 '67 - p346
SR - v49 - N 12 '66 - p53

MOYES, Patricia 1923-
BiE&WWA, ConAu 17R, EncMys,
WrDr 80

Helter-Skelter
BL - v64 - My 1 '68 - p1031
BS - v28 - Ap 1 '68 - p18
CSM - v60 - My 2 '68 - pB9

MOYES, Patricia (continued)
KR - v36 - F 15 '68 - p191
LJ - v93 - Ap 15 '68 - p1813
NYTBR - v73 - Ap 7 '68 - p26
SE - v33 - My '69 - p558
SLJ - v24 - F '78 - p35
SR - v51 - Jl 20 '68 - p31
TLS - Ap 3 '69 - p354

MUESNER, Anne Marie

The Picture Story Of Steve Cauthen
Hi Lo - v2 - N '80 - p4

MUNSHOWER, Suzanne   1945-
ConAu 97

John Travolta
Kliatt - v12 - Fall '78 - p30
SLJ - v26 - S '79 - p129

MUNSTERHJELM, Erik   1905-
ConAu 49, OxCan

A Dog Named Wolf
Teacher - v91 - F '74 - p97

MURPHY, Barbara Beasley   1933-
ConAu 41R, SmATA 5

Home Free
KR - v38 - F 1 '70 - p104
LJ - v95 - Je 15 '70 - p2309
SR - v53 - Ap 18 '70 - p37

No Place To Run
B&B - v6 - Je '78 - p3
BL - v74 - D 15 '77 - p157
BL - v74 - D 15 '77 - p197
CCB-B - v31 - D '77 - p64
EJ - v67 - F '78 - p79
HB - v53 - D '77 - p669
KR - v45 - Je 15 '77 - p628
PW - v212 - S 5 '77 - p73
SLJ - v24 - N '77 - p74

MURPHY, Shirley Rousseau   1928-
ConAu 21R, WhoAmW 79, WrDr 80

The Sand Ponies
CCB-B - v21 - Ja '68 - p80
KR - v35 - S 1 '67 - p1049
LJ - v92 - D 15 '67 - p4615

MURRAY, Michele   1933-1974
AuBYP SUP, ConAu 49, SmATA 7

The Crystal Nights
BL - v69 - Je 1 '73 - p944
BS - v33 - Je 15 '73 - p146
BW - My 4 '75 - p4
BW - v7 - My 13 '73 - p3
BW - v7 - N 11 '73 - p3C
CCB-B - v27 - S '73 - p15
CE - v50 - Ja '74 - p166
Comw - v99 - N 23 '73 - p216
KR - v41 - Ap 1 '73 - p397
KR - v41 - D 15 '73 - p1356
LJ - v98 - My 15 '73 - p1655
LJ - v98 - My 15 '73 - p1691
LJ - v98 - D 15 '73 - p3691
NO - v12 - D 29 '73 - p15
NYTBR - S 16 '73 - p8
PW - v203 - My 7 '73 - p65
TN - v30 - Je '74 - p434

MUSICK, Phil

The Tony Dorsett Story
BL - v74 - Ap 1 '78 - p1264
EJ - v67 - Ap '78 - p91
KR - v46 - Ja 1 '78 - p39
LJ - v103 - Ap 1 '78 - p771
SLJ - v24 - My '78 - p87

MYERS, Walter Dean   1937-
AuBYP SUP, ConAu 33R, SelBAA, WhoAm 76

Brainstorm
CCB-B - v31 - Ap '78 - p132
Hi Lo - v1 - N '79 - p4
JB - v43 - F '79 - p58
SLJ - v24 - N '77 - p60

MYRUS, Donald   1927-
AuBYP, ConAu 1R, SmATA 23

Ballads, Blues, And The Big Beat
BS - v26 - D 1 '66 - p341
CCB-B - v20 - D '66 - p61
CLW - v38 - Mr '67 - p484
CSM - v58 - N 3 '66 - pB8
Comw - v85 - N 11 '66 - p181
HB - v42 - D '66 - p725
KR - v34 - S 15 '66 - p990
NYTBR - v71 - N 6 '66 - p28

N

NAGEL, Shirley 1922-
ConAu 93

Escape From The Tower Of London
Hi Lo - v1 - F '80 - p4
Teacher - v96 - My '79 - p127

NAMIOKA, Lensey 1929-
ConAu 69

The Samurai And The Long-Nosed Devils
BL - v73 - N 15 '76 - p468
BL - v73 - N 15 '76 - p476
CCB-B - v30 - Ja '77 - p78
KR - v44 - Ag 1 '76 - p848
Kliatt - v13 - Spring '79 - p12

NATHAN, Dorothy d1966
ConAu 81, SmATA 15

The Shy One
CCB-B - v21 - S '67 - p14
KR - v34 - S 15 '66 - p979
LJ - v91 - O 15 '66 - p5234
NYTBR - v72 - Ja 22 '67 - p26
PW - v190 - O 17 '66 - p63

NAYLOR, Phyllis Reynolds 1933-
AuBYP SUP, ConAu 21R, IndAu
1917, SmATA 12, WrDr 80

No Easy Circle
BS - v33 - S 1 '73 - p257
LJ - v97 - S 15 '72 - p2965
NYTBR - S 3 '72 - p8

NEAL, Harry Edward 1906-
ConAu 5R, SmATA 5, WhoAm 78,
WrDr 80

Communication: From Stone Age To Space Age
CCB-B - v27 - Jl '74 - p182
LJ - v99 - Ap 15 '74 - p1231
SB - v10 - D '74 - p206

The Mystery Of Time
BL - v63 - S 1 '66 - p57
KR - v34 - F 15 '66 - p192
LJ - v91 - My 15 '66 - p2711
NYTBR - v71 - Ag 21 '66 - p20
SB - v2 - S '66 - p104

NEIGOFF, Mike 1920-
ConAu 5R, SmATA 13

Runner-Up
BL - v72 - S 15 '75 - p171
SLJ - v22 - D '75 - p70

Ski Run
LJ - v98 - My 15 '73 - p1706

NEIMARK, Paul
see Owens, Jessie (co-author)

NELSON, Cordner 1918-
ConAu 29R, WhoWest 78, WrDr 80

The Miler
BS - v29 - D 1 '69 - p354
KR - v37 - S 15 '69 - p1009
LJ - v94 - D 15 '69 - p4621

NELSON, Marg 1899-
AuBYP, ConAu 1R

Mystery At Land's End
BL - v57 - Jl 15 '61 - p704
KR - v29 - Ja 15 '61 - p61
LJ - v86 - Ap 15 '61 - p1697
SR - v44 - Je 24 '61 - p20

167

NESS, Evaline   1911-
ConAu 5R, IlsCB 1967, SmATA 1,
ThrBJA, TwCCW 78, WhoAm 78

*Amelia Mixed The Mustard And
Other Poems*
Am - v133 - D 6 '75 - p406
BL - v71 - My 15 '75 - p966
CCB-B - v28 - Jl '75 - p182
CLW - v47 - My '76 - p452
Cur R - v16 - F '77 - p47
HB - v51 - Ag '75 - p394
KR - v43 - Ap 1 '75 - p368
NYTBR - My 4 '75 - p24
PW - v207 - Ap 28 '75 - p44
SLJ - v21 - My '75 - p49
SR - v2 - My 31 '75 - p36
Teacher - v93 - F '76 - p29
Teacher - v94 - N '76 - p137

NEUFELD, John   1938-
AuBYP, ConAu 25R, SmATA 6

Edgar Allan
BL - v65 - F 1 '69 - p594
BL - v65 - Ap 1 '69 - p901
BS - v28 - Ja 1 '69 - p423
CCB-B - v22 - My '69 - p147
EJ - v58 - My '69 - p778
HB - v45 - Ap '69 - p172
KR - v36 - N 1 '68 - p1226
NYTBR - v73 - N 3 '68 - p33
NYTBR, pt.2 - F 13 '72 - p12
RT - v31 - My '78 - p915
SE - v33 - My '69 - p558
SR - v52 - Ja 18 '69 - p41
Teacher - v86 - Ap '69 - p184

Lisa, Bright And Dark
BS - v29 - Ja 1 '70 - p389
CCB-B - v23 - F '70 - p103
KR - v37 - O 15 '69 - p1124
LJ - v95 - F 15 '70 - p790
NYTBR - N 16 '69 - p52
NYTBR, pt.2 - N 9 '69 - p60

Sunday Father
NYTBR - Ja 30 '77 - p24
PW - v210 - N 22 '76 - p50
WLB - v51 - Ap '77 - p674

Touching
EJ - v59 - D '70 - p1303
KR - v38 - O 15 '70 - p1163

LJ - v95 - N 15 '70 - p4057
NYTBR - N 29 '70 - p38

NEVILLE, Emily Cheney   1919-
ConAu 5R, ConLC 12, MorBMP,
SmATA 1, ThrBJA, TwCCW 78

It's Like This, Cat
CSM - My 9 '63 - p3B
LJ - v88 - Jl '63 - p2782
LJ - v96 - Ja 15 '71 - p283
NYTBR, pt.2 - My 12 '63 - p2
SR - v46 - Jl 20 '63 - p34
TCR - v68 - O '66 - p90
TCR - v68 - F '67 - p450
TLS - Ap 16 '70 - p416

NEWBY, P H   1918-
BioIn 3, BioIn 10, ConAu 5R, ConLC
13, WrDr 80

The Spirit Of Jem
CSM - v59 - Ag 3 '67 - p11
KR - v35 - My 1 '67 - p566
LJ - v92 - D 15 '67 - p4625
Lis - v78 - N 16 '67 - p643
NYTBR - v72 - S 10 '67 - p38
NYTBR - v72 - N 5 '67 - p64
Obs - D 3 '67 - p26
SR - v50 - N 11 '67 - p50
TLS - N 30 '67 - p1145
TLS - D 4 '69 - p1384

NEWELL, Hope   1896-1965
ConAu 73, MorJA, SmATA 24

A Cap For Mary Ellis
CE - v46 - Ap '70 - p368
NYTBR - Ja 24 '54 - p22

NEWLON, Clarke
AuBYP SUP, ConAu 49, SmATA 6

Famous Mexican-Americans
BL - v69 - S 1 '72 - p42
BS - v32 - My 15 '72 - p98
CCB-B - v25 - Je '72 - p160
KR - v40 - Ja 1 '72 - p13
LJ - v98 - F 15 '73 - p656
SE - v37 - D '73 - p789
SR - v55 - My 20 '72 - p82

NEWMAN, Marvin

Africa's Animals
NYTBR - v72 - D 3 '67 - p12
SB - v3 - D '67 - p235

NEWMAN, Robert Howard 1909-
ConAu 1R, SmATA 4, ScF&FL 1,
ScF&FL 2

Night Spell
Am - v137 - D 3 '77 - p406
BB - v5 - Je '77 - p3
BL - v73 - Ap 15 '77 - p1268
HB - v53 - Ag '77 - p443
KR - v45 - Ap 15 '77 - p427
SLJ - v23 - My '77 - p78

The Twelve Labors Of Hercules
KR - v40 - My 15 '72 - p585
NYTBR - Ag 27 '72 - p24

NEWMAN, Shirlee P 1924-
AuBYP SUP, ConAu 5R, SmATA
10, WhoAmW 77

*Marian Anderson: Lady From
Philadelphia*
BL - v63 - S 1 '66 - p57
BS - v26 - Je 1 '66 - p102
Inst - v76 - Ag '66 - p217
KR - v34 - F 1 '66 - p115
LJ - v91 - Jl '66 - p3545
NYTBR - v71 - Jl 10 '66 - p38
PW - v189 - My 16 '66 - p80
SR - v49 - My 14 '66 - p42

NICKEL, Helmut

*Warriors And Worthies: Arms And
Armours Through The Ages*
A Lib - v1 - Ap '70 - p386
BL - v66 - Ja 15 '70 - p622
CCB-B - v24 - S '70 - p16
HB - v46 - Ap '70 - p176
LJ - v95 - My 15 '70 - p1912
LJ - v95 - My 15 '70 - p1946
SR - v53 - My 9 '70 - p69

NIELSEN, Virginia 1909-
ConAu X, SmATA X (also known as
McCall, Virginia Nielsen)

Keoni, My Brother
BL - v62 - Mr 15 '66 - p701
CCB-B - v19 - Ap '66 - p135
HB - v42 - F '66 - p65
see also McCall, Virginia Nielsen

NIXON, Joan Lowery 1927-
AuBYP SUP, ConAu 9R, SmATA 8

*The Kidnapping Of Christina
Lattimore*
BL - v75 - Mr 15 '79 - p1143
BW - My 13 '79 - pK3
KR - v47 - My 15 '79 - p580
NYTBR - My 13 '79 - p27
PW - v215 - F 12 '79 - p127

NOAILLES, R H
see Guilcher, Jean Michel (co-
author)

NOBLE, Iris 1922-
AuBYP, ConAu 1R, SmATA 5

*Cameras And Courage: Margaret
Bourke-White*
BL - v70 - S 1 '73 - p52
BS - v33 - Je 15 '73 - p146
KR - v41 - F 15 '73 - p199
LJ - v98 - Jl '73 - p2203
NYTBR - Jl 15 '73 - p8
PW - v203 - Je 4 '73 - p90

NOLAN, William Francis 1928-
ConAu 1R, ConSFA, EncMys, WrDr
80

*Carnival Of Speed: True
Adventures In Motor Racing*
KR - v41 - F 15 '73 - p199
LJ - v98 - My 15 '73 - p1705

NORBACK, Craig
see Norback, Peter (co-author)

NORBACK, Peter

Great Songs Of Madison Avenue
CSM - v68 - O 29 '76 - p26
Choice - v14 - Mr '77 - p55

NORRIS, Gunilla B
AuBYP SUP, SmATA 20

NORRIS, Gunilla B (continued)

The Good Morrow
BL - v65 - Jl 15 '69 - p1276
BW - v3 - My 4 '69 - p10
CCB-B - v23 - N '69 - p50
CSM - v61 - My 1 '69 - pB4
Comw - v91 - N 21 '69 - p254
HB - v45 - Ap '69 - p172
KR - v37 - F 15 '69 - p179
LJ - v94 - My 15 '69 - p2105
NYTBR - Je 8 '69 - p42
PW - v195 - My 5 '69 - p52
RR - v28 - Jl '69 - p700

NORRIS, Marianna
AuBYP SUP

Father And Son For Freedom
BL - v64 - My 1 '68 - p1048
KR - v36 - Ja 15 '68 - p61
LJ - v93 - F 15 '68 - p885

NORTH, Sterling   1906-1974
ConAu 5R, ConAu 53, SmATA 1,
ThrBJA, TwCCW 78, WhAm 6

Raccoons Are The Brightest People
BL - v63 - S 15 '66 - p88
BS - v26 - Ag 15 '66 - p186
CLW - v38 - N '66 - p210
CSM - v58 - S 8 '66 - p13
KR - v34 - Je 1 '66 - p566
KR - v34 - Je 15 '66 - p581
LJ - v91 - Jl '66 - p3457
LJ - v91 - O 15 '66 - p5270
NH - v76 - N '67 - p85
NYT - v115 - S 10 '66 - p27
NYTBR, pt.2 - F 16 '69 - p22
Nat R - v18 - N 15 '66 - p1182
PW - v189 - My 23 '66 - p81
PW - v192 - Jl 3 '67 - p62
PW - v194 - Jl 8 '68 - p166
SB - v2 - Mr '67 - p298
SR - v50 - S 30 '67 - p47

Rascal: A Memoir Of A Better Era
Atl - v212 - D '63 - p154
BS - v23 - S 1 '63 - p190
CC - v80 - Ag 7 '63 - p983
CSM - Ag 8 '63 - p11
HM - v227 - S '63 - p118
LJ - v88 - S 1 '63 - p3096
LJ - v88 - S 15 '63 - p3374

NYTBR - Ag 25 '63 - p24

NORTON, Alice Mary
see Norton, Andre

NORTON, Andre   (pseud.) 1912-
ConAu X, ConLC 12, ConSFA,
MorJA, SmATA 1, TwCCW 78,
WorAu (real name: Norton, Alice
Mary)

Catseye
BL - v58 - '61 - p2561
KR - v29 - Jl 15 '61 - p614
TLS - N 23 '62 - p914

Exiles Of The Stars
B&B - v17 - Je '72 - p72
BL - v67 - Je 15 '71 - p868
CCB-B - v24 - Jl '71 - p175
HB - v47 - Ag '71 - p389
KR - v39 - Mr 1 '71 - p243
LJ - v96 - Je 15 '71 - p2140
NS - v83 - Je 2 '72 - p759
Spec - v228 - Ap 22 '72 - p626
TLS - Ap 28 '72 - p480

Fur Magic
CSM - v61 - My 1 '69 - pB5
HB - v45 - Ap '69 - p172
LJ - v94 - F 15 '69 - p877
NS - v78 - O 31 '69 - p623
Obs - D 7 '69 - p31
TLS - Je 26 '69 - p689

The Opal-Eyed Fan
BL - v74 - O 15 '77 - p368
BS - v37 - F '78 - p342
KR - v45 - S 15 '77 - p1008
LJ - v102 - D 15 '77 - p2513
PW - v212 - O 3 '77 - p93

NURNBERG, Maxwell   1897-
ConAu 5R

Wonders In Words
BL - v65 - F 1 '69 - p595
CE - v46 - My '70 - p434
LJ - v94 - Mr 15 '69 - p1330
NYTBR - Ap 13 '69 - p30

NUSSBAUM, Albert F   1934-
ConAu 85

NUSSBAUM, Albert F (continued)

    Gypsy
      BL - v74 - Ja 15 '78 - p809
      BL - v75 - O 15 '78 - p357
    see also Frederick, Lee
           Hiller, Doris
           Martin, Albert
           Oreshnik, A F

O

OAKES, Vanya   1909-
AuBYP, ConAu 33R, SmATA 6,
WhoWest 76 (also known as Oakes,
Virginia Armstrong)

> *Willy Wong: American*
> BL - v47 - My 1 '51 - p316
> HB - v27 - Jl '51 - p248
> LJ - v76 - Ap 15 '51 - p713
> NYT - Ap 15 '51 - p18

O'BRIEN, Jack   1898-1938
AuBYP, MorJA (listed under
O'Brien, John Sherman)

> *Return Of Silver Chief*
> LJ - v69 - F 1 '44 - p120
> NYTBR - Mr 19 '44 - p27

O'BRIEN, Robert C   (pseud.) 1918?-
1973
ChLR 2, ConAu X, FourBJA,
SmATA 23, TwCCW 78 (real name:
Conly, Robert Leslie)

> *Z For Zachariah*
> Am - v133 - D 6 '75 - p403
> BB - v3 - My '75 - p4
> BL - v71 - Mr 1 '75 - p687
> BL - v73 - Mr 15 '77 - p1101
> BS - v35 - My '75 - p50
> CCB-B - v29 - N '75 - p51
> CLW - v47 - N '75 - p188
> EJ - v67 - D '78 - p83
> GP - v13 - Mr '75 - p2570
> HB - v51 - Je '75 - p276
> JB - v39 - Je '75 - p201
> KR - v43 - Ja 15 '75 - p85
> KR - v43 - F 15 '75 - p189
> Kliatt - v11 - Spring '77 - p7
> LJ - v100 - Ap 1 '75 - p694
> NYT - v125 - D 20 '75 - p25
> NYTBR - Mr 2 '75 - p8

NYTBR - Je 1 '75 - p29
NYTBR - N 16 '75 - p55
NYTBR - My 29 '77 - p23
Obs - Mr 30 '75 - p24
Obs - Jl 23 '78 - p21
PW - v207 - Ja 20 '75 - p77
PW - v207 - Ja 27 '75 - p278
SLJ - v21 - Mr '75 - p109
SLJ - v22 - D '75 - p32
Spec - v234 - Ap 12 '75 - p444
TLS - Ap 4 '75 - p360
TN - v32 - Ap '76 - p285
TN - v34 - Spring '78 - p265

O'CONNOR, Dick   1930-
ConAu 97

> *Rick Barry: Basketball Ace*
> BL - v73 - Jl 1 '77 - p1654
> KR - v45 - Mr 15 '77 - p293
> SLJ - v23 - My '77 - p80

O'CONNOR, Patrick   (pseud.) 1915-
ConAu X, EncMys, SmATA 2, WrDr
80 (real name: Wibberley, Leonard)

> *The Black Tiger*
> NYTBR - S 16 '56 - p38

> *Black Tiger At Lemans*
> BL - v54 - My 15 '58 - p539
> KR - v26 - Mr 15 '58 - p230
> LJ - v83 - My 15 '58 - p1610

> *A Car Called Camellia*
> BL - v67 - O 1 '70 - p142
> KR - v38 - My 15 '70 - p559
> LJ - v95 - D 15 '70 - p4377
> PW - v197 - Je 15 '70 - p65

> *Mexican Road Race*
> BL - v53 - Jl 1 '57 - p562
> KR - v25 - Ap 15 '57 - p309
> LJ - v82 - S 15 '57 - p2199

O'CONNOR, Patrick (continued)
　　SR - v40 - N 16 '57 - p90
　see also Wibberley, Leonard

O'DELL, Scott　1903?-
　ChLR 1, ConAu 61, MorJA, SmATA
　12, TwCCW 78, WhoWor 78

　　Black Pearl
　　　B&B - v17 - D '71 - pR16
　　　BL - v64 - D 1 '67 - p450
　　　BS - v27 - F 1 '68 - p431
　　　BW - v1 - N 5 '67 - p30
　　　CCB-B - v21 - D '67 - p64
　　　CE - v45 - F '69 - p338
　　　HB - v43 - O '67 - p603
　　　KR - v35 - S 1 '67 - p1058
　　　LJ - v92 - D 15 '67 - p4625
　　　NYTBR - v72 - N 5 '67 - p20
　　　NYTBR, pt.2 - N 5 '72 - p42
　　　Obs - Ag 4 '68 - p22
　　　PW - v192 - O 23 '67 - p52
　　　Par - v43 - Je '68 - p68
　　　SR - v50 - O 21 '67 - p43
　　　TLS - Je 6 '68 - p588
　　　TN - v24 - Ap '68 - p324

　　Child Of Fire
　　　BL - v71 - S 15 '74 - p93
　　　BS - v34 - O 15 '74 - p330
　　　BW - N 10 '74 - p6
　　　CCB-B - v28 - D '74 - p66
　　　CLW - v46 - My '75 - p453
　　　CLW - v47 - N '75 - p166
　　　Choice - v12 - N '75 - p1133
　　　Choice - v14 - N '77 - p1178
　　　Comw - v101 - N 22 '74 - p194
　　　HB - v50 - D '74 - p695
　　　KR - v42 - Ag 1 '74 - p810
　　　KR - v43 - Ja 1 '75 - p11
　　　LJ - v99 - S 15 '74 - p2295
　　　LJ - v99 - D 15 '74 - p3247
　　　NYTBR - N 3 '74 - p23
　　　NYTBR - N 3 '74 - p52
　　　NYTBR - D 1 '74 - p76
　　　NYTBR - Mr 12 '78 - p45
　　　PT - v8 - N '74 - p26
　　　PW - v205 - Jl 22 '74 - p70

　　Island Of The Blue Dolphins
　　　BL - v56 - Ap 1 '60 - p489
　　　HB - v36 - Ap '60 - p137
　　　LJ - v85 - Ap 15 '60 - p1702

　　　NYTBR - Mr 27 '60 - p40
　　　NYTBR, pt.2 - N 7 '71 - p46
　　　NYTBR, pt.2 - F 13 '72 - p14
　　　Obs - Ap 10 '66 - p18
　　　SR - v43 - My 7 '60 - p42
　　　Spec - Je 3 '66 - p706
　　　TLS - My 19 '66 - p442

　　Kathleen, Please Come Home
　　　BB - v6 - N '78 - p2
　　　BL - v74 - My 15 '78 - p1486
　　　CCB-B - v32 - S '78 - p15
　　　KR - v46 - Mr 15 '78 - p311
　　　NYTBR - Ap 30 '78 - p53
　　　PW - v213 - My 22 '78 - p233
　　　SLJ - v24 - My '78 - p78

　　The King's Fifth
　　　Atl - v218 - D '66 - p154
　　　B&B - v13 - D '67 - p43
　　　BL - v63 - D 15 '66 - p452
　　　CCB-B - v20 - Ja '67 - p78
　　　CLW - v39 - N '67 - p241
　　　CSM - v58 - N 3 '66 - pB12
　　　Comw - v85 - N 11 '66 - p175
　　　HB - v42 - D '66 - p721
　　　Inst - v83 - My '74 - p97
　　　KR - v34 - S 1 '66 - p913
　　　LJ - v92 - F 15 '67 - p897
　　　NYTBR - v72 - Ja 15 '67 - p28
　　　Obs - N 26 '67 - p28
　　　PW - v190 - O 10 '66 - p74
　　　SR - v49 - N 12 '66 - p53
　　　TLS - N 30 '67 - p1138
　　　TN - v23 - Ap '67 - p292

　　Sing Down The Moon
　　　BL - v67 - N 1 '70 - p230
　　　BL - v67 - Ap 1 '71 - p660
　　　BL - v69 - O 15 '72 - p178
　　　BW - v4 - N 8 '70 - p23
　　　CCB-B - v24 - Ja '71 - p78
　　　CLW - v42 - F '71 - p383
　　　CLW - v49 - D '77 - p212
　　　Comw - v93 - N 20 '70 - p202
　　　HB - v46 - D '70 - p623
　　　HT - v22 - D '72 - p891
　　　KR - v38 - O 15 '70 - p1149
　　　LJ - v95 - N 15 '70 - p4046
　　　NS - v84 - N 10 '72 - p694
　　　NYTBR - O 18 '70 - p34
　　　NYTBR, pt.2 - N 8 '70 - p38
　　　NYTBR, pt.2 - My 6 '73 - p28

O'DELL, Scott (continued)
    Obs - D 3 '72 - p38
    PW - v198 - S 28 '70 - p79
    SR - v53 - N 14 '70 - p38
    TLS - N 3 '72 - p1320

   Zia
    BB - v4 - My '76 - p4
    BL - v72 - Ap 15 '76 - p1188
    BW - My 2 '76 - pL2
    CCB-B - v29 - Jl '76 - p180
    CE - v53 - O '76 - p34
    EJ - v65 - O '76 - p88
    HB - v52 - Je '76 - p291
    JB - v41 - O '77 - p304
    J Read - v20 - My '77 - p732
    KR - v44 - Mr 15 '76 - p324
    Kliatt - v12 - Fall '78 - p13
    LA - v53 - S '76 - p701
    NO - v15 - Ag 21 '76 - p17
    NYTBR - My 2 '76 - p38
    Obs - Je 12 '77 - p25
    Obs - Je 26 '77 - p29
    PW - v209 - Ap 5 '76 - p101
    SLJ - v22 - My '76 - p62
    TLS - Jl 15 '77 - p860

O'DONOGHUE, Bryan   1921-
ConAu 77

   Wild Animal Rescue!
    KR - v39 - Je 1 '71 - p589
    LJ - v96 - S 15 '71 - p2920
    PW - v199 - Je 21 '71 - p71
    SB - v7 - D '71 - p264

OGAN, George F
see Ogan, Margaret E Nettles (co-
author)

OGAN, Margaret E Nettles   1923-
AuBYP SUP, ConAu 9R, SmATA 13

   Acuna Brutes
    KR - v41 - S 15 '73 - p1043
    LJ - v98 - My 15 '73 - p1706

   Desert Road Racer
    KR - v38 - S 15 '70 - p1050
    LJ - v95 - D 15 '70 - p4378

   Grand National Racer
    Cur R - v16 - D '77 - p360
    KR - v45 - F 15 '77 - p169

    SLJ - v24 - S '77 - p148
    SLJ - v24 - Mr '78 - p107

   Green Thirteen
    BL - v74 - Je 15 '78 - p1613
    Hi Lo - v1 - S '79 - p5
    NYTBR - Ap 30 '78 - p45
    SLJ - v24 - F '78 - p66

OGILVIE, Elisabeth   1917-
AuBYP, TwCA SUP, WhoAmW 77

   The Pigeon Pair
    BL - v64 - S 1 '67 - p66
    BS - v27 - My 1 '67 - p66
    HB - v43 - Je '67 - p354
    KR - v35 - F 15 '67 - p209
    LJ - v92 - My 15 '67 - p2031
    NYTBR, pt.2 - v72 - My 7 '67 - p8

O'HANLON, Jacklyn   1933-
ConAu X (also known as Meek,
Jacklyn O'Hanlon)

   Fair Game
    BS - v37 - Ag '77 - p141
    CCB-B - v31 - D '77 - p65
    EJ - v66 - N '77 - p81
    KR - v45 - Mr 15 '77 - p291
    NYTBR - My 1 '77 - p46
    PW - v211 - My 23 '77 - p247
    SLJ - v23 - My '77 - p70

OJIGBO, A Okion

   Young And Black In Africa
    BL - v68 - Mr 1 '72 - p566
    CCB-B - v25 - Je '72 - p161
    KR - v39 - O 1 '71 - p1084
    LJ - v96 - D 15 '71 - p4192
    NYTBR, pt.2 - N 7 '71 - p45
    SE - v37 - O '73 - p561

OLNEY, Ross Robert   1929-
AuBYP, ConAu 13R, SmATA 13,
WhoWest 78, WrDr 80

   A. J. Foyt: The Only Four Time
   Winner
    Hi Lo - v1 - S '79 - p4

   Auto Racing's Young Lions
    KR - v45 - Je 1 '77 - p585
    SLJ - v24 - S '77 - p134

OTFINOSKI, Steven (continued)

*Sky Ride And Other Exciting
Stories*
   Hi Lo - v1 - Ap '80 - p4

Village Of Vampires
   Hi Lo - v1 - D '79 - p4
   SLJ - v26 - D '79 - p82

*The Zombie Maker: Stories Of
Amazing Adventures*
   Hi Lo - v1 - Mr '80 - p5

OTTUM, Bob
  see Edwards, Phil (co-author)

OWEN, Evan

On Your Own
   Hi Lo - v1 - My '80 - p3
   SLJ - v25 - My '79 - p65

OWENS, Jesse   1913-
  McGEWB, SelBAA, WhoAm 78,
  WhoBlA 77

The Man Who Outran Hitler
   Kliatt - v14 - Winter '80 - p29

P

PACE, Mildred Mastin 1907-
AuBYP SUP, ConAu 5R

Wrapped For Eternity
BL - v70 - My 1 '74 - p1005
BL - v71 - Mr 15 '75 - p767
CCB-B - v28 - O '74 - p34
Choice - v12 - N '75 - p1133
GP - v16 - Mr '78 - p3271
JB - v42 - F '78 - p47
KR - v42 - Mr 15 '74 - p312
KR - v43 - Ja 1 '75 - p14
LJ - v99 - My 15 '74 - p1451
LJ - v99 - My 15 '74 - p1475
NYTBR - My 26 '74 - p8
NYTBR - N 3 '74 - p55
SB - v10 - My '74 - p58
SE - v39 - Mr '75 - p175
SLJ - v25 - S '78 - p43

PAINE, Roberta M 1925-
AuBYP SUP, ConAu 33R, SmATA
13, WhoAmW 77

Looking At Sculpture
BS - v28 - N 1 '68 - p325
BW - v2 - N 3 '68 - p6
NYTBR - v73 - N 3 '68 - p54
PW - v194 - N 4 '68 - p50
SR - v51 - N 9 '68 - p68

PAISLEY, Tom
see Bethancourt, T Ernesto

PALFREY, Sarah 1913?-
AuBYP SUP (also known as Cooke,
Sarah Fabyan)

Tennis For Anyone!
BL - v63 - Mr 15 '67 - p776
LJ - v92 - Ja 15 '67 - p352
PW - v190 - Ag 15 '66 - p65

PANATI, Charles 1943-
ConAu 81

Links
BL - v74 - Je 1 '78 - p1538
KR - v46 - F 1 '78 - p130
LJ - v103 - Ap 15 '78 - p898
PW - v213 - F 6 '78 - p90

PARKER, Richard 1915-
ConAu 73, SmATA 14, TwCCW 78,
WrDr 80

Quarter Boy
B&B - v22 - Je '77 - p74
BL - v73 - O 15 '76 - p325
CCB-B - v30 - Ap '77 - p131
CE - v54 - O '77 - p28
GP - v15 - My '76 - p2891
JB - v40 - O '76 - p283
KR - v44 - O 15 '76 - p1146
SLJ - v23 - S '76 - p136
TLS - Ap 2 '76 - p377

PARKINSON, Ethelyn M 1906-
AuBYP SUP, ConAu 49, SmATA 11,
WhoAm 78

Today I Am A Ham
BL - v64 - Jl 15 '68 - p1287
BS - v29 - Ja 1 '70 - p391
KR - v36 - Ap 1 '68 - p393
LJ - v93 - My 15 '68 - p2115

PASCAL, Francine

*My First Love And Other
Disasters*
BL - v75 - F 15 '79 - p936
CCB-B - v32 - Mr '79 - p123
KR - v47 - Jl 1 '79 - p745
NYTBR - Ap 29 '79 - p38
PW - v216 - Ja 8 '79 - p74

PASCAL, Francine (continued)
   SLJ - v25 - Mr '79 - p149

PATTEN, Lewis B 1915-
   ConAu 25R, WhoAm 78

      The Killings At Coyote Springs
      BL - v73 - My 1 '77 - p1329
      Kliatt - v12 - Spring '78 - p9

PATTERSON, Betty

      I Reached For The Sky
      LJ - v95 - O 15 '70 - p3635

PATTERSON, Doris T 1917-
   WhoAmW 64

      Your Family Goes Camping
      BL - v56 - D 15 '59 - p237

PATTERSON, Lillie
   AuBYP, ConAu 73, SmATA 14

      Frederick Douglass
      BL - v69 - My 1 '73 - p837
      JNE - v38 - Fall '69 - p420
      RR - v86 - Mr '69 - p172

      Martin Luther King, Jr.
      CCB-B - v23 - My '70 - p149
      LJ - v95 - O 15 '70 - p3603
      LJ - v95 - N 15 '70 - p4046
      NYTBR, pt.2 - My 4 '69 - p44
      RT - v32 - My '79 - p920

PATTERSON, Sarah 1959-

      The Distant Summer
      BL - v73 - S 15 '76 - p124
      BS - v36 - S '76 - p186
      EJ - v67 - Ja '78 - p91
      KR - v44 - Ap 1 '76 - p420
      LJ - v101 - Jl '76 - p1556
      NYTBR - O 10 '76 - p36
      PW - v209 - Ap 12 '76 - p59
      PW - v211 - My 2 '77 - p68
      SLJ - v22 - My '76 - p36
      SLJ - v22 - My '76 - p83
      TLS - Ap 23 '76 - p481

PATTON, A Rae 1908-
   AmM&WS 76P, ConAu 5R

      The Chemistry Of Life
      BL - v67 - My 1 '71 - p749
      HB - v47 - Ag '71 - p405
      KR - v38 - O 1 '70 - p1114
      LJ - v96 - Mr 15 '71 - p1129
      SB - v6 - D '70 - p223

PAULSEN, Gary 1939-
   ConAu 73, SmATA 22

      The Foxman
      BL - v73 - Je 15 '77 - p1576
      BS - v37 - O '77 - p204
      CCB-B - v31 - D '77 - p66
      EJ - v67 - F '78 - p81
      KR - v45 - Mr 15 '77 - p291
      SLJ - v23 - Mr '77 - p153

      The Green Recruit
      SLJ - v24 - My '78 - p88

      Tiltawhirl John
      KR - v46 - Ja 1 '78 - p8
      SLJ - v24 - N '77 - p75

PAYNE, Donald Gordon 1924-
   ConAu 13R, IntAu&W 77

      The Lost Ones
      Am - v121 - D 13 '69 - p596
      BL - v64 - Jl 1 '68 - p1220
     see also Cameron, Ian

PEARCE, W E 1907-
   AmM&WS 12P

      Transistors And Circuits:
      Electronics For Young
      Experimenters
      BL - v67 - Jl 1 '71 - p906
      KR - v39 - F 15 '71 - p184
      LJ - v96 - My 15 '71 - p1815
      SA - v225 - D '71 - p114
      SB - v7 - S '71 - p164
      WLB - v46 - Mr '72 - p613

PEASE, Howard 1894-1974
   BioIn 1, BioIn 2, ConAu 5R, JBA 51,
   SmATA 2, TwCCW 78

      The Jinx Ship
      BL - v24 - F '28 - p212
      SR - v4 - Ja 28 '28 - p558

PECK, Ira 1922-
ConAu 77

The Life And Words Of Martin Luther King, Jr.
NYTBR, pt.2 - My 4 '69 - p44

PECK, Richard 1934-
ConAu 85, SmATA 18, TwCCW 78, WrDr 80

Are You In The House Alone?
BL - v73 - O 15 '76 - p315
BL - v73 - O 15 '76 - p326
CCB-B - v30 - Mr '77 - p111
Comw - v104 - N 11 '77 - p731
EJ - v66 - S '77 - p84
EJ - v67 - Ja '78 - p91
EJ - v67 - My '78 - p90
HB - v53 - F '77 - p60
KR - v44 - S 1 '76 - p982
Kliatt - v12 - Winter '78 - p11
NYT - v126 - D 21 '76 - p31
NYTBR - N 14 '76 - p29
PW - v210 - S 13 '76 - p99
SLJ - v23 - D '76 - p69
SMQ - v8 - Fall '79 - p26
WCRB - v3 - S '77 - p58

Don't Look And It Won't Hurt
BW - v6 - N 5 '72 - p8
Choice - v14 - N '77 - p1178
KR - v40 - Ag 15 '72 - p949
LJ - v97 - D 15 '72 - p4080
NYTBR - N 12 '72 - p8
PW - v202 - S 25 '72 - p60

Dreamland Lake
BL - v70 - N 15 '73 - p335
BL - v70 - N 15 '73 - p342
CCB-B - v27 - Ja '74 - p83
KR - v41 - D 15 '73 - p1357
LJ - v98 - D 15 '73 - p3691
NYTBR - Ja 13 '74 - p10
NYTBR - F 23 '75 - p40
Teacher - v92 - Ap '75 - p110

Father Figure
BW - N 12 '78 - pE4
CCB-B - v32 - Ja '79 - p86
EJ - v68 - F '79 - p104
HB - v54 - D '78 - p647
Inst - v89 - Ja '80 - p112
NYTBR - S 30 '79 - p43

PW - v216 - Jl 16 '79 - p68
Par - v54 - Ja '79 - p20

Ghosts I Have Been
BL - v74 - O 1 '77 - p300
BL - v74 - Je 1 '78 - p1560
BW - D 11 '77 - pE4
CCB-B - v31 - Mr '78 - p117
EJ - v67 - S '78 - p90
HB - v54 - F '78 - p56
KR - v45 - S 15 '77 - p991
NYTBR - O 30 '77 - p34
NYTBR - N 13 '77 - p52
PW - v212 - Jl 11 '77 - p81
RT - v32 - O '78 - p43
SLJ - v24 - N '77 - p61
Teacher - v95 - O '77 - p159

Sounds And Silences: Poetry For Now
Am - v123 - D 5 '70 - p499
BL - v67 - N 1 '70 - p224
BW - v4 - N 8 '70 - p5
CCB-B - v24 - D '70 - p64
CSM - v63 - Ja 23 '71 - p13
EJ - v60 - S '71 - p829
KR - v38 - Jl 15 '70 - p750
LJ - v95 - N 15 '70 - p4058
NYTBR, pt.2 - N 8 '70 - p54
PW - v198 - Jl 27 '70 - p74
SR - v53 - S 19 '70 - p35
TN - v27 - Ja '71 - p209

Through A Brief Darkness
BL - v73 - D 15 '76 - p615
BS - v33 - Ja 15 '74 - p472
CCB-B - v27 - Mr '74 - p116
GP - v14 - Ap '76 - p2844
JB - v40 - O '76 - p283
KR - v41 - D 1 '73 - p1314
LJ - v99 - F 15 '74 - p582
TES - S 22 '78 - p23

PECK, Robert Newton 1928-
ConAu 81, SmATA 21, TwCCW 78, WrDr 80

Fawn
BL - v71 - Mr 15 '75 - p745
BS - v34 - F 15 '75 - p515
KR - v42 - D 1 '74 - p1271
KR - v42 - D 15 '74 - p1316
LJ - v100 - Mr 15 '75 - p603
NYTBR - F 2 '75 - p12

PECK, Robert Newton (continued)
    PW - v206 - D 9 '74 - p63

Millie's Boy
    BW - v7 - N 11 '73 - p3C
    JLH - v41 - S 15 '73 - p1044
    LJ - v98 - O 15 '73 - p3158
    PW - v204 - O 29 '73 - p36

PEDERSEN, Elsa   1915-
AuBYP, ConAu 1R, ForWC 70

Cook Inlet Decision
    NYTBR - My 12 '63 - p26

PEEKNER, Ray
see Paulsen, Gary (co-author) -
    The Green Recruit

PEET, Creighton   1899-1977
AuBYP, ConAu 69

*Man In Flight: How The Airlines
Operate*
    BL - v69 - D 15 '72 - p406
    CC - v89 - N 29 '72 - p1218
    CCB-B - v26 - D '72 - p63
    LJ - v98 - Ja 15 '73 - p269

PEI, Mario   1901-1978
ConAu 5R, ConAu 77, CurBio 68,
CurBio 78N, TwCA SUP, WhoAm 78

*Our Names: Where They Came
From And What They Mean*
    BL - v57 - F 1 '61 - p329
    CSM - F 2 '61 - p7
    KR - v28 - Ag 15 '60 - p689
    LJ - v85 - D 15 '60 - p4576
    NYTBR - Ap 9 '61 - p34
    SR - v43 - D 17 '60 - p35

PELTIER, Leslie C   1900-
AmM&WS 76P, BioIn 1, BioIn 7,
ConAu 17R, SmATA 13

*Guideposts To The Stars:
Exploring The Skies Throughout
The Year*
    BL - v69 - Mr 15 '73 - p698
    KR - v40 - D 1 '72 - p1363
    LJ - v98 - My 15 '73 - p1684
    S&T - v46 - Jl '73 - p44
    SB - v9 - My '73 - p68

TLS - Ap 6 '73 - p401

PENRY-JONES, J

*The Boys' Book Of Ships And
Shipping*
    LJ - v91 - Ap 15 '66 - p2223
    NYTBR - v71 - My 8 '66 - p25
    SB - v2 - S '66 - p88

PEPE, Philip   1935-
ConAu 25R, SmATA 20

Great Comebacks In Sport
    BL - v71 - Je 15 '75 - p1077
    LJ - v100 - Je 1 '75 - p1149

PERL, Lila
AuBYP, ConAu 33R, SmATA 6

Dumb Like Me, Olivia Potts
    CCB-B - v30 - D '76 - p64
    KR - v44 - S 1 '76 - p975
    SLJ - v23 - D '76 - p68

*Ghana And Ivory Coast: Spotlight
On West Africa*
    BL - v71 - My 1 '75 - p916
    HB - v51 - O '75 - p476
    KR - v43 - Ap 1 '75 - p390
    SLJ - v22 - S '75 - p124

That Crazy April
    Am - v131 - D 7 '74 - p373
    B&B - v23 - Jl '78 - p58
    BL - v70 - My 15 '74 - p1058
    CE - v51 - N '74 - p92
    CLW - v46 - F '75 - p316
    CLW - v47 - D '75 - p208
    Choice - v14 - N '77 - p1178
    GP - v14 - My '75 - p2640
    JB - v39 - Je '75 - p202
    KR - v42 - Ap 1 '74 - p364
    LJ - v99 - My 15 '74 - p1475
    PW - v205 - Je 10 '74 - p41
    TLS - Ap 4 '75 - p371

PERRY, Jesse
see Kinnick, B J (co-author)

PERRY, Richard
ConAu 41R

The World Of The Giant Panda
    BL - v66 - Mr 1 '70 - p813

PERRY, Richard (continued)
>   CSM - v62 - N 28 '69 - pB4
>   Choice - v6 - F '70 - p1777
>   LJ - v94 - N 1 '69 - p4017
>   NH - v79 - Ap '70 - p77
>   NYTBR - Jl 1 '73 - p8
>   Obs - N 30 '69 - p35
>   PW - v196 - Ag 18 '69 - p73
>   SB - v6 - S '70 - p149

PETERS, Elizabeth   (pseud.) 1927-
ConAu X, WrDr 80 (real name:
Mertz, Barbara Gross)

> *Summer Of The Dragon*
>   BL - v75 - My 1 '79 - p1348

PETERS, Elizabeth

> *Summer Of The Dragon*
>   KR - v47 - F 15 '79 - p217
>   LJ - v104 - My 1 '79   p1081
>   PW - v215 - Ap 2 '79 - p68

PETERSON, Helen Stone   1910-
ConAu 37R, SmATA 8, WhoAmW
77, WrDr 80

> *Susan B. Anthony*
>   Comw - v95 - N 19 '71 - p189
>   LJ - v97 - Jl '72 - p2486

PETRY, Ann   1912?-
ConAu 5R, ConLC 7, SelBAA,
SmATA 5, ThrBJA, TwCA SUP,
TwCCW 78

> *Harriet Tubman*
>   BS - v30 - F 1 '71 - p482
>   CSM - v61 - My 1 '69 - pB7

> *Tituba Of Salem Village*
>   Atl - v214 - D '64 - p163
>   BL - v69 - My 1 '73 - p839
>   CCB-B - v18 - Ja '65 - p78
>   CSM - F 25 '65 - p7
>   CSM - v57 - F 25 '65 - p7
>   CSM - v61 - My 1 '69 - pB7
>   HB - v41 - F '65 - p65
>   LJ - v89 - S 15 '64 - p3498
>   NYTBR, pt.2 - N 1 '64 - p8
>   SR - v47 - N 7 '64 - p55

PEVSNER, Stella
ConAu 57, SmATA 8

> *And You Give Me A Pain, Elaine*
>   BL - v75 - S 15 '78 - p224
>   KR - v46 - O 15 '78 - p1139
>   PW - v214 - O 23 '78 - p61
>   SLJ - v25 - N '78 - p77

> *Call Me Heller, That's My Name*
>   BL - v69 - Je 1 '73 - p950
>   CCB-B - v26 - Je '73 - p160
>   KR - v41 - Ap 1 '73 - p385
>   LJ - v98 - N 15 '73 - p3456
>   PW - v203 - Ap 16 '73 - p55

> *Keep Stompin' Till The Music
> Stops*
>   BL - v73 - My 1 '77 - p1355
>   CCB-B - v31 - S '77 - p24
>   CLW - v49 - F '78 - p313
>   Inst - v87 - N '77 - p160
>   KR - v45 - My 1 '77 - p486
>   SE - v41 - O '77 - p532
>   SLJ - v24 - S '77 - p134
>   WCRB - v4 - Mr '78 - p41

> *A Smart Kid Like You*
>   BB - v4 - Mr '76 - p4
>   BL - v71 - Jl 1 '75 - p1129
>   CCB-B - v29 - S '75 - p17
>   CLW - v47 - N '75 - p188
>   Comw - v102 - N 21 '75 - p569
>   J Read - v19 - F '76 - p421
>   KR - v43 - Ap 1 '75 - p375
>   NYTBR - N 16 '75 - p52
>   PW - v207 - Mr 31 '75 - p49
>   SLJ - v21 - My '75 - p58

PEYTON, K M   1929-
ChLR 3, ConAu 69, SmATA 15,
SouST, ThrBJA, TwCCW 78 (also
known as Peyton, Kathleen Wendy)

> *The Beethoven Medal*
>   BL - v69 - O 1 '72 - p140
>   BS - v32 - S 15 '72 - p284
>   BW - v6 - N 5 '72 - p8
>   CCB-B - v26 - S '72 - p14
>   CE - v49 - F '73 - p258
>   EJ - v61 - N '72 - p1261
>   HB - v48 - O '72 - p475
>   KR - v40 - Jl 1 '72 - p728
>   LJ - v97 - O 15 '72 - p3462

PEYTON, K M (continued)

    Lis - v86 - N 11 '71 - p661
    NO - v11 - N 18 '72 - p28
    NS - v82 - N 12 '71 - p661
    Obs - N 28 '71 - p35
    PW - v202 - Jl 17 '72 - p122
    Spec - v227 - N 13 '71 - p688
    TLS - O 22 '71 - p1318

    A Pattern Of Roses
    B&B - v18 - N '72 - pR6
    BL - v70 - S 15 '73 - p124
    BL - v70 - Mr 15 '74 - p827
    BS - v33 - O 15 '73 - p334
    CCB-B - v27 - N '73 - p49
    CSM - v65 - N 7 '73 - pB4
    CSM - v66 - D 5 '73 - pB12
    Choice - v12 - N '75 - p1133
    GW - v107 - D 16 '72 - p24
    HB - v49 - O '73 - p473
    KR - v41 - Ag 1 '73 - p819
    LJ - v98 - S 15 '73 - p2667
    LJ - v98 - D 15 '73 - p3691
    Lis - v88 - N 9 '72 - p644
    NS - v84 - N 10 '72 - p692
    Obs - N 26 '72 - p37
    Obs - Je 8 '75 - p23
    PW - v204 - S 17 '73 - p57
    Spec - v229 - N 11 '72 - p750
    TLS - N 3 '72 - p1324
    TN - v30 - N '73 - p82
    Teacher - v91 - N '73 - p130

    Pennington's Last Term
    A Lib - v3 - Ap '72 - p420
    BL - v67 - Jl 1 '71 - p906
    BL - v68 - Ap 1 '72 - p670
    BS - v31 - Ag 15 '71 - p235
    BW - v5 - My 9 '71 - p18
    CCB-B - v25 - S '71 - p13
    CE - v48 - N '71 - p100
    CLW - v43 - Mr '72 - p430
    EJ - v60 - N '71 - p1156
    HB - v47 - Ag '71 - p390
    KR - v39 - Ap 15 '71 - p443
    LJ - v96 - Je 15 '71 - p2140
    PW - v199 - My 31 '71 - p135
    SR - v54 - S 18 '71 - p49

PFEFFER, Susan Beth   1948-
ConAu 29R, SmATA 4, WhoAmW
77, WrDr 80

The Beauty Queen
    CCB-B - v28 - N '74 - p51
    KR - v42 - My 1 '74 - p489
    Kliatt - v11 - Spring '77 - p7
    LJ - v99 - S 15 '74 - p2296
    PW - v205 - Je 10 '74 - p41

Better Than All Right
    EJ - v62 - Ja '73 - p147
    KR - v40 - Jl 15 '72 - p808
    LJ - v98 - Mr 15 '73 - p1015
    NYTBR - N 12 '72 - p14

Starring Peter And Leigh
    BL - v75 - Je 1 '79 - p1486
    CCB-B - v32 - Jl '79 - p198
    SLJ - v25 - My '79 - p66

*Whatever Words You Want To
Hear*
    BS - v34 - S 15 '74 - p286
    KR - v42 - Ag 1 '74 - p811
    LJ - v99 - D 15 '74 - p3273
    PW - v206 - S 23 '74 - p155

PFLUG, Betsy

Egg-Speriment
    KR - v41 - Ap 1 '73 - p392
    LJ - v98 - O 15 '73 - p3140

PHELAN, Mary Kay   1914-
AuBYP SUP, ConAu 1R, SmATA 3,
WhoAmW 77, WrDr 80

Four Days In Philadelphia, 1776
    BL - v64 - Ja 1 '68 - p548
    BW - v1 - N 5 '67 - p40
    CE - v44 - Ap '68 - p502
    KR - v35 - S 15 '67 - p1152
    LJ - v92 - O 15 '67 - p3854
    NYTBR, pt.1 - v73 - F 25 '68 - p26

PHILBROOK, Clem   1917-
AuBYP, SmATA 24

Slope Dope
    KR - v34 - Jl 1 '66 - p631
    LJ - v91 - O 15 '66 - p5237

PHILLIPS, Betty Lou

*Earl Campbell, Houston Oiler
Superstar*
    BL - v76 - Ja 1 '80 - p670

PHILLIPS, Betty Lou (continued)
SLJ - v26 - Mr '80 - p135

PHILLIPS, Maxine

Your Rights When You're Young
BL - v76 - Jl 15 '80 - p1662
Hi Lo - v1 - D '79 - p5

PHIPSON, Joan   1912-
ConAu X, SmATA 2, ThrBJA,
TwCCW 78, WrDr 80 (also known as
Fitzhardinge, Joan Margaret)

The Family Conspiracy
Comw - v80 - My 22 '64 - p269
HB - v40 - Ap '64 - p179
LJ - v89 - Mr 15 '64 - p1452
NYTBR - Ap 5 '64 - p34
PW - v190 - Ag 1 '66 - p64
SR   v47   Je 27 '64 - p45
TLS - N 23 '62 - p894
TLS - S 20 '74 - p1005

PICARD, Barbara Leonie   1917-
ConAu 5R, SmATA 2, ThrBJA,
TwCCW 78, WrDr 80

One Is One
BL - v63 - Ja 15 '67 - p539
BS - v26 - D 1 '66 - p341
CCB-B - v20 - Ap '67 - p128
HB - v43 - F '67 - p73
HT - v15 - D '65 - p879
KR - v34 - Ag 15 '66 - p835
LJ - v91 - D 15 '66 - p6204
LR - v20 - Winter '65 - p271
NYTBR - v72 - Mr 26 '67 - p22
Obs - D 19 '65 - p23
Spec - N 12 '65 - p629
TLS - D 9 '65 - p1146

PIERIK, Robert   1921-
ConAu 37R, SmATA 13

Archy's Dream World
KR - v40 - Ja 1 '72 - p4
LJ - v97 - My 15 '72 - p1930

PIERSALL, James   1929-
WhoProB 73

Fear Strikes Out: The Jim Piersall
Story
BL - v51 - Je 1 '55 - p406
HB - v31 - D '55 - p469
KR - v23 - Ap 15 '55 - p288
LJ - v80 - Ap 15 '55 - p872

PIMLOTT, Douglas
see Rutter, Russell (co-author)

PINE, Tillie S   1896-
BkP, ConAu 69, SmATA 13

Rocks And How We Use Them
LJ - v93 - Ja 15 '68 - p284
SB - v4 - My '68 - p29

PINIAT, John

Going For The Win
BL - v74 - My 15 '78 - p1487

Rosina Torres
Hi Lo - v2 - N '80 - p5

PINKWATER, Daniel Manus   1941-
AuBYP SUP, ConAu 29R, SmATA
8, WhoE 75

The Hoboken Chicken Emergency
BL - v73 - Ap 15 '77 - p1268
BW - Mr 20 '77 - pH4
CCB-B - v30 - Je '77 - p163
CE - v54 - O '77 - p28
CSM - v69 - My 4 '77 - pB8
HB - v53 - Je '77 - p316
KR   v45   F 15 '77   p166
NW - v90 - Jl 18 '77 - p92
NYTBR - Mr 27 '77 - p44
New R - v177 - D 3 '77 - p28
RT - v31 - Ap '78 - p841
SLJ - v24 - S '77 - p134

Lizard Music
BL - v73 - S 1 '76 - p4126
BL - v73 - My 15 '77 - p1426
BW - F 13 '77 - pG10
CCB-B - v30 - Mr '77 - p112
HB - v53 - Ap '77 - p161
KR - v44 - Ag 1 '76 - p846
PW - v210 - O 18 '76 - p64
PW - v215 - Ap 23 '79 - p80
RT - v31 - O '77 - p19
SLJ - v23 - O '76 - p110

PINKWATER, Daniel Manus
(continued)
    Teacher - v95 - O '77 - p158

PLACE, Marion T 1910-
ConAu 1R, IndAu 1917, SmATA 3,
WhoPNW

    Frontiersman: The True Story Of
    Billy Dixon
      LJ - v92 - N 15 '67 - p4257
      NYTBR - v72 - Mr 26 '67 - p22

PLATT, Kin 1911-
AuBYP SUP, ConAu 17R, SmATA
21, WhoAm 74

    The Ape Inside Me
      BL - v76 - Ja 1 '80 - p662
      BS - v39 - F '80 - p410
      CBRS - v8 - N '79 - p29
      CCB-B - v33 - My '80 - p180
      Hi Lo - v1 - My '80 - p3
      KR - v48 - F 1 '80 - p136
      SLJ - v26 - N '79 - p92

    The Blue Man
      KR - v29 - Je 15 '61 - p501
      LJ - v86 - N 15 '61 - p4040
      NYTBR - S 24 '61 - p40

    Boy Who Could Make Himself
    Disappear
      BL - v65 - O 1 '68 - p190
      BS - v28 - Jl 15 '68 - p173
      BW - v2 - O 6 '68 - p20
      CCB-B - v22 - S '68 - p14
      KR - v36 - My 15 '68 - p556
      LJ - v93 - O 15 '68 - p3986
      SR - v51 - Ag 24 '68 - p43

    Chloris And The Creeps
      BS - v33 - Ag 15 '73 - p234
      BW - v7 - N 11 '73 - p3C
      CCB-B - v27 - Ja '74 - p84
      KR - v41 - F 15 '73 - p188
      LJ - v98 - Ap 15 '73 - p1389
      PW - v203 - My 7 '73 - p66

    Chloris And The Freaks
      BL - v72 - F 1 '76 - p762
      BL - v72 - F 1 '76 - p788
      CCB-B - v29 - Ap '76 - p131
      Cur R - v16 - F '77 - p48
      KR - v43 - D 15 '75 - p1379

NYTBR - N 16 '75 - p52
SLJ - v22 - D '75 - p32
SLJ - v22 - D '75 - p61

Dracula, Go Home!
    BL - v75 - My 15 '79 - p1435
    CBRS - v7 - My '79 - p99
    CCB-B - v33 - S '79 - p16
    Hi Lo - v1 - O '79 - p4
    SLJ - v25 - My '79 - p82

Headman
    EJ - v66 - Ja '77 - p65
    EJ - v67 - My '78 - p88
    KR - v43 - Jl 15 '75 - p783
    NYTBR - D 14 '75 - p8
    SLJ - v22 - D '75 - p61
    TN - v32 - Ap '76 - p285
    TN - v33 - Spring '77 - p288

Hey, Dummy
    BS - v31 - Ja 15 '72 - p471
    CCB-B - v25 - Je '72 - p162
    KR - v39 - N 15 '71 - p1213
    NYTBR - Mr 12 '72 - p8
    NYTBR - My 6 '73 - p28
    SMQ - v8 - Fall '79 - p27
    TN - v36 - Winter '80 - p208

Mystery Of The Witch Who
Wouldn't
    BS - v29 - D 1 '69 - p354
    KR - v37 - S 1 '69 - p939
    LJ - v94 - D 15 '69 - p4618

Run For Your Life
    BL - v74 - N 15 '77 - p545
    CCB-B - v31 - Ja '78 - p85
    Hi Lo - v1 - Mr '80 - p4
    SLJ - v24 - D '77 - p65

Sinbad And Me
    BS - v26 - O 1 '66 - p251
    KR - v34 - Jl 1 '66 - p630
    LJ - v91 - D 15 '66 - p6209
    NYTBR, pt.2 - v73 - F 25 '68 - p18
    SLJ - v24 - F '78 - p35
    Teacher - v92 - O '74 - p108

POLLACK, Philip

    Careers And Opportunities In
    Science
      LJ - v93 - F 15 '68 - p885
      SB - v3 - Mr '68 - p283

POLLOCK, Bruce

The Face Of Rock And Roll
LJ - v103 - D 15 '78 - p2532
SLJ - v25 - D '78 - p74

Me, Minsky And Max
BL - v75 - D 1 '78 - p610
HB - v54 - D '78 - p647
KR - v46 - D 1 '78 - p1312
SLJ - v25 - Ja '79 - p62

POLLOCK, Rollene

Flying Wheels
BL - v75 - Jl 15 '79 - p1622
Hi Lo - v1 - O '79 - p4

POMEROY, Pete (pseud.) 1925-
AuBYP SUP, ConAu X (real name:
Roth, Arthur J)

Wipeout!
LJ - v93 - My 15 '68   p2130
see also Roth, Arthur Joseph

POOLE, Gray
see Poole, Lynn (co-author)

POOLE, Josephine   1933-
ConAu 21R, SmATA 5, TwCCW 78,
WrDr 80

*Touch And Go: A Story Of
Suspense*
BL - v73 - Mr 15 '77 - p1094
BS - v36 - Mr '77 - p387
CCB B - v30 - D '76 - p15
Comw - v103 - N 19 '76 - p762
GP - v15 - N '76 - p2988
HB - v53 - F '77 - p60
JB - v41 - Ap '77 - p120
KR - v44 - Ag 1 '76 - p848
SLJ - v23 - D '76 - p69
TLS - D 10 '76 - p1548

POOLE, Lynn   1910-1969
ConAu 5R, CurBio 54, CurBio 69,
MorJA, SmATA 1, WhAm 5

Men Who Dig Up History
BL - v64 - Jl 15 '68 - p1283
BS - v28 - My 1 '68 - p66

CCB-B - v21 - Jl '68 - p180
CSM - v60 - My 2 '68 - pB6
KR - v36 - F 1 '68 - p127
LJ - v93 - Mr 15 '68 - p1140
SB - v4 - S '68 - p116
SR - v51 - Je 15 '68 - p33

PORCARI, Constance Kwolek
see Kwolek, Constance

POSELL, Elsa Z
AuBYP SUP, ConAu 1R, SmATA 3,
WhoAmW 74

This Is An Orchestra
KR - v41 - D 15 '73 - p1368
LJ - v99 - Mr 15 '74 - p894

POSEY, Jeanne K

The Horse Keeper's Handbook
LJ - v99 - N 1 '74 - p2868
RSR - v2 - O '74   p157

POST, Elizabeth L   1920-
ConAu 49, WhoAm 78

*The Emily Post Book Of Etiquette
For Young People*
BS - v27 - Ja 1 '68 - p394
KR - v35 - N 15 '67 - p1376
LJ - v93 - Ja 15 '68 - p310
PW - v192 - N 6 '67 - p50
SR - v51 - My 18 '68 - p64

POTTER, Charles Francis   1885-1962
NatCAB 52, WhoAm 4

*More Tongue Tanglers And A
Rigmarole*
CSM - My 7 '64 - p3B
HB - v40 - Je '64 - p277
SR - v47 - Ag 15 '64 - p45

POWERS, Bill   1931-
ConAu 77

Flying High
BL - v74 - Mr 15 '78 - p1198
CCB-B - v31 - Ap '78 - p133
Inst - v87 - My '78 - p113
SLJ - v24 - My '78 - p88

A Test Of Love
BL - v75 - Jl 15 '79 - p1622

POWERS, Bill (continued)
    CBRS - v7 - Spring '79 - p119
    CCB-B - v33 - S '79 - p16
    Hi Lo - v1 - S '79 - p5
    SLJ - v25 - My '79 - p75

    The Weekend
    BB - v6 - N '78 - p3
    BL - v74 - Ap 15 '78 - p1343
    CCB-B - v31 - Je '78 - p165
    CLW - v50 - N '78 - p182
    Cur R - v17 - My '78 - p127
    Hi Lo - v1 - S '79 - p2
    Kliatt - v14 - Spring '80 - p8
    NYTBR - Ap 30 '78 - p45
    SLJ - v25 - S '78 - p163

POYNTER, Margaret

    Crazy Minnie
    Hi Lo - v1 - Mr '80 - p4

PRAGER, Arthur

    World War II Resistance Stories
    BL - v75 - Jl 15 '79 - p1622
    CCB-B - v33 - S '79 - p16
    CLW - v51 - Ap '80 - p415
    SLJ - v26 - S '79 - p146

PRAGER, Emily
see Prager, Arthur (co-author)

PRESBERG, Miriam Goldstein
see Gilbert, Miriam

PRESTON, Edward (pseud.) 1925-
ConAu X (real name: Guess, Edward
Preston)

    *Martin Luther King: Fighter For
    Freedom*
    LJ - v96 - Ap 15 '71 - p1432

PRICE, Willard 1887-
ConAu 1R, WhoAm 76, WrDr 80

    Lion Adventure
    KR - v35 - Ap 1 '67 - p415
    PW - v191 - Je 5 '67 - p176
    TLS - My 25 '67 - p459

PRINCE, Alison 1931-
ConAu 29R

    The Turkey's Nest
    BL - v76 - Mr 15 '80 - p1044
    CBRS - v8 - Mr '80 - p79
    GP - v18 - N '79 - p3592
    HB - v56 - Je '80 - p308
    KR - v48 - Ap 1 '80 - p442
    SLJ - v26 - My '80 - p79
    TES - N 23 '79 - p31
    TLS - D 14 '79 - p124

PRINGLE, Laurence 1935-
ConAu 29R, FourBJA, SmATA 4,
WhoE 77

    Dinosaurs And Their World
    BL - v64 - My 15 '68 - p1096
    KR - v36 - Mr 1 '68 - p267
    LJ - v93 - Je 15 '68 - p2542
    PW - v193 - Ap 15 '68 - p98
    SB - v4 - S '68 - p114
    Teacher - v94 - Ja '77 - p134

PRONZINI, Bill 1943-
ConAu 49

    Midnight Specials
    BL - v74 - N 15 '77 - p529
    KR - v45 - Mr 15 '77 - p311
    KR - v45 - Ap 15 '77 - p439
    PW - v211 - Mr 28 '77 - p73
    WLB - v52 - D '77 - p307

PROUDFIT, Isabel 1898-
AuBYP, MorJA

    *Riverboy: The Story Of Mark
    Twain*
    BL - v37 - N 15 '40 - p123
    SR - v23 - N 16 '40 - p8

PURCELL, John
see Pollack, Philip (co-author)

PURDY, Susan 1939-
ConAu 13R, IlsCB 1957, SmATA 8,
WhoAmW 77

    Books For You To Make
    BL - v70 - Ja 1 '74 - p490
    BW - v7 - N 11 '73 - p5C
    KR - v41 - O 1 '73 - p1106
    LJ - v99 - Ja 15 '74 - p211

PYLE, Howard   1853-1911
  JBA 34, OxAm, SmATA 16,
  TwCCW 78A, WhAm 1, WhoChL

   The Merry Adventures Of Robin Hood
     B&B - v19 - O '73 - p137
     BL - v43 - Ja 1 '47 - p140
     Dr - Autumn '73 - p75
     LJ - v72 - Ja 1 '47 - p84
     Obs - Ag 10 '69 - p26
     TLS - D 3 '71 - p1509

R

RABE, Berniece Louise   1928-
ConAu 49, SmATA 7, WrDr 80

The Girl Who Had No Name
BL - v73 - Jl 1 '77 - p1654
CCB-B - v31 - Ja '78 - p85
HB - v53 - O '77 - p533
J Read - v22 - N '78 - p184
KR - v45 - Je 1 '77 - p581
LA - v55 - Ap '78 - p523
PW - v212 - Jl 4 '77 - p77
SLJ - v23 - My '77 - p71
Teacher - v95 - O '77 - p159

Naomi
BL - v71 - Je 1 '75 - p1016
BL - v73 - Mr 15 '77 - p1101
BS - v35 - S '75 - p169
CCB-B - v29 - D '75 - p69
Cur R - v16 - F '77 - p48
J Read - v20 - O '76 - p80
KR - v43 - Je 1 '75 - p612
NYTBR - Je 22 '75 - p8
PW - v207 - Je 30 '75 - p58
SLJ - v21 - Ap '75 - p69

Rass
BL - v69 - My 15 '73 - p909
BW - v7 - My 13 '73 - p3
KR - v40 - D 15 '72 - p1432
LJ - v98 - My 15 '73 - p1692
NYTBR - Ag 12 '73 - p8
PW - v203 - Ap 16 '73 - p55

Who's Afraid?
CBRS - v8 - Ag '80 - p139
Hi Lo - v2 - S '80 - p3
KR - v48 - Jl 1 '80 - p841

RABIN, Gil

False Start
BW - v3 - My 4 '69 - p28
CCB-B - v23 - F '70 - p105

CLW - v41 - Ap '70 - p534
KR - v37 - My 1 '69 - p515
LJ - v94 - O 15 '69 - p3835
LJ - v94 - D 15 '69 - p4582
LJ - v95 - F 15 '70 - p743
NYTBR - Ag 24 '69 - p20

RABINOWICH, Ellen

Rock Fever
BL - v76 - N 15 '79 - p297
Hi Lo - v1 - F '80 - p4
SLJ - v26 - F '80 - p60

Toni's Crowd
BL - v75 - O 15 '78 - p370
CCB-B - v32 - F '79 - p104
CLW - v51 - O '79 - p142
Hi Lo - v1 - O '79 - p5
Kliatt - v14 - Spring '80 - p8
SLJ - v25 - N '78 - p78

RADLAUER, Edward   1921-
AuBYP, ConAu 69, SmATA 15

Some Basics About Bicycles
BL - v75 - N 15 '78 - p552
J Read - v22 - My '79 - p773
SLJ - v25 - F '79 - p58

Some Basics About Motorcycles
BL - v75 - N 15 '78 - p552
J Read - v22 - My '79 - p773
SLJ - v25 - F '79 - p58

Some Basics About Skateboards
BL - v75 - N 15 '78 - p552
SLJ - v25 - F '79 - p58

Some Basics About Vans
BL - v75 - N 15 '78 - p552
SLJ - v25 - F '79 - p58

RAMSDELL, Sheldon
see Mergandahl, T E, Jr. (co-author)

RANDALL, Florence Engel 1917-
AuBYP SUP, BlkAW, ConAu 41R,
SmATA 5, WhoAmW 77

The Almost Year
A Lib - v3 - Ap '72 - p420
Am - v125 - D 4 '71 - p490
BL - v67 - Jl 15 '71 - p953
BL - v68 - Ap 1 '72 - p670
BS - v31 - My 15 '71 - p100
CCB-B - v25 - N '71 - p50
CE - v48 - Ja '72 - p208
CLW - v43 - N '71 - p174
CSM - v63 - Je 5 '71 - p21
Comw - v94 - My 21 '71 - p264
HB - v47 - Ag '71 - p392
KR - v39 - Mr 1 '71 - p243
LJ - v96 - My 15 '71 - p1782
LJ - v96 - My 15 '71 - p1816
LJ - v96 - D 15 '71 - p4159
NCW - v216 - Mr '73 - p92
NYTBR - Ap 11 '71 - p22
NYTBR, pt.2 - N 7 '71 - p28
PW - v199 - Ap 12 '71 - p83
TN - v28 - Ja '72 - p204

RAPPOPORT, Ken 1935-
ConAu 53

Diamonds In The Rough
SLJ - v25 - My '79 - p83
WCRB - v5 - S '79 - p19

RASKIN, Edith Lefkowitz
see Raskin, Joseph (co-author)

RASKIN, Joseph 1897-
ConAu 33R, SmATA 12, WhoWorJ
72

*Spies And Traitors: Tales Of The
Revolutionary And Civil Wars*
B&B - v5 - My '77 - p2
BL - v72 - Jl 15 '76 - p1597
Comw - v103 - N 19 '76 - p758
KR - v44 - Ap 1 '76 - p400
LA - v54 - Ja '77 - p82
SLJ - v23 - O '76 - p110

RAUCHER, Herman 1928-
ConAu 29R, SmATA 8, WhoE 77,
WrDr 80

Summer Of '42
Am - v124 - My 22 '71 - p549
B&B - v16 - S '71 - p51
BS - v30 - Mr 1 '71 - p527
KR - v39 - Ja 1 '71 - p23
LJ - v96 - My 1 '71 - p1638
LJ - v96 - My 15 '71 - p1831
LJ - v96 - D 15 '71 - p4161
NYTBR, pt.1 - My 2 '71 - p36
PW - v199 - Ja 18 '71 - p46
TLS - Ag 20 '71 - p987

RAVIELLI, Anthony 1916-
ConAu 29R, IlsCB 1967, SmATA 3,
ThrBJA

What Is Tennis?
BL - v74 - Ap 1 '78 - p1264
HB - v54 - Ap '78 - p183
SLJ - v24 - Mr '78 - p132

RAWLINGS, Marjorie 1896-1953
OxAm, ThrBJA, TwCCW 78,
TwCW, WhAm 3, YABC 1

The Yearling
Atl - Je '38
BL - v34 - Ap 15 '38 - p300
CSM - Ap 27 '38 - p11
Comw - v28 - Ap 29 '38 - p24
NYTBR - Ap 3 '38 - p2
Nat - v146 - Ap 23 '38 - p483
New R - v94 - Ap 27 '38 - p370
SR - v17 - Ap 2 '38 - p5
Spec - v161 - N 11 '38 - p824
TLS - D 24 '38 - p813
Time - v31 - Ap 4 '38 - p69
YR - v27 - Summer '38 - pR10

RAWLS, Wilson 1919-
AuBYP SUP, AuNews 1, ConAu 1R,
SmATA 22 (also known as Rawls,
Woodrow Wilson)

Summer Of The Monkeys
BL - v72 - Jl 1 '76 - p1523

Where The Red Fern Grows
BS - v34 - O 1 '74 - p311
NYTBR - S 8 '74 - p38

RAWSON, Ruth

Acting
BL - v67 - Ja 15 '71 - p394
EJ - v60 - N '71 - p1160

RAY, E Roy

What Does An Airline Crew Do?
BL - v65 - My 1 '69 - p1018
NYTBR - v73 - N 3 '68 - p58
SB - v5 - My '69 - p71

RAYMOND, Charles   (joint pseud.)
ConAu X (real names: Koch,
Charlotte; and Koch, Raymond)

The Trouble With Gus
BW - v2 - My 5 '68 - p34
CCB-B - v22 - O '68 - p32
CSM - v60 - My 2 '68 - pB1
KR - v36 - Ja 15 '68 - p58
LJ - v93 - Ja 15 '68 - p294

RAZZELL, Arthur G   1925-
AuBYP SUP, SmATA 11, WrDr 80

Three And The Shape Of Three:
Exploring Mathematics
BL - v66 - S 15 '69 - p139
LJ - v94 - N 15 '69 - p4300
SB - v5 - S '69 - p111

REED, Donald

Robert Redford
WCRB - v3 - My '77 - p24

REED, Fran

A Dream With Storms
BL - v76 - Ap 15 '80 - p1184
Hi Lo - v1 - D '79 - p3

REEDER, Colonel Red   1902-
AuBYP, ConAu 1R, SmATA 4 (also
known as Reeder, Russell P, Jr.)

West Point Plebe
CSM - N 10 '55 - p6B
KR - v23 - Je 1 '55 - p363
LJ - v80 - O 15 '55 - p2392
NYTBR - S 11 '55 - p28

REEMAN, Douglas   1925-
ConAu 1R, DcLEL 1940, WrDr 80

The Deep Silence
BL - v64 - Ap 15 '68 - p973
BS - v27 - F 15 '68 - p443
KR - v36 - Ja 1 '68 - p25
LJ - v93 - Ap 15 '68 - p1821
NYT - v117 - F 24 '68 - p27
NYTBR - v73 - Mr 3 '68 - p44
PW - v193 - Ja 15 '68 - p83
TN - v24 - Je '68 - p451

REES, David   1936-

Risks
GP - v16 - Ap '78 - p3282
JB - v42 - Je '78 - p167
PW - v214 - O 9 '78 - p77
TLS - Ap 7 '78 - p383

REEVES, John R T   1947-

Questions And Answers About Acne
KR - v45 - Ap 15 '77 - p438
SLJ - v24 - S '77 - p149

REIFF, Stephanie Ann   1948-
ConAu 93, ScF&FL 1

Secrets Of Tut's Tomb And The
Pyramids
Cur R - v217 - Ag '78 - p227
SLJ - v25 - S '78 - p43
SLJ - v25 - N '78 - p64

REIFF, Tana

The Family From Vietnam
BL - v76 - Ap 15 '80 - p1184
Hi Lo - Je '80 - p3

Juan And Lucy
BL - v76 - Ap 15 '80 - p1184
Hi Lo - Je '80 - p3

Mollie's Year
BL - v76 - Ap 15 '80 - p1184
Hi Lo - Je '80 - p3

A Place For Everyone
BL - v76 - Ap 15 '80 - p1184
Hi Lo - Je '80 - p3

The Shoplifting Game
BL - v76 - Ap 15 '80 - p1184

REIFF, Tana (continued)
  Hi Lo - Je '80 - p3

  So Long, Snowman
    BL - v76 - Ap 15 '80 - p1184
    Hi Lo - Je '80 - p3

  A Time To Choose
    BL - v76 - Ap 15 '80 - p1184
    Hi Lo - Je '80 - p3

REINGOLD, Carmel Berman
  AuBYP SUP

  *How To Cope: A New Guide To
  The Teen-Age Years*
    BS - v34 - Ap 15 '74 - p54
    KR - v42 - F 15 '74 - p195
    LJ - v99 - S 15 '74 - p2297

REISS, Bob

  Franco Harris
    BL - v74 - O 15 '77 - p381
    SLJ - v24 - D '77 - p65

REISS, Johanna 1929?-
  AuBYP SUP, ConAu 85, HerW,
  SmATA 18, TwCCW 78B

  The Upstairs Room
    B&B - v19 - Ja '74 - p84
    BL - v69 - O 15 '72 - p205
    BW - v7 - Mr 11 '73 - p13
    CCB-B - v26 - N '72 - p48
    CE - v49 - F '73 - p258
    CSM - v64 - N 8 '72 - pB7
    Comw - v97 - N 17 '72 - p158
    Econ - v249 - D 29 '73 - p61
    HB - v49 - F '73 - p50
    Inst - v82 - N '72 - p127
    KR - v40 - Ag 15 '72 - p949
    KR - v40 - D 15 '72 - p1420
    LJ - v97 - D 15 '72 - p4057
    NS - v86 - N 9 '73 - p704
    NYTBR - D 3 '72 - p82
    NYTBR, pt.2 - N 5 '72 - p3
    NYTBR, pt.2 - N 5 '72 - p29
    PW - v202 - S 25 '72 - p59
    SR - v1 - Ap 14 '73 - p87
    TLS - N 23 '73 - p1429
    TN - v29 - Ap '73 - p254
    Teacher - v90 - My '73 - p43

REIT, Seymour
  AuBYP SUP, SmATA 21

  *Growing Up In The White House:
  The Story Of The Presidents'
  Children*
    KR - v36 - S 1 '68 - p983
    LJ - v934 - N 15 '68 - p4422
    PW - v194 - O 14 '68 - p66

RENICK, Marion 1905-
  ConAu 1R, MorJA, OhA&B,
  SmATA 1

  Football Boys
    BL - v64 - F 15 '68 - p702
    KR - v35 - Ag 15 '67 - p960
    LJ - v92 - D 15 '67 - p4632

REUBEN, Michael
  see Hoard, Edison (co-author)

REYNOLDS, Marjorie 1903-
  AuBYP, ConAu 5R

  A Horse Called Mystery
    Teacher - v90 - D '72 - p69

REYNOLDS, Pamela

  *Will The Real Monday Please
  Stand Up?*
    CCB-B - v29 - O '75 - p31
    KR - v43 - Je 1 '75 - p612
    PW - v207 - Je 9 '75 - p63
    SLJ - v22 - O '75 - p81

RHODIN, Eric Nolan 1916-
  ConAu 1R

  The Good Greenwood
    BL - v68 - Ap 15 '72 - p718
    BL - v68 - Ap 15 '72 - p725
    BS - v33 - S 1 '73 - p259
    HB - v48 - F '72 - p59
    LJ - v96 - N 15 '71 - p3911

RICE, Earle, Jr.

  Tiger, Lion, Hawk
    BL - v74 - F 15 '78 - p997
    BL - v75 - O 15 '78 - p357
    Hi Lo - v1 - N '79 - p1
    TN - v36 - Winter '80 - p199

RICH, Elizabeth 1935-
ConAu 29R

Flying Scared: What It's Like To Be An Airline Hostess
BS - v32 - Ag 1 '72 - p221
BW - v7 - Je 24 '73 - p13
CSM - v64 - Jl 26 '72 - p9
KR - v40 - Je 1 '72 - p662
LJ - v97 - N 1 '72 - p3609
PW - v201 - My 29 '72 - p29

RICH, Mark

Diesel Trucks, On The Move
SLJ - v25 - Mr '79 - p143

RICHARD, Adrienne 1921-
AuBYP SUP, ConAu 29R, SmATA 5, WrDr 80

Into The Road
BL - v73 - Ja 1 '77 - p661
BL - v73 - Ja 1 '77 - p668
BS - v37 - Ap '77 - p31
CCB-B - v30 - Mr '77 - p113
GP - v16 - D '77 - p3219
HB - v53 - Ap '77 - p167
JB - v42 - F '78 - p48
KR - v44 - O 15 '76 - p1146
Kliatt - v13 - Winter '79 - p15
SLJ - v23 - D '76 - p62
TLS - O 28 '77 - p1274

Pistol
A Lib - v1 - Ap '70 - p386
A Lib - v5 - My '74 - p236
BL - v66 - N 1 '69 - p343
CCB-B - v23 - Mr '70 - p116
EJ - v59 - Ja '70 - p146
EJ - v63 - F '74 - p92
HB - v45 - D '69 - p679
KR - v37 - Ag 1 '69 - p784
LJ - v94 - O 15 '69 - p3841
NYTBR - N 30 '69 - p42
NYTBR, pt.2 - N 9 '69 - p60
PW - v196 - S 22 '69 - p85
SR - v53 - Ja 24 '70 - p75
TLS - Ap 28 '72 - p486

RICHARDS, Norman
AuBYP SUP

The Story Of Old Ironsides
LJ - v92 - N 15 '67 - p4254

The Story Of The Alamo
CE - v47 - Ja '71 - p212
LJ - v96 - F 15 '71 - p744

RICHMOND, Julius Benjamin
see Houser, Norman (co-author)

RICHTER, Conrad 1890-1968
ConAu 5R, ConAu 25R, SmATA 3, TwCA, TwCA SUP, WhAm 5

The Light In The Forest
Atl - v192 - Jl '53 - p80
BL - v49 - Mr 1 '53 - p213
BL - v49 - Je 15 '53 - p341
BL - v63 - Ja 1 '67 - p493
BL - v69 - O 15 '72 - p178
CC - v83 - D 7 '66 - p1510
CSM - Je 4 '53 - p13
HB - v29 - D '53 - p469
HB - v43 - Ap '67 - p222
KR - v21 - Ap 1 '53 - p231
LJ - v78 - My 15 '53 - p917
LJ - v78 - Je 15 '53 - p1165
LJ - v91 - D 15 '66 - p6210
NY - v29 - My 16 '53 - p153
NYTBR - My 17 '53 - p5
NYTBR - v71 - N 6 '66 - p68
Nat - v176 - Je 6 '53 - p488
SR - v36 - My 16 '53 - p12
YR - v42 - Summer '53 - p14

RICHTER, Hans Peter 1925-
ConAu 45, FourBJA, SmATA 6, TwCCW 78B, WhoWor 78

Friedrich
BL - v67 - Ap 1 '71 - p665
CCB-B - v24 - F '71 - p97
HB - v47 - Ap '71 - p173
KR - v38 - O 15 '70 - p1163
LJ - v96 - My 15 '71 - p1806
Lis - v86 - N 11 '71 - p661
NYTBR - Ja 10 '71 - p26
NYTBR, pt.2 - N 8 '70 - p34
PW - v199 - Ja 11 '71 - p63
TLS - D 3 '71 - p1512

RIEGER, Shay 1929-
ConAu 29R

RIEGER, Shay (continued)

Animals In Clay
BL - v67 - Jl 15 '71 - p956
HB - v47 - Je '71 - p300
PW - v200 - Jl 5 '71 - p50

RITCHIE-CALDER, Peter
see Calder, Ritchie

RIVERA, Geraldo 1943-
AuBYP SUP, BioNews 74, CurBio
75, IntMPA 78, NewYTET, WhoAm
78

*A Special Kind Of Courage:
Profiles Of Young Americans*
PW - v211 - Ap 4 '77 - p88
SLJ - v23 - Ja '77 - p108

ROBB, Mary K 1908-
ConAu P-2

Making Teen Parties Click
P&R - v1 - Je '66 - p532

ROBERTS, Charles G D 1860-1943
JBA 34, OxCan, TwCA, TwCA SUP,
TwCCW 78, WhAm 3

Red Fox
CSM - v64 - Ag 2 '72 - p11
CSM - v64 - D 4 '72 - p20
HB - v48 - Je '72 - p255
KR - v40 - My 1 '72 - p542
LJ - v97 - S 15 '72 - p2954
SB - v8 - S '72 - p157
Time - v99 - Je 12 '72 - p90

ROBERTS, Lawrence

Big Wheels
BL - v74 - N 15 '77 - p545
Cur R - v16 - D '77 - p361

ROBERTS, Nancy 1924-
AuBYP SUP, ConAu 9R, WhoAmW
77

Appalachian Ghosts
BL - v75 - N 15 '78 - p549

ROBERTSON, Keith 1914-
ConAu 9R, MorBMP, MorJA,
SmATA 1, TwCCW 78

Henry Reed's Big Show
BL - v67 - F 1 '71 - p452
CCB-B - v24 - Je '71 - p162
CE - v47 - Ap '71 - p377
HB - v47 - Ap '71 - p170
KR - v38 - N 1 '70 - p1193
LJ - v95 - D 15 '70 - p4355
LJ - v96 - Ja 15 '71 - p286

The Year Of The Jeep
BL - v64 - Je 15 '68 - p1188
BW - v2 - Jl 28 '68 - p14
HB - v44 - Ag '68 - p432
KR - v36 - Ap 15 '68 - p461
LJ - v93 - Je 15 '68 - p2549
PW - v193 - My 6 '68 - p45
SE - v33 - My '69 - p556

ROBINSON, Louie
see Ashe, Arthur (co-author)

ROBISON, Nancy 1934-
ConAu 93

Department Store Model
BL - v74 - O 15 '77 - p370
Cur R - v16 - D '77 - p361

Janet Guthrie: Race Car Driver
SLJ - v25 - My '79 - p86

*Nancy Lopez: Wonder Woman Of
Golf*
BL - v75 - Jl 15 '79 - p1632
SLJ - v25 - My '79 - p86

RODERUS, Frank 1942-
ConAu 89

Home To Texas
BL - v75 - N 1 '78 - p464

RODGERS, Mary 1931-
ConAu 49, ConLC 12, NotNAT,
SmATA 8, TwCCW 78, WhoAm 78

Freaky Friday
BL - v68 - Je 15 '72 - p910
BW - v6 - My 7 '72 - p5
CCB-B - v26 - S '72 - p15
CSM - v64 - My 4 '72 - pB5
Comw - v97 - N 17 '72 - p158
HB - v48 - Ag '72 - p378
KR - v40 - Mr 1 '72 - p267
LJ - v97 - Ap 15 '72 - p1608

RODGERS, Mary (continued)
NS - v86 - N 9 '73 - p700
NYTBR - Jl 16 '72 - p8
PW - v201 - F 14 '72 - p70
TLS - N 23 '73 - p1433
Teacher - v90 - My '73 - p73
Teacher - v95 - O '77 - p80
VV - v19 - D 16 '74 - p51

RODMAN, Bella 1903-
AuBYP SUP, ConAu P-2

Lions In The Way
BL - v63 - O 1 '66 - p168
CCB-B - v20 - S '66 - p19
CE - v43 - F '67 - p355
CLW - v38 - Ja '67 - p341
CSM - v58 - N 3 '66 - pB1
Comw - v85 - N 11 '66 - p176
HB - v42 - O '66 - p576
KR - v34 - My 1 '66 - p483
LJ - v91 - Jl '66 - p3546
NYTBR - v71 - My 8 '66 - p14
NYTBR - v72 - N 5 '67 - p54
PW - v191 - Mr 27 '67 - p64
SR - v49 - N 12 '66 - p54
TCR - v68 - F '67 - p451
TN - v23 - Ja '67 - p195

RODOWSKY, Colby F 1932-
ConAu 69, SmATA 21

P.S. Write Soon
Inter BC - v10 - #1 '79 - p26
JB - v43 - Ap '79 - p119
RT - v32 - D '78 - p364

What About Me?
JB - v41 - D '77 - p366
PW - v215 - Ja 22 '79 - p371

ROGER, Mae Durham
see Durham, Mae

ROGERS, James T 1921-
ConAu 45, WhoE 77

*The Pantheon Story Of
Mathematics For Young People*
Am - v115 - N 5 '66 - p557
BL - v63 - F 1 '67 - p584
BS - v26 - N 1 '66 - p296
CSM - v58 - N 3 '66 - pB10
Comw - v85 - N 11 '66 - p180

KR - v34 - S 1 '66 - p916
LJ - v92 - Mr 15 '67 - p1330
NYT - v116 - F 2 '67 - p26
NYTBR - v71 - N 6 '66 - p34
PW - v190 - O 3 '66 - p85
SB - v3 - My '67 - p13

Story Of Mathematics
NS - v75 - My 24 '68 - p698
TLS - Je 6 '68 - p596

ROLLINS, Charlemae 1897-1979
BlkAW, ConAu 9R, MorBMP,
SelBAA, SmATA 3

Famous American Negro Poets
BL - v62 - S 15 '65 - p101
BS - v25 - Ap 15 '65 - p55
CCB-B - v19 - O '65 - p38
CLW - v37 - O '65 - p153
KR - v33 - Mr 1 '65 - p247
LJ - v90 - Ap 15 '65 - p2042
NYTBR - v70 - My 9 '65 - p10

*Famous Negro Entertainers Of
Stage, Screen And TV*
BL - v63 - Je 15 '67 - p1102
BS - v27 - My 1 '67 - p66
CCB-B - v20 - Je '67 - p158
KR - v35 - Ap 1 '67 - p421
LJ - v92 - Je 15 '67 - p2454

ROMEIKA, William L
see Cook, Joseph J (co-author) -
Better Surfing For Boys

RONAN, Eve
see Ronan, Margaret (co-author)

RONAN, Margaret

Curse Of The Vampires
Kliatt - v14 - Spring '80 - p58

Superstars
Kliatt - v13 - Spring '79 - p33

ROSE, Karen

There Is A Season
BL - v64 - Mr 15 '68 - p870
CCB-B - v21 - F '68 - p100
CLW - v43 - F '72 - p331
KR - v35 - O 15 '67 - p1283
LJ - v92 - S 15 '67 - p3203

ROSE, Karen (continued)
    LJ - v95 - F 15 '70 - p743
    SR - v50 - D 16 '67 - p36

ROSEN, Winifred   1943-
ConAu 29R, SmATA 8

    Cruisin For A Bruisin
    CCB-B - v30 - F '77 - p97

ROSENBAUM, Eileen   1936-
AuBYP SUP, ConAu 21R

    The Kidnapers Upstairs
    CCB-B - v21 - Mr '68 - p115
    KR - v36 - Ja 1 '68 - p6
    LJ - v93 - Ap 15 '68 - p1803

ROSENBERG, Ethel Clifford   1915-
ConAu 29R, SmATA 3, WhoAmW
77

    *The Year Of The Three-Legged
    Deer*
    BL - v69 - N 1 '72 - p246
    CCB-B - v26 - Ja '73 - p73
    CLW - v44 - O '72 - p193
    KR - v40 - My 1 '72 - p536
    LJ - v97 - N 15 '72 - p3804
    NYTBR - Je 18 '72 - p8

ROSENBERG, Sharon   1942-
ConAu 57, SmATA 8

    *The Illustrated Hassle-Free Make
    Your Own Clothes Book*
    Atl - v227 - Ap '71 - p104
    B&B - v18 - Je '73 - p138
    LJ - v96 - Je 15 '71 - p2149
    LJ - v96 - D 15 '71 - p4161
    TN - v28 - Ja '72 - p208

ROSENBERG, Sondra

    Will There Never Be A Prince?
    CCB-B - v24 - S '70 - p19
    KR - v38 - F 15 '70 - p180
    LJ - v95 - D 15 '70 - p4355
    SR - v53 - My 9 '70 - p47

ROSENBLOOM, Joseph   1928-
ConAu 57, SmATA 21, WrDr 80

    Maximilian You're The Greatest
    BL - v75 - Jl 15 '79 - p1629

    Kliatt - v13 - Fall '79 - p26
    SLJ - v25 - My '79 - p82

ROSS, Pat

    *Young And Female: Turning
    Points In The Lives Of Eight
    American Women*
    BL - v69 - S 15 '72 - p102
    BW - v6 - My 7 '72 - p13
    CCB-B - v26 - O '72 - p30
    CSM - v64 - My 4 '72 - pB5
    EJ - v63 - Ap '74 - p90
    KR - v40 - Je 1 '72 - p633
    LJ - v97 - Je 15 '72 - p2244
    NYTBR, pt.2 - My 7 '72 - p24
    PW - v202 - Jl 31 '72 - p71
    SE - v37 - D '73 - p788

ROTH, Arnold   1929-
AuBYP SUP, ConAu 21R, SmATA
21, WhoE 77

    Pick A Peck Of Puzzles
    BL - v63 - Mr 15 '67 - p797
    CCB-B - v20 - F '67 - p97
    HB - v43 - F '67 - p75
    KR - v34 - S 1 '66 - p911
    LJ - v91 - O 15 '66 - p5260
    NYTBR - v71 - N 27 '66 - p42
    SR - v49 - N 12 '66 - p48

ROTH, Arthur Joseph   1925-
AuBYP SUP, ConAu 53

    Avalanche
    BL - v76 - Mr 15 '80 - p1045
    Inst - v89 - Ja '80 - p102
    Kliatt - v14 - Winter '80 - p14

    The Secret Lover Of Elmtree
    BL - v73 - O 15 '76 - p315
    BL - v73 - O 15 '76 - p326
    BS - v36 - Mr '77 - p387
    CCB-B - v30 - Ja '77 - p81
    EJ - v67 - Ja '78 - p92
    HB - v53 - F '77 - p61
    KR - v44 - Ag 15 '76 - p910
    NYTBR - N 28 '76 - p40
    SLJ - v23 - N '76 - p72

    Two For Survival
    BL - v73 - O 15 '76 - p326
    CCB-B - v30 - N '76 - p47

ROTH, Arthur Joseph (continued)
    CE - v53 - Ja '77 - p150
    HB - v52 - D '76 - p630
    KR - v44 - Ag 1 '76 - p849
    RT - v31 - Ap '78 - p839
    SLJ - v23 - O '76 - p111
see also Pomeroy, Pete

ROTH, Charles E 1934-

    Then There Were None
    KR - v45 - S 15 '77 - p993
    SB - v14 - S '78 - p115
    SLJ - v25 - N '78 - p68

ROTH, David

    The Winds Of Summer
    BS - v32 - Jl 15 '72 - p199
    CCB-B - v25 - Je '72 - p162
    KR - v40 - Mr 15 '72 - p336
    LJ - v97 - S 15 '72 - p2966
    TLS - Ap 28 '72 - p481

ROUNDS, Glen 1906-
ConAu 53, IlsCB 1967, JBA 51,
SmATA 8, TwCCW 78

    Stolen Pony
    KR - v37 - Ap 15 '69 - p443
    LJ - v94 - S 15 '69 - p3208

RUBENSTONE, Jessie 1912-
ConAu 69

    Knitting For Beginners
    BL - v70 - Ja 15 '74 - p545
    CCB-B - v27 - Ja '74 - p85
    CE - v50 - Mr '74 - p298
    KR - v41 - O 1 '73 - p1106
    LJ - v99 - F 15 '74 - p576
    NYTBR - N 4 '73 - p62

RUBIN, Arnold Perry 1946-
ConAu 69

    The Youngest Outlaws: Runaways In America
    Cur R - v16 - F '77 - p30
    TN - v34 - Fall '77 - p102

RUBLOWSKY, John 1928-
AuBYP SUP, ConAu 17R, WhoE 74

    Popular Music
    BL - v64 - Ap 15 '68 - p965
    Choice - v5 - Jl '68 - p634
    LJ - v92 - S 15 '67 - p3214
    LJ - v92 - N 1 '67 - p4002

RUBY, Lois 1942-
ConAu 97

    Arriving At A Place You've Never Left
    BL - v74 - O 1 '77 - p282
    BL - v74 - O 1 '77 - p302
    BS - v38 - Ap '78 - p13
    CCB-B - v31 - D '77 - p68
    Inst - v87 - My '78 - p123
    KR - v45 - D 1 '77 - p1271
    Kliatt - v14 - Spring '80 - p8
    WLB - v52 - D '77 - p337

RUCKMAN, Ivy

    Encounter
    BL - v75 - O 15 '78 - p369
    KR - v46 - N 1 '78 - p1194
    SLJ - v25 - N '78 - p78

RUFF, Peter

    Olivia Newton-John
    Kliatt - v14 - Winter '80 - p63
    SLJ - v26 - D '79 - p106

RUFFINS, Reynold
    see Sarnoff, Jane (co-author)

RUIZ, Ramon E
    see Atwater, James D (co-author)

RUMSEY, Marian 1928-
ConAu 21R, SmATA 16, Str&VC

    Lion On The Run
    BL - v69 - Je 1 '73 - p950
    CSM - v65 - My 2 '73 - pB4
    Inst - v83 - N '73 - p124
    KR - v41 - Ja 1 '73 - p6
    LJ - v98 - Jl '73 - p2197

RUSCH, Richard B

    Man's Marvelous Computer: The Next Quarter Century
    BL - v67 - Ap 1 '71 - p665

RUSCH, Richard B (continued)
>   KR - v38 - O 15 '70 - p1171
>   LJ - v96 - Mr 15 '71 - p1130
>   SB - v6 - Mr '71 - p294

RUSHING, Jane Gilmore   1925-
ConAu 49, WhoAm 78

>   *Mary Dove*
>   Am - v130 - My 4 '74 - p348
>   BS - v34 - Ap 15 '74 - p49
>   BW - S 14 '75 - p4
>   EJ - v65 - Ja '76 - p98
>   KR - v42 - Ja 1 '74 - p23
>   LJ - v99 - Mr 15 '74 - p777
>   LJ - v99 - S 15 '74 - p2305
>   NYTBR - Mr 17 '74 - p38
>   PW - v205 - Ja 21 '74 - p78

RUSSELL, Bill   1934-
CurBio 75, WebAB

>   *Go Up For Glory*
>   BL - v62 - Je 1 '66 - p940
>   BS - v26 - Ap 1 '66 - p19
>   KR - v34 - F 15 '66 - p212
>   KR - v34 - Mr 1 '66 - p255
>   LJ - v91 - Mr 15 '66 - p1440
>   NYTBR - v71 - Mr 20 '66 - p28
>   PW - v190 - O 17 '66 - p67
>   RR - v86 - Mr '69 - p171

RUSSELL, Patrick   (pseud.) 1942-
ConAu X, SmATA 4 (real name:
Sammis, John)

>   *The Tommy Davis Story*
>   Comw - v93 - F 26 '71 - p523
>   KR - v37 - Mr 15 '69 - p311
>   LJ - v94 - My 15 '69 - p2125
>   PW - v195 - Ap 21 '69 - p66
>   SR - v52 - Je 28 '69 - p38

RUTHERFORD, Douglas   (pseud.)
1915-
ConAu X, WrDr 80 (real name:
McConnell, John Douglas R)

>   *Killer On The Track*
>   CCB-B - v28 - Ap '75 - p137
>   KR - v42 - N 15 '74 - p1206

RUTLAND, Jonathan

>   *Ships*
>   BL - v73 - Ja 15 '77 - p720
>   SLJ - v23 - My '77 - p64

RUTTER, Russell J

>   *The World Of The Wolf*
>   BL - v64 - My 1 '68 - p1014
>   CE - v45 - S '68 - p42
>   LJ - v93 - Ap 1 '68 - p1493

S

SABIN, Francene
ConAu 69

Jimmy Connors: King Of The Courts
CE - v55 - Ja '79 - p171
KR - v46 - Mr 1 '78 - p251
SLJ - v24 - My '78 - p87

Set Point
BL - v74 - O 1 '77 - p303
KR - v45 - Je 1 '77 - p580
SLJ - v24 - S '77 - p136

SABIN, Louis   1930-
ConAu 69

The Fabulous Dr. J
SLJ - v23 - Mr '77 - p148

Johnny Bench: King Of Catchers
KR - v45 - Ap 1 '77 - p356
SLJ - v24 - S '77 - p136

Pele: Soccer Superstar
CE - v53 - Mr '77 - p262
SLJ   v23   Mr '77 - p148

SACHS, Marilyn   1927-
ChLR 2, ConAu 17R, FourBJA, SmATA 3, TwCCW 78, WhoAmW 75

Bus Ride
CBRS - v8 - Ag '80 - p139
CCB-B - v33 - Jl '80 - p222
Hi Lo - v2 - S '80 - p3
KR - v48 - Jl 1 '80 - p841
PW - v217 - Je 6 '80 - p82

Peter And Veronica
BL - v65 - My 15 '69 - p1078
BW - v3 - My 4 '69 - p10
CCB-B - v23 - Ap '70 - p133

CLW - v43 - F '72 - p331
CSM - v61 - My 1 '69 - pB4
GW - v103 - D 19 '70 - p21
HB - v45 - Je '69 - p312
KR - v37 - Mr 15 '69 - p305
LJ - v94 - Ap 15 '69 - p1785
LJ - v95 - F 15 '70 - p743
NYTBR - My 25 '69 - p32
PW - v195 - Mr 17 '69 - p57
SR - v52 - My 10 '69 - p57
TLS - O 30 '70 - p1267

A Summer's Lease
BL - v75 - Ap 1 '79 - p1220
HB - v55 - Je '79 - p311
KR - v47 - Je 15 '79 - p690
NYTBR - Ag 19 '79 - p20
PW - v215 - My 7 '79 - p84
SLJ - v25 - My '79 - p36
SLJ - v25 - My '79 - p75

SACKETT, Samuel J   1928-
ConAu 1R, SmATA 12, WrDr 80

Cowboys And The Songs They Sang
ABC - v18 - Ja '68 - p34
BL - v64 - N 1 '67 - p337
CCB-B - v20 - Jl '67 - p175
HB - v43 - Ag '67 - p481
KR - v35 - Ap 15 '67 - p504
LJ - v92 - Jl '67 - p2656
NYTBR - v72 - N 5 '67 - p65
NYTBR, pt.2 - v72 - My 7 '67 - p41
PW - v191 - My 8 '67 - p62
SR - v50 - Je 17 '67 - p36

SAGARIN, Edward
see Aymar, Brandt (co-author)

SAHADI, Lou

Pro Football's Gamebreakers
BL - v74 - Ja 1 '78 - p743
LJ - v102 - S 15 '77 - p1865
PW - v212 - Ag 22 '77 - p58
WCRB - v4 - Ja '78 - p56

SAINT GEORGE, Judith   1931-
ConAu 69, SmATA 13

The Halo Wind
BL - v75 - D 1 '78 - p619
CCB-B - v32 - F '79 - p105
HB - v55 - F '79 - p66
SLJ - v25 - D '78 - p56

Shadow Of The Shaman
BL - v74 - F 15 '78 - p1012
KR - v46 - Ja 15 '78 - p47
SLJ - v24 - My '78 - p85

SAMACHSON, Dorothy   1914-
AuBYP, ConAu 9R, ForWC 70,
SmATA 3

The First Artists
BL - v67 - O 1 '70 - p147
CCB-B - v24 - F '71 - p98
CSM - v62 - N 14 '70 - pB11
Inst - v130 - My '71 - p80
KR - v38 - S 15 '70 - p1056
LJ - v95 - N 15 '70 - p4059
LJ - v95 - D 15 '70 - p4326
SA - v223 - D '70 - p123
SB - v6 - D '70 - p195

SAMACHSON, Joseph
see Samachson, Dorothy (co-author)

SAMMIS, John
see Russell, Patrick

SAMUELS, Gertrude
ConAu 9R, NatPD, SmATA 17,
WhoAmW 77, WhoWorJ 72

Run, Shelley, Run!
Am - v130 - My 4 '74 - p350
BL - v70 - My 1 '74 - p996
BL - v71 - Mr 15 '75 - p748
BS - v34 - Ap 1 '74 - p7

CCB-B - v27 - Je '74 - p163
CSM - v66 - Ap 10 '74 - pF5
EJ - v64 - S '75 - p80
KR - v42 - Ja 15 '74 - p61
LJ - v99 - Ap 15 '74 - p1232
Ms - v3 - D '74 - p79
NY - v50 - D 2 '74 - p182
NYTBR - Ap 7 '74 - p8
PW - v205 - F 11 '74 - p65

SANDERLIN, Owenita   1916-
ConAu 17R, SmATA 11, WrDr 80

Tennis Rebel
BL - v74 - My 15 '78 - p1487
Hi Lo - v1 - D '79 - p3
NYTBR - Ap 30 '78 - p45
SLJ - v24 - My '78 - p88

SANT, Kathryn Storey

Desert Chase
BL - v76 - Mr 15 '80 - p1065

SARASON, Martin

A Federal Case
BL - v74 - Mr 15 '78 - p1179

SARGENT, Shirley   1927-
AuBYP, ConAu 1R, ForWC 70,
SmATA 11

Ranger In Skirts
CLW - v38 - Ja '67 - p342
LJ - v91 - N 15 '66 - p5765

SARNOFF, Jane   1937-
AuBYP SUP, ConAu 53, SmATA 10

A Great Aquarium Book: The
Putting-It-Together Guide For
Beginners
BL - v74 - S 1 '77 - p44
CCB-B - v31 - Ja '78 - p86
CE - v54 - N '77 - p90
HB - v54 - F '78 - p70
NYTBR - Ag 14 '77 - p27
PW - v211 - Je 13 '77 - p107
SLJ - v24 - O '77 - p117
Teacher - v95 - O '77 - p165
Teacher - v95 - My '78 - p21

SARNOFF, Paul 1918-
ConAu 5R

Ice Pilot: Bob Bartlett
KR - v34 - S 1 '66 - p911
LJ - v91 - D 15 '66 - p6205

SAROYAN, William 1908-1981
ConAu 5R, ConDr 77, ConLC 10,
CurBio 72, SmATA 23, TwCW,
WhoAm 78

My Name Is Aram
EJ - v63 - Ja '74 - p43

SASEK, Miroslav 1916-1980
BkP, ConAu 73, IlsCB 1967, SmATA
16, SmATA 23N, ThrBJA

This Is The United Nations
B&B - v13 - Jl '68 - p42
BL - v64 - Jl 15 '68 - p1288
BW - v2 - S 1 '68 - p12
CCB-B - v21 - Jl '68 - p181
HB - v44 - Ag '68 - p410
KR - v36 - My 15 '68 - p553
NYTBR - v73 - Je 23 '68 - p22
SE - v33 - My '69 - p563
SR - v51 - Je 15 '68 - p33
TLS - Je 6 '68 - p596

SAUNDERS, F Wenderoth
AmM&WS 73P

Machines For You
Am - v117 - N 4 '67 - p520
HB - v44 - F '68 - p57
KR - v35 - S 1 '67 - p1052
LJ - v93 - My 15 '68 - p2116
SB - v3 - D '67 - p259

SAVITT, Sam 1917-
ConAu 1R, SmATA 8, WhoAmA 78,
WhoE 77, WrDr 80

Sam Savitt's True Horse Stories
LJ - v96 - Mr 15 '71 - p1119
PW - v198 - D 28 '70 - p61

SAVITZ, Harriet May 1933-
AuBYP SUP, ConAu 41R, SmATA 5

The Lionhearted
EJ - v66 - Ja '77 - p65
Kliatt - v11 - Fall '77 - p8

On The Move
RT - v31 - Ap '78 - p804

Wheelchair Champions
BL - v74 - Mr 15 '78 - p1176
KR - v46 - My 15 '78 - p550
SLJ - v24 - My '78 - p88

SAYERS, Gale
see Griese, Bob (co-author)

SCHAEFER, Jack 1907-
ConAu 17R, SmATA 3, ThrBJA,
TwCCW 78, WhoAm 78

Shane
KR - v17 - S 15 '49 - p521
LJ - v74 - O 1 '49 - p1461
SR - v32 - D 3 '49 - p58

SCHATZ, Letta

Bola And The Oba's Drummers
BL - v64 - Mr 1 '68 - p787
CCB-B - v22 - S '68 - p16
Comw - v87 - N 10 '67 - p176
KR - v35 - Jl 15 '67 - p810

SCHEER, George 1917-
AuBYP SUP, ConAu 13R

Yankee Doodle Boy
HB - v41 - F '65 - p65
LJ - v89 - D 15 '64 - p5019
NYTBR, pt.2 - N 1 '64 - p56

SCHELL, Orville 1940-
AuBYP SUP, ConAu 25R, SmATA
10

*Modern China: The Story Of A
Revolution*
BL - v69 - O 1 '72 - p140
BS - v32 - My 15 '72 - p99
CCB-B - v26 - O '72 - p31
HB - v48 - Je '72 - p279
KR - v40 - My 15 '72 - p593
NYTBR - My 14 '72 - p8
Nat - v214 - Je 26 '72 - p829
PW - v202 - Jl 31 '72 - p71

SCHELLIE, Don 1932-

Kidnapping Mr. Tubbs
HB - v55 - O '78 - p527

SCHELLIE, Don (continued)
  KR - v46 - N 15 '78 - p1254
  SLJ - v25 - O '78 - p159

SCHIESEL, Jane
  AuBYP SUP

  The Otis Redding Story
    BS - v33 - D 15 '73 - p430
    KR - v41 - N 1 '73 - p1209
    LJ - v98 - D 15 '73 - p3715
    NYTBR - D 30 '73 - p10
    PW - v204 - Jl 23 '73 - p70

SCHMITZ, Dorothy Childers

  Dorothy Hamill: Skate To Victory
    Cur R - v16 - D '77 - p363
    SLJ - v24 - D '77 - p65

  Hang Gliding
    SLJ - v25 - F '79 - p58

SCHODER, Judith

  Brotherhood Of Pirates
    Hi Lo - v1 - Ja '80 - p4
    SLJ - v26 - Ja '80 - p75

SCHOEN, Barbara 1924-
  ConAu 21R, SmATA 13, WrDr 80

  Place And A Time
    BL - v64 - S 1 '67 - p56
    CCB-B - v20 - My '67 - p146
    CSM - v59 - My 4 '67 - pB10
    HB - v43 - Ap '67 - p214
    KR - v35 - Ja 15 '67 - p68
    LJ - v92 - My 15 '67 - p2033
    NYTBR - v72 - Ap 16 '67 - p22
    SR - v50 - Mr 18 '67 - p36

SCHOOR, Gene 1921-
  AuBYP, ConAu 29R, SmATA 3

  *The Jim Thorpe Story: America's
  Greatest Athlete*
    KR - v19 - S 1 '51 - p490
    LJ - v77 - Ja 1 '52 - p70
    NYTBR - Ja 27 '52 - p28

  *The Story Of Ty Cobb: Baseball's
  Greatest Player*
    BL - v48 - My 15 '52 - p302
    CSM - My 15 '52 - p11

    KR - v20 - Ap 1 '52 - p229
    LJ - v77 - My 1 '52 - p796
    NYTBR - Ap 6 '52 - p32
    PW - v192 - O 9 '67 - p62
    SR - v35 - My 10 '52 - p59

SCHRAFF, Anne E 1939-
  AuBYP SUP, ConAu 49

  The Day The World Went Away
    KR - v41 - My 1 '73 - p522
    LJ - v99 - S 15 '74 - p2297

SCHROEDER, Lynn
  see Ostrander, Sheila (co-author)

SCHULMAN, L M 1934-
  ConAu 33R, SmATA 13

  *The Loners: Short Stories About
  The Young And Alienated*
    BL - v66 - My 1 '70 - p1094
    CCB-B - v23 - Je '70 - p166
    LJ - v95 - My 15 '70 - p1956
    NYTBR - Mr 1 '70 - p34
    PW - v197 - Ja 26 '70 - p278
    SR - v53 - My 9 '70 - p70

SCHULZ, Charles M 1922-
  ConAu 9R, ConLC 12, CurBio 60,
  SmATA 10, ThrBJA, WhoAmA 78

  *Always Stick Up For The
  Underbird*
    SLJ - v24 - S '77 - p137

  Nobody's Perfect, Charlie Brown
    B&B - v14 - Ag '69 - p38

  *You're The Greatest, Charlie
  Brown*
    BS - v30 - Mr 1 '71 - p532
    SLJ - v26 - D '79 - p100

SCHURFRANZ, Vivian 1925-
  ConAu 61, SmATA 13

  Roman Hostage
    BB - v3 - O '75 - p4
    BL - v71 - Ap 15 '75 - p868
    CCB-B - v29 - N '75 - p53
    NYTBR - Ag 24 '75 - p8
    PW - v207 - Ap 28 '75 - p45
    SLJ - v21 - Ap '75 - p70

SCHURMAN, Dewey

Athletic Fitness
BL - v72 - N 1 '75 - p338
LJ - v100 - N 15 '75 - p2164

SCHWARTZ, Alvin   1927-
AuBYP SUP, ChLR 3, ConAu 13R,
SmATA 4, WhoE 77

Tomfoolery
KR - v41 - D 15 '73 - p1354
NYTBR - D 2 '73 - p79

*A Twister Of Twists, A Tangler Of
Tongues*
ANQ - v11 - Mr '73 - p110
BL - v69 - Ja 1 '73 - p451
BW - v6 - D 3 '72 - p20
CCB-B - v26 - Je '73 - p162
CE - v49 - F '73 - p258
HB - v49 - Ap '73 - p153
JAF - v86 - Ap '73 - p198
KR - v40 - O 1 '72 - p1149
LJ - v97 - D 1 '72 - p3911
LJ - v98 - My 15 '73 - p1685
NYT - v122 - D 13 '72 - p67
NYTBR - N 19 '72 - p8
NYTBR - D 3 '72 - p82
NYTBR, pt.2 - N 5 '72 - p29
PW - v202 - O 30 '72 - p56
RT - v32 - N '78 - p148
SR - v4 - My 28 '77 - p33
SR - v55 - D 9 '72 - p79
Teacher - v93 - Mr '76 - p18

*Witcracks: Jokes And Jests From
American Folklore*
BL - v70 - D 15 '73 - p446
CCB-B - v27 - Mr '74 - p117
HB - v50 - F '74 - p62
Inst - v83 - My '74 - p96
JAF - v87 - Jl '74 - p246
LJ - v98 - D 15 '73 - p3709
NYT - v123 - D 10 '73 - p35
SWR - v1 - D 4 '73 - p28

SCHWEITZER, Byrd Baylor
see Baylor, Byrd

SCOGGIN, Margaret C   1905-1968
BioIn 2, BioIn 8, CurBio 52, CurBio
68

Escapes And Rescues
BL - v56 - Jl 1 '60 - p663
HB - v36 - Ag '60 - p317
LJ - v85 - Jl '60 - p2684

*More Chucklebait: Funny Stories
For Everyone*
BL - v46 - N 1 '49 - p84
CSM - N 17 '49 - p10
HB - v25 - N '49 - p541
KR - v17 - S 1 '49 - p477
LJ - v74 - D 1 '49 - p1830
NYT - O 23 '49 - p50

SCOPPETTONE, Sandra   1936-
AuBYP SUP, ConAu 5R, NatPD,
SmATA 9

Happy Endings Are All Alike
CCB-B - v32 - Ja '79 - p86
CLW - v50 - O '78 - p117
Inter BC - v10 - #6 '79 - p16
SLJ - v25 - F '79 - p65
WLB - v53 - D '78 - p341

The Late Great Me
BS - v36 - My '76 - p40
KR - v43 - N 15 '75 - p1304
KR - v43 - D 1 '75 - p1344
NYTBR - F 22 '76 - p38
PW - v208 - N 10 '75 - p47
SLJ - v22 - Ja '76 - p58

SCOTT, Ann Herbert   1926-
AuBYP SUP, BkP, ConAu 21R,
FourBJA

Sam
BL - v64 - F 15 '68 - p702
BW - v2 - Ap 7 '68 - p14
CCB-B - v21 - F '68 - p100
Inst - v77 - F '68 - p190
LJ - v93 - F 15 '68 - p862
Par - v43 - Ag '68 - p76

SCOTT, John   1912-1976
ConAu 5R, ConAu 69, SmATA 14,
WhoAm 74

China: The Hungry Dragon
BL - v64 - Ja 15 '68 - p589

SCOTT, John (continued)
BS - v27 - Ja 1 '68 - p392
CCB-B - v21 - Je '68 - p165
KR - v35 - N 15 '67 - p1376
LJ - v93 - Ja 15 '68 - p310
NYTBR - v72 - N 5 '67 - p32
SR - v51 - My 11 '68 - p42
SS - v59 - N '68 - p281

SCOTT, John Anthony   1916-
AuBYP SUP, ConAu 9R, DrAS 78H,
SmATA 23

Fanny Kemble's America
BL - v70 - S 1 '73 - p48
CCB-B - v27 - N '73 - p52
CE - v50 - N '73 - p102
CSM - v65 - N 7 '73 - pB6
Comw - v99 - N 23 '73 - p217
HB - v49 - D '73 - p599
KR - v41 - My 15 '73 - p572
LJ - v98 - My 15 '73 - p1656
LJ - v98 - My 15 '73 - p1692
LJ - v98 - D 15 '73 - p3691
NYTBR - Jl 15 '73 - p8
NYTBR - N 4 '73 - p52

SCOTT, William R

Lonesome Traveler
BL - v67 - S 15 '70 - p83
BS - v30 - Je 15 '70 - p119
LJ - v95 - My 15 '70 - p1970
LJ - v95 - Je 1 '70 - p2180
LJ - v95 - D 15 '70 - p4328
PW - v197 - F 23 '70 - p150

SCUDDER, Mildred Lee
see Lee, Mildred

SEARIGHT, Mary Williams   1918-
ConAu 29R, SmATA 17, WhoAmW
77

Your Career In Nursing
BL - v67 - D 1 '70 - p305
BL - v74 - D 15 '77 - p678
BS - v30 - O 15 '70 - p299
KR - v45 - N 15 '77 - p1210
LJ - v95 - D 15 '70 - p4368
SB - v6 - D '70 - p248
SLJ - v24 - Mr '78 - p139

SEAVER, Tom
see Drucker, Malka (co-author) -
*Tom Seaver: Portrait Of A
Pitcher*

SEED, Suzanne   1940-
AuBYP SUP, WhoAmW 77

Saturday's Child
AB - v52 - D 10 '73 - p2022
CCB-B - v26 - Jl '73 - p176
CSM - v67 - Ja 22 '75 - p8
Comw - v99 - N 23 '73 - p218
EJ - v63 - Ap '74 - p90
Inst - v83 - N '73 - p126
KR - v41 - Ap 15 '73 - p466
KR - v41 - D 15 '73 - p1361
LJ - v98 - My 15 '73 - p1692
NYTBR - Jl 15 '73 - p8
PW - v203 - Mr 12 '73 - p64

SEEWAGEN, George L

Tennis
BL - v65 - F 1 '69 - p596
KR - v36 - Ap 15 '68 - p474
LJ - v93 - My 15 '68 - p2128

SEGAL, Erich   1937-
ASpks, ConAu 25R, ConLC 10,
CurBio 71, WhoAm 78, WhoWorJ 72

Love Story
A Lib - v1 - Jl '70 - p715
Am - v122 - My 2 '70 - p478
Atl - v225 - Je '70 - p124
B&B - v16 - O '70 - p36
BL - v66 - Ap 15 '70 - p1022
BL - v67 - S 1 '70 - p54
BL - v67 - Ap 1 '71 - p654
BL - v67 - Jl 15 '71 - p934
BL - v68 - Jl 15 '72 - p980
BS - v29 - Mr 15 '70 - p474
CSM - v62 - Ap 30 '70 - p11
EJ - v62 - N '73 - p1189
HB - v46 - Ap '70 - p188
KR - v37 - D 1 '69 - p1287
LJ - v95 - F 1 '70 - p514
LJ - v95 - My 15 '70 - p1971
LJ - v95 - D 15 '70 - p4328
Lis - v85 - Ap 1 '71 - p420
NO - v9 - F 23 '70 - p19
NS - v80 - Ag 28 '70 - p249

SEGAL, Erich (continued)
NW - v75 - Mr 9 '70 - p94
NY - v46 - F 28 '70 - p116
NY - v46 - O 24 '70 - p170
NYT - v119 - F 13 '70 - p35
NYTBR - Mr 8 '70 - p31
Obs - Ag 23 '70 - p23
Obs - Ja 10 '71 - p23
PW - v196 - D 1 '69 - p39
PW - v198 - O 19 '70 - p55
SR - v53 - D 26 '70 - p30
Spec - v225 - Ag 29 '70 - p217
TLS - S 4 '70 - p965
TN - v27 - Ap '71 - p309

SEIDELMAN, James E   1926-
AuBYP, ConAu 25R, SmATA 6

Creating Mosaics
BL - v64 - Ap 1 '68 - p935
CC - v84 - D 13 '67 - p1602
KR - v35 - Ag 15 '67 - p963
LJ - v92 - D 15 '67 - p4618

Creating With Clay
KR - v35 - S 1 '67 - p1052

Creating With Paint
LJ - v93 - Ja 15 '68 - p295

Creating With Paper
Inst - v77 - Ap '68 - p155
KR - v35 - Ag 15 '67 - p963
LJ - v92 - D 15 '67 - p4618
SR - v51 - F 10 '68 - p70

SELDEN, George   1929-
ConAu X, FourBJA, MorBMP,
SmATA 4, TwCCW 78 (also known
as Thompson, George Selden)

The Cricket In Times Square
BL - v57 - D 15 '60 - p250
CSM - N 3 '60 - p1B
Comw - v73 - N 18 '60 - p207
GW - D 1 '61 - p6
HB - v36 - O '60 - p407
LJ - v85 - D 15 '60 - p4570
NS - v62 - N 10 '61 - p704
NYTBR, pt.2 - N 13 '60 - p50
NYTBR, pt.2 - N 8 '70 - p6
PW - v198 - O 19 '70 - p56
SR - v43 - N 12 '60 - p94
Spec - N 10 '61 - p682

Tucker's Countryside
BW - v3 - Jl 27 '69 - p12
CCB-B - v23 - D '69 - p64
Comw - v90 - My 23 '69 - p303
HB - v45 - Ag '69 - p412
KR - v37 - Ap 15 '69 - p443
LJ - v94 - Je 15 '69 - p2504
LJ - v94 - D 15 '69 - p4582
NO - v8 - Je 9 '69 - p23
NYTBR, pt.2 - My 4 '69 - p26
NYTBR, pt.2 - N 9 '69 - p62
PW - v195 - My 19 '69 - p70
SR - v52 - Je 28 '69 - p39

SELF, Margaret Cabell   1902-
AuBYP, ConAu 5R, OhA&B,
SmATA 24, WhoAm 78

*Sky Rocket: The Story Of A Little
Bay Horse*
Am - v123 - D 5 '70 - p497
BL - v67 - Mr 15 '71 - p621
BS - v30 - D 15 '70 - p415
LJ - v96 - Jl '71 - p2375
PW - v198 - S 28 '70 - p80

SELLERS, Naomi
ConAu 1R, ForWC 70

Cross My Heart
BL - v50 - S 15 '53 - p38
HB - v29 - D '53 - p470
KR - v21 - Je 15 '53 - p360
LJ - v78 - O 1 '53 - p1702
NYT - Ag 16 '53 - p14

SELSAM, Millicent E   1912-
BkP, ChLR 1, ConAu 9R, MorJA,
SmATA 1

Milkweed
BL - v64 - D 1 '67 - p451
CCB-B - v21 - O '67 - p33
CSM - v60 - D 21 '67 - p11
HB - v43 - O '67 - p607
Inst - v77 - D '67 - p124
KR - v35 - Ag 15 '67 - p963
LJ - v92 - O 15 '67 - p3842
NY - v43 - D 16 '67 - p163
SA - v217 - D '67 - p145
SB - v3 - D '67 - p234
SR - v50 - Ag 19 '67 - p35

SENN, J A

    The Wolf King And Other True
    Animal Stories
      Hi Lo - v1 - Ap '80 - p3

SETH, Marie

    Dream Of The Dead
      BL - v74 - D 15 '77 - p679

SEULING, Barbara   1937-
ConAu 61, SmATA 10

    The Last Cow On The White
    House Lawn
      BL - v75 - S 1 '78 - p53
      BW - S 10 '78 - pE6
      KR - v46 - Jl 15 '78 - p752
      PW - v213 - My 15 '78 - p104
      SLJ - v25 - S '78 - p148

SEYMOUR, William Kean   1887-
ConAu 9R, DcLEL, LongCTC, Who
74

    Happy Christmas
      BS - v28 - O 15 '68 - p298
      LJ - v93 - O 15 '68 - p3992
      LJ - v93 - N 15 '68 - p4300
      NYTBR - v73 - D 1 '68 - p76
      TLS - O 3 '68 - p1108

SHAPIRO, Milton J   1926-
AuBYP, ConAu 81

    All-Stars Of The Outfield
      BL - v67 - O 15 '70 - p196
      BS - v30 - Je 1 '70 - p106
      CCB-B - v24 - N '70 - p47
      KR - v38 - Ap 15 '70 - p471
      LJ - v95 - My 15 '70 - p1964
      PW - v197 - Je 15 '70 - p65
      SR - v53 - Je 27 '70 - p38

    Jackie Robinson Of The Brooklyn
    Dodgers
      PW - v192 - Jl 24 '67 - p58

SHAPIRO, Neal

    The World Of Horseback Riding
      BL - v73 - Mr 15 '77 - p1095

      LJ - v101 - D 15 '76 - p2594
      SLJ - v23 - Mr '77 - p148

SHAW, Arnold   1909-
AuBYP SUP, ConAu 1R, SmATA 4,
WhoWor 78

    The Rock Revolution: What's
    Happening In Today's Music
      AB - v44 - S 15 '69 - p775
      BL - v66 - S 15 '69 - p122
      CCB-B - v23 - O '69 - p30
      KR - v37 - Ap 1 '69 - p391
      LJ - v94 - Ap 15 '69 - p1612
      LJ - v94 - S 15 '69 - p3236
      NY - v45 - D 13 '69 - p212
      SN - v85 - Mr '70 - p36
      SR - v52 - S 13 '69 - p37

SHAW, Dale   1927-

    Titans Of The American Stage
      BL - v68 - Mr 1 '72 - p561
      BL - v68 - Mr 1 '72 - p567
      KR - v39 - O 15 '71 - p1136
      LJ - v97 - Ja 15 '72 - p291

SHAW, Richard   1923-
ConAu 37R, SmATA 12, WrDr 80

    Call Me Al Raft
      BS - v35 - F '76 - p363
      BS - v72 - D 15 '75 - p581
      KR - v43 - Jl 15 '75 - p783
      PW - v208 - D 1 '75 - p66
      SLJ - v22 - S '75 - p126

    Shape Up, Burke
      BL - v72 - My 1 '76 - p1271
      BS - v36 - Ja '77 - p324
      CCB-B - v30 - O '76 - p32
      J Read - v21 - O '77 - p86
      KR - v44 - My 15 '76 - p601
      PW - v210 - Jl 19 '76 - p132
      SLJ - v22 - Ap '76 - p93

SHEA, George

    Big Bad Ernie
      Hi Lo - v1 - Ja '80 - p4

    I Died Here
      Hi Lo - v1 - O '79 - p3
      SLJ - v26 - D '79 - p82

SHEA, George (continued)

Nightmare Nina
Hi Lo - v1 - F '80 - p4

SHEFFIELD, Janet N   1926-
ConAu 65

Not Just Sugar And Spice
CCB-B - v29 - Ap '76 - p133
KR - v43 - N 1 '75 - p1230
SLJ - v22 - Ja '76 - p50

SHELLEY, Mary   1797-1851
BrAu 19, HerW, OxEng, WhoHr&F,
WhoSciF

Frankenstein
CF - v56 - D '76 - p64
Choice - v7 - Mr '70 - p80
Choice - v11 - Je '74 - p603
KR - v41 - Ag 1 '73 - p840
SLP - v246 - Ag '74 - p90
TLS - O 16 '69 - p1215
Teacher - v92 - F '75 - p38
VV - v19 - Jl 25 '74 - p25

SHELTON, William   1919-
AuBYP SUP, AuNews 1, ConAu 5R,
SmATA 5, WhoS&SW 78

Flights Of The Astronauts
Am - v108 - Je 1 '63 - p807
CSM - My 9 '63 - p7B
Comw - v78 - My 24 '63 - p261
LJ - v88 - Ap 15 '63 - p1780

SHEMIN, Margaretha   1928-
ConAu 13R, SmATA 4

The Empty Moat
BL - v66 - F 1 '70 - p672
CLW - v42 - O '70 - p138
HB - v45 - D '69 - p679
KR - v37 - N 15 '69 - p1203
LJ - v94 - D 15 '69 - p4614
PW - v197 - Je 1 '70 - p67
TN - v26 - Je '70 - p426

The Little Riders
HB - v40 - F '64 - p59
LJ - v88 - D 15 '63 - p4858
NYTBR - Ja 19 '64 - p20
TLS - N 26 '64 - p1083

SHEPHERD, Elizabeth
AuBYP SUP, ConAu 33R, SmATA 4

The Discoveries Of Esteban The Black
CSM - v63 - Mr 20 '71 - p13
LJ - v95 - D 15 '70 - p4357
NYTBR - O 4 '70 - p30

SHERBURNE, Zoa Morin   1912-
ConAu 1R, FourBJA, SmATA 3,
WhoPNW

The Girl In The Mirror
Am - v115 - N 5 '66 - p553
BL - v63 - N 1 '66 - p327
BS - v26 - N 1 '66 - p296
CCB-B - v20 - N '66 - p48
CSM - v58 - N 3 '66 - pB12
KR - v34 - Ag 1 '66 - p764
LJ - v91 - N 15 '66 - p5765
NYTBR - v71 - N 6 '66 - p20
SR - v49 - O 22 '66 - p61

The Girl Who Knew Tomorrow
Am - v123 - D 5 '70 - p498
BL - v66 - Je 15 '70 - p1274
BS - v30 - My 1 '70 - p63
J Read - v22 - N '78 - p128
KR - v38 - Mr 1 '70 - p250
LJ - v95 - D 15 '70 - p4368

Leslie
EJ - v62 - Mr '73 - p480
KR - v40 - O 1 '72 - p1154
LJ - v98 - Ja 15 '73 - p270

Too Bad About The Haines Girl
BL - v63 - Jl 1 '67 - p1141
BS - v26 - Mr 1 '67 - p443
CCB-B - v20 - My '67 - p146
CSM - v59 - My 4 '67 - pB10
EJ - v56 - N '67 - p1222
J Ho E - v61 - S '69 - p478
J Read - v22 - N '78 - p128
KR - v35 - Mr 15 '67 - p349
LJ - v92 - Ap 15 '67 - p1753
NYTBR - v72 - Mr 5 '67 - p30
NYTBR - v72 - N 5 '67 - p64
SR - v50 - Mr 18 '67 - p36
SR - v52 - Jl 19 '69 - p42

Why Have The Birds Stopped Singing?
BL - v70 - Jl 1 '74 - p1202

SHERBURNE, Zoa Morin (continued)
J Read - v22 - N '78 - p127
KR - v42 - Mr 15 '74 - p301
LJ - v99 - My 15 '74 - p1488

SHERMAN, D R 1934-
ConAu 13R

Brothers Of The Sea
BL - v63 - N 15 '66 - p364
BS - v26 - N 1 '66 - p285
KR - v34 - Jl 15 '66 - p712
LJ - v91 - O 15 '66 - p4977
NYTBR - v71 - S 25 '66 - p53
PW - v190 - Jl 18 '66 - p74
TLS - O 6 '66 - p922

SHEVELSON, Joseph

Roller Skating
Hi Lo - v1 - Ap '80 - p4
SLJ - v26 - S '79 - p147

SHIRER, William 1904-
ConAu 9R, CurBio 62, DcLB 4,
OxAm, TwCA SUP, WhoWor 78

Rise And Fall Of Adolph Hitler
BL - v57 - Je 15 '61 - p641
CSM - My 11 '61 - p4B
HB - v37 - Ag '61 - p351
KR - v29 - F 1 '61 - p114
LJ - v86 - Ap 15 '61 - p1698
NYTBR, pt.2 - My 14 '61 - p12
Time - v78 - Ag 4 '61 - p73

SHORE, June Lewis
AuBYP SUP, AuNews 1

Summer Storm
BL - v74 - S 1 '77 - p44
CCB-B - v30 - Je '77 - p166
PW - v211 - F 14 '77 - p83
SLJ - v23 - My '77 - p71

SHOTWELL, Louisa R 1902-
ConAu 1R, MorBMP, SmATA 3,
ThrBJA, TwCCW 78

Adam Bookout
BL - v64 - Ja 15 '68 - p595
BW - v1 - N 5 '67 - p22
CCB-B - v21 - F '68 - p100
CE - v44 - My '68 - p561

CSM - v60 - F 1 '68 - p11
Comw - v87 - N 10 '67 - p177
Comw - v89 - F 21 '69 - p644
HB - v44 - F '68 - p67
KR - v35 - O 15 '67 - p1272
LJ - v92 - N 15 '67 - p4255
NYTBR - v72 - N 5 '67 - p43
PW - v192 - S 18 '67 - p67
SR - v50 - O 21 '67 - p43

SHREVE, Susan Richards

*The Nightmares Of Geranium
Street*
BW - Ap 8 '79 - pL2
RT - v32 - F '79 - p607

SIEGAL, Mordecai

The Good Dog Book
BL - v74 - D 1 '77 - p609
KR - v45 - Ag 1 '77 - p844
Kliatt - v13 - Spring '79 - p57
PW - v211 - Je 20 '77 - p65
SR - v5 - N 26 '77 - p40

SIEGEL, Bertram M
see Stone, A Harris (co-author) -
Take A Balloon

SIEGEL, Dorothy Schainman 1932-
ConAu 9R, ForWC 70, WhoAmW 72

*Winners: Eight Special Young
People*
BL - v74 - Ap 15 '78 - p1341

SILVERBERG, Robert 1930?-
ConAu 1R, ConLC 7, ConSFA,
SmATA 13, ThrBJA, WhoAm 78

The Auk, The Dodo And The Oryx
BL - v63 - Jl 15 '67 - p1191
CCB-B - v20 - Jl '67 - p176
Inst - v130 - Ap '71 - p136
KR - v35 - Ap 1 '67 - p432
LJ - v92 - Je 15 '67 - p2464
NYTBR, pt.2 - v72 - My 7 '67 - p34
SB - v3 - S '67 - p135
SR - v50 - Je 17 '67 - p36

Planet Of Death
LJ - v92 - N 15 '67 - p4257
NYTBR - v72 - Mr 26 '67 - p22

SILVERBERG, Robert (continued)
NYTBR - v72 - N 5 '67 - p64

Three Survived
KR - v37 - Ap 15 '69 - p453
LJ - v94 - Ap 15 '69 - p1800
PW - v195 - Ap 7 '69 - p56

Vanishing Giants: The Story Of The Sequoias
BW - v3 - Jl 6 '69 - p10
CSM - v61 - My 15 '69 - p11
KR - v37 - Ap 1 '69 - p391
LJ - v94 - D 15 '69 - p4614
SB - v5 - S '69 - p150

World's Fair 1992
LJ - v95 - Je 15 '70 - p2316
NYTBR - S 20 '70 - p47

SILVERSTEIN, Alvin 1933-
AuBYP SUP, ConAu 49, SmATA 8

Alcoholism
ACSB - v9 - Spring '76 - p39
CLW - v47 - My '76 - p452
Cur R - v16 - Ag '77 - p175
KR - v43 - N 1 '75 - p1245
NYTBR - Ja 18 '76 - p12
SB - v12 - S '76 - p100
SLJ - v22 - F '76 - p49

Bionics
BL - v67 - F 1 '71 - p453
CE - v47 - My '71 - p438
KR - v38 - S 15 '70 - p1057
LJ - v96 - My 15 '71 - p1817
SB - v6 - Mr '71 - p327

The Chemicals We Eat And Drink
BL - v70 - N 1 '73 - p294
CCB-B - v27 - F '74 - p101
HB - v50 - Ap '74 - p171
KR - v41 - Ap 1 '73 - p393
KR - v41 - D 15 '73 - p1355
LJ - v99 - Mr 15 '74 - p894
SB - v10 - My '74 - p64

Heart Disease
BL - v73 - Ja 1 '77 - p669
CCB-B - v30 - My '77 - p150
SB - v13 - S '77 - p86
SLJ - v23 - Mr '77 - p148

The Left-Hander's World
BL - v74 - Ja 1 '78 - p749
CCB-B - v31 - Je '78 - p166
HB - v54 - Je '78 - p308
SB - v14 - S '78 - p69
SLJ - v24 - Ap '78 - p88

SILVERSTEIN, Virginia B
see Silverstein, Alvin (co-author)

SIMON, Hilda 1921-
ConAu 77, FourBJA, IlsCB 1967

Chameleons And Other Quick-Change Artists
BL - v70 - F 15 '74 - p652
BL - v70 - F 15 '74 - p659
BS - v33 - D 1 '73 - p404
LJ - v99 - F 1 '74 - p374
SB - v10 - S '74 - p132

SIMON, R E
see Davis, Charles (co-author)

SIMON, Ruth 1918-
AuBYP

A Castle For Tess
KR - v35 - My 15 '67 - p602
LJ - v92 - N 15 '67 - p4270

SIMS, William

West Side Cop
LJ - v96 - Ap 15 '71 - p1514

SINGER, Isaac Bashevis 1904-
ChLR 1, ConAu 1R, ConLC 11, CurBio 69, SmATA 3, ThrBJA, TwCCW 78

Zlateh The Goat And Other Stories
Am - v115 - N 5 '66 - p554
Atl - v218 - D '66 - p150
BL - v63 - N 15 '66 - p378
BS - v26 - D 1 '66 - p342
CCB-B - v20 - Ja '67 - p79
CE - v44 - D '67 - p262
CSM - v58 - N 3 '66 - pB10
Comw - v85 - N 11 '66 - p174
HB - v42 - D '66 - p712
KR - v34 - O 1 '66 - p1045
LJ - v91 - D 15 '66 - p6197

SINGER, Isaac Bashevis (continued)
    NYRB - v7 - D 15 '66 - p29
    NYTBR - v71 - O 9 '66 - p34
    NYTBR - v71 - D 4 '66 - p66
    PW - v190 - O 10 '66 - p74
    SR - v49 - N 12 '66 - p49
    TCR - v68 - D '66 - p275
    TN - v23 - Ja '67 - p196

SKIDMORE, Hubert 1909?-1946
ConBio 46, DcNAA, WhoAm 2

    River Rising
    BL - v36 - S '39 - p19
    HB - v15 - S '39 - p302
    LJ - v64 - S 1 '39 - p663
    NYTBR - Ag 20 '39 - p10

SKIPPER, G C
see Sims, William (co-author)

SKIRROW, Desmond

    The Case Of The Silver Egg
    B&B - v12 - Mr '67 - p60
    BL - v65 - Ja 1 '69 - p499
    CSM - v58 - N 3 '66 - pB4
    HB - v45 - Ap '69 - p173
    KR - v36 - O 15 '68 - p1164
    Obs - D 4 '66 - p28
    PW - v194 - O 7 '68 - p54

SKULICZ, Matthew 1944-
ConAu 37R

    Right On, Shane
    KR - v39 - D 1 '71 - p1261
    LJ - v97 - Ap 15 '72 - p1619
    NYTBR - Je 18 '72 - p8

SLOANE, Eugene A 1926-
ConAu 65

    The Complete Book Of Bicycling
    A Lib - v4 - F '73 - p98
    BL - v67 - F 15 '71 - p467
    BW - v6 - Ja 2 '72 - p6
    LJ - v95 - D 1 '70 - p4191
    LJ - v96 - Ja 15 '71 - p294
    LJ - v96 - Mr 1 '71 - p792
    LJ - v97 - Ap 15 '72 - p1388
    NYTBR - Je 4 '72 - p8
    NYTBR - Je 2 '74 - p14
    PW - v197 - Je 8 '70 - p156

    Trav - v136 - Jl '71 - p77
    WSJ - v176 - N 5 '70 - p14
    WSJ - v176 - D 8 '70 - p22

SLOTE, Alfred 1926-
AuBYP SUP, SmATA 8

    The Hotshot
    BL - v73 - My 15 '77 - p1424
    BW - Mr 11 '79 - pF2
    CCB-B - v30 - Jl '77 - p180
    Hi Lo - v1 - S '79 - p6
    NYTBR - O 9 '77 - p28
    RT - v31 - Ap '78 - p842
    SLJ - v23 - My '77 - p80
    Teacher - v96 - My '79 - p125

    My Father, The Coach
    CCB-B - v26 - N '72 - p49
    KR - v40 - S 1 '72 - p1028
    KR - v40 - D 15 '72 - p1414
    LJ - v97 - D 15 '72 - p4088
    Teacher - v91 - Ap '74 - p87
    Teacher - v93 - S '75 - p57

    My Trip To Alpha I
    BL - v75 - O 15 '78 - p391
    CCB-B - v32 - Ja '79 - p88
    KR - v46 - N 15 '78 - p1249
    SLJ - v25 - O '78 - p150

    Stranger On The Ball Club
    BL - v67 - Mr 15 '71 - p622
    CCB-B - v24 - D '70 - p67
    LJ - v95 - D 15 '70 - p4378
    SR - v54 - Jl 17 '71 - p36
    Spectr - v47 - Mr '71 - p46
    Teacher - v93 - S '75 - p57

SMARIDGE, Norah Antoinette 1903-
AuBYP, ConAu 37R, SmATA 6

    The Mystery At Greystone Hall
    Hi Lo - v1 - F '80 - p3
    SLJ - v26 - D '79 - p99

    The Teen-Ager's Guide To
    Collecting Practically Anything
    BL - v69 - Mr 1 '73 - p645
    Hob - v78 - Ap '73 - p157
    KR - v40 - N 1 '72 - p1255
    LJ - v98 - Mr 15 '73 - p1016
    PW - v202 - D 18 '72 - p40

SMITH, Beatrice Schillinger
ConAu 57, SmATA 12

 The Road To Galveston
  BL - v70 - F 15 '74 - p659
  LJ - v99 - My 15 '74 - p1476

SMITH, Dennis E 1938-

 Report From Engine Co. 82
  AC - v87 - S '72 - p80
  A Lib - v3 - Je '72 - p682
  Am - v126 - My 20 '72 - p541
  BL - v68 - Ap 15 '72 - p693
  BS - v31 - F 1 '72 - p491
  BS - v33 - Ag 1 '73 - p215
  BW - v6 - Mr 12 '72 - p8
  BW - v7 - Ap 15 '73 - p13
  Comw - v97 - F 2 '73 - p399
  EJ - v62 - My '73 - p827
  HB - v48 - O '72 - p495
  JGE - v25 - Jl '73 - p155
  LJ - v97 - F 1 '72 - p492
  LJ - v97 - Jl '72 - p2496
  LJ - v97 - D 15 '72 - p4059
  NO - v11 - Mr 4 '72 - p23
  NW - v79 - Ja 24 '72 - p72
  NY - v47 - F 19 '72 - p116
  NYT - v121 - F 1 '72 - p35
  NYTBR - Ap 16 '72 - p20
  PW - v202 - D 11 '72 - p37
  SR - v55 - Ap 8 '72 - p68
  SR - v55 - D 2 '72 - p89
  TN - v29 - Ap '73 - p258
  Time - v99 - F 28 '72 - p82

SMITH, Doris Buchanan 1934-
AuBYP SUP, ConAu 69

 Up And Over
  BL - v72 - My 1 '76 - p1271
  HB - v52 - Ag '76 - p408
  KR - v44 - Mr 1 '76 - p262
  SLJ - v23 - S '76 - p139

SMITH, Howard K 1914-
BioNews 74, ConAu 45, CurBio 76,
IntMPA 78, WhoWor 78

 Washington, D.C.: The Story Of
 Our Nation's Capital
  BL - v64 - O 15 '67 - p275
  BS - v27 - My 1 '67 - p67
  HB - v43 - Ag '67 - p485

  KR - v35 - Mr 15 '67 - p356
  LJ - v92 - My 15 '67 - p2034
  NYTBR - v72 - My 28 '67 - p20
  PW - v191 - My 29 '67 - p64
  SR - v50 - Je 17 '67 - p36

SMITH, James P

 Pete Rose
  BL - v73 - Je 15 '77 - p1572
  SLJ - v23 - My '77 - p81

SMITH, Jay H

 Chris Evert
  BL - v72 - O 15 '75 - p307
  SLJ - v22 - D '75 - p69

 Olga Korbut
  CCB-B - v29 - O '75 - p34
  SLJ - v22 - S '75 - p96

SMITH, John
 see Seymour, William (co-author)

SMITH, LeRoi Tex 1934-
AuBYP SUP, ConAu 29R, WhoWest
74

 Fixing Up Motorcycles
  BL - v70 - Ap 1 '74 - p844
  KR - v41 - Jl 1 '73 - p744
  LJ - v99 - Ap 1 '74 - p1048
  LJ - v99 - Ap 15 '74 - p1239

 Make Your Own Hot Rod
  BL - v68 - Ja 15 '72 - p407
  BL - v68 - Ja 15 '72 - p431
  LJ - v96 - O 1 '71 - p3150
  LJ - v96 - N 15 '71 - p3919

SMITH, Moyne
AuBYP

 Seven Plays And How To Produce
 Them
  BL - v64 - Jl 15 '68 - p1288
  CCB-B - v22 - O '68 - p34
  KR - v36 - Je 1 '68 - p611
  LJ - v93 - Ap 15 '68 - p1816
  SR - v51 - O 19 '68 - p37

SMITH, Nancy Covert 1935-
ConAu 57, SmATA 12

SMITH, Nancy Covert (continued)

Josie's Handful Of Quietness
CLW - v47 - D '75 - p235
SLJ - v22 - S '75 - p112

SMITH, Pauline Coggeshall 1908-
ConAu 29R

Brush Fire!
BL - v75 - Je 15 '79 - p1533
Hi Lo - v1 - S '79 - p2
SLJ - v26 - S '79 - p148

SMITH, Robert 1905-

*Hit Hard! Throw Hard!: The
Secrets Of Power Baseball*
BL - v74 - O 1 '77 - p303
KR - v45 - Ag 15 '77 - p855
SLJ - v24 - D '77 - p63

SMITH, Sally Liberman 1929-
ConAu 21R

Nobody Said It's Easy
BL - v61 - My 15 '65 - p915
CE - v42 - F '66 - p382
Choice - v2 - Jl '65 - p325
LJ - v90 - F 1 '65 - p657

SMITS, Ted 1905-
ConAu 77, WhoAm 78

Soccer For The American Boy
LJ - v95 - D 15 '70 - p4382
Teacher - v95 - My '78 - p109

SNOW, Donald Clifford
see Fall, Thomas

SNOW, Edward Rowe 1902-
ConAu 9R, CurBio 58

*Supernatural Mysteries And Other
Tales*
KR - v42 - O 1 '74 - p1095
PW - v206 - D 30 '74 - p97

SNYDER, Anne 1922-
ConAu 37R, SmATA 4, WrDr 80

First Step
CCB-B - v29 - Je '76 - p165
Kliatt - v11 - Winter '77 - p8

*My Name Is Davy. I'm An
Alcoholic*
BS - v37 - Jl '77 - p127
CCB-B - v30 - Jl '77 - p180
EJ - v66 - S '77 - p77
KR - v45 - Ja 15 '77 - p49
Kliatt - v12 - Fall '78 - p14
NYTBR - My 1 '77 - p46
PW - v211 - Ja 17 '77 - p84
SLJ - v23 - F '77 - p74
WLB - v52 - My '78 - p721

SNYDER, Gerald Seymour 1933-
ConAu 61

*The Right To Be Let Alone:
Privacy In The United States*
BL - v71 - Je 15 '75 - p1077
KR - v43 - Mr 15 '75 - p321
SLJ - v22 - S '75 - p126

SNYDER, Zilpha Keatley 1927-
ConAu 9R, MorBMP, SmATA 1,
ThrBJA, TwCCW 78

Black And Blue Magic
BL - v62 - My 1 '66 - p878
CCB-B - v20 - N '66 - p48
HB - v42 - Je '66 - p308
Inst - v75 - Je '66 - p139
KR - v34 - F 1 '66 - p108
LJ - v91 - Ap 15 '66 - p2214
NYTBR - v71 - Jl 24 '66 - p22

The Egypt Game
BL - v63 - My 15 '67 - p998
CCB-B - v20 - Je '67 - p160
HB - v43 - Ap '67 - p209
KR - v35 - F 15 '67 - p200
LJ - v92 - Ap 15 '67 - p1742
NYTBR - v72 - Jl 23 '67 - p22
NYTBR, pt.2 - N 5 '72 - p42
PW - v191 - Ap 24 '67 - p95
Par - v43 - Je '68 - p68
SR - v50 - My 13 '67 - p55

Eyes In The Fishbowl
BL - v64 - My 15 '68 - p1097
CCB-B - v21 - Jl '68 - p181
CSM - v60 - My 2 '68 - pB9
EJ - v58 - F '69 - p297
HB - v44 - Ap '68 - p182
KR - v36 - F 1 '68 - p124
LJ - v93 - Ap 15 '68 - p1804

SNYDER, Zilpha Keatley (continued)
    NYTBR - v73 - My 26 '68 - p30
    PW - v193 - Mr 11 '68 - p49
    SR - v51 - My 11 '68 - p41

SOBOL, Donald J 1924-
  ConAu 1R, FourBJA, SmATA 1,
  TwCCW 78, WhoAm 78

    Encyclopedia Brown Gets His
    Man
      BL - v64 - F 1 '68 - p643
      CC - v84 - D 13 '67 - p1602
      CSM - v59 - O 5 '67 - p10
      KR - v35 - O 1 '67 - p1209
      LJ - v92 - N 15 '67 - p4271
      NYTBR - v72 - N 5 '67 - p44
      PW - v193 - Ja 8 '68 - p67

SOBOL, Ken 1938-
  WrDr 80

    The Clock Museum
      CC - v84 - D 13 '67 - p1602
      KR - v35 - O 1 '67 - p1214
      LJ - v92 - D 15 '67 - p4618
      SB - v3 - D '67 - p206

SORENSEN, Robert

    Shadow Of The Past: True Life
    Sports Stories
      Hi Lo - v1 - Mr '80 - p5

SORENSEN, Virginia E 1912-
  ConAu 13R, MorBMP, MorJA,
  SmATA 2, TwCA SUP, TwCCW 78,
  WhoAm 78

    Miracles On Maple Hill
      BL - v53 - S 1 '56 - p30
      Comw - v65 - N 16 '56 - p184
      Inst - v82 - N '72 - p136
      KR - v24 - Ag 1 '56 - p519
      LJ - v81 - S 15 '56 - p2045
      NS - v73 - My 26 '67 - p732
      NYTBR - Ag 26 '56 - p28
      TLS - My 25 '67 - p449

SORRENTINO, Joseph N 1930?-
  ConAu 49, SmATA 6, WhoWest 78

    Up From Never
      BL - v68 - Ap 1 '72 - p665

    BS - v31 - Ja 1 '72 - p448
    KR - v39 - Jl 1 '71 - p731
    KR - v39 - Jl 15 '71 - p752
    LJ - v96 - S 1 '71 - p2630
    NYTBR - Ap 9 '78 - p39
    PW - v200 - Jl 5 '71 - p44
    PW - v203 - Mr 19 '73 - p74
    TN - v28 - Ap '72 - p313

SORTOR, Toni 1939-
  ConAu 61, SmATA 12 (also known as
  Sortor, June Elizabeth)

    Adventures Of B.J., The Amateur
    Detective
      KR - v43 - Je 15 '75 - p661
      SLJ - v21 - My '75 - p70

SOULE, Gardner 1913-
  AuBYP SUP, ConAu 5R, SmATA 14

    UFO's And IFO's: A Factual
    Report On Flying Saucers
      BL - v64 - Mr 1 '68 - p788
      KR - v35 - D 1 '67 - p1430
      LJ - v92 - D 15 '67 - p4628

SOUTH, Wesley W 1919-
  WhoBlA 77

    Up From The Ghetto
      Bl W - v19 - Jl '70 - p84
      EJ - v60 - My '71 - p657

SPARKS, Beatrice 1918-
  ConAu 97 (revealed as the author of
  Go Ask Alice, published anony-
  mously)

    Go Ask Alice
      CSM - N 11 '71 - pB6
      LJ - v97 - Mr 15 '72 - p1174

    Jay's Journal
      Hi Lo - v2 - S '80 - p1
    see also Anonymous

SPEARE, Elizabeth 1908-
  ConAu 1R, CurBio 59, MorBMP,
  MorJA, SmATA 5, TwCCW 78

    Witch Of Blackbird Pond
      BL - v55 - D 15 '58 - p222
      CSM - D 18 '58 - p7
      HB - v34 - D '58 - p472

SPEARE, Elizabeth (continued)
    KR - v26 - Ag 1 '58 - p548
    LJ - v83 - D 15 '58 - p3579
    NYTBR, pt.2 - N 2 '58 - p24
    SE - v23 - D '59 - p406
    SR - v41 - N 1 '58 - p62

SPENCE, Martha

There Really Is Sound
    Hi Lo - v2 - O '80 - p4

SPENCER, John Wallace

Limbo Of The Lost
    PW - v204 - Jl 23 '73 - p72
    Yacht - v132 - Jl '72 - p74

SPENCER, Zane   1935-
    ConAu 89

Branded Runaway
    BL - v76 - Jl 15 '80 - p1673
    Hi Lo - v2 - S '80 - p4
    SLJ - v26 - Ag '80 - p71

SPIEGELMAN, Judith M
    ConAu 21R, SmATA 5

With George Washington At Valley Forge
    CCB-B - v21 - F '68 - p101

SPINO, Michael

Running Home
    LJ - v103 - Ja 1 '78 - p102

SPLAVER, Sarah   1921-
    AuBYP SUP, ConAu 85, WhoAmW 77, WhoE 77, WhoWorJ 72

Your Career If You're Not Going To College
    BL - v68 - D 1 '71 - p329
    PGJ - v51 - D '72 - p290

SPRAGUE, Gretchen   1926-
    AuBYP, ConAu 13R

A Question Of Harmony
    BL - v62 - N 1 '65 - p269
    BS - v25 - My 15 '65 - p101
    CCB-B - v18 - Je '65 - p155
    HB - v41 - Je '65 - p285

    KR - v33 - F 1 '65 - p111
    LJ - v90 - Ap 15 '65 - p2038
    NYTBR - v70 - My 9 '65 - p26

SPRAGUE, Jane

That New Girl
    WLB - v51 - F '77 - p491

SPRINGER, Marilyn Harris
    see Harris, Marilyn

SPYKER, John Howland

Little Lives
    BL - v75 - Ja 1 '79 - p738
    BOT - v20 - F '79 - p57
    LJ - v104 - F 15 '79 - p515
    Time - v113 - Mr 12 '79 - p94
    VV - v24 - F 12 '79 - p90
    WCRB - v5 - Ja '79 - p26

SPYRI, Johanna   1827?-1901
    BioIn 3, BioIn 4, JBA 51, OxGer, SmATA 19, WhoChL

Heidi
    B&B - v14 - Ag '69 - p46
    NYTBR - N 13 '55 - p42

STADTMAUER, Saul A

Visions Of The Future: Magic Boards
    SLJ - v24 - My '78 - p64

STAFFORD, Jean   1915-1979
    ConAu 1R, ConAu 85, ConNov 76, DcLB 2, OxAm, SmATA 22N

Elephi, The Cat With The High I.Q.
    NYTBR - S 16 '61 - p38
    PW - v190 - Ag 29 '66 - p351

STAMBLER, Irwin   1924-
    AuBYP, ConAu 5R, SmATA 5, WrDr 80

Weather Instruments: How They Work
    KR - v36 - Mr 15 '68 - p349
    LJ - v93 - O 15 '68 - p3974
    SB - v4 - My '68 - p33

STANFORD, Don   1918-
ConAu 53, WrDr 80

The Red Car
BL - v51 - D 15 '54 - p178
KR - v22 - Jl 15 '54 - p441
NYTBR, pt.2 - N 14 '54 - p8
SR - v37 - N 13 '54 - p94

STANGER, Margaret A

That Quail, Robert
BL - v63 - O 1 '66 - p146
BS - v26 - S 1 '66 - p200
BW - v2 - Mr 3 '68 - p18
HB - v43 - Ap '67 - p215
KR - v34 - Je 15 '66 - p609
LJ - v91 - Jl '66 - p3458
LJ - v91 - S 15 '66 - p4374
PW - v193 - Ja 15 '68 - p87
SB - v2 - Mr '67 - p297
TLS - N 2 '67 - p1046

STEELE, William O   1917-1979
ConAu 5R, MorJA, SmATA 1,
TwCCW 78, WhoAm 78

The Old Wilderness Road
LJ - v94 - F 15 '69 - p888
NO - v8 - Ap 28 '69 - p19
NYTBR - v73 - N 3 '68 - p26

STEIN, Cathi

Elton John
WLB - v51 - D '76 - p314

STEIN, R Conrad
see Hannahs, Herbert (co-author)
Hardin, Gail (co-author)

STEINBECK, John   1902-1968
ConAu 1R, ConAu 25R, ConLC 13,
OxAm, SmATA 9, WhAm 5,
WhoTwCL

The Pearl
Atl - v180 - D '47 - p138
BL - v44 - D 15 '47 - p152
Comw - v47 - Ja 23 '48 - p377
KR - v15 - O 1 '47 - p551
LJ - v72 - N 1 '47 - p1540
NY - v23 - D 27 '47 - p59
NYTBR - N 30 '47 - p4

New R - v117 - D 22 '47 - p28
SR - v30 - N 22 '47 - p14
Time - v50 - D 22 '47 - p90

Travels With Charley
Atl - v210 - Ag '62 - p138
BL - v58 - Jl 1 '62 - p748
BL - v58 - Jl 15 '62 - p784
CSM - Ag 2 '62 - p7
KR - v30 - Mr 1 '62 - p272
LJ - v87 - Je 15 '62 - p2378
NY - v38 - S 8 '62 - p152
NYTBR - Jl 29 '62 - p5
SR - v45 - S 1 '62 - p31
Spec - O 19 '62 - p604
TLS - N 2 '62 - p843
Time - v80 - Ag 10 '62 - p70

STERLING, Philip   1907-
ConAu 49, SmATA 8

*Four Took Freedom: The Lives Of
Harriet Tubman, Frederick
Douglas, Robert Small, And
Blanche K. Bruce*
NYTBR - v117 - Je 7 '68 - p37

*Quiet Rebels: Four Puerto Rican
Leaders*
KR - v36 - S 1 '68 - p993
PW - v194 - Ag 5 '68 - p59

Sea And Earth
BL - v67 - D 1 '70 - p305
CCB-B - v24 - N '70 - p49
CE - v47 - Mr '71 - p316
CSM - v62 - My 7 '70 - pB7
Comw - v92 - My 22 '70 - p250
HB - v46 - Je '70 - p304
KR - v38 - My 15 '70 - p568
LJ - v95 - S 15 '70 - p3068
NYTBR - My 10 '70 - p26
PW - v197 - Je 1 '70 - p68
SB - v6 - S '70 - p133
SR - v53 - S 19 '70 - p35

STERNE, Emma   1894-1971
ConAu 5R, MorJA, SmATA 6,
TwCA, TwCA SUP

The Long Black Schooner
CSM - v60 - N 7 '68 - pB12
Comw - v91 - F 27 '70 - p584
NYTBR - v73 - My 5 '68 - p49

STEVENSON, William 1925-
ConAu 13R, TwCCW 78, WrDr 80

The Bushbabies
BL - v62 - N 15 '65 - p333
CLW - v37 - F '66 - p379
CSM - v57 - N 4 '65 - pB9
HB - v41 - D '65 - p613
Inst - v75 - F '66 - p160
KR - v33 - Ag 15 '65 - p821
LJ - v91 - Mr 15 '66 - p1710
NYTBR - v70 - D 26 '65 - p18
Punch - v250 - Ap 20 '66 - p594
SR - v49 - Ja 22 '66 - p45
TLS - My 19 '66 - p437

STEWART, Jo

The Promise Ring
BL - v75 - Je 15 '79 - p1533
Hi Lo - v1 - O '79 - p3

STEWART, Mary Florence Elinor
1916-
ConAu 1R, ConLC 7, SmATA 12,
TwCW, WhoAmW 77, WorAu

Ludo And The Star Horse
BL - v71 - My 15 '75 - p967
GP - v15 - Mr '77 - p3077
KR - v43 - Ap 1 '75 - p376
PW - v207 - Ap 28 '75 - p45
SLJ - v22 - S '75 - p112
TLS - D 6 '74 - p1380

STEWART, Ramona 1922-
ASpks, ConAu 1R, ForWC 70

Sixth Sense
KR - v47 - Ja 1 '79 - p32
PW - v215 - Ja 15 '79 - p115

STINE, H William

Best Friend
BL - v74 - Je 15 '78 - p1613
Cur R - v17 - My '78 - p87

STINE, Megan
see Stine, H William (co-author)

STOCKDALE, Bill
see Butterworth, Ben (co-author) -
Danger In The Mountains
The Desert Chase
The Diamond Smugglers
The Island Of Helos
Jim And The Dolphin
Jim And The Sun Goddess
Jim In Training
The Missing Aircraft
Prisoner Of Pedro Cay
The Shipwreckers
The Sniper At Zimba
The Temple Of Mantos

STODDARD, Hope 1900-
AuBYP, ConAu 49, SmATA 6

Famous American Women
BL - v67 - O 1 '70 - p141
BS - v30 - Jl 1 '70 - p147
CCB-B - v24 - O '70 - p34
KR - v38 - My 15 '70 - p569
LJ - v95 - S 15 '70 - p3068
PW - v197 - Je 1 '70 - p68
SR - v53 - Ag 22 '70 - p53

STOLZ, Mary Slattery 1920-
ConAu 5R, ConLC 12, MorBMP,
MorJA, SmATA 10, TwCCW 78,
WhoAm 78

And Love Replied
BL - v55 - D 1 '58 - p188
HB - v34 - D '58 - p489
KR - v26 - Ag 15 '58 - p609
LJ - v83 - D 15 '58 - p3581
NYTBR - N 9 '58 - p48
SR - v41 - N 1 '58 - p62

By The Highway Home
BL - v68 - Ja 1 '72 - p395
BL - v68 - Ja 15 '72 - p431
BS - v31 - N 15 '71 - p387
CCB-B - v25 - Mr '72 - p115

STOLZ, Mary Slattery (continued)
CE - v49 - O '72 - p30
CLW - v43 - Ap '72 - p481
CSM - v63 - N 11 '71 - pB5
HB - v47 - O '71 - p486
KR - v39 - Ag 15 '71 - p883
LJ - v96 - O 15 '71 - p3480
NYTBR - Ag 24 '71 - p8
PW - v200 - S 20 '71 - p49
SR - v54 - N 13 '71 - p61
Teacher - v91 - N '73 - p131

Cat In The Mirror
BB - v4 - F '76 - p4
BL - v72 - Ja 1 '76 - p628
CCB-B - v29 - D '75 - p70
HB - v51 - D '75 - p597
KR - v43 - S 1 '75 - p999
LA - v53 - My '76 - p522
PW - v208 - Ag 18 '75 - p68
SLJ - v22 - O '75 - p102
SLJ - v25 - S '78 - p43

The Edge Of Next Year
BL - v71 - S 15 '74 - p102
BS - v34 - Ja 15 '75 - p475
CCB-B - v28 - Mr '75 - p123
Choice - v12 - N '75 - p1134
Choice - v14 - N '77 - p1178
EJ - v64 - Ap '75 - p90
HB - v50 - O '74 - p144
KR - v42 - O 15 '74 - p1111
Kliatt - v13 - Fall '79 - p14
LJ - v99 - D 15 '74 - p3273
PT - v9 - Jl '75 - p95
PW - v206 - Ag 5 '74 - p58

Hospital Zone
BL - v53 - O 15 '56 - p97
HB - v32 - D '56 - p463
KR - v24 - Ag 15 '56 - p578
LJ - v81 - D 15 '56 - p3002
NYTBR, pt.2 - N 18 '56 - p10
SR - v39 - N 17 '56 - p70

In A Mirror
Atl - v192 - D '53 - p98
BL - v50 - O 1 '53 - p59
HB - v29 - O '53 - p360
HB - v29 - D '53 - p469
KR - v21 - Jl 15 '53 - p431
LJ - v78 - O 15 '53 - p1862
NYTBR, pt.2 - N 15 '53 - p10
SR - v36 - N 14 '53 - p68

Leap Before You Look
BS - v32 - Ja 15 '73 - p483
CCB-B - v26 - S '72 - p18
CE - v49 - D '72 - p146
KR - v40 - Ap 15 '72 - p486
LJ - v97 - S 15 '72 - p2967
NYTBR - S 3 '72 - p8
SR - v55 - Je 17 '72 - p75

The Sea Gulls Woke Me
BL - v48 - O 15 '51 - p69
CSM - S 13 '51 - p13
HB - v27 - S '51 - p335
KR - v19 - Jl 1 '51 - p322
LJ - v76 - D 1 '51 - p2017
NYTBR - S 16 '51 - p28
SR - v34 - O 20 '51 - p39

To Tell Your Love
BL - v47 - S 15 '50 - p45
BL - v47 - O 1 '50 - p63
HB - v26 - S '50 - p384
KR - v18 - Ag 1 '50 - p424
LJ - v75 - N 1 '50 - p1914
NYTBR - O 8 '50 - p34
SR - v33 - N 11 '50 - p50

A Wonderful, Terrible Time
BL - v64 - D 15 '67 - p504
BW - v1 - N 5 '67 - p22
CCB-B - v21 - F '68 - p102
CE - v46 - Ap '70 - p367
Comw - v87 - N 10 '67 - p176
Comw - v89 - F 21 '69 - p647
HB - v43 - D '67 - p754
Inst - v77 - Ap '68 - p155
KR - v35 - S 15 '67 - p1136
LJ - v92 - O 15 '67 - p3856
NYTBR - v72 - N 5 '67 - p43
PW - v192 - N 27 '67 - p43

STONAKER, Frances Benson
AuBYP SUP

Famous Mathematicians
KR - v34 - Ja 15 '66 - p61
LJ - v91 - My 15 '66 - p2713
SB - v2 - D '66 - p175

STONE, A Harris
AuBYP SUP

Plants Are Like That
BL - v65 - S 15 '68 - p124

STONE, A Harris (continued)
    CE - v46 - S '69 - p38
    CSM - v60 - My 2 '68 - pB8
    KR - v36 - Mr 1 '68 - p267
    LJ - v93 - Ap 15 '68 - p1804
    SB - v5 - My '69 - p50
    TLS - D 4 '69 - p1401

   Rocks And Rills: A Look At
   Geology
    BL - v64 - N 1 '67 - p339
    CCB-B - v21 - O '67 - p34
    CE - v45 - O '68 - p92
    HB - v43 - O '67 - p611
    KR - v35 - Je 15 '67 - p699
    LJ - v92 - O 15 '67 - p3856
    SA - v217 - D '67 - p142
    SB - v3 - D '67 - p217
    SR - v50 - Jl 22 '67 - p43

   Take A Balloon
    KR - v35 - O 1 '67 - p1214
    LJ - v93 - Ja 15 '68 - p296
    PW - v192 - N 13 '67 - p80
    SB - v3 - Mr '68 - p299

STONE, Patti   1926-
  ConAu 5R

   Judy George: Student Nurse
    BS - v26 - My 1 '66 - p59
    CCB-B - v20 - Ja '67 - p81
    KR - v34 - Ja 15 '66 - p64
    LJ - v91 - My 15 '66 - p2713

STONE, Willie   (pseud.)
  (Real name: Moore, Chuck)

   I Was A Black Panther
    BW - v4 - N 8 '70 - p12
    Comw - v93 - N 20 '70 - p202
    EJ - v60 - F '71 - p275
    LJ - v96 - F 15 '71 - p736

STORR, Catherine   1913-
  ConAu 13R, SmATA 9, TwCCW 78,
  WrDr 80

   Thursday
    B&B - v20 - Ja '75 - p81
    BL - v69 - N 15 '72 - p303
    BS - v32 - O 15 '72 - p340
    CE - v49 - Ap '73 - p376
    HB - v49 - Ap '73 - p148

    KR - v40 - Jl 1 '72 - p730
    LJ - v97 - O 15 '72 - p3465
    Lis - v86 - N 11 '71 - p661
    NS - v82 - N 12 '71 - p661
    NYTBR - O 1 '72 - p8
    NYTBR, pt.2 - N 5 '72 - p28
    PW - v202 - Ag 14 '72 - p46
    Spec - v227 - N 13 '71 - p696
    TLS - O 22 '71 - p1318

STOUTENBURG, Adrien Pearl   1916-
  ConAu 5R, ConP 75, SmATA 3,
  ThrBJA, WhoAm 78, WrDr 80

   American Tall Tale Animals
    BL - v64 - Jl 1 '68 - p1237
    LJ - v93 - O 15 '68 - p3974
    NYTBR - v73 - My 5 '68 - p34
    PW - v193 - Je 3 '68 - p129

   American Tall Tales
    BL - v63 - S 15 '66 - p123
    HB - v42 - Ag '66 - p432
    Inst - v76 - Ag '66 - p217
    LJ - v91 - Jl '66 - p3554
    NYTBR - v71 - My 8 '66 - p33
    PW - v189 - My 9 '66 - p79
see also Kendall, Lace

STRANGER, Joyce   (pseud.)
  ConAu X, TwCCW 78, WrDr 80
  (real name: Wilson, Joyce Muriel)

   Rex
    BL - v64 - Mr 1 '68 - p769
    BS - v28 - My 15 '68 - p91
    BW - v2 - Je 16 '68 - p6
    HB - v44 - Je '68 - p342
    KR - v36 - F 15 '68 - p208
    LJ - v93 - My 1 '68 - p1920
    LJ - v93 - My 15 '68 - p2133
    NYTBR - v73 - Ap 21 '68 - p54
    PW - v193 - F 12 '68 - p71
    PW - v194 - Ag 12 '68 - p55
    SR - v51 - N 9 '68 - p70

STREATFEILD, Noel   1897-
  ConAu 81, JBA 51, SmATA 20,
  TwCCW 78, WhoChL

   Thursday's Child
    B&B - v16 - N '70 - p58
    B&B - v18 - My '73 - p125
    BL - v67 - Je 15 '71 - p873

STREATFEILD, Noel (continued)
    BS - v31 - Ap 15 '71 - p47
    BW - v5 - My 9 '71 - p17
    Comw - v94 - My 21 '71 - p267
    GW - v103 - D 19 '70 - p21
    HB - v47 - Je '71 - p294
    KR - v39 - Mr 1 '71 - p237
    LJ - v96 - Je 15 '71 - p2142
    NS - v80 - N 6 '70 - p611
    PW - v199 - Mr 15 '71 - p73
    Spec - v225 - D 5 '70 - pR8
    TLS - O 30 '70 - p1263

STRESHINSKY, Shirley
see Elder, Lauren (co-author)

STUART, Morna   1905-
  Au & Wr 71

    Marassa And Midnight
      CCB-B - v21 - Ap '68 - p134
      HT - v16 - D '66 - p865
      KR - v35 - Jl 15 '67 - p817
      LJ - v92 - S 15 '67 - p3191
      TLS - N 24 '66 - p1084
      TN - v24 - Je '68 - p448

STUBENRAUCH, Bob
  AuBYP SUP

    Where Freedom Grew
      BS - v30 - N 15 '70 - p358
      BW - v4 - N 8 '70 - p20
      LJ - v95 - D 15 '70 - p4357
      NYTBR, pt.2 - N 8 '70 - p3
      PW - v198 - N 9 '70 - p61

STURTZEL, Howard Allison
see Annixter, Paul

STURTZEL, Jane Levington
see Annixter, Jane

SUHL, Yuri   1908-
  ChLR 2, ConAu 45, SmATA 8,
  WhoWorJ 72

    On The Other Side Of The Gate
      BB - v3 - My '75 - p3
      BL - v71 - Ap 15 '75 - p869
      BL - v73 - Ap 1 '77 - p1178
      BS - v35 - Jl '75 - p96
      CCB-B - v29 - S '75 - p20

      Cur R - v17 - O '78 - p343
      EJ - v66 - Ja '77 - p65
      HB - v51 - Je '75 - p271
      Inst - v84 - My '75 - p106
      JB - v42 - Ag '78 - p210
      KR - v43 - F 1 '75 - p128
      Kliatt - v11 - Winter '77 - p8
      NYTBR - D 28 '75 - p10
      PW - v207 - Ap 21 '75 - p47
      SLJ - v21 - Mr '75 - p110

    Uncle Misha's Partisans
      BL - v70 - N 1 '73 - p294
      CCB-B - v27 - Ja '74 - p87
      CE - v50 - F '74 - p230
      CSM - v65 - N 7 '73 - pB4
      GP - v14 - My '75 - p2632
      HB - v50 - F '74 - p54
      KR - v41 - Ag 15 '73 - p888
      LJ - v98 - Jl '73 - p2197
      Obs - Jl 20 '75 - p23
      TLS - Jl 11 '75 - p764
      TN - v30 - Ap '74 - p309

SULLIVAN, George Edward   1927-
  AuBYP, ConAu 13R, SmATA 4,
  WrDr 80

    Bert Jones: Born To Play Football
      BL - v74 - Ja 1 '78 - p751
      KR - v45 - N 15 '77 - p1209
      SLJ - v24 - D '77 - p64

    Better Swimming And Diving For
    Boys And Girls
      BL - v64 - Mr 1 '68 - p788
      LJ - v92 - D 15 '67 - p4634

    The Complete Book Of Autograph
    Collecting
      BL - v68 - F 1 '72 - p464
      BL - v68 - F 1 '72 - p467
      Comw - v95 - N 19 '71 - p191
      Hob - v77 - Mr '72 - p158
      Hob - v83 - S '78 - p106
      LJ - v97 - Jl '72 - p2491
      NYTBR - N 21 '71 - p8

    Modern Olympic Superstars
      CCB-B - v33 - S '79 - p20
      Hi Lo - v1 - O '79 - p5
      SLJ - v25 - My '79 - p85

SULLIVAN, George Edward
(continued)

The Picture Story Of Catfish Hunter
  BL - v73 - Jl 15 '77 - p1731
  KR - v45 - Ap 15 '77 - p433
  SLJ - v24 - S '77 - p138

Pitchers And Pitching
  BL - v69 - S 1 '72 - p43
  CSM - v64 - My 4 '72 - pB6
  KR - v40 - Mr 15 '72 - p340
  LJ - v97 - My 15 '72 - p1930

Pro Football's Greatest Upsets
  LJ - v97 - My 15 '72 - p1931

Rise Of The Robots
  BL - v67 - My 15 '71 - p800
  BS - v31 - My 15 '71 - p100
  CLW - v43 - D '71 - p224
  LJ - v96 - My 15 '71 - p1817
  SB - v7 - D '71 - p186

Understanding Architecture
  BL - v68 - S 1 '71 - p60
  CCB-B - v25 - D '71 - p65

Wilt Chamberlain
  LJ - v96 - My 15 '71 - p1824
see also Seewagen, George L (co-
author)

SULLIVAN, Mary Beth

Feeling Free
  BL - v75 - Jl 15 '79 - p1631
  CBRS - v7 - Ag '79 - p140
  CCB-B - v33 - N '79 - p59
  KR - v47 - Ag 1 '79 - p859
  Kliatt - v14 - Winter '80 - p34
  SB - v15 - Mr '80 - p224
  SLJ - v26 - O '79 - p156

SULLIVAN, Mary Wilson   1907-
ConAu 73, SmATA 13

Bluegrass Iggy
  BL - v72 - Ja 1 '76 - p629
  KR - v43 - Ag 15 '75 - p919
  SLJ - v22 - D '75 - p55

The Indestructible Old-Time String Band
  KR - v43 - Jl 1 '75 - p714

NYTBR - S 7 '75 - p20
PW - v208 - Jl 14 '75 - p60
SLJ - v522 - S '75 - p113

What's This About Pete?
  CCB-B - v30 - Ja '77 - p83
  KR - v44 - Ap 15 '76 - p484
  SLJ - v22 - Mr '76 - p118

SULLIVAN, Navin   1929-
Au&Wr 71, ConAu 5R

Pioneer Astronomers
  CSM - Jl 16 '64 - p5
  HB - v40 - Ag '64 - p393
  LJ - v89 - S 15 '64 - p3499
  NH - v73 - N '64 - p6
  SA - v211 - D '64 - p147
  S&T - v29 - Ap '65 - p238

SULLIVAN, Wilson

Franklin Delano Roosevelt
  BL - v67 - S 1 '70 - p59
  BS - v30 - My 1 '70 - p63
  Comw - v92 - My 22 '70 - p251
  KR - v38 - My 15 '70 - p569
  LJ - v95 - D 15 '70 - p4369
  NYTBR - Ag 9 '70 - p22
  NYTBR, pt.2 - N 8 '70 - p36
  PW - v197 - Je 1 '70 - p68
  SR - v53 - O 24 '70 - p67

SUMMERS, James Levingston   1910-
AuBYP, ConAu 13R, MorJA

The Iron Doors Between
  BS - v28 - O 1 '68 - p279
  BW - v2 - N 3 '68 - p18
  HB - v44 - O '68 - p576
  KR - v36 - Ag 1 '68 - p825
  LJ - v93 - S 15 '68 - p3327

You Can't Make It By Bus
  CCB-B - v23 - Ja '70 - p89
  CSM - v61 - N 6 '69 - pB9
  EJ - v63 - Ja '74 - p62
  KR - v37 - N 15 '69 - p1204
  LJ - v95 - Ja 15 '70 - p257
  LJ - v96 - Ja 15 '71 - p282
  NYTBR, pt.2 - N 9 '69 - p48

SUNG, Betty Lee   1924-
AmM&WS 78S, ConAu 25R

SUNG, Betty Lee (continued)

The Chinese In America
BL - v69 - Ja 1 '73 - p451
BL - v69 - F 15 '73 - p553
CE - v49 - Mr '73 - p324
KR - v40 - Ag 15 '72 - p946
LJ - v98 - My 15 '73 - p1692
SE - v37 - D '73 - p789

SURGE, Frank   1931-
ConAu 69, SmATA 13

Famous Spies
CCB-B - v22 - Jl '69 - p182
LJ - v94 - O 15 '69 - p3824

Western Outlaws
LJ - v94 - D 15 '69 - p4609

SWARTHOUT, Glendon Fred   1918-
ConAu 1R, ConNov 76, FourBJA,
WhoWest 74, WrDr 80

Bless The Beasts And Children
BL - v66 - Je 1 '70 - p1195
BL - v66 - Je 15 '70 - p1274
BL - v67 - Ap 1 '71 - p655
BS - v29 - Mr 1 '70 - p450
HM - v240 - Ap '70 - p107
KR - v38 - Ja 1 '70 - p24
KR - v38 - F 1 '70 - p119
LJ - v95 - Mr 1 '70 - p915
LJ - v95 - Ap 15 '70 - p1661
LJ - v95 - My 15 '70 - p1913
LJ - v95 - D 15 '70 - p4328
NO - v9 - Je 1 '70 - p17
NYTBR - Ap 5 '70 - p30
PW - v197 - Ja 19 '70 - p79
PW - v198 - O 5 '70 - p64
SR - v53 - My 2 '70 - p29
Spec - v225 - D 5 '70 - pR22
TN - v27 - Ap '71 - p309

Whichaway
BL - v63 - N 15 '66 - p378
BS - v26 - N 1 '66 - p296
CCB-B - v20 - Ap '67 - p130
KR - v34 - S 1 '66 - p915
LJ - v92 - Ja 15 '67 - p348
LJ - v98 - O 15 '73 - p3163
NYTBR - v71 - N 6 '66 - p12
NYTBR - v71 - D 4 '66 - p66
Nat R - v18 - D 13 '66 - p1285

Obs - D 3 '67 - p26
PW - v190 - O 10 '66 - p74
SR - v50 - Mr 18 '67 - p36

SWARTHOUT, Kathryn
see Swarthout, Glendon Fred (co-
author) - *Whichaway*

SWEENEY, Karen O'Connor   1938-
ConAu 89

Entertaining
Inst - v87 - My '78 - p116
SLJ - v25 - S '78 - p149

SWENSON, May   1919-
ConAu 5R, ConLC 4, ConP 75,
SmATA 15, WhoAm 78, WorAu

Poems To Solve
BL - v63 - Ap 1 '67 - p847
BS - v26 - D 1 '66 - p342
CLW - v38 - Ja '67 - p338
HB - v43 - F '67 - p77
Inst - v76 - F '67 - p186
KR - v34 - N 1 '66 - p1146
LJ - v92 - Ja 15 '67 - p348
PS - v42 - Spring '68 - p86

SWIFT, Helen Miller   1914-
AuBYP, ConAu 1R

Head Over Heels
KR - v35 - D 15 '67 - p1477
LJ - v93 - Ja 15 '68 - p311

T

TABRAH, Ruth M 1921-
ConAu 13R, LEduc 74, SmATA 14,
WhoAmW 75

> *Hawaii Nei*
> BL - v64 - Ja 15 '68 - p595
> CCB-B - v21 - N '67 - p49
> KR - v35 - S 1 '67 - p1065
> LJ - v92 - N 15 '67 - p4265
> SR - v50 - Ag 19 '67 - p35
> TN - v24 - Je '68 - p448

TATE, Joan 1922-
ConAu 49, SmATA 9, TwCCW 78,
WrDr 80

> *Tina And David*
> BS - v33 - O 15 '73 - p334
> CCB-B - v27 - My '74 - p151
> KR - v41 - S 1 '73 - p973
> LJ - v99 - Ja 15 '74 - p219

TAVES, Isabella 1915-
ConAu 21R, WhoAmW 75

> *Not Bad For A Girl*
> CCB-B - v26 - N '72 - p50
> EJ - v61 - N '72 - p1262
> Inst - v82 - N '72 - p126
> KR - v40 - Je 1 '72 - p624
> LJ - v97 - My 15 '72 - p1930
> NYTBR, pt.2 - My 7 '72 - p24

TAYLOR, David

> *Is There A Doctor In The Zoo?*
> BL - v74 - My 1 '78 - p1398
> HB - v55 - O '78 - p547
> KR - v46 - Ap 1 '78 - p426
> KR - v46 - My 15 '78 - p556
> Kliatt - v13 - Fall '79 - p33
> LJ - v103 - My 1 '78 - p967
> PW - v213 - Ap 3 '78 - p75

SB - v15 - My '79 - p37
SLJ - v25 - N '78 - p85
WLB - v53 - F '79 - p464

TAYLOR, Dawson 1916-
AmSCAP 66, ConAu 13R

> *Aim For A Job In Automotive*
> *Service*
> BL - v65 - S 15 '68 - p111
> LJ - v93 - S 15 '68 - p3327

TAYLOR, Lester Barbour, Jr. 1932-
ODwPR 79

> *Rescue! True Stories Of Heroism*
> BL - v75 - O 15 '78 - p388
> CBRS - v7 - Ja '79 - p50
> CLW - v51 - N '79 - p181

TAYLOR, Mildred
AuBYP SUP, ConAu 85, SelBAA,
SmATA 15

> *Roll Of Thunder, Hear My Cry*
> BW - Ap 23 '78 - pE2
> CLW - v49 - D '77 - p212
> CSM - v70 - O 23 '78 - pB9
> GP - v16 - Ap '78 - p3283
> JB - v42 - F '78 - p51
> NYTBR - Mr 19 '78 - p51
> Obs - D 11 '77 - p31
> TLS - D 2 '77 - p1415

TAYLOR, Theodore 1921-
ConAu 21R, FourBJA, SmATA 5,
TwCCW 78, WrDr 80

> *Air Raid: Pearl Harbor*
> BL - v68 - O 15 '71 - p206
> CCB-B - v25 - O '71 - p35
> CE - v48 - F '72 - p260
> KR - v39 - Je 1 '71 - p598

TAYLOR, Theodore (continued)
 LJ - v97 - Je 15 '72 - p2244
 NYTBR - Jl 11 '71 - p8
 NYTBR, pt.2 - N 7 '71 - p30
 SR - v54 - Ag 21 '71 - p27
 TN - v28 - Je '72 - p435

The Cay
 A Lib - v1 - Ap '70 - p387
 Am - v121 - D 13 '69 - p594
 BL - v65 - Jl 15 '69 - p1277
 BS - v30 - N 15 '70 - p363
 BW - v3 - My 4 '69 - p36
 CCB-B - v22 - Jl '69 - p183
 CLW - v41 - F '70 - p383
 GW - v103 - D 19 '70 - p21
 HB - v45 - O '69 - p537
 KR - v37 - My 15 '69 - p560
 LJ - v94 - Je 15 '69 - p2505
 LJ - v94 - D 15 '69 - p4583
 Lis - v84 - N 12 '70 - p671
 NS - v80 - N 6 '70 - p610
 NYTBR - Je 29 '69 - p26
 NYTBR, pt.2 - N 9 '69 - p61
 NYTBR, pt.2 - N 8 '70 - p6
 Obs - D 6 '70 - p27
 PW - v195 - Je 9 '69 - p63
 SR - v52 - Je 28 '69 - p39
 TLS - O 30 '70 - p1258
 TN - v26 - Ja '70 - p208

Teetoncey
 BL - v71 - S 1 '74 - p47
 CCB-B - v28 - N '74 - p56
 HB - v50 - O '74 - p145
 KR - v42 - Jl 15 '74 - p744
 LJ - v99 - O 15 '74 - p2749
 NYTBR - O 6 '74 - p8
 PW - v206 - D 2 '74 - p62
 Teacher - v93 - Ap '76 - p121

TEALL, Kaye M

TV Camera Three
 BL - v74 - Ap 15 '78 - p1343

Witches Get Everything
 Hi Lo - v1 - My '80 - p3

TERASAKI, Gwen

Bridge To The Sun
 BL - v54 - S 1 '57 - p8
 CSM - S 25 '57 - p9

NYT - O 13 '57 - p6
SR - v40 - S 7 '57 - p20

TERHAAR, Jaap   1922-
ConAu 37R, FourBJA, SmATA 6
(sometimes cited as Haar, Jaap Ter)

The World Of Ben Lighthart
 BL - v74 - S 15 '77 - p193
 BS - v37 - Ag '77 - p141
 CCB-B - v30 - Jl '77 - p182
 CLW - v49 - O '77 - p140
 EJ - v66 - S '77 - p77
 KR - v45 - Je 1 '77 - p582
 LA - v54 - N '77 - p948

TERRY, Luther L   1911-
AmM&WS 76P, ConAu P-2, CurBio
61, SmATA 11, WhoAm 78

To Smoke Or Not To Smoke
 BL - v66 - Ja 15 '70 - p622
 BS - v29 - D 1 '69 - p355
 KR - v37 - N 15 '69 - p1212
 LJ - v95 - Mr 15 '70 - p1207
 LJ - v96 - O 15 '71 - p3436
 NYTBR - Ja 25 '70 - p26

TERZIAN, James P   1915-
AuBYP SUP, ConAu 13R, SmATA
14

*Mighty Hard Road: The Story Of
Cesar Chavez*
 BL - v67 - Mr 1 '71 - p563
 BL - v68 - Je 15 '72 - p895
 BL - v70 - O 15 '73 - p226
 BS - v31 - Mr 1 '72 - p547
 CC - v87 - D 16 '70 - p1516
 Inst - v82 - N '72 - p136
 KR - v38 - N 15 '70 - p1258
 LJ - v96 - Mr 15 '71 - p1130
 NYTBR, pt.2 - N 8 '70 - p46
 PW - v198 - N 9 '70 - p60

Pete Cass: Scrambler
 PW - v194 - O 7 '68 - p55

THALER, Susan   1939-
ConAu 21R

Rosaria
 Atl - v117 - N 4 '67 - p517
 BS - v27 - O 1 '67 - p264

THALER, Susan (continued)
>CCB-B - v21 - Ja '68 - p86
>KR - v35 - Ag 1 '67 - p887
>LJ - v92 - N 15 '67 - p4266

THOGER, Marie 1923-
ConAu 25R

>*Shanta*
>KR - v36 - Ja 1 '68 - p6
>LJ - v93 - F 15 '68 - p874
>NS - v73 - My 26 '67 - p732
>TLS - N 24 '66 - p1084

THOMAS, Allison

>*Sandy: The Autobiography Of A Dog*
>BL - v74 - My 1 '78 - p1404
>KR - v46 - Mr 1 '78 - p291
>PW - v213 - Ap 24 '78 - p75
>SLJ - v25 - N '78 - p56

THOMAS, Charles
see Hibbert, Christopher (co-author)

THOMAS, Dian 1945-
ConAu 65

>*Roughing It Easy*
>CSM - v68 - Ag 3 '76 - p21
>RSR - v2 - O '74 - p35

THOMPSON, Estelle

>*Hunter In The Dark*
>BL - v75 - Ap 15 '79 - p1276
>BW - F 18 '79 - pE7
>WLB - v53 - My '79 - p641

THOMPSON, George Selden
see Selden, George

THOMPSON, Jean 1933-

>*Brother Of The Wolves*
>BL - v75 - D 15 '78 - p691
>CBRS - v7 - F '79 - p70
>EJ - v68 - F '79 - p102
>SE - v43 - Ap '79 - p301
>SLJ - v25 - N '78 - p69

THOMPSON, Vivian Laubach 1911-
AuBYP, ConAu 1R, SmATA 3,
WhoAmW 75, WrDr 80

>*Hawaiian Tales Of Heroes And Champions*
>BL - v68 - Mr 1 '72 - p567
>CCB-B - v26 - O '72 - p32
>CE - v49 - O '72 - p30
>HB - v48 - F '72 - p46
>KR - v39 - O 15 '71 - p1129
>LJ - v97 - Ap 15 '72 - p1610

THOMSON, Peter 1913-
AuBYP, ConAu 5R

>*Cougar*
>KR - v36 - Ja 1 '68 - p7

THORN, John 1947-
ConAu 97

>*A Century Of Baseball Lore*
>KR - v42 - My 15 '74 - p575
>LJ - v99 - Je 15 '74 - p1726
>LJ - v99 - O 15 '74 - p2753
>PW - v205 - Mr 25 '74 - p55

THRASHER, Crystal Faye 1921-
ConAu 61

>*The Dark Didn't Catch Me*
>BL - v71 - Ap 1 '75 - p820
>CCB-B - v29 - D '75 - p71
>CE - v52 - Ja '76 - p156
>CLW - v47 - O '75 - p133
>CSM - v67 - My 7 '75 - pB2
>Comw - v102 - N 21 '75 - p569
>HB - v51 - Je '75 - p272
>J Read - v19 - Ja '76 - p331
>KR - v43 - Mr 1 '75 - p240
>NYT - v125 - D 20 '75 - p25
>NYTBR - Mr 30 '75 - p8
>NYTBR - Je 1 '75 - p28
>NYTBR - N 16 '75 - p54
>NYTBR - D 7 '75 - p66
>PW - v207 - F 10 '75 - p56
>SLJ - v21 - Ap '75 - p60

THYPIN, Marilyn

>*Checking And Balancing*
>BL - v76 - My 15 '80 - p1360
>SLJ - v26 - Ag '80 - p79

THYPIN, Marilyn (continued)

Good Buy! Buying Home Furnishings
  BL - v76 - Je 15 '80 - p1524
  SLJ - v26 - Ag '80 - p79

Health Care For The Wongs: Health Insurance, Choosing A Doctor
  BL - v76 - Je 15 '80 - p1524
  SLJ - v26 - Ag '80 - p79

Leases And Landlords: Apartment Living
  BL - v76 - My 15 '80 - p1360
  SLJ - v26 - Ag '80 - p79

More Food For Our Money: Food Buying, Planning, Nutrition
  BL - v75 - Je 15 '79 - p1533

Put Your Money Down
  BL - v75 - Je 15 '79 - p1533

State Your Claim! Small Claims Court
  BL - v76 - Je 15 '80 - p1525
  SLJ - v26 - Ag '80 - p79

Wheels And Deals: Buying A Car
  BL - v75 - Jl 15 '79 - p1622
  SLJ - v26 - S '79 - p149

TITLER, Dale Milton   1926-
AuBYP SUP, ConAu 81

Haunted Treasures
  KR - v44 - S 15 '76 - p1043

Unnatural Resources: True Stories Of American Treasure
  BL - v70 - D 1 '73 - p389
  CLW - v45 - Mr '74 - p399
  Inst - v83 - N '73 - p128
  KR - v41 - Ag 15 '73 - p887
  LJ - v99 - Ja 15 '74 - p213

Wings Of Adventure
  BL - v68 - My 15 '72 - p786
  CSM - v64 - F 10 '72 - p11
  LJ - v96 - D 15 '71 - p4094
  PW - v200 - N 15 '71 - p68

TOEPFER, Ray Grant   1923-
ConAu 21R

Liberty And Corporal Kincaid
  BL - v64 - Je 15 '68 - p1189
  BS - v27 - F 1 '68 - p431
  KR - v35 - D 1 '67 - p1426

TOLAN, Stephanie S   1942-
ConAu 77

The Liberation Of Tansy Warner
  BL - v76 - Jl 15 '80 - p1678
  CBRS - v8 - Ag '80 - p139
  KR - v48 - Jl 15 '80 - p914

TOMERLIN, John   1930-
AuBYP SUP

The Fledgling
  BL - v65 - N 1 '68 - p316
  BS - v28 - Ag 1 '68 - p195
  CCB-B - v22 - F '69 - p102
  CSM - v60 - N 7 '68 - pB11
  KR - v36 - Jl 1 '68 - p699
  LJ - v93 - S 15 '68 - p3327
  SR - v51 - N 9 '68 - p69

The Nothing Special
  BL - v65 - My 15 '69 - p1079
  CSM - v61 - My 1 '69 - pB10
  KR - v37 - F 15 '69 - p186
  LJ - v94 - Ap 15 '69 - p1801
  PW - v195 - Ap 21 '69 - p66

TOPPIN, Edgar Allan
  see Dobler, Lavinia (co-author)
    Drisko, Carol F (co-author)

TOWNSEND, John Rowe   1922-
ChLR 2, ConAu 37R, FourBJA, SmATA 4, SouST, TwCCW 78

Good-Bye To The Jungle
  BL - v64 - S 1 '67 - p67
  BS - v27 - My 1 '67 - p67
  HB - v43 - Je '67 - p355
  Inst - v76 - Je '67 - p144
  KR - v35 - F 15 '67 - p212
  LJ - v92 - My 15 '67 - p2032
  NY - v43 - D 16 '67 - p164
  NYTBR - v72 - N 5 '67 - p64
  NYTBR, pt.2 - v72 - My 7 '67 - p12
  PW - v191 - Mr 20 '67 - p61
  SR - v50 - Ap 22 '67 - p100

TOWNSEND, John Rowe (continued)

Good Night, Prof, Dear
BL - v67 - Je 1 '71 - p832
BL - v68 - Ap 1 '72 - p665
BW - v5 - My 9 '71 - p18
CCB-B - v24 - Jl '71 - p179
CSM - v63 - My 6 '71 - pB6
HB - v47 - Je '71 - p294
KR - v39 - Ja 15 '71 - p57
LJ - v96 - Ap 15 '71 - p1520
NYTBR, pt.2 - My 2 '71 - p18
PW - v199 - Mr 22 '71 - p53
SR - v54 - My 15 '71 - p45
TN - v28 - Ap '72 - p314

Hell's Edge
BL - v65 - Jl 15 '69 - p1277
BS - v29 - Je 1 '69 - p103
CCB-B - v23 - S '69 - p19
KR - v37 - Ap 15 '69 - p454
NYTBR - Ag 31 '69 - p16
PW - v195 - My 12 '69 - p58

Pirate's Island
B&B - v13 - My '68 - p46
BL - v64 - Ap 15 '68 - p999
BW - v2 - My 5 '68 - p24
CCB-B - v21 - Jl '68 - p182
CSM - v60 - My 2 '68 - pB10
HB - v44 - Ag '68 - p423
KR - v36 - Mr 1 '68 - p263
LJ - v93 - Ap 15 '68 - p1805
Lis - v79 - My 16 '68 - p643
NS - v75 - My 24 '68 - p695
NY - v44 - D 14 '68 - p208
NYTBR - v73 - My 26 '68 - p30
Obs - Ap 14 '68 - p27
PW - v193 - F 5 '68 - p66
SR - v51 - My 11 '68 - p40
TLS - Mr 14 '68 - p254

The Summer People
BL - v69 - N 1 '72 - p241
BL - v69 - N 1 '72 - p247
BS - v32 - S 15 '72 - p285
CCB-B - v26 - D '72 - p67
Comw - v97 - N 17 '72 - p157
GW - v107 - D 16 '72 - p23
HB - v49 - Ap '73 - p129
KR - v40 - S 15 '72 - p1107
KR - v40 - D 15 '72 - p1422
LJ - v98 - Mr 15 '73 - p1016
NS - v84 - N 10 '72 - p692

NYTBR - N 19 '72 - p10
NYTBR, pt.2 - N 5 '72 - p28
Obs - N 26 '72 - p37
PW - v202 - O 16 '72 - p49
SR - v55 - D 9 '72 - p79
Spec - v229 - N 11 '72 - p750
TLS - N 3 '72 - p1324
TN - v29 - Je '73 - p358

Trouble In The Jungle
A Lib - v1 - Ap '70 - p387
BL - v65 - My 1 '69 - p1019
BW - v3 - My 4 '69 - p28
CCB-B - v23 - F '70 - p106
CSM - v61 - My 1 '69 - pB7
HB - v45 - Ap '69 - p174
KR - v37 - Mr 1 '69 - p238
LJ - v94 - My 15 '69 - p2073
LJ - v94 - My 15 '69 - p2119
LJ - v94 - D 15 '69 - p4583
PW - v195 - Mr 17 '69 - p57

TREADWAY, Rudy Peeples
AuBYP SUP

Go To It, You Dutchman! The Story Of Edward Bok
CCB-B - v23 - S '69 - p19
KR - v37 - Ap 1 '69 - p392
LJ - v94 - N 15 '69 - p4304
PW - v195 - Mr 10 '69 - p74

TREGASKIS, Richard   1916-1973
ConAu 1R, ConAu 45, SmATA 3,
WhAm 6, WhoWor 74

John F. Kennedy And PT-109
BL - v67 - Ap 15 '62 - p580
CSM - My 10 '62 - p8B
LJ - v87 - Ap 15 '62 - p1697
NYTBR - F 25 '62 - p36

TREMAIN, Rose   1943-
ConAu 97

Sadler's Birthday
BL - v73 - Je 1 '77 - p1484
KR - v45 - Mr 15 '77 - p308
LJ - v102 - Ap 15 '77 - p950
Lis - v95 - Ap 22 '76 - p518
NY - v53 - Ag 1 '77 - p68
NYTBR - Jl 24 '77 - p14
Obs - Ap 25 '76 - p27
PW - v211 - Mr 28 '77 - p73

TREMAIN, Rose (continued)
    TLS - Ap 30 '76 - p507

TUCK, Jay Nelson

    Heroes Of Puerto Rico
      BL - v69 - Ja 15 '73 - p478

TUNIS, Edwin   1897-1973
  ChLR 2, ConAu 5R, ConAu 45,
  IlsCB 1967, MorJA, SmATA 1,
  SmATA 24N

    Chipmunks On The Doorstep
      A Lib - v3 - Ap '72 - p421
      BL - v67 - Jl 15 '71 - p956
      BL - v68 - Ap 1 '72 - p670
      CCB-B - v25 - S '71 - p17
      CE - v48 - N '71 - p106
      CLW - v43 - Ap '72 - p480
      HB - v47 - Ag '71 - p397
      Inst - v81 - Je '72 - p66
      KR - v39 - Ap 15 '71 - p441
      LJ - v96 - Je 15 '71 - p2134
      NYT - v121 - D 16 '71 - p67
      NYTBR - My 16 '71 - p8
      NYTBR, pt.2 - N 7 '71 - p30
      PW - v199 - Je 21 '71 - p71
      SA - v225 - D '71 - p108
      SB - v7 - D '71 - p249
      SR - v54 - Jl 17 '71 - p37
      TN - v28 - Ja '72 - p204

TUNIS, John R   1889-1975
  ConAu 57, ConAu 61, ConLC 12,
  MorJA, TwCA SUP, TwCCW 78

    All-American
      Atl - v170 - D '42 - p149
      BL - v39 - O 1 '42 - p37
      CC - v59 - S 30 '42 - p1187
      CSM - D 10 '42 - p16
      Comw - v37 - N 20 '42 - p116
      HB - v18 - N '42 - p425
      LJ - v67 - O 15 '42 - p897
      LJ - v67 - N 1 '42 - p958
      NY - v18 - D 12 '42 - p111
      NYTBR - N 1 '42 - p9
      SR - v25 - N 14 '42 - p26
      SR - v25 - D 5 '42 - p60

    Go, Team, Go
      BL - v50 - Ap 1 '54 - p303
      CSM - My 13 '54 - p12

      HB - v30 - Ap '54 - p105
      KR - v22 - Ja 1 '54 - p4
      LJ - v79 - Ap 15 '54 - p791
      NYTBR - F 28 '54 - p24
      SR - v37 - Mr 20 '54 - p53
      SR - v37 - Je 19 '54 - p40

    His Enemy, His Friend
      Am - v117 - N 4 '67 - p518
      BL - v64 - Mr 1 '68 - p788
      BS - v27 - N 1 '67 - p315
      BW - v1 - N 19 '67 - p24
      CCB-B - v21 - F '68 - p102
      CLW - v39 - D '67 - p298
      CSM - v59 - N 2 '67 - pB13
      Comw - v87 - N 10 '67 - p181
      EJ - v63 - F '74 - p91
      HB - v44 - F '68 - p51
      KR - v35 - S 15 '67 - p1147
      LJ - v93 - F 15 '68 - p890
      LJ - v95 - O 15 '70 - p3610
      NYTBR - v72 - O 29 '67 - p44
      NYTBR - v72 - N 5 '67 - p64
      NYTBR, pt.2 - N 8 '70 - p30
      NYTBR, pt.2 - F 13 '72 - p14
      PW - v192 - O 23 '67 - p52
      SR - v51 - Mr 16 '68 - p39

    The Kid Comes Back
      BL - v43 - S '46 - p20
      HB - v22 - N '46 - p469
      KR - v14 - S 1 '46 - p426
      LJ - v71 - N 1 '46 - p1547
      NYTBR - N 10 '46 - p5
      NYTBR - S 11 '77 - p61
      SR - v29 - N 9 '46 - p54

    World Series
      BL - v38 - S '41 - p18
      LJ - v66 - S 1 '41 - p737
      NYTBR - O 19 '41 - p10
      NYTBR - S 11 '77 - p61

TURNER, Alice K   1940-
  ConAu 53, SmATA 10, WhoAm 78

    Yoga For Beginners
      KR - v41 - Ag 15 '73 - p891
      LJ - v99 - Mr 15 '74 - p905
      PW - v204 - Ag 13 '73 - p54

TURNER, William O   1914-
  AuNews 1, ConAu 1, IntAu&W 77,
  WrDr 80

TURNER, William O (continued)

The Treasure Of Fan-Tan Flat
   NYTBR - Je 4 '61 - p18

TURNGREN, Annette   1902-1980
   AuBYP, ConAu 9R, MnnWr, MorJA,
   SmATA 23N

Mystery Plays A Golden Flute
   BS - v29 - Je 1 '69 - p103
   KR - v37 - Ap 15 '69 - p454
   LJ - v94 - My 15 '69 - p2124
   PW - v195 - Ap 7 '69 - p56

Mystery Walks The Campus
   CSM - N 15 '56 - p15
   KR - v24 - Jl 15 '56 - p481
   LJ - v82 - F 15 '57 - p596

U

UCHIDA, Yoshiko 1921-
ConAu 13R, MorJA, SmATA 1,
TwCCW 78

Journey Home
   BL - v75 - D 15 '78 - p691
   CBRS - v7 - Ja '79 - p50
   CCB-B - v32 - Ap '79 - p146
   CE - v55 - Ap '79 - p298
   KR - v47 - Ja 1 '79 - p6
   LA - v56 - My '79 - p546
   Par - v54 - Ap '79 - p24
   SE - v43 - Ap '79 - p298
   SLJ - v25 - Ja '79 - p58
   WCRB - v5 - Ja '79 - p54

Journey To Topaz
   BL - v68 - Ja 1 '72 - p395
   BW - v5 - N 7 '71 - p14
   CCB-B - v25 - D '71 - p66
   HB - v47 - D '71 - p615
   Inst - v81 - N '71 - p133
   NYTBR - Mr 12 '72 - p8
   PW - v200 - S 6 '71 - p51
   SR - v54 - D 11 '71 - p46

Samurai Of Gold Hill
   BL - v69 - F 15 '73 - p553
   BL - v69 - F 15 '73 - p575
   CCB-B - v26 - My '73 - p147
   HB - v49 - F '73 - p51
   KR - v40 - N 1 '72 - p1241
   SE - v37 - D '73 - p789

UHLICH, Richard

*Twenty Minutes To Live And
Other Tales Of Suspense*
   Hi Lo - v1 - Ja '80 - p3

ULYATT, Kenneth 1920-
ConAu 61, SmATA 14

Outlaws
   BL - v74 - Jl 1 '78 - p1682
   GP - v15 - Ap '77 - p3091
   JB - v41 - Je '77 - p186
   SLJ - v25 - S '78 - p165

UNKELBACH, Kurt 1913-
AuBYP SUP, ConAu 21R, SmATA
4, WhoE 74

The Dog Who Never Knew
   KR - v35 - N 15 '67 - p1370
   LJ - v93 - S 15 '68 - p3327
   PW - v193 - My 27 '68 - p58

How To Bring Up Your Pet Dog
   BL - v69 - N 15 '72 - p303

UNTERMEYER, Louis 1885-1977
ConAu 5R, ConAu 73, CurBio 78,
OxAm, SmATA 2, TwCW,
WhoWorJ 72

*The Firebringer And Other Great
Stories*
   BL - v65 - Mr 1 '69 - p756
   LJ - v94 - F 15 '69 - p889
   NYTBR - v73 - N 3 '68 - p46

URQUHART, David Inglis

*The Internal Combustion Engine
And How It Works*
   BL - v70 - Ja 15 '74 - p546
   KR - v41 - O 15 '73 - p1169
   LJ - v99 - F 15 '74 - p577

V

VAN DUYN, Janet 1910-
ConAu 69, SmATA 18

> *Builders On The Desert*
> KR - v42 - Ap 15 '74 - p431
> LJ - v99 - O 15 '74 - p2743
> SB - v10 - D '74 - p249
> SE - v39 - Mr '75 - p175
> SLJ - v25 - S '78 - p43

VAN LAWICK-GOODALL, Jane
see Lawick-Goodall, Jane Van

VAN RYZIN, Lani

> *Cutting A Record In Nashville*
> BL - v76 - Je 15 '80 - p1525
> Hi Lo - v2 - N '80 - p3

VAN STEENWYK, Elizabeth
AuBYP SUP

> *Dorothy Hamill: Olympic Champion*
> Hi Lo - v1 - S '79 - p4

> *Mystery At Beach Bay*
> Hi Lo - v1 - Ja '80 - p4

VASS, George 1927-
ConAu 37R

> *Reggie Jackson: From Superstar To Candy Bar*
> SLJ - v25 - My '79 - p86

> *Steve Garvey: The Bat Boy Who Became A Star*
> SLJ - v25 - My '79 - p86

VENN, Mary Eleanor
see Adrian, Mary

VENTURO, Betty Lou Baker
see Baker, Betty

VERDICK, Mary 1923-
ConAu 1R

> *On The Ledge And Other Action Packed Stories*
> Hi Lo - v1 - Ap '80 - p4

> *Write For The Job*
> Hi Lo - v2 - S '80 - p6

VERRAL, Charles Spain 1904-
AuBYP, ConAu P-1, SmATA 11,
WhoE 77, WrDr 80

> *Babe Ruth: Sultan Of Swat*
> BL - v73 - D 15 '76 - p612
> Comw - v103 - N 19 '76 - p764
> SLJ - v23 - Ja '77 - p90

VINING, Elizabeth Gray
see Gray, Elizabeth Janet

VROMAN, Mary Elizabeth 1923-
1967
BlkAW, SelBAA

> *Harlem Summer*
> BL - v69 - My 1 '73 - p839
> CCB-B - v20 - Jl '67 - p177
> LJ - v92 - S 15 '67 - p3206
> NYTBR, pt.2 - My 4 '69 - p6
> NYTBR, pt.2 - v72 - My 7 '67 - p16
> SR - v50 - My 13 '67 - p57
> TN - v24 - N '67 - p100

W

WAGMAN, John
see Pollock, Bruce (co-author) -
The Face Of Rock And Roll

WALDEN, Amelia Elizabeth 1909-
ConAu 1R, CurBio 56, MorJA,
SmATA 3, WhoAm 78

Basketball Girl Of The Year
BS - v30 - Jl 1 '70 - p147
KR - v38 - F 1 '70 - p112
LJ - v95 - My 15 '70 - p1965
NYTBR - Ap 19 '70 - p26

Go, Philips, Go!
BL - v70 - Je 1 '74 - p1101
BL - v70 - Je 1 '74 - p1107
KR - v42 - Mr 15 '74 - p309
LJ - v99 - My 15 '74 - p1490

A Name For Himself
CCB-B - v21 - Ja '68 - p87
EJ - v56 - N '67 - p1222
KR - v35 - Mr 1 '67 - p280
LJ - v92 - Jl '67 - p2660

A Spy Case Built For Two
CCB-B - v22 - Je '69 - p166
KR - v37 - F 15 '69 - p187
LJ - v94 - My 15 '69 - p2124
PW - v195 - Ap 7 '69 - p56

The Spy Who Talked Too Much
BS - v28 - Je 1 '68 - p115
CSM - v60 - My 2 '68 - pB9
KR - v36 - Ja 15 '68 - p59

Valerie Valentine Is Missing
KR - v39 - S 1 '71 - p955
LJ - v96 - D 15 '71 - p4199
PW - v200 - S 20 '71 - p49

Walk In A Tall Shadow
BW - v2 - D 3 '68 - p18

CLW - v41 - F '70 - p390
KR - v36 - O 1 '68 - p1122
NYTBR - v73 - N 24 '68 - p42

When Love Speaks
NYTBR - F 4 '62 - p26

WALDRON, Ann 1924-
ConAu 13R, SmATA 16, WhoAm 76

The Luckie Star
BL - v73 - Jl 1 '77 - p1656
CCB-B - v31 - O '77 - p39
CLW - v49 - F '78 - p313
KR - v45 - Ap 15 '77 - p428
SLJ - v24 - S '77 - p138

WALKER, Barbara J

The Picture Life Of Jimmy Carter
BL - v73 - My 15 '77 - p1423
SLJ - v23 - My '77 - p57

WALKER, Nona

The Medicine Makers
BS - v26 - Jl 1 '66 - p143
SB - v2 - S '66 - p139

WALKER, Sloan

*The One And Only Crazy Car
Book*
KR - v41 - D 1 '73 - p1314
LJ - v99 - Ap 15 '74 - p1216

WALLACE, Lew 1827-1905
DcLEL, JBA 34, OxAm, Pen AM,
WhAm 1

Ben-Hur
BW - v6 - S 17 '72 - p15
BW - v6 - D 3 '72 - p20
CR - v221 - O '72 - p216

237

WALLACE, Lew (continued)
  KR - v40 - Jl 1 '72 - p730

WALLACH, Theresa

  Easy Motorcycle Riding
    LJ - v96 - My 1 '71 - p294
    LJ - v96 - My 15 '71 - p1825

WALLER, Leslie 1923-
  AuBYP SUP, ConAu 1R, SmATA 20

  New Sound
    BL - v65 - Jl 15 '69 - p1272
    CCB-B - v22 - Jl '69 - p184
    KR - v37 - Ap 15 '69 - p455
    LJ - v94 - Mr 15 '69 - p1345
    NS - v79 - F 13 '70 - p226
    Obs - Mr 8 '70 - p30
    SR - v52 - My 10 '69 - p60
    TLS - Mr 12 '70 - p287

  Overdrive
    B&B - v14 - Ag '69 - p48
    KR - v35 - O 15 '67 - p1284
    LJ - v92 - N 15 '67 - p4257
    NS - v77 - My 16 '69 - p699
    NYTBR - v72 - N 5 '67 - p16

WALSH, Jill Paton
  ChLR 2, ConAu X, FourBJA,
  SmATA 4 (also known as Paton
  Walsh, Gillian)

  Fireweed
    B&B - v15 - F '70 - p36
    BL - v66 - Je 1 '70 - p1218
    BL - v67 - Ap 1 '71 - p661
    BW - v4 - My 17 '70 - p3
    CCB-B - v24 - N '70 - p51
    CSM - v62 - My 7 '70 - pB6
    Comw - v92 - My 22 '70 - p248
    HB - v46 - Je '70 - p283
    KR - v38 - Mr 15 '70 - p330
    LJ - v95 - My 15 '70 - p1912
    LJ - v95 - My 15 '70 - p1957
    NYTBR - Jl 5 '70 - p14
    NYTBR, pt.2 - N 8 '70 - p34
    PW - v197 - My 18 '70 - p38
    SR - v53 - My 9 '70 - p69

  Unleaving
    B&B - v21 - Je '76 - p48
    BL - v72 - Je 1 '76 - p1401

    BL - v72 - Je 1 '76 - p1410
    BW - My 2 '76 - pL3
    BW - D 12 '76 - pH4
    CCB-B - v30 - D '76 - p67
    CSM - v68 - Jl 1 '76 - p23
    Comw - v103 - N 19 '76 - p763
    GP - v15 - S '76 - p2938
    GW - v114 - My 2 '76 - p23
    HB - v52 - Ag '76 - p408
    JB - v40 - O '76 - p292
    KR - v44 - My 15 '76 - p601
    Kliatt - v12 - Winter '78 - p11
    NO - v15 - Ag 21 '76 - p17
    NYTBR - Ag 8 '76 - p18
    NYTBR - N 14 '76 - p52
    PW - v209 - Ap 5 '76 - p102
    SLJ - v22 - My '76 - p35
    SLJ - v22 - My '76 - p74
    TLS - Ap 2 '76 - p375

WALTERS, Hugh (pseud.) 1910-
  AuBYP, ConSFA (real name:
  Hughes, Walter Llewellyn)

  The Mohole Menace
    CLW - v41 - D '69 - p260
    CSM - v61 - My 1 '69 - pB5
    KR - v36 - Ag 15 '68 - p909
    LJ - v94 - F 15 '69 - p889

WAMPLER, Jan

  *All Their Own: People And The
  Places They Build*
    BL - v73 - Jl 1 '77 - p1618
    HE - v38 - Mr 4 '78 - p812
    Kliatt - v12 - Fall '78 - p52
    Nat - v224 - Ap 2 '77 - p408
    SA - v236 - Je '77 - p136
    TLS - D 23 '77 - p1494
    WCRB - v4 - My '78 - p52

WARD, Herman 1914-
  ConAu 5R, DrAS 78E

  Poems For Pleasure
    BS - v23 - Jl 15 '63 - p148
    HB - v39 - O '63 - p522
    LJ - v88 - S 15 '63 - p3371
    NYTBR - Ag 4 '63 - p24

WARNER, Lucille Schulberg
  ConAu 69

WARNER, Lucille Schulberg
(continued)

From Slave To Abolitionist
BL - v73 - D 15 '76 - p612
BS - v37 - Ap '77 - p31
CCB-B - v30 - Ap '77 - p134
CE - v54 - Ja '78 - p142
HB - v53 - Ap '77 - p174
KR - v44 - S 15 '76 - p1049
LA - v54 - Ap '77 - p444
RT - v31 - Mr '78 - p709
SLJ - v23 - Ja '77 - p106

WARREN, Fred
AuBYP SUP

The Music Of Africa
BL - v67 - Mr 1 '71 - p563
KR - v38 - D 1 '70 - p1299
LJ - v96 - F 15 '71 - p729

WARWICK, Dolores
ConAu X, DrAS 78E (also known as
Frese, Dolores Warwick)

Learn To Say Goodbye
BL - v68 - F 1 '72 - p464
Comw - v95 - N 19 '71 - p188
KR - v39 - S 15 '71 - p1023
LJ - v97 - F 15 '72 - p788
PW - v200 - S 20 '71 - p49

WATERS, John F 1930-
AuBYP SUP, ConAu 37R, SmATA
4, WhoE 77, WrDr 80

What Does An Oceanographer Do?
BL - v66 - Je 1 '70 - p1218
CCB-B - v24 - N '70 - p51
KR - v38 - F 1 '70 - p109
SB - v6 - S '70 - p126
SR - v53 - Ap 18 '70 - p37

WATKINS, William Jon 1942-
ConAu 41R

A Fair Advantage
BL - v72 - F 15 '76 - p851
KR - v43 - D 15 '75 - p1384
SLJ - v22 - Ap '76 - p79

WATSON, Sally 1924-
ConAu 5R, FourBJA, SmATA 3

Jade
BS - v28 - Mr 1 '69 - p491
BW - v3 - Jl 6 '69 - p10
CCB-B - v22 - Ap '69 - p135
CSM - v61 - My 1 '69 - pB6
HB - v45 - Ap '69 - p181
LJ - v94 - F 15 '69 - p889
SR - v52 - F 22 '69 - p47

WATTS, K G O
see Razzell, Arthur G (co-author)

WAYNE, Bennett

Adventure In Buckskin
Hi Lo - v1 - My '80 - p4
LJ - v98 - S 15 '73 - p2659

Big League Pitchers And Catchers
Hi Lo - Je '80 - p4
LJ - v99 - S 15 '74 - p2281

The Founding Fathers
SLJ - v22 - N '75 - p68

Four Women Of Courage
Hi Lo - v1 - My '80 - p4

*Indian Patriots Of The Eastern
Woodlands*
J Read - v20 - My '77 - p732
SLJ - v23 - N '76 - p64

The Super Showmen
SLJ - v21 - Mr '75 - p102

Three Jazz Greats
BL - v74 - Ap 15 '78 - p1330
LJ - v98 - O 15 '73 - p3151
M Ed J - v60 - Ja '74 - p94

*Women Who Dared To Be
Different*
BL - v72 - My 1 '76 - p1247
LJ - v98 - S 15 '73 - p2659

Women With A Cause
BL - v72 - D 15 '75 - p583
SLJ - v22 - D '75 - p56

WEAVER, Robert G 1920-
DrAS 78E, IlsBYP

Nice Guy, Go Home
CCB-B - v22 - S '68 - p19
KR - v36 - F 1 '68 - p125

WEAVER, Robert G (continued)
    LJ - v93 - Ap 15 '68 - p1818
    NYTBR - v73 - Ap 28 '68 - p30

WEBER, Bruce

    All-Pro Basketball
    SLJ - v25 - My '79 - p84

WEEKS, Morris, Jr.

    Hello, Puerto Rico
    BL - v69 - Ja 15 '73 - p479
    KR - v40 - Ap 1 '72 - p415
    LJ - v97 - F 15 '72 - p781
    LJ - v97 - Je 15 '72 - p2244

WEINGARDEN, M

    First Payday
    Hi Lo - v2 - S '80 - p6

WEIR, LaVada
ConAu 21R, SmATA 2, WrDr 80

    The Roller Skating Book
    Hi Lo - v1 - Ap '80 - p4
    SLJ - v26 - Ag '80 - p72

    Skateboards And Skateboarding
    BL - v73 - Je 15 '77 - p1578
    BW - Ap 10 '77 - pE10
    EJ - v66 - N '77 - p81
    KR - v45 - Ap 1 '77 - p357
    PW - v211 - My 2 '77 - p70
    SLJ - v24 - S '77 - p128
    SR - v5 - N 26 '77 - p42
    Teacher - v95 - O '77 - p167

WEISS, Ann E 1943-
ConAu 45

    Save The Mustangs!
    BL - v70 - Mr 15 '74 - p825
    BW - My 19 '74 - p3
    KR - v42 - F 15 '74 - p190
    PW - v205 - My 20 '74 - p64

WEISS, David
AuBYP SUP

    The Great Fire Of London
    BL - v65 - Ap 15 '69 - p951
    BS - v28 - Ja 1 '69 - p423
    CSM - v60 - N 7 '68 - pB12

    LJ - v94 - F 15 '69 - p889

WEISS, Harvey 1922-
ConAu 5R, IlsCB 1967, SmATA 1,
ThrBJA, WhoAmA 78

    Collage And Construction
    BL - v66 - My 15 '70 - p1163
    CCB-B - v24 - N '70 - p52
    Comw - v92 - My 22 '70 - p253
    HB - v46 - O '70 - p493
    KR - v38 - Mr 1 '70 - p248
    LJ - v95 - Je 15 '70 - p2310
    NYTBR - Ag 23 '70 - p20
    PW - v197 - Je 15 '70 - p66
    SR - v53 - My 9 '70 - p46

    *Motors And Engines And How
    They Work*
    BL - v65 - Jl 15 '69 - p1277
    CCB-B - v23 - Mr '70 - p122
    CE - v46 - F '70 - p267
    CSM - v61 - My 1 '69 - pB8
    KR - v37 - My 15 '69 - p573
    LJ - v94 - O 15 '69 - p3825
    LJ - v94 - D 15 '69 - p4583
    NYTBR - Jl 27 '69 - p18
    SA - v221 - D '69 - p146
    SB - v5 - My '69 - p68
    TLS - Jl 5 '74 - p725

    Sailing Small Boats
    BL - v64 - F 15 '68 - p703
    LJ - v93 - Ja 15 '68 - p311
    NYTBR - v73 - Ap 7 '68 - p26
    SB - v4 - My '68 - p59
    Yacht - v123 - My '68 - p88

WELLS, H G 1866-1946
OxEng, SmATA 20, TwCA, TwCA
SUP, WhoSciF, WhoTwCL

    *The Time Machine. The War Of
    The Worlds*
    Choice - v14 - Jl '77 - p686
    WLB - v52 - D '77 - p307

WELLS, Robert 1913-
AuBYP

    What Does A Test Pilot Do?
    KR - v37 - D 1 '69 - p1274
    SB - v5 - Mr '70 - p343

WELLS, Rosemary   1943-
ConAu 85, FourBJA, IlsCB 1967,
SmATA 18

None Of The Above
BL - v71 - S 15 '74 - p94
BS - v34 - F 15 '75 - p519
BW - N 10 '74 - p8
CCB-B - v28 - Ap '75 - p139
Comw - v101 - N 22 '74 - p194
EJ - v65 - Ja '76 - p98
KR - v42 - O 1 '74 - p1067
KR - v43 - Ja 1 '75 - p12
LJ - v99 - N 15 '74 - p3059
LJ - v99 - D 15 '74 - p3248
NYTBR - N 24 '74 - p8
PW - v206 - Ag 5 '74 - p58

WERNER, Herma   1926-
ConAu 85

The Dragster
BL - v75 - Ap 15 '79 - p1290
Hi Lo - v1 - D '79 - p5
see also Piniat, John (co-author)

WERSBA, Barbara   1932-
ChLR 3, ConAu 29R, SmATA 1,
ThrBJA, TwCCW 78

The Dream Watcher
B&B - v14 - Ag '69 - p48
BL - v65 - N 1 '68 - p304
BW - v2 - N 3 '68 - p18
HB - v44 - O '68 - p567
KR - v36 - S 1 '68 - p988
LJ - v93 - S 15 '68 - p3328
LJ - v96 - Ja 15 '71 - p283
NS - v78 - O 31 '69 - p623
NYTBR - v73 - N 3 '68 - p2
NYTBR, pt.2 - N 5 '72 - p42
Obs - Ag 3 '69 - p25
SR - v51 - N 9 '68 - p69
TLS - Je 26 '69 - p686
Teacher - v86 - Ap '69 - p184

Run Softly, Go Fast
BL - v67   Ap 1 '71 - p655
CCB-B - v24 - F '71 - p100
Comw - v93 - N 20 '70 - p202
EJ - v60 - Ap '71 - p530
EJ - v63 - My '74 - p90
HB - v46 - D '70 - p624
J Read - v22 - N '78 - p130

KR - v38 - O 15 '70 - p1164
LJ - v96 - F 15 '71 - p738
NYTBR - N 22 '70 - p38
TN - v27 - Ap '71 - p309

WHEELER, W H

Counterfeit!
SLJ - v26 - D '79 - p98

WHIPPLE, Dorothy Vermilya   1900-
WhoAmW 72

*Is The Grass Greener?: Answers To
Questions About Drugs*
BL - v68 - N 1 '71 - p243
BL - v68 - Ap 1 '72 - p665
KR - v39 - Ap 1 '71 - p384
LJ - v96 - Jl '71 - p2291
NYTBR, pt.2 - My 2 '71 - p32
SB - v7 - Mr '72 - p321
TN - v28 - Ap '72 - p314

WHITE, E B   1899-
ChLR 1, ConAu 13R, ConLC 10,
MorJA, OxAm, SmATA 2, TwCCW
78 (full name: White, Elwyn Brooks)

The Trumpet Of The Swan
Am - v123 - D 5 '70 - p496
Atl - v226 - S '70 - p123
BL - v67 - S 1 '70 - p59
BW - v4 - My 17 '70 - p4
CCB-B - v24 - O '70 - p35
CSM - v62 - Jl 25 '70 - p13
Comw - v93 - N 20 '70 - p201
HB - v46 - Ag '70 - p391
Inst - v80 - Ag '70 - p173
KR - v38 - Ap 15 '70 - p455
LJ - v95 - Jl '70 - p2537
LJ - v95 - D 15 '70 - p4327
NO - v9 - Ag 10 '70 - p21
NS - v80 - N 6 '70 - p611
NY - v46 - D 5 '70 - p217
NYRB - v15 - D 17 '70 - p10
NYTBR - Je 28 '70 - p4
NYTBR - D 6 '70 - p58
NYTBR, pt.2 - N 8 '70 - p38
PW - v197 - Ap 20 '70 - p62
Par - v45 - O '70 - p20
SR - v53 - Je 27 '70 - p39
Spec - v225 - D 5 '70 - pR19
TLS - D 11 '70 - p1458

WHITE, E B (continued)
Teacher - v91 - My '74 - p81
Time - v96 - D 21 '70 - p68
WSJ - v176 - Jl 14 '70 - p16

WHITE, Florence Meiman   1910-
ConAu 41R, IntAu&W 77, SmATA
14

Cesar Chavez: Man Of Courage
LJ - v98 - N 15 '73 - p3460
Teacher - v91 - S '73 - p143

Escape! The Life Of Harry Houdini
CCB-B - v32 - Jl '79 - p204
Hi Lo - v1 - S '79 - p6
KR - v47 - My 1 '79 - p521

Malcolm X: Black And Proud
SLJ - v22 - N '75 - p84

WHITE, Robb   1909-
ChLR 3, ConAu 1R, JBA 51,
SmATA 1, WhoAm 78

Deathwatch
BL - v68 - Jl 15 '72 - p1000
BS - v32 - Je 15 '72 - p152
EJ - v61 - N '72 - p1260
HB - v48 - O '72 - p475
KR - v40 - Mr 15 '72 - p336
LJ - v97 - Je 15 '72 - p2245
NYTBR - Je 4 '72 - p28
NYTBR, pt.2 - My 7 '72 - p4
NYTBR, pt.2 - N 5 '72 - p26
PW - v201 - My 15 '72 - p54
TN - v29 - Ap '73 - p258

The Frogmen
BS - v33 - Je 15 '73 - p146
CE - v50 - N '73 - p98
KR - v41 - My 1 '73 - p522
LJ - v98 - N 15 '73 - p3471
NYTBR - S 16 '73 - p12

The Long Way Down
B&B - v6 - Je '78 - p5
BL - v74 - O 15 '77 - p370
BS - v37 - Mr '78 - p400
CCB-B - v31 - My '78 - p150
KR - v45 - D 1 '77 - p1271
SLJ - v24 - N '77 - p77

No Man's Land
BS - v29 - D 1 '69 - p355
KR - v37 - O 15 '69 - p1124
LJ - v95 - Ja 15 '70 - p258
NY - v45 - D 13 '69 - p203

Up Periscope
Atl - v198 - D '56 - p104
BL - v53 - N 1 '56 - p122
HB - v32 - O '56 - p363
KR - v24 - Je 15 '56 - p406
LJ - v81 - O 15 '56 - p2473
NYTBR - S 23 '56 - p32
SR - v39 - N 17 '56 - p71

WHITE, Wallace   1930-

One Dark Night
BL - v76 - O 15 '79 - p347
CBRS - v8 - O '79 - p20
Hi Lo - v1 - F '80 - p5
SLJ - v26 - O '79 - p162

WHITEFORD, Andrew Hunter   1913-
AmM&WS 76P, ConAu 45, WhoAm
78

North American Indian Arts
BL - v68 - S 15 '71 - p101
CSM - v63 - Jl 10 '71 - p15
LJ - v96 - O 15 '71 - p3480
PW - v198 - D 7 '70 - p51
SA - v225 - D '71 - p109
WLB - v46 - S '71 - p83

WHITEHEAD, Robert J
see Bamman, Henry (co-author) -
Viking Treasure

WHITELEY, Opal
REnAL

Opal
CSM - v68 - O 4 '76 - p23
KR - v44 - Ag 1 '76 - p900
Kliatt - v12 - Winter '78 - p25
LJ - v101 - O 15 '76 - p2168
NYTBR - N 21 '76 - p61
PW - v210 - Jl 12 '76 - p66

WHITNEY, David C   1921-
ConAu 9R, DrAS 78H, WhoAm 78

WHITNEY, David C (continued)

First Book Of Facts And How To Find Them
BL - v63 - Ja 1 '67 - p492
CCB-B - v20 - D '66 - p64
CE - v44 - N '67 - p190
CSM - v58 - N 3 '66 - pB8
LJ - v91 - O 15 '66 - p5242
NYTBR - v71 - N 6 '66 - p54
SR - v49 - N 12 '66 - p49

WHITNEY, Phyllis A 1903-
ConAu 1R, EncMys, JBA 51,
SmATA 1, TwCCW 78, WhoAm 78

Hunter's Green
BL - v64 - Jl 1 '68 - p1221
BS - v28 - My 1 '68 - p61
KR - v36 - F 15 '68 - p213
KR - v36 - Mr 1 '68 - p279
LJ - v93 - Je 1 '68 - p2262
LJ - v93 - Jl '68 - p2740
PW - v193 - Ja 29 '68 - p92
TN - v25 - N '68 - p1

Mystery Of The Haunted Pool
BL - v57 - F 15 '61 - p368
CSM - N 23 '60 - p11
HB - v37 - F '61 - p52
KR - v28 - Jl 15 '60 - p560
LJ - v85 - S 15 '60 - p3227
NYTBR - F 19 '61 - p40
SR - v44 - Je 24 '61 - p20

Secret Of The Emerald Star
Kliatt - v13 - Spring '79 - p15

Secret Of The Tiger's Eye
Kliatt - v13 - Winter '79 - p17

Step To The Music
KR - v21 - O 15 '53 - p699
LJ - v78 - N 15 '53 - p2047
NYTBR - D 27 '53 - p14
SR - v36 - N 14 '53 - p70

WIBBERLEY, Leonard 1915-
ChLR 3, ConAu 5R, EncMys,
MorJA, SmATA 2, TwCCW 78,
WrDr 80

Flint's Island
B&B - v19 - O '73 - p120
BL - v68 - Jl 1 '72 - p943

BW - v6 - My 7 '72 - p13
CCB-B - v26 - O '72 - p34
CSM - v64 - My 4 '72 - pB5
HB - v48 - O '72 - p471
KR - v40 - Mr 15 '72 - p336
LJ - v97 - My 15 '72 - p1918
NYTBR - N 26 '72 - p8
TLS - S 28 '73 - p1117

Meeting With A Great Beast
B&B - v18 - Mr '73 - p75
BL - v68 - D 15 '71 - p354
BL - v68 - Mr 1 '72 - p562
BS - v31 - N 15 '71 - p385
BW - v6 - Mr 12 '72 - p7
KR - v39 - S 1 '71 - p967
LJ - v96 - N 1 '71 - p3641
LJ - v96 - D 15 '71 - p4206
NYTBR - D 19 '71 - p20
PW - v200 - S 27 '71 - p64
TLS - O 10 '72 - p1375

Perilous Gold
BL - v74 - Jl 15 '78 - p1729
KR - v46 - Ag 1 '78 - p812
PW - v213 - Je 19 '78 - p100
SLJ - v25 - S '78 - p166

Sea Captain From Salem
BL - v57 - Jl 1 '61 - p674
CSM - My 11 '61 - p5B
HB - v37 - Ag '61 - p349
KR - v29 - F 1 '61 - p112
LJ - v86 - My 15 '61 - p1998
NYTBR, pt.2 - My 14 '61 - p18
see also O'Connor, Patrick

WIDDER, Arthur 1928-
ConAu 5R

Adventures In Black
NYTBR - D 16 '62 - p25

WIENER, Joan
see Rosenberg, Sharon (co-author)

WIER, Ester 1910-
ConAu 9R, SmATA 3, ThrBJA,
TwCCW 78

The Loner
Am - v108 - Je 1 '63 - p806
CSM - My 9 '63 - p4B
Comw - v78 - My 24 '63 - p256

WIER, Ester (continued)
  HB - v39 - Ag '63 - p392
  LJ - v88 - My 15 '63 - p2154
  NYTBR, pt.2 - My 12 '63 - p2
  Obs - Ap 10 '66 - p20
  SR - v46 - Je 22 '63 - p47
  TCR - v68 - F '67 - p451
  TLS - My 19 '66 - p431

 The Winners
  CCB-B - v22 - O '68 - p36
  KR - v36 - Ap 1 '68 - p404
  LJ - v93 - Je 15 '68 - p2549

WIGHT, James Alfred
see Herriot, James

WILBUR, Richard   1921-
ConAu 1R, ConLC 9, ConP 75,
CurBio 66, SmATA 9, TwCA SUP,
WhoAm 78

 Opposites
  BL - v70 - Mr 15 '74 - p828
  BW - v7 - F 18 '73 - p15
  BW - v7 - S 9 '73 - p8
  CCB-B - v26 - Jl '73 - p180
  CSM - v66 - D 5 '73 - pB12
  Choice - v12 - N '75 - p1134
  HB - v49 - Ag '73 - p388
  HR - v26 - Autumn '73 - p588
  NY - v49 - D 3 '73 - p214
  NYTBR - Jl 1 '73 - p8
  NYTBR - N 4 '73 - p57
  PW - v203 - Je 25 '73 - p73
  SLJ - v25 - N '78 - p31
  TN - v30 - Ja '74 - p206
  Teacher - v91 - D '73 - p73

WILCOX, Collin   1924-
ConAu 21R, ScF&FL 1

 The Watcher
  BL - v74 - Ap 15 '78 - p1327
  KR - v46 - Ja 1 '78 - p21
  LJ - v103 - Mr 1 '78 - p589
  New R - v179 - N 4 '78 - p53
  PW - v213 - Ja 2 '78 - p62

WILDER, Laura Ingalls   1867-1957
ChLR 2, HerW, JBA 51, SmATA 15,
TwCCW 78, WhAm 3, WhoChL

 The First Four Years
  B&B - v19 - O '73 - p137
  BL - v67 - Ap 15 '71 - p705
  CCB-B - v24 - My '71 - p147
  CE - v48 - O '71 - p34
  CSM - v63 - My 6 '71 - pB2
  HB - v47 - Je '71 - p289
  Inst - v82 - N '72 - p136
  Inst - v130 - Je '71 - p74
  KR - v39 - Ja 15 '71 - p58
  LJ - v96 - My 15 '71 - p1818
  Life - v71 - Jl 2 '71 - p12
  NO - v10 - Mr 15 '71 - p19
  NYRB - v18 - Ap 20 '72 - p13
  NYTBR - Mr 28 '71 - p28
  PW - v199 - Mr 22 '71 - p53
  SR - v54 - Mr 20 '71 - p31
  TLS - S 28 '73 - p1116
  Teacher - v90 - Ja '73 - p90
  Time - v97 - Mr 15 '71 - p92

 The Little House Books
  NYRB - v18 - Ap 20 '72 - p13
  NYTBR, pt.2 - F 13 '72 - p12

 Little House In The Big Woods
  LJ - v98 - O 15 '73 - p3163

WILFORD, John Noble   1933-
AuBYP SUP, ConAu 29R, WhoE 74

 We Reach The Moon
  B&B - v15 - O '69 - p62
  BL - v66 - Mr 15 '70 - p874
  BL - v66 - Mr 15 '70 - p930
  BL - v70 - S 15 '73 - p127
  BS - v29 - Ja 1 '70 - p391
  BW - v3 - Ag 10 '69 - p13
  CCB-B - v24 - Jl '70 - p187
  LJ - v95 - Ja 15 '70 - p170
  LJ - v95 - Ap 15 '70 - p1649
  LJ - v98 - S 15 '73 - p2669
  NYTBR - v74 - D 21 '69 - p12
  S&T - v39 - Mr '70 - p184
  S&T - v39 - Ap '70 - p248
  SB - v6 - My '70 - p67
  SR - v52 - O 25 '69 - p33
  SR - v53 - My 9 '70 - p47
  TN - v28 - Ap '72 - p292
  TN - v28 - Ap '72 - p302

WILLIAMS, Amelia
see Compton, Margaret

WILLIAMS, Brian

Aircraft
BB - v5 - Ap '77 - p3

WILLIAMS, Gurney, Iii   1941-
ConAu 69

Ghosts And Poltergeists
BL - v76 - O 1 '79 - p282

WILLIAMS, Jay   1914-1978
ConAu 1R, ConAu 81, CurBio 78,
FourBJA, SmATA 3, SmATA 24N,
TwCCW 78

The Horn Of Roland
KR - v36 - O 1 '68 - p1120
NYTBR - v73 - N 3 '68 - p46

Life In The Middle Ages
Am - v115 - N 5 '66 - p556
B&B - v13 - D '67 - p44
BL - v63 - Ja 1 '67 - p492
BS - v26 - O 1 '66 - p252
CC - v83 - D 7 '66 - p1509
CCB-B - v21 - N '67 - p51
CLW - v38 - Ja '67 - p339
CSM - v58 - N 3 '66 - pB9
Comw - v85 - N 11 '66 - p178
HB - v43 - F '67 - p86
KR - v34 - S 15 '66 - p988
LJ - v91 - O 15 '66 - p5257
NS - v74 - N 3 '67 - p604
NY - v42 - D 17 '66 - p240
NYTBR - v71 - N 6 '66 - p39
Obs - D 3 '67 - p26
PW - v190 - O 17 '66 - p63
TCR - v68 - N '66 - p184
TLS - N 30 '67 - p1159

WILSON, Holly
AuBYP

Snowbound In Hidden Valley
NYTBR - My 26 '57 - p26

WILSON, Joyce Muriel Judson
see Stranger, Joyce

WILSON, Mitchell A   1913-1973
ConAu 1R, ConAu 41R, ConNov 72,
OxAm

*Seesaws To Cosmic Rays: A First
View Of Physics*
BL - v64 - O 15 '67 - p276
CCB-B - v20 - Jl '67 - p178
CLW - v39 - Ja '68 - p375
Inst - v77 - O '67 - p175
KR - v35 - My 15 '67 - p613
LJ - v92 - Jl '67 - p2661
NYTBR, pt.2 - v72 - My 7 '67 - p43
PW - v191 - Je 5 '67 - p177
SB - v3 - S '67 - p108
SR - v50 - My 13 '67 - p58

WILSON, Pat

*Young Sportsman's Guide To
Water Safety*
LJ - v92 - Ja 15 '67 - p352

WILSON, Tom

Encore! Encore!
Kliatt - v14 - Winter '80 - p73

This Book Is For The Birds
Kliatt - v14 - Spring '80 - p59

WINDSOR, Patricia   1938-
ConAu 49, WrDr 80

The Summer Before
BL - v69 - Jl 1 '73 - p1019
BS - v33 - Je 15 '73 - p147
CCB-B - v27 - S '73 - p20
Comw - v99 - N 23 '73 - p216
EJ - v64 - Ja '75 - p112
KR - v41 - My 15 '73 - p569
PW - v203 - Je 18 '73 - p70
TLS - D 5 '75 - p1455

WINTHROP, Elizabeth   1948-
ConAu X, SmATA 8 (also known as
Mahony, Elizabeth Winthrop)

*A Little Demonstration Of
Affection*
BB - v3 - Ag '75 - p4
BL - v71 - Ap 15 '75 - p869
BS - v35 - Jl '75 - p95
BW - Jl 13 '75 - p4
CCB-B - v28 - Jl '75 - p188

WINTHROP, Elizabeth (continued)
KR - v43 - Ap 1 '75 - p387
Kliatt - v11 - Spring '77 - p9
NYTBR - My 4 '75 - p30
PW - v207 - Je 16 '75 - p82
SLJ - v22 - S '75 - p128
SLJ - v22 - D '75 - p32

WITHERIDGE, Elizabeth
AuBYP SUP, MnnWr

And What Of You, Josephine
Charlotte?
BW - v3 - S 7 '69 - p16
CLW - v41 - D '69 - p261
Comw - v90 - My 23 '69 - p298
KR - v37 - Mr 15 '69 - p317
NYTBR - Ap 6 '69 - p18
PW - v195 - My 5 '69 - p52
RR - v28 - Jl '69 - p700

WITHERS, Carl A 1900-1970
AuBYP, ConAu 73, SmATA 14

The American Riddle Book
NYTBR - S 19 '54 - p26

WOHL, Gary
see Chodes, John (co-author)
Edwards, Audrey (co-author)
Reiss, Bob (co-author)

WOJCIECHOWSKA, Maia 1927-
ChLR 1, ConAu 9R, CurBio 76,
HerW, SmATA 1, ThrBJA, TwCCW
78

Don't Play Dead Before You Have
To
CCB-B - v24 - Ja '71 - p83
CE - v47 - D '70 - p160
EJ - v60 - F '71 - p277
KR - v38 - My 15 '70 - p560
LJ - v95 - Je 15 '70 - p2316
NYTBR - Ag 16 '70 - p22
SR - v53 - N 14 '70 - p77

A Kingdom In A Horse
Am - v113 - N 20 '65 - p640
BS - v25 - D 1 '65 - p360
CCB-B - v19 - Ap '66 - p140
CLW - v37 - Mr '66 - p478
CSM - v57 - N 4 '65 - pB11
Inst - v75 - F '66 - p160

Inst - v82 - N '72 - p136
KR - v33 - O 1 '65 - p1046
LJ - v90 - D 15 '65 - p5533
NYTBR - v70 - N 7 '65 - p20
Teacher - v90 - Ap '73 - p90

Shadow Of A Bull
HB - v40 - Je '64 - p293
LJ - v89 - Mr 15 '64 - p1470
NW - v65 - Mr 15 '65 - p102
NY - v40 - D 5 '64 - p224
NYTBR - Mr 22 '64 - p22
NYTBR, pt.2 - N 5 '72 - p42
Par - v40 - N '65 - p153
SR - v47 - Ap 25 '64 - p40
SR - v48 - Mr 27 '65 - p32
TCR - v68 - O '66 - p90

A Single Light
BL - v64 - Jl 1 '68 - p1236
BW - v2 - My 5 '68 - p22
CCB-B - v21 - Jl '68 - p183
HB - v44 - Je '68 - p331
Inst - v78 - O '68 - p158
KR - v36 - Mr 15 '68 - p344
LJ - v93 - Jl '68 - p2738
NYTBR - v73 - My 5 '68 - p3
NYTBR, pt.2 - F 13 '72 - p14
PW - v193 - Mr 25 '68 - p49
PW - v199 - Je 7 '71 - p58
SR - v51 - My 11 '68 - p42

Tuned Out
BS - v28 - N 1 '68 - p326
CCB-B - v22 - F '69 - p104
CSM - v60 - N 7 '68 - pB12
EJ - v58 - My '69 - p779
J Read - v22 - N '78 - p127
KR - v36 - O 1 '68 - p1123
LJ - v94 - Ja 15 '69 - p316
NYTBR - v73 - N 24 '68 - p42
NYTBR, pt.2 - F 15 '70 - p22
PW - v196 - Jl 28 '69 - p59
SR - v51 - N 9 '68 - p70
SR - v52 - Jl 19 '69 - p42

WOLFSON, Victor 1910-
ConAu 33R, NotNAT, TwCA SUP,
WhoWorJ 72

The Man Who Cared: A Life Of
Harry S. Truman
BS - v26 - Je 1 '66 - p103
KR - v34 - Ja 15 '66 - p61

WOLFSON, Victor (continued)
LJ - v92 - F 15 '67 - p900
NYTBR - v71 - My 8 '66 - p22

WOLITZER, Hilma 1930-
ConAu 65, WrDr 80

Out Of Love
BW - v10 - Mr 2 '80 - p13
Kliatt - v14 - Winter '80 - p15
PW - v215 - Je 18 '79 - p94

WOOD, Dorothy
see Wood, Frances (co-author)

WOOD, Frances

*Forests Are For People: The
Heritage Of Our National Forests*
BL - v67 - Ap 15 '71 - p699
BS - v31 - Ap 15 '71 - p47
KR - v38 - Ja '71 - p64
SB - v7 My '71 - p82

WOOD, James Playsted 1905-
ConAu 9R, FourBJA, SmATA 1,
WhoAm 78, WrDr 80

This Is Advertising
BS - v28 - N 1 '68 - p326

WOOD, Nancy 1936-
ConAu 21R, SmATA 6

Hollering Sun
BL - v68 - Jl 1 '72 - p943
BL - v69 - O 15 '72 - p178
BS - v32 - N 15 '72 - p396
CCB-B - v26 - Ja '73 - p84
CE - v49 - N '72 - p88
KR - v40 - Ap 1 '72 - p415
KR - v40 - D 15 '72 - p1426
LJ - v97 - S 15 '72 - p2957
LJ - v97 - D 15 '72 - p4058
NYTBR - Ag 13 '72 - p8
PW - v202 - Jl 31 '72 - p70
SE - v37 - D '73 - p789

WOOD, Paul W 1922-
ConAu 61

Stained Glass Crafting
BL - v64 - Je 15 '68 - p1166
LJ - v93 - F 15 '68 - p892

WOOD, Phyllis Anderson 1923-
AuBYP SUP, ConAu 37R, WrDr 80

Andy
CCB-B - v25 - O '71 - p36
KR - v39 - Ja 15 '71 - p58
LJ - v96 - F 15 '71 - p738
PW - v199 - Mr 15 '71 - p73

*A Five-Color Buick And A Blue-
Eyed Cat*
CLW - v47 - D '75 - p235
KR - v43 - Ap 15 '75 - p467
Kliatt - v11 - Fall '77 - p9
SLJ - v21 - Ja '75 - p58

Get A Little Lost, Tia
BL - v75 - S 15 '78 - p181
CBRS - v7 - F '79 - p70
Hi Lo - v1 - S '79 - p5
SLJ - v25 - Ja '79 - p63

*I Think This Is Where We Came
In*
BL - v72 - Je 1 '76 - p1410
Cur R - v16 - D '77 - p360
KR - v44 - Ap 1 '76 - p407
Kliatt - v12 - Winter '78 - p12
SLJ - v22 - Mr '76 - p119

Song Of The Shaggy Canary
BL - v70 - My 15 '74 - p1060
CCB-B - v28 - Ja '75 - p88
CLW - v47 - N '75 - p166
KR - v42 - Mr 15 '74 - p310
LJ - v99 - Ap 15 '74 - p1234

Win Me And You Lose
Hi Lo - v2 - N '80 - p6

WOODFORD, Peggy 1937-
WrDr 80

Please Don't Go
A Lib - v5 - O '74 - p493
BL - v69 - Je 1 '73 - p951
BW - v7 - My 13 '73 - p5
HB - v49 - Je '73 - p277
KR - v41 - F 15 '73 - p196
Obs - N 26 '72 - p37
Spec - v229 - N 11 '72 - p748
TLS - D 8 '72 - p1497

WORMSER, Richard 1908-
ConSFA, IntMPA 78

WORMSER, Richard (continued)

The Black Mustanger
A Lib - v3 - Ap '72 - p421
Am - v125 - D 4 '71 - p490
BL - v67 - Jl 15 '71 - p956
BL - v68 - Ap 1 '72 - p670
CCB-B - v25 - D '71 - p68
KR - v39 - Ap 1 '71 - p369
LJ - v96 - Je 15 '71 - p2134
PW - v199 - Ap 26 '71 - p60
TN - v28 - Ja '72 - p205

WORTHLEY, Jean Reese   1925-
ConAu 77

The Complete Family Nature Guide
CSM - v68 - Je 21 '76 - p18
LJ - v101 - Ap 15 '76 - p1035
SB - v13 - My '77 - p40

WOSMEK, Frances   1917-
ConAu 29R, WrDr 80

Never Mind Murder
BL - v74 - N 1 '77 - p471
KR - v45 - D 1 '77 - p1272
SLJ - v24 - D '77 - p62

WRIGHT, Elinor Bruce
see Lyon, Elinor

WRIGHT, Enid Meadowcroft
see Meadowcroft, Enid LaMonte

WRIGHTSON, Patricia   1921-
ConAu 45, FourBJA, SmATA 8,
SouST, TwCCW 78

A Racecourse For Andy
BL - v64 - My 1 '68 - p1049
BL - v65 - Ap 1 '69 - p902
BW - v2 - My 5 '68 - p2
BW - v2 - My 5 '68 - p3
CCB-B - v21 - Je '68 - p167
HB - v44 - Je '68 - p326
KR - v36 - F 15 '68 - p184
LJ - v93 - Ap 15 '68 - p1806
SR - v51 - My 11 '68 - p40
TN - v25 - Ja '69 - p206

WUORIO, Eva-Lis   1918-
AuBYP SUP, ConAu 77, CreCan 1,
ThrBJA

Save Alice!
BL - v65 - Ja 15 '69 - p548
CCB-B - v22 - F '69 - p104
CSM - v60 - N 7 '68 - pB14
KR - v36 - N 1 '68 - p1228
LJ - v94 - F 15 '69 - p890
PW - v194 - O 14 '68 - p65

WYLER, Rose   1909-
BkP, SmATA 18, ThrBJA (also
known as Ames, Rose Wyler)

The First Book Of Science Experiments
BL - v67 - My 1 '71 - p752
SB - v7 - My '71 - p16

WYNDHAM, Lee   (pseud.) 1912-1978
ConAu 5R, MorJA, SmATA 1,
SmATA 23N, TwCCW 78, WhoE 74
(real name: Hyndman, Jane Andrews)

Candy Stripers
BL - v55 - Ja 1 '59 - p244
KR - v26 - Ag 15 '58 - p610
LJ - v83 - D 15 '58 - p3581

WYSS, Johann David   1743-1818
CasWL, OxGer, WhoChL

The Swiss Family Robinson
BS - v31 - F 15 '72 - p524
NYTBR - D 21 '13 - p756
TLS - D 11 '70 - p1446

Y

YADIN, Yigael   1917-
ConAu 9R, CurBio 66, WhoWor 78,
WhoWorJ 72

The Story Of Masada
AJA - v71 - Jl '67 - p324
Atl - v219 - Ja '67 - p121
BL - v63 - D 1 '66 - p407
BS - v26 - N 1 '66 - p292
BS - v29 - My 1 '69 - p59
BW - v3 - Jl 13 '69 - p16
Choice - v4 - Ap '67 - p205
Econ - v221 - D 3 '66 - p1037
HT - v17 - Ja '67 - p64
KR - v37 - Ap 1 '69 - p384
LJ - v91 - D 1 '66 - p5965
LJ - v92 - Ja 15 '67 - p361
Lis - v77 - Ja 12 '67 - p66
NS - v72 - D 2 '66 - p832
NYTBR - v71 - D 4 '66 - p56
NYTBR - Jl 13 '69 - p26
Obs - S 11 '66 - p27
PW - v190 - S 19 '66 - p71
PW - v195 - Mr 24 '69 - p55
SR - v49 - N 26 '66 - p39
TLS - D 8 '66 - p1154
Time - v88 - D 9 '66 - p120
WSJ - v47 - Ja 27 '67 - p6

YATES, Brock
see Garlits, Don (co-author)

YATES, Elizabeth   1905-
ConAu 13R, JBA 51, MorBMP,
SmATA 4, TwCA SUP, TwCCW 78,
WhoAm 78

Skeezer: Dog With A Mission
CCB-B - v27 - Ja '74 - p88
PW - v205 - Ja 28 '74 - p301

YEP, Laurence Michael   1948-
ChLR 3, ConAu 49, SmATA 7,
WhoAm 78

Child Of The Owl
BB - v5 - S '77 - p4
BL - v73 - Ap 1 '77 - p1173
DS - v37 - Jl '77 - p128
BW - My 1 '77 - pE1
BW - D 11 '77 - pE4
CCB-B - v30 - Ap '77 - p135
CE - v54 - O '77 - p30
CLW - v49 - N '77 - p189
CSM - v69 - My 4 '77 - pB2
Comw - v104 - N 11 '77 - p731
Cur R - v16 - Ag '77 - p206
EJ - v67 - F '78 - p100
HB - v53 - Ag '77 - p447
Inst - v86 - My '77 - p119
KR - v45 - F 1 '77 - p99
LA - v54 - O '77 - p809
NYTBR - My 22 '77 - p29
NYTBR - N 13 '77 - p50
New R - v177 - D 3 '77 - p28
PW - v211 - F 28 '77 - p123
SE - v41 - O '77 - p531
SLJ - v23 - Ap '77 - p73
SLJ - v23 - My '77 - p36

YERKOW, Charles   1912-
AuBYP SUP

Automobiles: How They Work
LJ - v92 - My 15 '67 - p2024
SB - v2 - D '66 - p225

YOLEN, Jane H   1939-
ConAu 13R, FourBJA, SmATA 4,
TwCCW 78, WhoAm 78

Friend: The Story Of George Fox And The Quakers
BL - v68 - Ap 1 '72 - p663

YOLEN, Jane H (continued)
    BL - v68 - Ap 1 '72 - p680
    BS - v32 - Ap 15 '72 - p47
    CCB-B - v26 - O '72 - p35
    CLW - v43 - My '72 - p535
    CSM - v64 - My 4 '72 - pB5
    KR - v40 - Ja 15 '72 - p77
    LJ - v97 - Je 15 '72 - p2245
    LJ - v97 - D 15 '72 - p4058
    NYTBR - S 10 '72 - p8

YORK, Carol Beach   1928-
AuBYP SUP, ConAu 1R, SmATA 6

*Takers And Returners: A Novel Of
Suspense*
    CCB-B - v27 - N '73 - p55
    KR - v41 - Ja 1 '73 - p9
    LJ - v98 - Ap 15 '73 - p1392

YOUD, Samuel
see Christopher, John

YOUNG, Al   1939-
BlkAW, ConAu 29R, ConNov 76,
SelBAA, WhoAm 78

Snakes
    B&B - v16 - Ag '71 - p34
    BL - v67 - N 1 '70 - p215
    BL - v67 - N 15 '70 - p265
    BL - v67 - Ap 1 '71 - p655
    BW - v4 - My 17 '70 - p6
    KR - v38 - F 15 '70 - p204
    KR - v38 - Mr 15 '70 - p335
    LJ - v95 - Ap 15 '70 - p1505
    NY - v46 - Jl 11 '70 - p77
    NYTBR - My 17 '70 - p38
    PW - v197 - F 9 '70 - p76
    SR - v53 - Ag 22 '70 - p55
    TLS - Jl 30 '71 - p881
    TN - v27 - Ap '71 - p309
    Time - v95 - Je 29 '70 - p76

YOUNG, Jean

Woodstock Craftsman's Manual
    BS - v32 - Jl 15 '72 - p191
    CCB-B - v26 - O '72 - p36
    CSM - v64 - N 8 '72 - p8
    Cr H - v32 - O '72 - p8
    Hob - v77 - O '72 - p158
    Inst - v82 - Ag '72 - p176

    LJ - v97 - Ag '72 - p2571
    LJ - v97 - N 15 '72 - p3823
    LJ - v97 - D 15 '72 - p4059
    NYTBR - Jl 2 '72 - p8
    PW - v201 - Je 12 '72 - p65

YOUNG, Mary

Singing Windows
    NYTBR - Ap 22 '62 - p20

YOUNG, Percy M   1912-
AuBYP, ConAu 13R, OxMus,
WhoMus 72

World Conductors
    BL - v62 - Jl 15 '66 - p1085
    HB - v42 - Je '66 - p326
    KR - v34 - Ja 1 '66 - p14
    LJ - v91 - My 15 '66 - p2715

Z

ZAGOREN, Ruby 1922-1974
AuBYP, ConAu P-1, WhoAmW 74

*Venture For Freedom: The True
Story Of An African Yankee*
BL - v65 - Jl 1 '69 - p1229
BW - v3 - Ag 3 '69 - p13
LJ - v95 - Jl '70 - p2537
NYTBR, pt.2 - My 4 '69 - p20
PW - v195 - My 19 '69 - p71

ZANGER, Jack 1926?-1970
BioIn 8

*Great Catchers Of The Major
Leagues*
CSM - v62 - My 7 '70 - pB7
LJ - v95 - My 15 '70 - p1964
SR - v53 - Je 27 '70 - p38

ZIEMIAN, Joseph 1922-1971
ConAu 65

*The Cigarette Sellers Of Three
Crosses Square*
BL - v72 - S 15 '75 - p170
CCB-B - v29 - Mr '76 - p120
Kliatt - v11 - Spring '77 - p22
LA - v54 - Ja '77 - p83
Obs - Je 21 '70 - p31
PW - v211 - My 2 '77 - p70
SLJ - v22 - N '75 - p95

ZIM, Herbert S 1909-
BkP, ChLR 2, ConAu 13R, JBA 51,
SmATA 1, WhoAm 78

Life And Death
BL - v66 - Jl 1 '70 - p1343
BW - v4 - My 17 '70 - p30
CCB-B - v24 - O '70 - p36
CSM - v62 - My 7 '70 - pB1
KR - v38 - Ap 1 '70 - p388

LJ - v95 - S 15 '70 - p3056
NYTBR - Ap 26 '70 - p30
NYTBR, pt.2 - N 8 '70 - p38
PW - v197 - Ap 27 '70 - p79
SB - v6 - S '70 - p137
SR - v53 - Je 27 '70 - p39

Your Brain And How It Works
CCB-B - v26 - O '72 - p36
CLW - v44 - N '72 - p248
KR - v40 - Mr 15 '72 - p333
LJ - v97 - S 15 '72 - p2957
TLS - Je 15 '73 - p689

ZIM, Sonia Bleeker
see Zim, Herbert S (co-author) -
Life And Death

ZINDEL, Paul 1936-
ChLR 3, ConAu 73, ConDr 77,
ConLC 6, CurBio 73, SmATA 16,
TwCCW 78

Confessions Of A Teenage Baboon
BS - v37 - F '78 - p368
BW - D 11 '77 - pE4
CCB-B - v31 - My '78 - p151
EJ - v67 - S '78 - p90
EJ - v68 - O '79 - p103
JB - v42 - Ag '78 - p214
J Read - v22 - F '79 - p477
KR - v45 - S 15 '77 - p996
Kliatt - v13 - Winter '79 - p17
PW - v212 - S 19 '77 - p146
SLJ - v24 - N '77 - p78
TES - Ag 4 '78 - p18
TLS - Ap 7 '78 - p383

I Never Loved Your Mind
BS - v30 - Jl 1 '70 - p147
BS - v31 - Mr 1 '72 - p547
EJ - v59 - D '70 - p1305
KR - v38 - My 15 '70 - p560

ZINDEL, Paul (continued)
>   LJ - v95 - Je 15 '70 - p2317
>   LJ - v96 - Ja 15 '71 - p283
>   NY - v46 - D 5 '70 - p218
>   NYRB - v15 - D 17 '70 - p10
>   NYTBR, pt.2 - My 24 '70 - p14
>   NYTBR, pt.2 - N 8 '70 - p34
>   Obs - Ap 4 '71 - p36
>   PW - v197 - Ap 13 '70 - p85
>   TLS - Ap 2 '71 - p385
>   TN - v30 - Ja '74 - p197

>   *My Darling, My Hamburger*
>   BS - v29 - D 1 '69 - p356
>   CCB-B - v24 - S '70 - p20
>   Comw - v91 - N 21 '69 - p257
>   EJ - v59 - D '70 - p1305
>   HB - v46 - Ap '70 - p171
>   KR - v37 - N 15 '69 - p1204
>   LJ - v94 - N 15 '69 - p4303
>   NYTBR - D 7 '69 - p68
>   NYTBR, pt.2 - N 9 '69 - p2
>   NYTBR, pt.2 - N 9 '69 - p60
>   NYTBR, pt.2 - N 7 '71 - p47
>   Obs - Ap 19 '70 - p29
>   PW - v196 - S 22 '69 - p85
>   PW - v199 - Je 7 '71 - p58
>   SR - v54 - O 23 '71 - p87
>   TES - Jl 7 '78 - p30
>   TLS - Ap 16 '70 - p416

>   *Pardon Me, You're Stepping On*
>   *My Eyeball*
>   BL - v73 - O 1 '76 - p246
>   BL - v73 - O 1 '76 - p258
>   BS - v36 - Mr '77 - p389
>   CCB-B - v30 - Ap '77 - p136
>   CLW - v50 - O '78 - p104
>   CSM - v68 - N 3 '76 - p20
>   Comw - v103 - N 19 '76 - p763
>   EJ - v66 - S '77 - p84
>   GP - v15 - Ja '77 - p3041
>   HB - v52 - O '76 - p505
>   JB - v41 - Je '77 - p188
>   KR - v446 - Ag 1 '76 - p849
>   NYT - v126 - D 21 '76 - p31
>   NYTBR - N 14 '76 - p29
>   NYTBR - N 14 '76 - p52
>   NYTBR - O 23 '77 - p51
>   Obs - N 28 '76 - p31
>   PW - v210 - Ag 9 '76 - p78
>   SLJ - v23 - O '76 - p121
>   TLS - D 10 '76 - p1549

>   *The Pigman*
>   BL - v65 - Ja 1 '69 - p493
>   BS - v28 - N 1 '68 - p327
>   CCB-B - v22 - Ap '69 - p136
>   EJ - v61 - N '72 - p1163
>   HB - v45 - F '69 - p61
>   J Read - v22 - N '78 - p129
>   KR - v36 - O 1 '68 - p1123
>   LJ - v93 - N 15 '68 - p4425
>   NS - v77 - My 16 '69 - p698
>   NYTBR - v73 - N 3 '68 - p2
>   NYTBR, pt.2 - N 8 '70 - p30
>   NYTBR, pt.2 - F 13 '72 - p14
>   Obs - Jl 4 '76 - p19
>   PW - v194 - S 30 '68 - p61
>   SR - v52 - Ja 18 '69 - p41
>   Spec - v222 - My 16 '69 - p657
>   TLS - Ap 3 '69 - p354

>   *The Undertaker's Gone Bananas*
>   BL - v75 - S 1 '78 - p42
>   CCB-B - v32 - O '78 - p40
>   KR - v46 - S 15 '78 - p1022
>   PW - v213 - Je 26 '78 - p117
>   SLJ - v25 - O '78 - p160
>   WCRB - v4 - N '78 - p81

ZISTEL, Era
ConAu 25R

>   *Hi Fella*
>   CLW - v49 - My '78 - p455
>   KR - v45 - Ag 15 '77 - p853

TITLE INDEX

The Autobiography Of Miss Jane Pitman - Gaines, Ernest J

Automobiles: How They Work - Yerkow, Charles

Avalanche - Roth, Arthur Joseph

Avalanche Dog - Bartos-Hoeppner, Barbara

Babe Ruth And Hank Aaron: The Home Run Kings - Haskins, James

Babe Ruth: Sultan Of Swat - Verral, Charles Spain

Baby Needs Shoes - Carlson, Dale Bick

Backfield Challenge - Gault, William Campbell

Backward In Time - Kelley, Leo P

Bad Boy, Good Boy - Ets, Marie Hall

Bad Henry: An Authorized Hank Aaron Story - Baldwin, Stan

Bad Moon - Bromley, Dudley

A Bag Of Marbles - Joffo, Joseph

Ballads, Blues, And The Big Beat - Myrus, Donald

The Ballet Family - Allan, Mabel Esther

Balto - Anderson, Lavere

Barbara Jordan: Speaking Out - Haskins, James

The Baseball Bargain - Corbett, Scott

Baseball: Hall Of Fame, Stories Of Champions - Epstein, Sam

Baseball My Way - Morgan, Joe

Baseball's Greatest Sluggers - Libby, Bill

Baseball's Ten Greatest Pitchers - Felser, Larry

Baseball's Youngest Big Leaguers - Devaney, John

Basic Training - Holmes, Burnham

Basketball Girl Of The Year - Walden, Amelia Elizabeth

Battery Mates - Cox, William R

The Bayeux Tapestry: The Story Of The Norman Conquest, 1066 - Denny, Norman George

Be A Winner In Soccer - Coombs, Charles Ira

Be A Winner In Track And Field - Coombs, Charles Ira

Beat The Turtle Drum - Greene, Constance C

Beauty Is No Big Deal: The Common Sense Beauty Book - Lawson, Donna

The Beauty Queen - Pfeffer, Susan Beth

Bee - Cohen, Peter Zachary

Beethoven - Jacobs, David

The Beethoven Medal - Peyton, K M

Behind The Scenes In A Car Factory - Harris, Leon

Behind The Scenes In A Department Store - Harris, Leon

Behind The Scenes Of Television Programs - Harris, Leon

Behind The Wheel - Jackson, Robert Blake

Belonging - Kent, Deborah

Ben-Hur - Wallace, Lew

Benjamin Banneker: The Man Who Saved Washington - Lewis, Claude

Benny - Cohen, Barbara

The Bermuda Triangle And Other Mysteries Of Nature - Dolan, Edward Francis, Jr.

Bert Jones: Born To Play Football - Sullivan, George Edward

Best Friend - Stine, H William

The Best Of Bicycling - Leete, Harley M

Best Wishes, Amen - Morrison, Lillian

Better Camping For Boys - Kenealy, James P

Better Gymnastics For Boys - Claus, Marshall

Better Scuba Diving For Boys - Horner, Dave

Better Surfing For Boys - Cook, Joseph Jay

Better Swimming And Diving For Boys And Girls - Sullivan, George Edward

Better Tennis For Boys And Girls - Hopman, Harry

Better Than All Right - Pfeffer, Susan Beth

Between Friends - Garrigue, Sheila

Beyond The Dream: Occasional Heroes Of Sports - Berkow, Ira

258

The Boyhood Of Grace Jones - Langton, Jane

The Boys' Book Of Ships And Shipping - Penry-Jones, J

The Boys' Sherlock Holmes - Doyle, Arthur Conan

Brady - Fritz, Jean

Brainstorm - Myers, Walter Dean

Branded Runaway - Spencer, Zane

The Brave Balloonists: America's First Airmen - Douty, Esther Morris

Break A Leg, Betsy Maybe! - Kingman, Lee

A Breath Of Air And A Breath Of Smoke - Marr, John S

Brian Piccolo: A Short Season - Morris, Jeannie

Brian's Song - Blinn, William

Bridge To The Sun - Terasaki, Gwen

Bridges And How They Are Built - Goldwater, Daniel

The Bridges At Toko-Ri - Michener, James A

Brother Of The Wolves - Thompson, Jean

Brotherhood Of Pirates - Schoder, Judith

Brothers And Sisters: Modern Stories By Black Americans - Adoff, Arnold

Brothers Of The Sea - Sherman, D R

Brown Rabbit: Her Story - Morse, Evangeline

Bruce Jenner - Chodes, John

Brush Fire! - Smith, Pauline Coggeshall

Buckaroo - McKimmey, James

The Bucket Of Thunderbolts - Olsen, Gene

Bugs In Your Ears - Bates, Betty

Builders On The Desert - Van Duyn, Janet

A Building Goes Up - Kahn, Ely Jacques

Bull Pen Hero - Etter, Lester Frederick

Burn Out - Kropp, Paul

The Burning Glass - Johnson, Annabel

The Burning Thorn: An Anthology Of Poetry - Greaves, Griselda

Bus Ride - Sachs, Marilyn

The Bushbabies - Stevenson, William

But I'm Ready To Go - Albert, Louise

By Crumbs, It's Mine - Beatty, Patricia Robbins

By Secret Railway - Meadowcroft, Enid LaMonte

By The Highway Home - Stolz, Mary Slattery

C. C. Poindexter - Meyer, Carolyn

The Cage - Brown, Roy Frederick

Calendar - Adler, Irving

Call Me Al Raft - Shaw, Richard

Call Me Heller, That's My Name - Pevsner, Stella

Call Me Moose - Cone, Molly Lamken

The Call Of The Wild - London, Jack

Calling Earth - Land, Charles

Cameras And Courage: Margaret Bourke-White - Noble, Iris

Campus Mystery - Brisco, Patty

Can You Sue Your Parents For Malpractice? - Danziger, Paula

Canalboat To Freedom - Fall, Thomas

Canary Red - McKay, Robert W

A Candle In Her Room - Arthur, Ruth M

Candle In The Mist - Means, Florence Crannell

Candy Stripers - Wyndham, Lee

Canyon Winter - Morey, Walter Nelson

A Cap For Mary Ellis - Newell, Hope

Captain - Hall, Lynn

The Captains - Clary, Jack

Captive Thunder - Butler, Beverly

A Car Called Camellia - O'Connor, Patrick

Careers And Opportunities In Science - Pollack, Philip

Careers For Dog Lovers - Hall, Lynn

Careers In Sports - McGonagle, Bob

Carnival Of Speed: True Adventures In Motor Racing - Nolan, William Francis

The Case Of The Missing Link - Clymer, Eleanor

The Case Of The Silver Egg - Skirrow, Desmond

Title Index

Clyde's Clam Farm - Harmon, Lyn

The Coach Nobody Liked - Carson, John F

Cockle Stew And Other Rhymes - Massie, Diane Redfield

Codes, Ciphers, And Secret Writing - Gardner, Martin

Coins You Can Collect - Hobson, Burton

Collage And Construction - Weiss, Harvey

Collision Course - Hinton, Nigel

Colonizing Space - Bergaust, Erik

The Color Of Man - Cohen, Robert C

Come Alive At 505 - Brancato, Robin Fidler

The Comeback Guy - Frick, Constance H

Commander Of The Flying Tigers: Claire Lee Chennault - Archibald, Joe

Communication - Adler, Irving

Communication: From Stone Age To Space Age - Neal, Harry Edward

Compacts, Subs And Minis - Abodaher, David J

The Complete Book Of Autograph Collecting - Sullivan, George Edward

The Complete Book Of Bicycling - Sloane, Eugene A

The Complete Family Nature Guide - Worthley, Jean Reese

Computer - Jones, Weyman B

Computers: Tools For Today - DeRossi, Claude J

Confessions Of A Teenage Baboon - Zindel, Paul

Confessions Of A Toe-Hanger - Harris, Christie

Conqueror Of The Clouds - Hallstead, William Finn, III

Constance: A Story Of Early Plymouth - Clapp, Patricia

The Contender - Lipsyte, Robert

Cook Inlet Decision - Pedersen, Elsa

Cool Cat - Bonham, Frank

The Corduroy Road - Clyne, Patricia Edwards

Cougar - Thomson, Peter

Count Me Gone - Johnson, Annabel

Counterfeit! - Wheeler, W H

Cowboys And The Songs They Sang - Sackett, Samuel J

Crash Dive - Frederick, Lee

Crazy Eights - Dana, Barbara

Crazy Minnie - Poynter, Margaret

Crazy To Race - Butterworth, W E

Creating Mosaics - Seidelman, James E

Creating With Clay - Seidelman, James E

Creating With Paint - Seidelman, James E

Creating With Paper - Seidelman, James E

Creatures From UFO's - Cohen, Daniel

The Creep - Dodson, Susan

The Cricket In Times Square - Selden, George

Cross My Heart - Sellers, Naomi

The Crossbreed - Eckert, Allan W

Cruisin For A Bruisin - Rosen, Winifred

The Crystal Image: A Poetry Anthology - Janeczko, Paul

The Crystal Nights - Murray, Michele

Curse Not The Darkness - Hoard, Edison

The Curse Of King Tut And Other Mystery Stories - Hogan, Elizabeth

Curse Of The Vampires - Ronan, Margaret

The Curse Of The Viking Grave - Mowat, Farley

The Custer Wolf: Biography Of An American Renegade - Caras, Roger A

Cutting A Record In Nashville - Van Ryzin, Lani

Daddy Was A Number Runner - Meriwether, Louise

Daisy Summerfield's Style - Goffstein, M B

Dale DeArmond: A First Book Collection Of Her Prints - DeArmond, Dale

Dance - Biemiller, Ruth

A Dance To Still Music - Corcoran, Barbara

Dandelion Wine - Bradbury, Ray

Title Index

How To Star In Football - Masin, Herman L

How To Understand Auto Racing - Olney, Ross Robert

How To Watch Wildlife - Burness, Gordon

The Human Body: The Hand - Elgin, Kathleen

Hunger For Racing - Douglas, James M

Hunter In The Dark - Thompson, Estelle

Hunter's Green - Whitney, Phyllis A

Hurry Home, Candy - Dejong, Meindert

Hut School And The Wartime Home-Front Heroes - Burch, Robert

I Am The Darker Brother - Adoff, Arnold

I Died Here - Shea, George

I Don't Belong Here - French, Dorothy Kayser

I, Dwayne Kleber - Connor, James, III

I Gotta Be Free - Hallman, Ruth

I Heard The Owl Call My Name - Craven, Margaret

I Know What You Did Last Summer - Duncan, Lois

I Never Loved Your Mind - Zindel, Paul

I Reached For The Sky - Patterson, Betty

I Think This Is Where We Came In - Wood, Phyllis Anderson

I Wanna Go Home! - Ketcham, Hank

I Was A Black Panther - Stone, Willie

I Will Go Barefoot All Summer For You - Lyle, Katie Letcher

I Would Rather Be A Turnip - Cleaver, Vera

The Ice Ghosts Mystery - Curry, Jane Louise

Ice Pilot: Bob Bartlett - Sarnoff, Paul

If I Love You, Am I Trapped Forever? - Kerr, M E

If The Earth Falls In - Clark, Mavis Thorpe

I'll Always Get Up - Brown, Larry

I'll Get There. It Better Be Worth The Trip - Donovan, John

I'll Love You When You're More Like Me - Kerr, M E

The Illustrated Bird - Oster, Maggie

The Illustrated Hassle-Free Make Your Own Clothes Book - Rosenberg, Sharon

I'm Deborah Sampson: A Soldier In The War Of The Revolution - Clapp, Patricia

I'm Really Dragged, But Nothing Gets Me Down - Hentoff, Nat

In A Mirror - Stolz, Mary Slattery

In Her Father's Footsteps - Bradbury, Bianca

In Orbit - Morris, Wright

In Spite Of All Terror - Burton, Hester

In Summertime It's Tuffy - Angell, Judie

In The Shadow Of Man - Lawick-Goodall, Jane Van

In The Steps Of The Great American Museum Collector, Carl Ethan Akeley - Clark, James L

Incredible Animals - Meyers, James

The Incredible Detectives - Caufield, Don

The Incredible Journey - Burnford, Sheila

The Indestructible Old-Time String Band - Sullivan, Mary Wilson

India: Now And Through Time - Galbraith, Catherine Atwater

Indian Patriots Of The Eastern Woodlands - Wayne, Bennett

Indian Warriors And Their Weapons - Hofsinde, Robert

Indy - Gerber, Dan

Inside Basketball - Bethel, Dell

Inside The Gate - Lawrence, Mildred

The Internal Combustion Engine And How It Works - Urquhart, David Inglis

Into Exile - Lingard, Joan

Into The Road - Richard, Adrienne

Introducing Archaeology - Magnusson, Magnus

Introducing The Earth - Matthews, William H, III

Title Index

Mystery On The Night Shift - Dee, M M

Mystery Plays A Golden Flute - Turngren, Annette

Mystery Walks The Campus - Turngren, Annette

A Name For Himself - Walden, Amelia Elizabeth

Nancy Lopez: Wonder Woman Of Golf - Robison, Nancy

Naomi - Rabe, Berniece Louise

Napoleon - Komroff, Manuel

The Narc - Butterworth, W E

Narc One Going Down - Cunningham, Chet

The Nashville Sound - Hemphill, Paul

Nat Love, Negro Cowboy - Felton, Harold W

The Natural Superiority Of The Left-Hander - DeKay, James T

Negroes Of Achievement In Modern America - Flynn, James J

Nerves - DelRey, Lester

Never Mind Murder - Wosmek, Frances

The New American Continent - Carlisle, Norman V

The New Life - La Vida Neuva: The Mexican-Americans Today - Dobrin, Arnold

New Sound - Waller, Leslie

The New World Of Computers - Lewis, Alfred

The New World Of Helicopters - Delear, Frank J

New York - Bliven, Bruce, Jr.

New York City Too Far From Tampa Blues - Bethancourt, T Ernesto

Nice Guy, Go Home - Weaver, Robert G

Night Fall - Aiken, Joan

Night Of Fire And Blood - Kelley, Leo P

Night Spell - Newman, Robert Howard

A Night To Remember - Lord, Walter

Nightmare Nina - Shea, George

The Nightmares Of Geranium Street - Shreve, Susan Richards

Nikki 108 - Blue, Rose

Nilda - Mohr, Nicholasa

Nine Black American Doctors - Hayden, Robert Carter

The Nitty Gritty - Bonham, Frank

No Easy Circle - Naylor, Phyllis Reynolds

No Man For Murder - Ellis, Melvin Richard

No Man's Land - White, Robb

No Moon On Graveyard Head - Dorian, Edith

No Place To Hide - Fries, Chloe

No Place To Run - Murphy, Barbara Beasley

No Promises In The Wind - Hunt, Irene

No Rent To Pay - Jackson, Anita

No Talent Letterman - Jackson, Caary Paul

Nobody Has To Be A Kid Forever - Colman, Hila

Nobody Knows But Me - Bunting, Eve

Nobody Promised Me - Mack, John

Nobody Said It's Easy - Smith, Sally Liberman

Nobody Waved Good-Bye - Haggard, Elizabeth

Nobody's Perfect, Charlie Brown - Schulz, Charles M

Nolle Smith: Cowboy, Engineer, Statesman - Gugliotta, Bobette

None Of The Above - Wells, Rosemary

The Nonsense Book Of Riddles, Rhymes, Tongue Twisters, Puzzles And Jokes From American Folklore - Emrich, Duncan

Noodles, Nitwits, And Numskulls - Leach, Maria

The No-Return Trail - Levitin, Sonia

North American Indian Arts - Whiteford, Andrew Hunter

North Of Danger - Fife, Dale

North To Freedom - Holm, Anne S

North To Oak Island - Bromley, Dudley

North Town - Graham, Lorenz Bell

Northlight, Lovelight - Folch-Ribas, Jacques

Not Bad For A Girl - Taves, Isabella

Not Just Sugar And Spice - Sheffield, Janet N

The Nothing Special - Tomerlin, John

Now Or Never - Halacy, Daniel Stephen, Jr.

Nurse In Training - Laklan, Carli

Nurses And What They Do - Kay, Eleanor

Nursing As A Career - Chandler, Caroline A

O Captain: The Death Of Abraham Lincoln - Hayman, LeRoy

The Ocean World - Kovalik, Vladimir

Of Course You Can Sew! - Corrigan, Barbara

Offensive Football - Griese, Bob

Oh, Rick! - Bunting, Eve

The Old Wilderness Road - Steele, William O

Old Yeller - Gipson, Fred

Olga Korbut - Smith, Jay H

Olivia Newton-John - Ruff, Peter

On Astrology - Livingston, Peter

On City Streets - Larrick, Nancy

On ESP - Curtis, Robert H

On My Own - Davis, Charles

On Stage: Flip Wilson - Braun, Thomas

On The Ledge And Other Action Packed Stories - Verdick, Mary

On The Move - Savitz, Harriet May

On The Other Side Of The Gate - Suhl, Yuri

On The Red World - Kelley, Leo P

On The Way Up: What It's Like To Be In The Minor Leagues - Klein, Dave

On Your Own - Owen, Evan

Once Upon The Little Big Horn - Lampman, Evelyn Sibley

The One And Only Crazy Car Book - Walker, Sloan

One Cool Sister And Other Modern Stories - Mooney, Thomas J

One Dark Night - White, Wallace

One Day For Peace - Crosby, Alexander L

One Is One - Picard, Barbara Leonie

One More Flight - Bunting, Eve

One Punch Away - Greenya, John

One Summer In Between - Mather, Melissa

Onion Journey - Cunningham, Julia Woolfolk

Opal - Whiteley, Opal

The Opal-Eyed Fan - Norton, Andre

Opposites - Wilbur, Richard

Orders To Vietnam - Butterworth, W E

Orphans Of The Wind - Haugaard, Erik Christian

The Otis Redding Story - Schiesel, Jane

Our Eddie - Ish-Kishor, Sulamith

Our Fragile Earth - Helfman, Elizabeth S

Our John Willie - Cookson, Catherine McMullen

Our Names: Where They Came From And What They Mean - Lambert, Eloise

Our Names: Where They Came From And What They Mean - Pei, Mario

Out From Under: Benito Juarez And Mexico's Struggle For Independence - Atwater, James D

Out Loud - Merriam, Eve

Out Of Love - Wolitzer, Hilma

Out Of Step With The Dancers - Howard, Elizabeth

Out Of The Earth I Sing: Poetry And Songs Of Primitive Peoples Of The World - Lewis, Richard

Out Of The Sun - Bova, Ben

The Outcasts - Mannix, Daniel

Outlaw Red - Kjelgaard, Jim

Outlaws - Ulyatt, Kenneth

The Outsiders - Hinton, S E

Overdrive - Waller, Leslie

The Overland Launch - Hodges, C Walter

P.S. Write Soon - Rodowsky, Colby F

Pablo Picasso - Greenfeld, Howard

Pacemaker Story Books - Crosher, G R

The Pai-Pai Pig - Anderson, Joy

Title Index

Rattlesnake Run - Lazarus, Keo

Read For The Job - Hermann, Charles F

Reading, Writing, Chattering Chimps - Amon, Aline

Real Ghosts - Cohen, Daniel

The Red Car - Stanford, Don

Red Fox - Roberts, Charles G D

Red Sky At Morning - Bradford, Richard

Red Sky At Night - Bradbury, Bianca

Redcoat In Boston - Finlayson, Ann

Reflections On A Gift Of Watermelon Pickle And Other Modern Verse - Dunning, Stephen

Reggie Jackson: From Superstar To Candy Bar - Vass, George

Reggie Jackson: The Three Million Dollar Man - Allen, Maury

Remove Protective Coating A Little At A Time - Donovan, John

Report From Engine Co. 82 - Smith, Dennis E

Report On Planet Three And Other Speculations - Clarke, Arthur C

Rescue! True Stories Of Heroism - Taylor, Lester Barbour, Jr.

Return Of Silver Chief - O'Brien, Jack

Rex - Stranger, Joyce

Rich And Famous: The Further Adventures Of George Stable - Collier, James Lincoln

Rick Barry: Basketball Ace - O'Connor, Dick

Rico's Cat - Brookins, Dana

Rider's Rock - Lyon, Elinor

Right On, Shane - Skulicz, Matthew

The Right To Be Let Alone: Privacy In The United States - Snyder, Gerald Seymour

Ring The Judas Bell - Forman, James

Rise And Fall Of Adolph Hitler - Shirer, William

Rise Of The Robots - Sullivan, George Edward

Rising Damp - Corcoran, Barbara

The Rising Of The Lark - Moray, Ann

Risks - Rees, David

River Of The Wolves - Meader, Stephen W

River Rats, Inc. - George, Jean Craighead

River Rising - Skidmore, Hubert

Riverboy: The Story Of Mark Twain - Proudfit, Isabel

The Road From West Virginia - Hardin, Gail

Road Race Round The World: New York To Paris, 1908 - Jackson, Robert Blake

Road Racing In America - Engel, Lyle Kenyon

The Road To Galveston - Smith, Beatrice Schillinger

Roads: From Footpaths To Thruways - Doherty, C H

The Robber Ghost - Anckarsvard, Karin

Robert Frost: America's Poet - Faber, Doris

Robert Redford - Reed, Donald

Roberta Flack - Morse, Charles

The Robot People - Bunting, Eve

Rock Fever - Rabinowich, Ellen

The Rock Revolution: What's Happening In Today's Music - Shaw, Arnold

Rocket Pioneer - Coombs, Charles Ira

Rocket Ship Galileo - Heinlein, Robert A

Rocketship: An Incredible Journey Through Science Fiction And Science Fact - Malone, Robert

Rocks And How We Use Them - Pine, Tillie S

Rocks And Rills: A Look At Geology - Stone, A Harris

Rocky - Libby, Bill

Rod Carew - Batson, Larry

Roger Williams, Defender Of Freedom - Edwards, Cecile Pepin

Roll Of Thunder, Hear My Cry - Taylor, Mildred

Roller Hockey - Hollander, Zander

Roller Skating - Shevelson, Joseph

The Roller Skating Book - Weir, LaVada

The Roman Empire - Asimov, Isaac

Title Index

Title Index

Turkeys, Pilgrims, And Indian Corn - Barth, Edna

Tutankhamun And The Mysteries Of Ancient Egypt - Knapp, Ron

The Twelve Labors Of Hercules - Newman, Robert Howard

The Twelve Million Dollar Note - Kraske, Robert

Twenty Minutes To Live And Other Tales Of Suspense - Uhlich, Richard

21 Kinds Of American Folk Art And How To Make Each One - Kinney, Jean

The Twenty-Third Street Crusaders - Carson, John F

A Twister Of Twists, A Tangler Of Tongues - Schwartz, Alvin

'Twixt Twelve And Twenty - Boone, Pat

Two Blocks Apart: Juan Gonzales And Peter Quinn - Mayerson, Charlotte Leon

Two Different Girls - Bunting, Eve

Two For Survival - Roth, Arthur Joseph

Two For The Road - Keller, Roseanne

Two Sieges Of The Alamo - Alter, Robert Edmond

Two Tickets To Freedom - Freedman, Florence B

UFO's And IFO's: A Factual Report On Flying Saucers - Soule, Gardner

The Ugly American - Lederer, William

Uncle Misha's Partisans - Suhl, Yuri

Under Pressure - Herbert, Frank

Under The Influence - Butterworth, W E

Undercover Cat Prowls Again - Gordon, Gordon

Underground Man - Meltzer, Milton

The Undersea People - Bunting, Eve

The Underside Of The Leaf - Goffstein, M B

Understanding Architecture - Sullivan, George Edward

Understanding Sex - Guttmacher, Alan F

The Undertaker's Gone Bananas - Zindel, Paul

The Unfinished March: The History Of The Negro In The United States, Reconstruction To World War I - Drisko, Carol F

The United States In The Civil War - Lawson, Donald Elmer

The United States In The Spanish-American War - Lawson, Donald Elmer

Unleaving - Walsh, Jill Paton

Unnatural Resources: True Stories Of American Treasure - Titler, Dale Milton

Unusual Aquarium Fishes - Fletcher, Alan Mark

Up A Road Slowly - Hunt, Irene

Up And Over - Smith, Doris Buchanan

Up From Never - Sorrentino, Joseph N

Up From The Ghetto - Drotning, Phillip T

Up From The Ghetto - South, Wesley W

Up In Seth's Room - Mazer, Norma Fox

Up Periscope - White, Robb

Up The Down Staircase - Kaufman, Bel

The Ups And Downs Of Jorie Jenkins - Bates, Betty

The Upstairs Room - Reiss, Johanna

VD: The Silent Epidemic - Hyde, Margaret Oldroyd

Vacation In Space - Kelley, Leo P

Valerie Valentine Is Missing - Walden, Amelia Elizabeth

Vampires - Garden, Nancy

Vanishing Giants: The Story Of The Sequoias - Silverberg, Robert

Vans: The Personality Vehicles - Dexler, Paul R

Vendetta - Deane, Shirley

Venture For Freedom: The True Story Of An African Yankee - Zagoren, Ruby

Very Far Away From Anywhere Else - LeGuin, Ursula Kroeber

Vicky Barnes, Junior Hospital Volunteer - Colver, Alice Ross

Vida Blue: Coming Up Again - Kowet, Don

Viking Treasure - Bamman, Henry A

PW	Publishers Weekly	SS	Social Studies
Pac A	Pacific Affairs	SWR	Southwest Review
Par	Parents Magazine	Sci	Science
Pet PM	Petersen's Photographic Magazine	Spec	Spectator
Poet	Poetry	Spectr	Spectrum
Prog	Progressive	TCR	Teachers College Record
Punch	Punch	TES	Times Educational Supplement
RR	Review for Religious	TLS	Times Literary Supplement
RSR	Reference Services Review	TN	Top of the News
RT	Reading Teacher	Teacher	Teacher
SA	Scientific American	Time	Time
S&T	Sky and Telescope	Trav	Travel-Holiday
SB	Science Books and Films	VQR	Virginia Quarterly Review
SE	Social Education	VV	Village Voice
SEP	Saturday Evening Post	WCRB	West Coast Review of Books
SLJ	School Library Journal	WLB	Wilson Library Bulletin
SMQ	School Media Quarterly	WSJ	Wall Street Journal
SN	Saturday Night	YR	Yale Review
SR	Saturday Review	Yacht	Yachting

ABBREVIATIONS OF MONTHS USED IN CITATIONS

Ja	January	Jl	July
F	February	Ag	August
Mr	March	S	September
Ap	April	O	October
My	May	N	November
Je	June	D	December